CHILDREN
& MOVEMENT

CHILDREN & MOVEMENT

Physical Education in the Elementary School

Jennifer Wall
McGill University

Nancy Murray
Brock University

Wm. C. Brown Publishers

Book Team

Editor *Chris Rogers*
Developmental Editor *Sue Pulvermacher-Alt*
Production Editor *Linda M. Meehan*
Designer *Ben Neff*
Art Editor *Janice M. Roerig*
Permissions Editor *Vicki Krug*
Visuals Processor *Joyce E. Watters*

Wm. C. Brown Publishers

President *G. Franklin Lewis*
Vice President, Editor-in-Chief *George Wm. Bergquist*
Vice President, Director of Production *Beverly Kolz*
Vice President, National Sales Manager *Bob McLaughlin*
Director of Marketing *Thomas E. Doran*
Marketing Communications Manager *Edward Bartell*
Marketing Manager *Kathy Law Laube*
Production Editorial Manager *Colleen A. Yonda*
Production Editorial Manager *Julie A. Kennedy*
Publishing Services Manager *Karen J. Slaght*
Manager of Visuals and Design *Faye M. Schilling*

CONTENTS

Preface xi

PREFACE  □ □ □

In a physical education program we try to consider the needs of every child, rather than only those of the elite few who are highly skilled. To promote skill development in the areas of dance, games, and gymnastics a variety of teaching methods are used. Cognitive understanding of movement skill is important and movement concepts should become familiar to both the children and the teacher.

This book has been written for use in professional programs preparing teachers for elementary schools. The intent is to provide a solid foundation for the development of an effective physical education program for children. The material presented is **one** way of approaching elementary physical education. We believe that, as educators, we must be able to select and design a variety of learning experiences for our students. These learning experiences must be designed so that students become skillful to the limit of their individual abilities while fostering understanding of movement concepts. Teachers need to make decisions so that students are appropriately challenged and achieve success. Children's innate love of movement must be fostered so that they develop positive attitudes toward physical activity. The most important thing is that we, as teachers, become knowledgeable about **children, movement,** and **teaching.**

The book is organized into four sections: Foundations, Dance, Games, and Gymnastics. The following is a visual representation of the text organization.

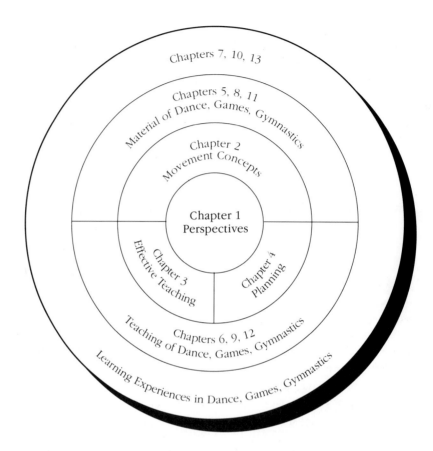

Chapters 7, 10, 13

Chapters 5, 8, 11
Material of Dance, Games, Gymnastics

Chapter 2
Movement Concepts

Chapter 1
Perspectives

Chapter 3
Effective Teaching

Chapter 4
Planning

Chapters 6, 9, 12
Teaching of Dance, Games, Gymnastics

Learning Experiences in Dance, Games, Gymnastics

**Section I:
Foundations**

This section introduces the foundations of the elementary school physical education program. Chapter 1 outlines the importance of physical education and presents information about the child. The content of the program presented in chapter 2 and the teaching methods discussed in chapter 3 may be applied to any physical activity. Planning for physical education, essential for quality programming, is the focus of chapter 4.

After reading this section, you should be able to explain the following to your peers and parents of children in your school:

1. the characteristics and goals of a quality physical education program;
2. the movement concepts derived from Rudolf Laban's study of human movement;
3. the various teaching methods used to promote children's skill development;
4. the ways in which the physical education program may be planned and evaluated.

This section deals with the dance component of the elementary school physical education program. Chapter 5 discusses the material of dance as it relates to singing games, folk dance, and creative dance. Chapter 6 focuses upon the teaching skills and strategies employed in dance lessons. Chapter 7 provides sample lesson plans and progressions.

Section II: Dance

After reading this section, you should be able to explain the following to your peers and parents of children in your school:

1. the types of dance experiences that should be included in an elementary school physical education program;
2. the application of movement concepts in the dance context;
3. the teaching skills that are specific to the dance situation;
4. how dance lessons are developed so that learning may be progressive.

This section deals with the games component of the elementary school physical education program. Chapter 8 discusses the material of games as it relates to low-organization, lead-up, and formal games. Chapter 9 focuses upon the teaching skills and strategies employed in games lessons. Chapter 10 provides sample lesson plans and progression.

Section III: Games

After reading this section you should be able to explain the following to your peers and parents of children in your school:

1. the types of games experiences that should be included in an elementary school physical education program;
2. the application of movement concepts in the games context;
3. the teaching skills that are specific to the games situation;
4. how games lessons are developed so that learning may be progressive.

This section deals with the gymnastics component of the elementary school physical education program. Chapter 11 discusses the material of gymnastics. Chapter 12 focuses upon the teaching skills and strategies employed as the children work on the floor and on small and large apparatus. Chapter 13 provides sample lesson plans and progressions.

Section IV: Gymnastics

After reading this section, you should be able to explain the following to your peers and parents of children in your school:

1. the types of gymnastics experiences that should be included in an elementary school physical education program;
2. the application of movement concepts in the gymnastics context;
3. the teaching skills that are specific to the gymnastics situation;
4. how gymnastics lessons are developed so that learning may be progressive.

The following schema is offered as an alternative to the previous organization and it also shows the relationship among the topics.

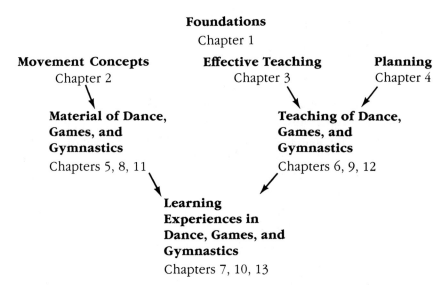

Throughout the text there are boxes with specific bits of information. The "To Do" boxes reinforce an idea being discussed and may be used for in-class activities or as mini-assignments. "Remember That" boxes are just that: small pieces of information we should keep in mind as we teach. "Fitness Facts" boxes highlight a fitness element related to participation in dance, games, or gymnastics activities, and "Safety Tips" provide help with organization during lessons.

We have tried to make the book easy to read by writing in a personal style, including photographs, figures, and tables, and providing chapter summaries, review questions, and related readings.

We hope each of these elements clarifies, reinforces, and extends the ideas in the text.

Many people are involved in the production of a book, and it is not possible to thank all of them individually. We hope they will accept our thanks in this general form.

Special recognition and thanks go to the following:

Pat Jeffries, Diane Bruman-Whyte, Leila Hofmeister, and Lorraine Munro, our typists, who coped with our numerous requests to "change this" and "rush that" with good humor;

Our reviewers, who provided us with valuable feedback:

Larry Albertson, University of Wisconsin–River Falls

Stuart Robbins, York University

Paula Dee Welch, University of Florida

Peter Werner, University of South Carolina

David Docherty, University of Victoria

David Bean, University of Calgary

Dorothy Kozeluh, Chicago State University

Kate Barrett, University of North Carolina

The editorial staff at Wm. C. Brown Publishers, who have been very supportive throughout the project;

The following principals, who allowed us to come into their schools and take photographs:

Richard McGrail, Spring Gardens Elementary School, Dollard des Ormeaux, Quebec;

Del Needham, Douglas Park School, Regina, Saskatchewan;

Vern Johnstone, Davin School, Regina, Saskatchewan;

Ginette Gingras, Anne Browne, and Sayla McCowan, teachers at the above schools, for generously giving up their lesson and lunch times;

Maureen Pritchard's class at Massey School, Regina, Saskatchewan, for the drawings for the section opener collages;

The children, for sharing their skills;

Jane Hodge, McGill University, Montreal, Quebec, who contributed material for chapter 3 and section III. She willingly listened and suggested refinement as ideas were considered in their rough states;

Len Gusthart, University of Saskatchewan, Saskatoon, Saskatchewan, who also provided material for chapter 3; and

Cyndi McNiven, for her movement knowledge and enthusiastic support during the preparation of the manuscript.

Special appreciation is extended to Ken Murray, Scott, and Julia, for their patience and understanding.

CHILDREN & MOVEMENT

SECTION

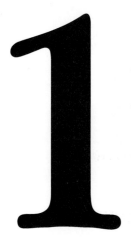

What is important in physical education today is that we increase the number of people who are skilled in working with children in a loving, caring environment and in helping them learn about physical education.

Siedentop, D., J. Herkowitz, and J. Rink. 1984. Elementary Physical Education Methods. *Englewood Cliffs, N.J.: Prentice-Hall.*

FOUNDATIONS

CHAPTER

1

PERSPECTIVES

Teaching physical education to children in elementary school is a stimulating, interesting, and satisfying challenge. It is a situation where both
the teacher and the children can interact in a lively and fun manner. The
lessons should be enjoyable, happy times for both you and the children.

> Making discoveries about what one's body can do, becoming
> skilled, inventing ways of getting on and off an obstacle, creating
> one's own dance, maybe sharing the creation with a friend, are all
> rewarding experiences (Wall 1981).

Children love to move. They love to learn. As we observe children
playing in the street or playground, we see that they move with total
involvement. Movement is often enjoyed for the sheer pleasure of the
sensations arising rather than for the specific purpose of "doing" something. Because movement is at the very core of our being, it is vitally
important that all children have the opportunity to both learn to move
and move to learn. As teachers we have a responsibility to foster a love
of physical activity so that children develop worthwhile skills and form
a basis and appreciation for movement that will last throughout their
lives.

Physical education is a time for doing. All children would rather do
than watch or listen. Children naturally enjoy the lively atmosphere of
the gymnasium or outdoors, and the freedom from the confines of the
classroom. Equipment and other stimuli provide new challenge in
movement and children look forward to the opportunity to work alone
or with others. As a classroom teacher, you have the advantage of children being naturally eager to participate in your lessons.

This chapter is intended to provide you with a basic understanding
of how we can meet children's educational needs through physical education. We will first consider why physical education is important as a
school subject.

The Importance of Physical Education

Physical education makes a unique contribution to a child's education
because it promotes the acquisition of physical skills and increased
physical abilities. Rich experiences in dance, games, and gymnastics
provide children with the joy of acquiring skills in both expressive and
functional movement, in cooperative and competitive situations, with
other children and alone. Skills are explored, practiced, and mastered
without equipment, with small equipment, and on large apparatus. Children will develop economy and efficiency of movement. The acquisition
of skill may elicit in the child a feeling of the kinesthetic—the powerful
feeling that the movement was "right."

Physical education is vital in the elementary school program as it has
a paramount role in maintaining and/or enhancing children's fitness
levels. Children's active, spontaneous play contributes to their growth

Children naturally enjoy physical education.

and health (Bailey et al. 1986). Frequent physical education classes are also important for wellness and the establishment of a healthy lifestyle. Every child should be offered the opportunity to benefit from engaging in regular, vigorous physical activity.

Most children, including the mentally and physically handicapped, enjoy moving and want to become more competent and versatile as they plan and work with different challenges in different environments. Possession of physical skill is important for social reasons. Skillful movers are usually highly sociable children so they are readily accepted into peer groups. Children recognize and appreciate competency in their peers and wish to be identified with competent children. Movement skills, therefore, may influence the friendships children develop. Children's abilities or inabilities may affect their popularity, self-confidence, self-image, and the competency to pursue new challenges and goals.

Because we pursue only those goals that we feel are attainable, it is vital that children experience success in physical education. In order for them to develop motor skills and wholesome attitudes toward physical activity, a well-rounded program that provides for individual differences and encourages each child to succeed is extremely important. This implies that children are not to be expected to perform at the same level. Teachers set problem-solving tasks to which there are numerous acceptable movement responses. As part of this process it is vitally important that each child receives feedback and reinforcement in every class.

Table 1.1

▼▼▼▼   ▼

Goals of physical education

1. Acquire useful physical skills.
2. Acquire knowledge and understanding of movement.
3. Be able to apply knowledge of movement in varied situations.
4. Enhance physical growth and development.
5. Maintain or enhance fitness.
6. Develop positive lifetime attitudes toward physical activity.
7. Promote positive self-esteem, self-worth.
8. Acquire desirable social skills.
9. Enhance creative abilities.
10. Develop an aesthetic appreciation for movement.

▼▼▼▼   ▼

As long ago as 1951, Van Hagen et al. wrote:

> Educators have long recognized the need for a thorough program of physical education during the early years of childhood. These are the years of rapid growth and development when strength and stamina are acquired to form a healthy body. These are the years when posture habits are being formed and fundamental motor skills are being learned to give the individual poise, grace, and bodily efficiency. Physical education, with its many kinds of activities offered to develop the whole child, has an important place in the program of the elementary school.

The goals of physical education programs are varied and diverse (see table 1.1), and a quality physical education program will strive to meet them.

Our aim as teachers is to provide worthwhile physical activities that encourage children to become skillful movers in a variety of situations. Movement tasks that are challenging, fun, and rewarding will promote positive life-long attitudes toward personal fitness, physical education, and leisure.

Where Have We Come From?

To explain some of the diversity in today's literature about elementary school physical education, it may be valuable for you to understand a little of its recent history.

European gymnastic systems, the emergence of sports, and an emphasis on the military were characteristics of physical education at the beginning of the 20th century. Termed physical training, students performed routine exercises in order to become physically fit. The teaching methodology most commonly employed was a command style, where the teacher set specific skills or exercises to be learned and the class was expected to meet specific standards.

Children learn by doing.

To Do

Think back as far as you can to your earliest school experiences.
What did you learn by **doing?**

Several factors contributed to the transition from physical training to physical education. Immigrants from Germany had been influenced by the German gymnastic clubs; the Swedish and Danish brought to North America their systematic exercises; and all immigrants contributed to the cultural mosaic with their national folk dances. The additional influence of strongly emerging games and sports in North American society accelerated progress toward "education" rather than "training."

Before the second World War, Rudolf Laban, an Austrian dancer, escaped from Nazi Germany and fled with some of his colleagues to England, where he pursued his interest in "dance for all."

> He postulated that, in addition to the fact that human movement was governed by physical laws, it also contained four principles which could best be comprehended by movement experiences (Hill 1979).

These four principles—body concepts, effort concepts, spatial concepts, and relationship concepts—deal with what the body does, where it moves, how it moves, and with whom or what it moves. (See chapter 2 for a thorough discussion of these principles.)

Laban was an inspiring individual who ". . . began to have profound influence on the teaching of physical education in general and dance and gymnastics in particular" (Wall 1981). In Britain many of the male teachers of physical training had gone to war and women (who were largely untrained) replaced men in educational settings. Some of these women had trained with Laban and employed his movement principles when teaching children.

There began a growing concern

> . . . about the value of teaching isolated, unnatural movement patterns to children, children who, when left to play alone, exhibited exciting movement phrases (Wall 1981).

The countryside of wartime Britain, scattered with commando equipment, offered children new challenges.

> They swung and balanced, climbed, dropped from improbable heights and extremely important, if left to themselves and not interfered with by adults, were sensible about taking safety precautions. Such equipment could be modified, set up in playgrounds and school halls, and in this way, physical education would be in a position to provide its own materials for learning . . .
> So, these three quite diverse happenings—teachers with an understanding of Laban's principles, changes in philosophy about how children learn and the introduction of much freer forms of activity, all became consolidated into what was to result in a new thrust in physical education (Hill 1979).

Exchanges between Britain and the United States also influenced the changes in physical education. Many teachers who had studied with Laban immigrated to Canada and the United States, employing his movement concepts in their programs. At the same time, American teaching

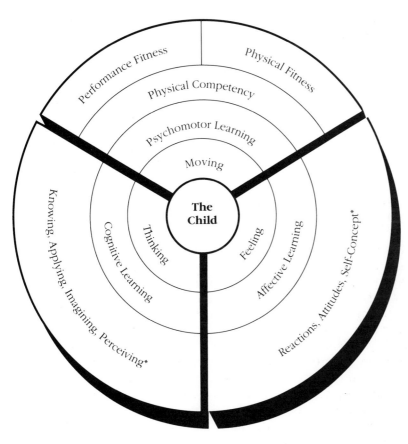

* Not all concepts are stated here.

Figure 1.1 The moving, thinking, feeling child

methodology was evolving, and American teachers who had traveled to Britain offered their insights into effective teaching methods. Thus the marriage began—the use of Laban's concepts for content, with an array of teaching styles to create a positive learning environment to meet all children's needs. The result was much more effective physical education programs.

More recently we have become acutely aware of the role of physical education in children's lives. Physical fitness is of significant concern to us all and our aim is to promote total health and wellness in our programs. Our goal is to offer equal opportunity to both boys and girls, disabled and able-bodied, so that all may enjoy an active, healthy lifestyle.

Children are complex beings whose thoughts, feelings, and actions are constantly in a state of flux. Because of the dynamic nature of children as they grow and mature, change in one element often affects the others. Thus, it is a "whole" child whom we must educate, not merely the physical or bodily aspect of the child (see figure 1.1).

The Moving, Thinking, Feeling Child

a.

b.

We are concerned with both
(a) **cognitive** abilities and
(b) **affective** abilities.

You will very likely study, or may have already studied some child psychology, so only a cursory overview on cognitive or affective development will be included here. While some important points will be discussed briefly in this chapter, you will see how we apply cognitive and affective development theory in the teaching chapters on dance, games, and gymnastics.

The Moving Child

Our primary goal as teachers of physical education is, of course, to educate children as they move, termed the *psychomotor development* of the child.

In order to understand psychomotor development, we first need to appreciate some basic concepts that affect children's progression through various stages in the process of acquiring movement competency. These concepts, termed *principles of development,* are outlined for you.

Principles of Development

Each of us grows and physically matures in much the same way. Our growth and development is largely predetermined. Under normal circumstances, we learn to walk at about twelve months, run at age three, skip at age six. Why?

We are concerned with **psychomotor** abilities.

Cephalocaudal Development When the child is born, the head constitutes approximately one-quarter of the total length of the body. Thus, the center of gravity is high and makes balance difficult. For example, children use the fewest body parts to throw or catch a ball. No steps are taken and their bodies are firmly planted on the ground. As the preschooler learns to run, strides are short and the feet are placed wide apart, rather than one in front of the other. As children mature, the whole body becomes involved in the action. Usually, the arms, shoulders, and hips rotate, and a step is taken to throw, kick, and strike.

Proximodistal Development In utero, the trunk develops prior to the limbs and extremities. As a result, children are able to gain control over the trunk of their body before limbs, hands, and feet. This concept infers that control proceeds from mass (gross muscles) to specific (fine muscle). For a child, large movements are much easier than fine, precise movements.

Balance is difficult for young
children because of their
physical proportions.

When a child enters kindergarten, an array of gross motor skills have
been mastered and many others are being acquired. The delight these
children experience in gross motor activities is obvious. They seem to
speak and react with their entire body; running, jumping, climbing, hopping, leaping, skipping, and galloping engrosses their whole being. Fine
motor skills, such as cutting, pasting, printing, drawing, coloring, and
tracing, are much slower to develop and require much practice.

A quality elementary physical education program will take both gross
and fine motor control into account. Gross motor activities slowly give
way to skills that require both gross and fine muscle control. When children gain control over their bodies, they will want to spend more time
handling objects. The simple skill of running and stopping emerges, to
be utilized later in a game situation where the child runs, stops, dodges
an opponent, and catches then aims the ball at a target. Gross motor
skills demonstrated without equipment progress to a combination of
gross and fine motor skills with equipment. The skills demanded of the
child should always proceed from simple to complex.

Each child is unique.

Each Child is Unique There will be some children who are advanced in their motor development and skills, while others will lag behind. This is due to many factors. Some children may have experienced a growth spurt. These children are constantly accommodating their movements to rapidly changing physical proportions. Still others may be small and physically immature. Often these smaller children are agile and quick, excelling at dance and gymnastics activities. An eight-year-old child highly skilled in catching and throwing will not necessarily be equally adept at striking or kicking skills. Although some of the movement patterns and spatial strategies may be similar, direct transfer does not usually occur.

It is quite remarkable that despite all of the obvious differences between children, the process of skill acquisition is relatively predictable as children grow and mature. Table 1.2 outlines this process, in which basic movements progress to complex movements and finally to refined movement skills. In the elementary years, gross motor activities that require primarily large muscle control are developed through the nonmanipulative activities of locomotion, balancing, and weightbearing. As some degree of proficiency is acquired, children will be challenged by manipulative activities, most of which require a degree of fine motor skill. Specialized skills emerge as children discover efficient and effective movements in dance, gymnastics, and games.

The Process of Skill Acquisition

REMEMBER THAT

Physically or mentally handicapped children may be developmentally delayed in relation to their peers. While this, of course, depends on the handicapping condition, children may "catch up" in due time or reach a plateau at some point in the continuum of skill acquisition.

Table 1.2

▼▼▼▼   ▼

Process of skill acquisition

Basic Gross Motor Activities		Complex Fine Motor Activities		Refined Specialized Skills
Require large muscle control		*Require small muscle control*		*Require fine and gross muscle control*
Arms	Shoulders	Fingers	Toes	
Legs	Hips	Hands	Feet	
Trunk	Back	Wrists	Ankles	
		Neck		
Nonmanipulative Activities		**Manipulative Activities**		
Develop control of the body		*Develop control of objects*		*Ability to control both the body and objects*
1. Locomotion:		1. Projecting:		
walking	running	throwing	rolling	
rolling	skipping	bouncing	kicking	
jumping	climbing	2. Receiving:		
galloping	sliding	catching	trapping	
leaping	hopping	3. Retaining:		
2. Balancing		dribbling	carrying	
3. Weightbearing:				
hanging	stretching			
swinging	twisting			
gripping	contracting			

▼▼▼▼   ▼

Physical Competency

Physical competency enables us to acquire skills more readily. Here we refer to the body's fitness level as well as its ability to respond to the demands of physical performance. The latter we term *performance fitness* (see figure 1.2).

Physical Fitness One of the primary objectives of the physical education program should be to increase—or at least maintain—each child's level of fitness. Because one's fitness level is highly affected by level of activity, genetic endowments, and nutrition, the fitness level of each child differs.

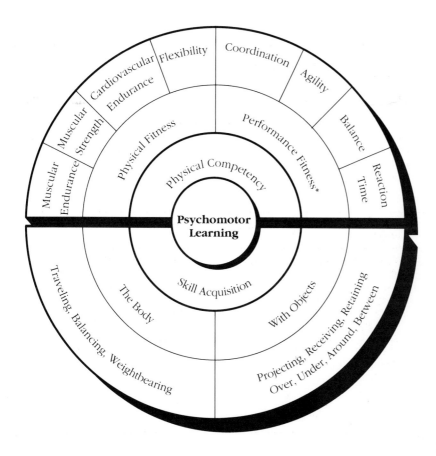

* Not all performance skills are stated here.

Figure 1.2 The psychomotor domain

Within any typical class, there will be a child who runs the fastest, another who is declared the strongest, and possibly another who boasts being able to do the "splits." Each of these children is demonstrating an admirable ability in one of the four components of fitness. These are:

1. cardiovascular endurance
2. muscular endurance
3. muscular strength
4. flexibility

Jogging promotes
cardiovascular endurance.

In order to maintain or increase one's fitness level, at least twenty minutes of activity three or four times a week, which increases the heart rate significantly, is necessary. Thus, regular physical education classes are essential if this objective of increased fitness is to be realized.

1. **Cardiovascular Endurance**—This refers to the body's ability to pump blood from the heart in order to serve the muscles with oxygen over a long period of time. Any strenuous activity engaged in over three minutes that significantly increases the heart rate is considered beneficial to the cardiovascular system. This is aerobic activity. Examples of these low-power output activities are running, swimming, skipping, or biking for an extended period of time.

In the physical education lesson, the introductory activity serves to warm up the student—a vitally important component of fitness. Cardiovascular activity may also be found in games lessons where a great deal of running is involved.

2. **Muscular Endurance**—This refers to the individual's ability to use particular muscles repeatedly. Most activities that tax the cardiovascular system also tax the particular muscles necessary to complete the exercise. Examples of these high-power output activities include practicing a handstand or cartwheel repeatedly, climbing a high rope, or jumping over and over again.

   Gymnastic activities that involve taking weight on the hands promote muscular endurance of the arms. In the games lesson, the repeated serving of a volleyball or throwing and catching of a playground ball require muscular endurance of the upper body. Leaping, jumping, and balancing activities in the dance lesson require muscular endurance of the legs.

3. **Muscular Strength**—Strength refers to a muscle's ability to work over a short period of time (ten seconds to three minutes). This is anaerobic activity. Muscular strength refers to the maximum force exerted by a muscle when contracted maximally. Examples of activities that require muscular strength are sprinting a short distance, lifting a heavy object, and opening an uncooperative jar.

   In dance, games, and gymnastics, the ability to jump high and with ease is an asset. This requires strength. Whether maintaining an unusual body shape in dance, balancing on the hands in gymnastics, or holding a defensive position in games, strength is an important aspect of fitness to consider.

4. **Flexibility**—This term refers to the range of motion about a particular joint of the body. Touching your toes is a common exercise. This is an indication of hip and lower back flexibility. While children are extremely flexible, it is evident that the body loses some flexibility due to the growth and maturation process. It appears that our level of flexibility may be in part due to genetic endowment as well as environmental factors or the activities in which we engage. If, for example, a child has been involved in gymnastics, ballet, wrestling, or diving, a higher level of flexibility may carry over into his or her adult life. Males are usually less flexible simply because typically male-oriented activities do not require good flexibility and thus

Rope climbing requires muscular endurance.

Hip and leg flexibility are required to do the splits.

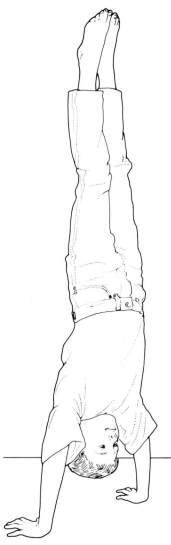

Headstands require muscular strength.

flexibility is not worked on during training. It is a fallacy that increased muscle mass reduces flexibility. If movements that increase flexibility are not practiced, then a reduced level of flexibility may be anticipated. It is important for every teacher to include activities that promote flexibility both to increase range of motion and reduce the possibility of injury.

Flexibility is primarily developed in physical education through dance and gymnastic activities that stretch the muscles. A "cold" muscle (one which has not been exercised) must never be bounced, but rather stretched for 20–30 seconds and released.

Performance Fitness This relates to the individual's ability to participate with ease and efficiency. Performance fitness (also termed movement ability) components include such things as coordination, reaction time, agility, and speed. While individuals who jog regularly may be highly physically fit, they may lack in performance fitness. Another individual who leads a sedentary lifestyle and is quite physically unfit may be quite adept in performance fitness (see figure 1.2).

To Do

1. Run up and down a set of stairs until you are tired. Was it your legs that "gave out"? If so, your muscular endurance in your legs wasn't equal to your cardiovascular endurance. If your chest hurt and you had "no air," it was your cardiovascular system that couldn't keep up to the muscular endurance in your legs.

2. Place one hand on the back of your neck, your other hand on your back. Slowly move your hands toward each other. Can you touch your fingertips together? If so, then you have good shoulder flexibility.

3. How many sit-ups can you do in thirty seconds? How many push-ups can you do in thirty seconds? These exercises will tax your muscular strength and endurance.

▼▼▼▼   ▼

The Thinking Child

Physical education has a special role in cognitive development. We call the subject physical **education,** which implies the transmission and reception of knowledge and thought, and the application of concepts. Thought (conscious or subconscious) should accompany all motion and difficult movements and sequences require refined thought.

In physical education we focus on the specific concepts of body, space, effort, and relationships (see chapter 2). Because of their relevance to all movement, these concepts form the basis of the subject. One of the objectives of physical education is for children to understand the principles governing movement, for this understanding promotes progression in physical skill.

The physical education program should aim to promote cognitive development in many ways. Even as the class enters the activity area or outdoor setting, children adapt to a new learning environment—one of large spaces, various equipment, and a modified set of behavioral guidelines.

As learning begins, a specialized vocabulary is used and language is developed. Because the aim is to structure lessons around a specific movement concept, all activity should pertain to that concept. Children will gain insight by responding to the task and receiving feedback as movement concepts are studied.

The child must use cognitive
abilities in movement
activities.

The range of task structure, from being closed, so that there is little or no choice of response, to open, which allows for much individual interpretation, encourages the child to think as the problem is solved (see chapter 3). While the task may be as wide in scope as "practice what you learned yesterday," or more clearly defined ("work with your ball at a high level"), the child must consciously decide which movements are appropriate.

We often ask questions of the class to reinforce and clarify facts and concepts, and their application and the development of creativity. Some examples follow.

1. Where should you look if you are "pressing"?
2. What would your pathway look like if you were to "meander"?
3. Can you clap to this music?
4. Change your punching action so that it is very s-l-o-w. What word can you use to describe this new movement?
5. We absorb force when we bend our arms in catching a ball. How can you absorb force when you jump?

6. Why do we use our arms to jump higher?
7. How can you use the space more effectively when you are passing the ball around an opponent?
8. Which rolls, a ball or a box? What body shape do you need to roll smoothly?
9. How should you place your hands so that you have a firm base in a headstand?
10. What kind of a body shape is best when you want to be very stable?

Thus, the cognitive domain is educated. Quality movement is a major objective of any physical education program and is the result of creating, analyzing, memorizing, concentrating, and applying knowledge.

Attitudes, moods, self-concept, and social awareness affect all of our feelings. Sometimes called "gut reactions," the source of our feelings may be very spontaneous or may be the result of expertise or experience. While the affective domain has been largely ignored in the educational curricula of the past, educators are becoming increasingly aware of the vital importance of enhancing the child's self-awareness.

The Feeling Child

The environment of the physical education class affects the feelings of every child. Teachers who encourage and appreciate individual differences will foster desirable attitudes towards physical education. Our ultimate goal is to develop a warm, positive class environment in which everyone may be prepared to risk without fear of ridicule.

For this reason, teachers must aim to treat all children as unique human beings. The teacher who praises each and every positive effort helps to create a friendly atmosphere where children feel welcome. In a class of this sort, self-esteem and social graces are enhanced.

Positive teacher behavior includes calling children by their names, ensuring that various children are "leaders," and that children are not being singled out for negative reasons. Therefore, activities such as elimination games are unacceptable as they detect the lesser skilled children and punish them through exclusion from the activity. Children may in subtle or obvious ways be reprimanded for their weak skill level. They need as much opportunity for skill acquisition as their more talented peers. The process may become cyclical in nature, as illustrated in figure 1.3.

A positive learning environment is one in which all children may succeed at their own level. Children readily accept the talents of their peers, and teachers need not feel apprehensive about praising individual children for their unique abilities whether they be very small or quite significant.

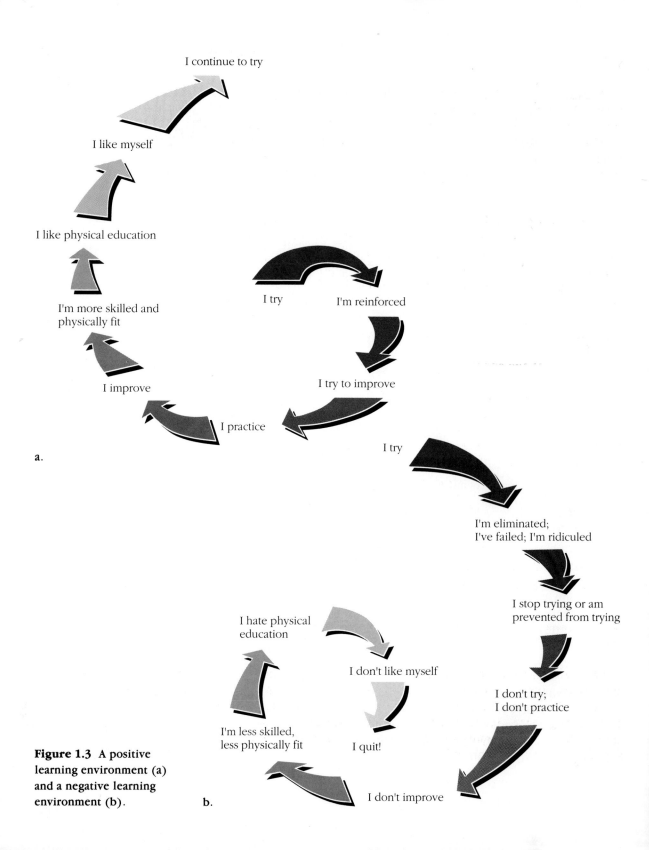

I continue to try

I like myself

I like physical education

I'm more skilled and physically fit

I improve

I practice

I try

I'm reinforced

I try to improve

I try

a.

I'm eliminated;
I've failed; I'm ridiculed

I stop trying or am prevented from trying

I don't try;
I don't practice

I hate physical education

I don't like myself

I quit!

I'm less skilled,
less physically fit

I don't improve

Figure 1.3 A positive learning environment (a) and a negative learning environment (b).

b.

Because children learn from observing and interacting with their peers, observation and close student interaction (e.g., "help your friend improve the end of his or her sequence") is of tremendous value for skill development. Teachers may stop a class to point out quality movement or a unique response to the task. Because we do not expect every child to work at a specified skill level nor respond in the same manner, every child in the class should be offered the opportunity to demonstrate occasionally.

Appropriate social groupings are very important. A positive learning environment will be the result of careful planning of who goes into what group as well as spatial placing of the students. A space overcrowded with gymnastic apparatus and lacking in safety is not conducive to positive or happy peer interaction. When a game is played with too many children it restricts activity and the children's resulting boredom may lead to negative peer interaction. In dance, creating groups that are too large will result in lack of cooperation, because of the children's difficulty of dealing with too many people and ideas. Thus, the teacher must be cognizant of age appropriate social groupings (see table 1.3).

Research has resulted in greater understanding of the cognitive, affective, and psychomotor development of children, helping us to identify needs of different stages as well as to recognize that children do not have the same likes, abilities, motivation, and skills. We are more accepting of individual differences; indeed, we often encourage variations in performance more than discourage them. The "miniature adult" idea has long since passed, but we must avoid falling into the trap of underestimating children's capabilities. This may result in our under-challenging them and/or accepting poor quality performance. When skilled teachers combine:

> **t**heir theoretical knowledge of growth and development;
>
> **w**hat they know of the individual children they are teaching;
>
> **m**ovement knowledge; and
>
> **t**eaching knowledge;

they are then able to offer exciting lessons in dance, games, and gymnastics.

Characteristics of Children

Despite obvious individual differences within a class of children, various age groups generally exhibit predictable cognitive, social, and physical behaviors. A sequential physical education program based on knowledge of the general characteristics of particular age groups is most valuable. Table 1.3 illustrates characteristics, implications, and activity suggestions for ages 5 through 12.

Table 1.3

▼▼▼▼   ▼

Physical, cognitive, and social development of children, as
related to age

Age 5

Characteristics	Physical development Implications	Activity suggestions
Need vigorous activity	Daily lessons of 20–30 minutes will promote healthy growth and development	Every child should engage in maximum activity for a maximum amount of time
Growth rate is decreasing	General movement abilities are improving	Body awareness activities—body parts, weightbearing, locomotion
Percentage of muscle mass is increasing, body fat is decreasing	Children are becoming stronger, more agile, and are very flexible	Dance, gymnastic, and locomotor activities to promote agility and flexibility
Lacks muscular endurance	Children tire easily and may require moments of rest	Alternate periods of intense activity with periods of a less strenuous nature
Center of gravity is still high	Sense of equilibrium is developing, balance is sometimes difficult	Rolling, hopping, leaping, jumping— weightbearing on various body parts promote good balance
Energy is directed toward mastering bodily control, and to a lesser extent, control of objects	Activity without equipment is important	Locomotor activities in dance, games, and gymnastics should be stressed
Gross motor skills are much easier than fine motor skills	Children can handle their body much better than with objects	Gross motor activities, nonmanipulative activities
Most can run with adult form	Running may be utilized in activities	Stopping, starting, dodging, changing direction, pathways, and speed in running. Chasing games are a favorite
Some locomotor movements are still being acquired	Much time should be spent on locomotor activities	Rolling, jumping, hopping, leaping, skipping, and galloping, presented in various ways
Beginning of object handling	Manipulation of objects is difficult:	More time should be spent on nonmanipulative skills than manipulative skills

Table 1.3—*Continued*

▼▼▼▼   ▼

Age 5

Characteristics	*Physical development Implications*	*Activity suggestions*
	—may throw and strike (project) with some proficiency	Throw with small balls, strike with a large bat or hand at a stationary ball
	—may catch and trap (receive) with difficulty	Catching and trapping is easiest when rolled or bounced with a large ball

Characteristics	*Cognitive development Implications*	*Activity suggestions*
	—may bounce and dribble (retain) with difficulty	Large balls should be used. A predictable surface such as the wall or floor should be used in initial development of ball skills
Children may excel in one skill and find another difficult	Teacher should allow for and anticipate individual differences	Skilled children should be given additional challenges, lesser skilled children should be encouraged but not pressured
Children have a short attention span	Change activities/tasks often	Directions for and duration of, activities must be brief. Children may need to be reminded of task
Amount of concentration varies	Are prone to accidents, may forget easily, can't work alone for lengthy periods	Remind children of task, safety procedures
Repetition is enjoyed and provides security	Routines are necessary; favorite activities are enjoyed repeatedly	Establish routine, repeat favorite activities, repeat mastered skills
Wants to be always involved	Equipment for every child and a variety	Each child should be as active as possible with his/her own equipment

Table 1.3—*Continued*
▼▼▼▼   ▼

Age 5

Characteristics	Cognitive development Implications	Activity suggestions
Are eager to learn	Enjoy solving problems, discovering	Problem-solving is ideal with much exploration, time to discover Apply Laban's concepts of body, effort, space, and relationships
Enjoy music, rhythmic activities	Keep good time to rhythmic music, creating own rhythms	Music and percussion instruments may be used extensively in activities
Are imaginative, love dramatics	Enjoy the expressive nature of dance	Foster use of the imagination, creativity, and dramatics
General lack of fear	Children should work within their capabilities	Children should be taught safety rules and procedures to prevent injuries

Characteristics	Social development Implications	Activity suggestions
Are very egocentric	Cooperation with a partner may be difficult	Working alone is best; short periods of working with a partner
	Have difficulty in seeking a team goal	Team games present a problem because the child is not always active
	Scores are not important	Racing and chasing games (tag) are appropriate
Need approval and much praise	Provide experiences that will challenge the child, yet foster success	Give praise for quality work, good efforts, and recent accomplishments
Are learning to share, take turns	Will share and take turns if the activity is appropriate	Children should not be forced to work with others

Ages 6 and 7

Characteristics	Physical development Implications	Activity suggestions
Need vigorous activity	Daily lessons of 30 minutes will ensure healthy development	Every child should engage in maximum activity for a maximum amount of time
Steady gains in height and weight	Health improves, children are stronger and more physically adept	Much repetition of previously acquired skills in new and varied situations

Table 1.3—*Continued*

▼▼▼▼   ▼

Ages 6 and 7

Characteristics	Physical development Implications	Activity suggestions
Legs are still short in relation to trunk, however, legs are growing rapidly	Children may appear awkward at times, adept at others	Much activity to enhance control of the body and to a lesser extent, control of objects
Center of gravity is near adult location	Activities requiring balance are important	Repeat simple challenges requiring good balance, introduce new ones on floor and apparatus
Improved ability to focus eyes and track objects	Manipulation of objects is steadily improving	Catching, trapping with feet, dribbling with hands or feet are appropriate activities
Enjoys constant activity, has sudden bursts of energy	Should have maximum activity within lesson	Directions should be short, each child should have equipment
Is mastering or has mastered most locomotor movements	Running, skipping, galloping, hopping, leaping, jumping, and rolling play a large role in the program	Much repetition of locomotor activities in dance, games, and gymnastics
Skill and control is developing in gross motor activities	Repeat gross motor skills acquired; practice new gross motor skills	Create new balances, shapes, or ways of travelling on body parts, in new directions and pathways, on or with various equipment
Manipulative skills are slowly developing	Children vary in their ability to manipulate equipment. Most can kick, bounce a ball, throw, catch	Manipulate equipment with various body parts Extensions such as paddles, sticks, and racquets are often too difficult Batting is appropriate if the ball is stationary
Fine motor skills are slowly developing	Activities requiring small muscle control are difficult	Ball activities are important, but bean bags, hoops, and skipping ropes should be used as well to encourage fine muscle control

Table 1.3—*Continued*

▼▼▼▼   ▼

Ages 6 and 7

Characteristics	Physical development Implications	Activity suggestions
Abilities of males and females is not different	Differences in ability due to the child's sex are not apparent	All children should be encouraged to participate to their best ability

Characteristics	Cognitive development Implications	Activity suggestions
Attention span is still short	Lessons should be short with varied activities	Change activities/tasks often. Keep directions short and simple
Has improved reasoning powers	May be reasoned with effectively	Will understand clear, short directions and explanations
Discourages easily, has strong desire to please others	Needs praise, encouragement, understanding	Each child should receive positive reinforcement; children should not be singled out for negative reasons
Is imaginative and creative, enjoys dramatics	Activities should foster creativity and imagination	Create games, dance, and gymnastics sequences Dramatic movement is enjoyed
"Why?" is often asked	The program should encourage reasoning, problem-solving, memory	Set tasks utilizing problem-solving, limitation methods of teaching
Memory is improving, though may lapse	A well-planned program should provide for continuity, building on previous work	Children may require reminders for safety, sequence work, previous activities
Has a greater purpose in work than at age 5	Has a tremendous desire to learn new skills and master others	Repeat body and space concepts without equipment Provide much time for work with equipment in various ways
Concepts of time, weight, and space are developing	Concepts of time, weight, and space should be included	Concepts of fast and slow, heavy and light, directions, pathways, and levels should be explored
Responds well to rhythmic music	Various kinds of recorded music as well as percussion instruments are enjoyed	Dance activities should involve the use of music

Table 1.3—*Continued*

▼▼▼▼ ▼

Ages 6 and 7

Characteristics	Social development Implications	Activity suggestions
Sense of humor is not mature	Children will laugh at silly situations, slapstick humor	Sarcasm will be perceived as ridicule
Transition period between individual and group play	Would rather play alone or with one other, but groups of 3 or 4 may be suitable at times	Children should work primarily alone or with one other; groups of 5 or more are ineffective
Friendships shift continually	Teacher should allow for spontaneous groupings	Sensitivity to children's social preferences is important
Little differentiation between friends of same or opposite sex	Children will gladly play with a member of the opposite sex	Pairing children is not a problem due to gender
Will recognize that some children are more skilled than others	Program should allow for individual differences	Children should be openly praised for skill, although every child needs praise and reinforcement
Children are usually in awe of teacher, may be intimidated by teacher who knows all	Teacher should be aware of this responsibility	Children should be free to ask questions and the teacher to openly admit mistakes or lack of knowledge

Ages 8 and 9

Characteristics	Physical development Implications	Activity suggestions
Need vigorous activity	Lessons should be 30–45 minutes long, at least three times a week	Maximum amount of children should participate for a maximum amount of time
Height and weight gain is strong and steady	Children have good balance, agility, flexibility, strength	Previously learned skills may be utilized in more challenging ways
Upper body is in good proportion to lower body	Balance is excellent and should be applied in dance, games, and gymnastic activities	Balance activities that challenge the student in both body and object handling should be included
Usually little difference in physique of males and females, though there may be some early maturing 9-year-olds	Males and females should engage in all activities together	Both males and females should be exposed to a wide range of activities

Table 1.3—*Continued*
▼▼▼▼   ▼

Ages 8 and 9

Characteristics	Physical development Implications	Activity suggestions
Physiological growth changes occur in female from 8–12; in males from 9–13	Some early maturers experience hormonal imbalances	Activities that provide for differences in physical and emotional maturity, such as creating games, gymnastic, and dance sequences, and playing cooperative games
Distinct individual differences due to physical maturation and past experience	Children need a well-balanced program	Challenging, success-oriented activities in dance, games, and gymnastics
Are active and energetic, may be overactive with hurried carelessness	Much activity, encouragement to tenaciously pursue new skills and sequences	Working alone or in pairs to maximize activity and skill development
Eye-hand, eye-foot coordination is quite good	Skills with equipment can begin to progress to being sport-specific	Ball control with feet and hands alone, with a partner, and in small groups
	Include extensions such as racquets, paddles, sticks, and scoops in program	Working alone and with a partner, cooperatively and competitively, with extensions
Locomotor skills are being refined	Activities in dance, games, and gymnastics become more dissimilar and complex	Locomotion that involves apparatus, equipment, and other children
Fine motor control is developing	Activities that require use of small muscles of hands, wrists, feet, ankles	Gestures, balancing, body parts leading the action in dance Gripping, releasing with feet and hands, balancing in gymnastics Throwing, catching, kicking, striking, controlling different objects with different implements in games

Table 1.3—*Continued*

▼▼▼▼   ▼

Ages 8 and 9

Characteristics	Cognitive development Implications	Activity suggestions
Desires quality approval, wants to do things well	All children should experience success	Success-oriented teaching methods with encouragement Children should not be made to conform to set standards and expectations, nor singled out for lack of ability (as in relays)
Memory sharpens	Children can concentrate, maintain interest for longer periods of time	Lessons should be from 30–45 minutes in length
Decrease in egocentricity	Children can appreciate, empathize with others	Can work well in pairs or groups up to 4 in dance, games, and gymnastics
Thought processes begin to be adultlike	Problem-solving and concept development may be more complex	Enjoy creating sequences, game strategy Combinations of concepts make lessons both mentally and physically demanding
Distinct individual differences in personality, interest	Are aware of own abilities and interests; self-concept is being established	Personalities may harmonize or clash; teacher should carefully structure groups
\ Winning and losing are of tremendous importance	May be aggressive, quarrelsome; may argue over fairness	Rules must be established and adhered to; disciplinary measures should be consistent and fair

Characteristics	Social development Implications	Activity suggestions
Children are between childhood and adolescence	Want responsibility, adult privileges but may not have maturity to handle it	Teacher's guidance and supervision is crucial
\ Awareness of peers is increasing	Peer acceptance and pressure may be more important than adults'	Activities should reinforce the self-image of both males and females

Table 1.3—*Continued*

▼▼▼▼   ▼

Ages 8 and 9

Characteristics	Social development Implications	Activity suggestions
Clubs, gangs begin to form of one sex	Children enjoy being a member of a group, team	May work well in groups of 4 in games activities; in dance and gymnastics, partner work is best
Friendships are almost exclusive to same sex	Teacher needs sensitivity when forming groups, teams so all children feel accepted	Children should not be forced into working with partner of opposite sex if they don't wish to (i.e., folk dancing)
Becoming aware of sexual roles, separate interests of sexes	Boys tend to enjoy rough play, strong vigorous movement; girls tend to enjoy social interaction, fine motor movements, and attention to details	Dance activities should appeal to boys' masculine nature; games activities should be structured so that girls will experience and progress in their skill. Avoid playing "boys against girls"
Role models from the community, television, or movies become important	Children may attempt to emulate the behavior of role models	Role models may be used to the teacher's advantage to develop or provide impetus to an activity (i.e., "Sugar Ray Leonard jumped rope to train, let's all jump rope")

Ages 10 through 12

Characteristics	Physical development Implications	Activity suggestions
Need vigorous activity	Lessons should be 30–60 minutes long and at *least* three times per week	Children should experience maximum activity for a maximum amount of time
Individual differences become obvious	Wide differences in physical stature, abilities within class	Children should be able to work at their own level and progress at their own rate
Rapid development in strength, control of gross and fine muscles	Complex skills are being refined and may be applied to specific sports	Judicious instruction and expected level of performance in sports skills must account for individual differences

Table 1.3—*Continued*

▼▼▼▼   ▼

Ages 10 through 12

Characteristics	Physical development Implications	Activity suggestions
Girls tend to be taller and heavier than boys	Girls are usually more mature both physically and socially	Girls may need extra encouragement at times to participate fully due to self-consciousness
Flexibility may begin to decrease, especially in boys who naturally tend not to pursue activities which tax flexibility	Girls may begin to show greater ability than boys in activities that require flexibility	Persistence of teacher for both males and females to pursue dance and gymnastic activities that require flexibility
		Muscles should not be bounced to increase the flexibility of a joint, rather a stretch should be held for 15–20 seconds and released
		Teacher should encourage challenging balances, shapes, transference of weight, and unique use of body parts to promote flexibility

Characteristics	Cognitive development Implications	Activity suggestions
Enjoys some intellectual activities, appreciates and can apply abstract concepts. Fact retention increases	Program should be intellectually stimulating	Children can readily apply and utilize concepts learned previously, such as biomechanical factors and movement concepts. Teacher may discuss fitness principles and their implications in the program
		Children may wish to pursue learning about the history of particular sports, professional athletes, etc.
		Rules become increasingly important

Table 1.3—*Continued*

▼▼▼▼   ▼

Ages 10 through 12

Characteristics	Cognitive development Implications	Activity suggestions
Enjoy contests	Contests may be used more frequently in games activities	Large- and small-group contests are appropriate occasionally, when children have mastered the skills required
Increased interest in hobbies, extracurricular activities	Some children may be highly skilled in specific sports	Additional challenges should be provided for the highly skilled. This may include having the highly skilled help the lesser-skilled children

Characteristics	Social development Implications	Activity suggestions
Egocentricity decreases	Usually conforms well to authority, though children may sometimes find conflicting reactions to adult standards	Rules, procedures should be well-established and enforced Some adults are highly respected; teacher must earn children's respect
Definite groups form according to age and sex	May display antagonism towards opposite sex	Groups should be created with prudence Classes should be mixed; however, occasionally separating the sexes may increase skill development and productivity
Seeks group approval	Aware of group reactions, group standards	Teacher should structure activities with children's preferences in mind
Role models play an important part in child's world	Athletic role models should be incorporated, discussed when appropriate	Incorporate children's interests in games, dance stimuli, and dance themes
Children are establishing values	Children may be swayed easily by the opinions, values of respected others	Teacher must be fair, encouraging, and positive

Table 1.3—*Continued*

▼▼▼▼   ▼

Ages 10 through 12

Characteristics	*Social development Implications*	*Activity suggestions*
Males and females develop separate interests	Boys tend to be extremely competitive and value high skill; girls fluctuate in friendships and value skill to a lesser degree	Boys may need encouragement to play fairly, to include others; girls may need encouragement to participate fully
Desire to be popular, need to assert self	Program should utilize problem-solving teaching methods and provide for individual differences where all can succeed	Peer observation should be utilized but children should not be forced to demonstrate if they would prefer not
		Every child should be recognized for achievements at all levels of skill

▼▼▼▼   ▼

Summary

A quality physical education program has tremendous value for all children. While gaining useful physical skills and improving fitness, children may learn movement concepts and other cognitive skills that increase their ability to participate in groups and get along with others. The rich variety found in dance, games, and gymnastics experiences allows all children to benefit from a diverse program.

Contemporary physical education has evolved from physical training programs, which stressed calisthenics, to a focus upon movement concepts and individualized learning. The physical education program should promote useful physical skills, enhance physical fitness, promote an understanding of movement principles, and increase the child's self-esteem. The content of physical education is based upon four movement concepts as postulated by Rudolf Laban. The teaching method should be varied according to the needs of the children.

Teachers should be aware of educating the "whole" child, through dance, games, and gymnastics activities that enhance the cognitive, affective, and psychomotor domains. While all children progress through the same stages of physical growth and development, individual children progress at different rates.

Review Questions

1. Why should physical education be included in the elementary school program?
2. What are some of the objectives of the elementary school program?
3. What contribution did Rudolf Laban make towards physical education?
4. What is the affective domain? How may it be enhanced in physical education?
5. What is the psychomotor domain and its component parts of physical and movement competency?
6. Discuss three principles of growth and development, and their implications for the physical education teacher.

References

Bailey, D. A., A. D. Martin, and J. L. Howie. 1986. Physical Activity, Nutrition, Bone Density and Osteoporosis. *Australian Journal of Science and Medicine in Sport.* 18:3, 3–8.

Hill, R. 1979. Movement Education: What's in a Name? *Canadian Association of Health, Physical Education and Recreation Journal.* 46:1, 18–24.

Van Hagan, W., G. Dexter, and J. F. Williams. 1951. *Physical Education in the Elementary School.* Sacramento: California State Department of Education.

Wall, J. 1981. *Beginnings.* Montreal: McGill University.

Related Readings

Anderson, D. 1986. A Successful Program. Elementary Physical Education. *Journal of Physical Education, Recreation and Dance.* 57:6, 43–44, 60.

Bressan, E. 1986. Children's Physical Education Designed to Make a Difference. *Journal of Physical Education, Recreation and Dance.* 57:2, 26–28.

Dalley, M. 1985. Physical Activity for the Very Young. *Canadian Association of Health, Physical Education and Recreation Journal.* 51:8, 13–17.

Rupnow, E. 1980. Eliminating Sex Role Stereotyping in Elementary Physical Education. *Journal of Health, Physical Education and Recreation.* 51:6, 38.

Seefeldt, V. 1984. Physical Fitness in Preschool and Elementary School Aged Children. *Journal of Physical Education, Recreation and Dance.* 55:9, 33–37.

Verabioff, L. 1986. Can We Justify Daily Physical Education? *Canadian Association of Health, Physical Education and Recreation Journal.* 52:2, 8–11.

For those interested in pursuing the historical aspects of elementary physical education since 1945 there is extensive material housed at the University of North Carolina, Greensboro, North Carolina.

CHAPTER

2

UNDERSTANDING MOVEMENT

The physical education program we propose for children in elementary schools is based on *movement concepts,* which are studied in the context of three distinct movement forms: dance, games, and gymnastics. This is a skill-oriented program, dependent on our understanding and recognizing individual differences in performance levels. We try to help all children maximize their different movement abilities, and the expectation is that children will have different levels of competency (indeed, they may develop quite different skill vocabularies) in the areas of dance, games, and gymnastics.

One of our responsibilities is to help children develop positive attitudes toward an active lifestyle. We hope that children will enjoy their physical education lessons and will wish to be active at other times. We hope this enjoyment will continue throughout their lives. The need for specific fitness programs should, therefore, be reduced. In today's society the conundrum has been whether one is taught physical skills in order to improve one's level of fitness, or whether one is fit because one enjoys participating in various movement forms. We lean toward the latter.

The Movement Concepts

Rudolf Laban 1879–1958

Functional and Expressive Movement

Our physical education program is based on Rudolf Laban's *descriptive analysis of human movement.* Laban was interested in the conscious control of human movement, our ability to develop a variety of movement responses, and, unlike the animals, to select and change these responses at will. The concept of us as thinking, feeling, doing beings is central to his movement analysis.

Over the years many educators in Britain, Canada, and the United States have used Laban's movement concepts as the "content" of their physical education programs for students at all levels of education. When Laban's movement concepts form the basis of the physical education program, a conscious attempt is made to help the students understand the movement concepts so they can:

1. apply the concepts in dance, games, and gymnastics;
2. become skillful in dance, games, and gymnastics activities; and
3. appreciate the different movement forms arising.

These are three major long-term objectives of our program.

Functional and expressive movement are two important dimensions to Laban's descriptive analysis of movement. In reality the two are inseparable, but in order to discuss them it is necessary to present them as two distinct ideas.

When, for example, is running dancelike or expressive? What differentiates it from the very functional action used when trying to catch a bus? Do we consciously select the running skill appropriate for each situation? Laban's analysis of human movement helps us to understand, observe, distinguish between, select, and classify actions.

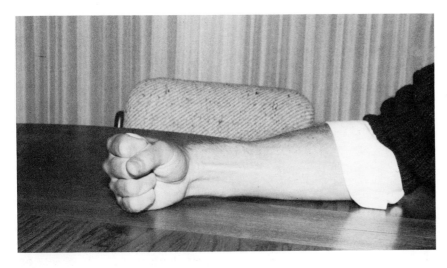

Figure 2.1 Is this expressive or functional?

The descriptive analysis begins with the premise that there are two dimensions to our movement lives:

1. "the *doing,* which encompasses all those movements necessary for the development and preservation of life in an objective way" (Wall 1983);
2. the *dancing,* including all movements concerned with feelings, expression, communication, personality, and the subjective component of our being.

The factor that differentiates between one movement activity and another is our intention as we move; an action can be functional in one context and expressive in another. To illustrate this idea, clench one hand, making a fist, and pound the little finger side (figure 2.1). What is your intention behind the action, and the context in which the action is used? It could be that you are trying to make a stamp stick on an envelope, a very functional action, or you may be making a very dogmatic statement and this gesture is used to reinforce what you are saying, in which case the action is expressive (see figure 2.2).

Why is it important for us to understand this distinction between functional and expressive movement? Because it helps us to:

1. appreciate the nature of the movement forms we are teaching;
2. define more specific objectives for our lessons;
3. elicit from the children movement responses appropriate for the context in which they are employed; and
4. select vocabulary related to the different movement forms (see table 2.1).

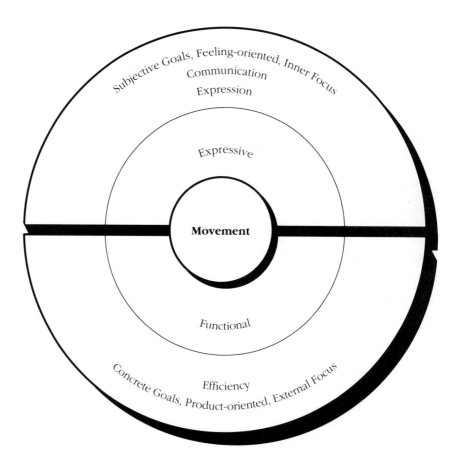

Figure 2.2 The expressive and functional aspects of movement and suggested criteria for classification of actions according to intention(s) behind the movement

To Do

The following actions may be **functional** or **expressive,** depending on the intention behind them and the context in which they are used. Suggest situations in which they are first employed functionally and then expressively.

Stamping a foot
Clapping your hands
Walking backward
A sudden turning action

Table 2.1

A semantic comparison of dance, games, and gymnastics

Movement Form (Perception)	Body Concepts—Verbs		Effort and Spatial Concepts—Adverbs
Dance *(expressive)*	Neutral:	Descriptive:	Qualifying:
	run	flee	smoothly
	walk	creep	angrily
	jump	bounce	hesitatingly
	turn	spin	forcefully
Games *(functional)*	Nonmanipulative:		Quantifying:
	run		quickly
	jump		slowly
	guard		faster
	pivot		stronger
	swerve		
	Manipulative:		
	catch		
	throw		
	kick		
	strike		
	volley		
Gymnastics *(functional)*	Neutral:		Quantifying/qualifying:
	hang		quickly
	balance		smoothly
	jump		slowly
	roll		strongly

In dance lessons we are trying to develop skillful use of the body as an instrument of expression, a carrier of ideas and abstractions. There will be a decided qualitative and aesthetic stress in our teaching. Games and gymnastics are movement forms in which the skills are used in very functional, concrete ways—to catch a ball, avoid an opponent, walk along a narrow bar, jump over a box. Beyond this, the two movement forms differ considerably. In games the body is employed as a tool, or a means to an end, the end being to score in some way. In gymnastics, the actions are ends in themselves as the gymnast asks, "Can I balance on two different body parts or hang upside-down suspended by one knee or leap across this gap?" When teaching games and gymnastics, we are concerned with improving the efficiency of each movement, and increasing the versatility and adaptability of the children. Our teaching will have a quantitative, functional emphasis.

Table 2.2

▼▼▼▼▼   ▼

Laban's four movement concepts

Body concepts: activity-oriented
Telling us what the whole body and/or specific parts are doing
Effort concepts: quantity/quality-oriented
Telling us what the movement is like, what dynamics are used
Spatial concepts: place- and pattern-oriented
Telling us where the movement is, how it moves through the environment
Relationship concepts: people- and things-oriented
Telling us what interaction is occurring between people and objects in the environment

▼▼▼▼▼   ▼

The Four Movement Concepts

Laban's descriptive analysis of human movement allows us to describe any human action in terms of four major concepts (table 2.2). These concepts give us the answers to the following four questions:

1. What is the body doing? **(body concepts)**
2. What is the dynamic content or quality of the movement? **(effort concepts)**
3. Where is the movement occurring? **(spatial concepts)**
4. With whom or to what is the mover relating? **(relationship concepts)**

Besides being able to describe any movements, we can also teach a new skill, and develop and/or change existing skills by using these concepts to modify and refine the movement patterns of the learner. The concepts provide us with the framework to:

1. structure learning tasks in all aspects of the physical education program;
2. observe and analyze movement;
3. communicate with others by using an accepted terminology; and
4. evaluate the content of the physical education program (Logsdon et al. 1984).

A number of authors (Holbrooke 1973; Logsdon et al. 1984; Russell 1975; Stanley 1977; Wall 1983) have developed schema to illustrate, explain, and clarify the components of the movement concepts. Initially they appear to be very simple ideas; however, do not be deceived by the apparent simplicity of Laban's descriptive analysis. You will understand the potential of the ideas only if you have used the movement concepts for your own skill development in the areas of dance, games, and gymnastics. Your own movement experiences are key toward the development of your teaching skills.

The four major concepts will be introduced separately and discussed as they relate to movement in a general way. In chapters 5, 8, and 11 you will find the same concepts explained as they relate specifically to the three movement forms—dance, games, and gymnastics—that are the core of the physical education program.

Awareness of the body concepts provide us with an understanding of our physical selves. Being familiar with our physical structure is a prerequisite for the acquisition and refinement of all motor skills. Very young children spend a considerable amount of time "discovering" their bodies. Babies open and close their hands, carefully watching the action all the time. They hold onto their feet and put them into their mouths. At an early age many playful activities involve identifying and naming different body parts.

Body Concepts

You may like to think of the body as a puppet or doll that has the same number and types of joints as humans. You can manipulate these inanimate objects in many ways, making them "do" many human actions and activities. Unlike the puppet or doll, we learn, through experience, to control our bodies so that we can consciously produce a specific action or combination of actions. To do this, we must know what is possible, either through discovery or by being told. Figure 2.3 shows four components of body concepts, each of which can be subdivided further.

The Body in Action The structure of our bodies is such that every movement we make or posture we assume is some combination of three basic actions: bending, stretching, and twisting. These words describe what we observe when the joints move in a particular way.

Bending Bending is the result of a joint, or series of joints, flexing. The body becomes rounded or angular as the extremities are brought nearer the center of the body and there is an accompanying inward focus. Some authors use the word "curling" interchangeably with bending. Curling has a more rounded connotation; bending is more angular. Maybe bending relates more to an action at an isolated joint, whereas "curling represents a more total involvement of many joints" (Logsdon et al. 1984).

Stretching When we stretch, the joint action is that of extension and the body parts move away from the body center, highlighting either the length and linear quality of the body or the width and flatness of the body. There tends to be an outward focus when stretching.

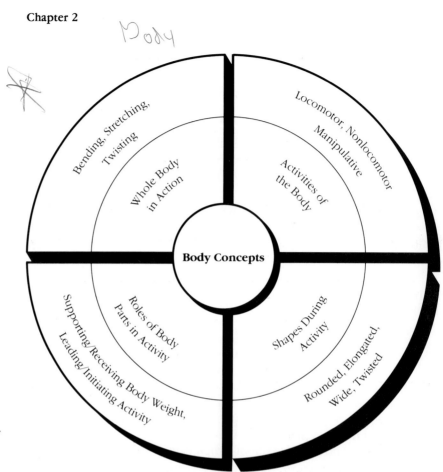

Figure 2.3 Components of the body concept of movement

Twisting The joint action of rotation can result in twisting, but only when one body part is fixed and kept still, and other parts rotate to face a new direction. To illustrate this, take a short length of paper, about the length of a finger, and hold it at each end between finger and thumb. Rotate both hands evenly away from you and toward you; the paper does not change. Now keep one hand still and rotate the other; the paper will twist. It will twist even more if you simultaneously rotate both hands in opposite directions.

Activities As the body bends, stretches, and twists, different **activities** arise. Three groups of activities form the core of dance, games, and gymnastics. These are:

1. locomotor activities
2. nonlocomotor activities
3. manipulative activities

Each group has a specialized vocabulary, which is detailed in chapters 5, 8, and 11.

To Do

1. Slowly lower your weight onto a chair, focusing on the bending actions occurring at your knees and hips. Feel the relaxation of the muscles involved when your weight is shifted from your feet to your hips.
2. Turn to look at someone or something behind you as you are sitting. What action occurs in your spine? Be aware of the counteraction in the hip region. If you look over your left shoulder what do you feel happening in your left thigh (knee to hip)? Right thigh?

▼▼▼▼   ▼

To Do

Recall two or three recent situations in which you ran (e.g., to catch up with a friend on a busy street). Describe the running skills(s) you needed to be successful. Are the skills the same or different in each situation? How versatile are you when running?

▼▼▼▼   ▼

Locomotor Activities These activities are concerned with traveling, or moving the body from place to place. The purpose of locomotion is to "go somewhere" through the general space. In our everyday lives we probably use walking more than any other form of locomotion. Young children may choose to skip along the sidewalk or run to keep up with their adult companion. Today we see more adults running as they jog to keep fit. When jogging, the focus of attention is less on the *where* of running and more on *how far* or *how long* we can run.

Forms of locomotion are explored in dance mainly because of the rhythmic nature of the activity, which is clearly seen in many folk dances, and the inherent expression in different forms of locomotion, seen more in creative dance.

A variety of running skills are developed for the purpose of playing games, and the variations in the skill depend on the nature of the game and the different roles of the players in the teams. Compare, for example, the running skills of a quarterback with the running skills of a wide receiver, or the running skills of a squash player with those of a soccer player. They are very different.

The gymnastics program really exploits our locomotor potential as we roll, climb, jump, slide, swing, or go under, across, between, and along various apparatus arrangements that are designed to challenge and excite.

Nonlocomotor Activities These are activities that occur in our personal space. The everyday activity of changing our position from standing to sitting or lying is nonlocomotor. There are two aspects to this kind of activity:

1. supporting the body weight and the resulting stillness; and
2. transferring the weight from one body part to another, resulting in changes in position.

Both of these ideas are important in dance and gymnastics and there is a considerable challenge in finding different ways of supporting ourselves and transferring weight (see chapter 11).

Examples of other nonlocomotor activities include the gestures we make as we speak, the way we turn our head or whole body to look in a different direction, our posture as we sit in a chair. Some may occur as we walk along the street; for example, we may turn to look at someone and use hand gestures as we speak. Thus, two or more components of a concept can occur simultaneously.

Manipulative Activities Activities used to control other objects are called manipulative. When we are very skilled, we almost forget the object is there, but in the initial stages of learning the skill our attention is focused exclusively on the object. Professional athletes and magicians are prime examples of people highly skilled in manipulative activities.

When we are very young, there is a large vocabulary of manipulative skills to be learned: managing a spoon, buttoning, tying shoelaces, using scissors, and holding a pencil, to name but a few. We take our ability to perform these activities for granted until we hurt or lose the use of a hand or arm. We then discover how complex and important these skills are. Some amputees and people born without hands learn to use their feet with the same degree of dexterity as those who have hands. Some people can paint exquisitely by holding a paintbrush in their mouths.

The games portion of the physical education program includes a large range of manipulative skills, which Mauldon and Redfern (1969) categorized into three groups:

1. sending away an object
2. receiving an object
3. traveling with an object

This categorization is discussed fully in chapter 8.

Body Shapes This concept may be less obvious in our daily lives than the previous two ideas. There are times when we consciously change the shape of our bodies; for example, trying to squeeze into an already full elevator, or, as children do, going through a hole in a fence to retrieve a ball thrown accidentally into a neighbor's yard.

Rounded body shape when jumping.

Defending the space.

On very windy and wet days we round our bodies to protect ourselves from the elements, as we do if someone throws a ball inaccurately in our direction and we dodge to avoid being hit. Shape is interrelated with the basic actions of bending, stretching, and twisting, resulting from the appropriate selection and combination of them. Indeed, we often describe shapes in terms of the actions used to achieve them, as in "look at that twisted shape." While in motion, our bodies are constantly assuming and passing through a variety of shapes, to which we may pay little attention.

Role of Body Parts in Activity The integrated involvement of various body parts during activity is often termed *coordination*. In much of our daily lives there is more than one body part involved, but when we concentrate on learning a new skill or improving an already known one, it is sometimes necessary to isolate a single part. As teachers we must be able to recognize the roles various body parts play.

Leading Activity In a welcoming or greeting gesture you can clearly see your hands leading your whole body, similar to reaching out to lift an object. Notice how baseball players' hands lead them as they go to catch flyballs. In gymnastics, the hands lead the body into a handstand,

Elongation of body when catching a ball above one's head.

Twisted body shapes.

and, once balanced upside down, the feet lead the body into an upright position. In dance, many different body parts may lead an action and considerable time is spent exploring expressions arising, especially in creative dance, when activities are led by different parts.

Initiating Activity It may be more difficult to observe which body parts *initiate* activity than which parts lead. To illustrate the concept, sit on a chair with your weight evenly distributed between your hips and your feet flat on the floor. Try to stand up, first by pushing your feet against the floor and then lifting your hips off the seat. Do it a second time, initiating the action in your hips. We think you will find this second method more efficient and comfortable than the first.

Changes in direction and momentum are produced by initiating activity in different parts of the body. If you have the opportunity to watch highly skilled figure skaters on television, notice how the leg not bearing weight is used to initiate turning. In dance, games, and gymnastics, the

To Do

Do these activities yourself, then watch a friend. Discuss what you saw and the differences you felt.

1. Sit before a mirror; feel and watch the differences in your expression when you make the following gestures:
   a. palm of hand moving toward the mirror, fingers toward the ceiling
   b. fingers moving toward the mirror, palm toward the ceiling
2. Keeping weight on your feet, crouch low. Begin to rise
   a. with your head leading the action
   b. with one elbow leading the action

▼▼▼▼   ▼

arms are important when jumping as they can be used to add momentum and increase the flight. Insufficient attention is often paid to this component of movement. This may be partly due to our inability to observe accurately.

Supporting and Receiving Weight These two concepts are taken together because, though different in intention, they are closely allied. Once weight is received it must be supported, even if only for a fleeting moment. It is in the area of dance and gymnastics that considerable time is spent improving and extending the ability to support and receive body weight.

The ability to support weight leads to balancing and suspending actions. We need to learn how to receive weight, absorb force, and reduce impact after actions such as jumping, transferring weight from one body part to another (as in a cartwheel), or hanging from a bar by our hands.

There are some situations in both dance and gymnastics when we are responsible for receiving and/or supporting all or part of someone else's weight. These are very challenging situations that demand considerable concentration and respect for other people.

During games activities, we learn to receive balls of various kinds. We have to be able to absorb the impact directly, with our hands, or indirectly, through a glove, stick, or other piece of equipment. Our reaction to the oncoming object depends on the speed with which it has been sent, the level at which it will arrive, and its size, shape, and weight. The appropriate amount of muscle relaxation, together with the controlled bending of the receiving limbs, results in our being able to gain and retain control of the ball.

Use of body parts to suspend weight.

Effort Concepts

The concepts inherent in the word effort are probably the least understood of Laban's principles. Initially it appears to be a very simple notion: there are four motion factors (time, weight, space, and flow) and movements are either <u>fast or slow, strong or light</u>, direct or flexible, bound or free (see figure 2.4).

You are directed to the original writing on the subject, *Effort* by Laban and Lawrence (1947), but the following quotation may help to reinforce the notion that Laban meant something far more complex than simple changes in speed, etc.

> Few people realize that their contentment in work and their happiness in life, as well as any personal or collective success, is conditioned by the perfect development and use of their individual efforts. But what effort really is and how this essential function of man could be assessed and adapted to the specific necessities of life remains for most people an unsolved problem (Laban and Lawrence 1947).

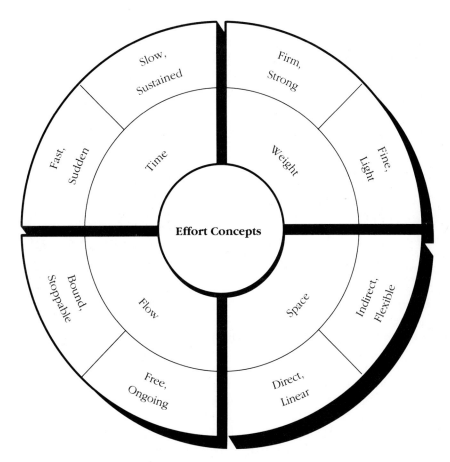

Figure 2.4 The four motion factors and the extremes of each

To relate effort to the physical manifestation, Laban and Lawrence state

A person's efforts are visibly expressed in the rhythms of his bodily motion. A rhythm may consist of strong, quick and direct movements. People who are strong, quick and direct can easily be distinguished from those with sensitive fine touch, sustained consideration and a flexible approach to decisions and actions. People thus endowed look and move differently from the strong quick and direct people (Laban and Lawrence 1947).

Effort Attitudes After years of studying human movement in many different situations, Laban concluded that we have two opposite attitudes toward the four motion factors (figure 2.4). He called one attitude indulging and the other fighting (see table 2.3).

Table 2.3

▼▼▼▼   ▼

Attitudes toward the motion factors and the resulting dynamics

	Indulging Words	Fighting Words
Time	Slow	Fast
	Lingering	Abrupt
	Sustained	Sudden
Weight	Fine	Firm
	Gentle	Powerful
	Delicate	Strong
Space	Flexible	Linear
	Roundabout	Straight
	Indirect	Direct
Flow	Free	Bound
	Ongoing	Stoppable
	Unrestrained	Restrained

▼▼▼▼   ▼

Indulging Attitude When we combine some or all of the motion factors in a specific movement in this way, we might consider that we are using more of each factor in the action. This is a satisfactory analogy with time, space, and flow. An action can be slow and last a long time, therefore incorporating two aspects of the **time** factor: speed and duration. An action with less speed and more duration is called *sustained*.

We indulge in the motion factor *space* if our movement takes up more area, is roundabout in its route, and there is no apparent focus. Watch someone using flamboyant gestures. These are often flexible as is the arm action when throwing a ball overhand. The quality changes to direct (fighting) at the moment of release as there is a specific focus to the action—the target at which the thrower is aiming.

When indulging in the use of *flow,* the sensation is of the body's energy streaming from within to the periphery and beyond. The movement will be fluent and feel free, and the focus will tend to be outside ourselves. Flow is less physical than the other three factors and is more related to our emotions, and it is manifest through the dynamics of our actions.

The idea of indulging in the *weight* factor may be a little more difficult to understand, as indulging in weight implies enjoying the sensations of being weightless, free from the pull of gravity and able to use muscle power with very delicate results. One of the best examples is of the classical ballet dancer, who is very strong, yet gives the impression of being very light. In the everyday world we see people "indulging" in the weight factor when they are picking up very delicate objects, threading a needle, or maybe lowering themselves to sit on a rickety chair. In this last example, there is very strong muscular action, which prevents gravity from

To Do

Contrast indulging (*a* and *b*) with fighting (*c* and *d*) the weight factor.

  a. Focus on your hands and gently touch fingertips together.
  b. Tap a balloon so that it floats slowly upward; use fingers, elbows, wrists.
  c. Stand tall, feet about shoulder-width apart, arms above the head and hands clasped; look up to ceiling.
  Pull strongly as if clasping a rope that is trying to pull you up to the ceiling. Release and breathe; repeat.
  d. Push a heavy piece of furniture, e.g., a piano. In *a* and *c*, the resistance is produced within the body, with opposing muscle groups working against each other.
  In *b* and *d,* the resistance is from outside the body.

▼▼▼▼　　　　　　　　　　　　　　　　　　　　▼

bringing the full body weight onto the chair all at once. When we do sit on the chair, we may still try to support some of our weight, and the sitting will feel tentative.

Fighting Attitude This attitude is opposite to indulging and results in very different qualities of action. Some functional actions need the fighting extreme of the weight factor in order to be efficient. Shot-putters and weight lifters attempt to exert maximum power, which is applied in different ways to achieve very different results.

The preceding examples indicate a fighting attitude toward the *weight* factor: when the mover is "feeling" his weight, the sensation is one of great power, alertness, and solidity. Gravity helps us as we stabilize ourselves and pull against its force. It is a very different sensation from complete relaxation when the muscles do not support the body weight; gravity takes over and the sensation is of heaviness and lethargy.

A fighting attitude toward *time* is seen when we move quickly, suddenly, or abruptly in a way that suggests we wish to finish the action. Excitement, agitation, nervousness, anger, and frustration are inner states that may be conveyed through sudden actions. Two examples of functional tasks that utilize this motion factor are the quick footwork needed in many ball games and the sudden hand movement used when trying to catch a fly.

Figure 2.4 will remind you that linear and direct are the qualities of fighting *space*. The limb or body as a whole moves through the space, disturbing it as little as possible. One literally takes the shortest route.

To Do

Contrast indulging (*a* and *b*) with fighting (*c*) the time factor.
Write the word **time.**

  a. Slowly.
  b. Focus on how long you can take to write it. Remember to keep the pen moving, as stopping en route changes the dynamics.
  c. Make a series of dots (. . .) as quickly as you can. Make sure the pen comes off the paper after each one and that there are no smudges.

▼▼▼▼▼   ▼

To Do

Contrast indulging (*a, b,* and *c*) with fighting (*d, e,* and *f*) the space factor.

  a. Put a screw into a piece of wood.
  b. Flick some ash or dust off your clothes.
  c. Jump and wiggle while in the air. Land on both feet.
  d. Pick up a pen or other object from a table.
  e. Hammer a nail into a piece of wood.
  f. Walk through a partially open doorway.

▼▼▼▼▼   ▼

Threading shoelaces or a needle are good examples of functional actions that require this quality of movement. There is a two-dimensional aspect of the fighting movement, whereas indulging implies moving into the third dimension, as the body parts twist and untwist.

Retiring, hesitant people tend to move in a linear fashion, their movements being more unobtrusive than those of ebullient people, all of whom tend to use more space as they move flexibly.

Flow is the motion factor responsible for the degree of control (or lack of) that we have as we move. As with all factors, our ability to shift between the extremes of free, ongoing movement, and bound, stoppable movement determines how skilled we are. "The capacity for control increases with the awareness of the degrees of control representing the fine shades between the contrasts of fluent flow and bound flow movement" (Laban and Lawrence 1947). Movement that can be stopped at any moment has the quality of bound flow. The mover is anticipating the need to stop and therefore withholds the energy flow. People with

---

To Do

Contrast indulging (*b* and *d*) with fighting (*a* and *c*) the flow factor.

   a. Using children's building blocks, build as high a tower as possible. Be aware of change in sensation as the tower becomes taller and less stable.
   b. Knock it down!
   c. Walk quickly along a very crowded street.
   d. Walk quickly along an empty street.

▼▼▼▼   ▼

poor eyesight exhibit bound-flow quality as they move in unfamiliar surroundings, as do many children who are unsure walking along a narrow ledge such as a balance beam. During most actions the degree of flow will fluctuate, and as we become more sure of what we are doing, we often increase the flow and the movement becomes fluid.

Spatial Concepts

The focus of our attention now shifts from ourselves, and our physical being, to the environment or space in which we are moving. We are concerned now with where we have been and where we are going. In dance, games, and gymnastics lessons, we aim to develop skill and knowledge about using space efficiently and effectively (see figure 2.5).

General Space This refers to the area in which we are; it may be a small room, a large games field, or a cafeteria. There may be clearly visible boundaries or none, in which case we may wish to establish some.

The point of reference for all general spatial decisions is the environment. We know where the center of the space is, that up is toward the ceiling or sky, and down toward the floor or ground.

As we move throughout general space we can concentrate on one or more of the following four components:

   1. levels
   2. extensions
   3. floor pathways
   4. air patterns

Levels This refers to how close to the floor or how far away from the floor we are as we move. As individuals, we have "level preferences"—some of us enjoy being low and are seemingly more earthbound, while others prefer being high and more remote from the earth. This preference may also be a function of age. Watch preschoolers as they play. They spend a lot of time crouching on, sitting on, and scrambling across the floor. Older children, in contrast, are tempted to climb and reach

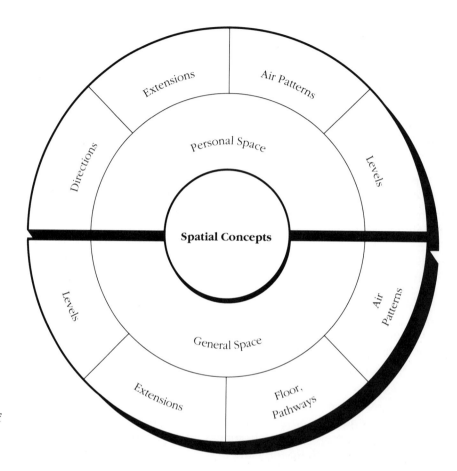

Figure 2.5 Components of the spatial concept of movement

heights that sometimes scare adults as we supervise their activities. In gymnastics, we structure different environments that offer different levels, or heights, for the children to explore. Once they feel confident and are skillful at one level, we may encourage them to challenge themselves by doing the same activity at a higher level.

In games playing, we say "keep the ball low" or "send it higher"; therefore, the children have to know how to control the ball at different levels.

Extensions In general space, the concept of extension applies mostly to locomotor actions. It describes the amount of space a movement pattern uses. The key words are "small" and "large"; "short" and "long." The appropriate pair depends on the activity. For example, you can run and trace a small circle on the floor, or you can trace a large circle. A jump may take you a short distance or it may take you a long distance through the space, as when long jumping.

Floor Pathways All locomotor actions trace a pattern on the floor. When walking along a crowded street, we may trace a very erractic pathway as we try to avoid other people. In contrast, figure skaters spend hours practicing tracing accurate designs on the ice. The resulting design is a combination of two kinds of lines, straight and curved. Football and basketball players learn to run patterns so that plays are predictable.

Air Patterns This concept is exploited in black-light theater productions and artistic films tracing the pathways of movement through the general space.

In games, children learn to control the pathway of balls as they throw them at different targets. In gymnastics, attention needs to be paid to the pathway taken by the body as it is launched into space, for example, in a dive roll. To encourage an inverted V-shaped pathway a rolled mat is sometimes placed near the takeoff. In dance, a group may run in the general space and create an air pattern that gives the impression of a whirlpool. An understanding of air patterns and the skill to produce specific ones increase the effectiveness of movement in objective and expressive situations.

Personal Space Laban called our personal space the kinesphere, which really is a more appropriate term to use. If you can visualize your "sphere of movement" being similar to a huge bubble of space surrounding you, the boundaries of which are determined by your fullest reach in every direction, then you will have no problem understanding personal space. Our point of reference as we make spatial decisions is now our own bodies, so where is up? down? Astronauts working in a gravity-free environment cannot be upside-down. For them, as for us when relating to our personal space, up is always toward the head and down is toward the feet.

Figure 2.5 shows four components of personal space.

Directions There are six basic directions we can move: forward, backward, left, right, up, and down. We sometimes combine two directions; for example, we need to move our arms forward and upward when taking a free throw in basketball. We combine three directions in a gesture of supplication, where the hands move upward, forward, and sideways. The resulting expression is quite different from that which arises when the hands move upward and sideways—try it.

Two directions combined in gesture—**up** and **sideways**.

Three directions combined in gesture—**up, forward,** and **sideways**.

Levels *Level* implies an area of space in relation to our body structure. The low level is below the hips, the area usually occupied by our legs. The medium level can be considered to be the area between hips and shoulder girdle. The area above the shoulders is called the high level, and is the more natural area for the arms and head. Changing from one level to another is often accompanied by changes in body shape, but it is possible to focus and imply a specific level with minimal change of position and shape.

Two directions, **forward** and **sideways,** combined in gesture.

To Do

Stand naturally and focus on a spot on the floor. Sense the accompanying downward "pull." Then focus upward. Is there any change of sensation throughout your body?

▼▼▼▼   ▼

In dance, expression changes when movements are performed at different levels. A low, turning action may appear sinister or express fear, depending on the context. A high level turn may communicate a feeling of release or freedom.

Some dance forms utilize specific levels. Classical ballet dancers prefer the high level, seeming to free themselves from the pull of gravity. Some jazz and modern dancers exploit the low level, emphasizing our relationship with the earth.

Extensions Gestures made by the arms and/or legs may be near the body or far away, be small in size or large. These are all aspects of extension in the personal space. In situations where we apply force to project (throw) an object with a hand, we may bring the arm close to the body in preparation for the action and follow through. The total size of the arm action will depend on several factors, including the weight of the object to be projected, the distance, and the speed we want it to travel. We reach out to catch a high ball (far), we bring our hands close to the body center to look at something small (near). In dance, children enjoy stepping with "giant strides" and contrasting them with "small steps."

Figure 2.6 Relationship concepts

Table 2.4

▼▼▼▼   ▼

Some of the different relationships in the three curriculum areas—dance, games, and gymnastics

	People in the Environment	Objects and Sounds in the Environment
Dance	Cooperative; ranging from dancing with a partner to being part of a large group	Different kinds of accompaniment, props, and costumes
Games	Cooperative; with a partner or teammates Competitive; playing 1 vs. 1, 2 vs. 1, 2 vs. 2, etc.	Games equipment, referee's whistle, boundaries of the playing area, goals, nets, etc.
Gymnastics	Cooperative; partner work, small groups	Apparatus arrangements

▼▼▼▼   ▼

Air Patterns The concept is identical to that in general space but is restricted to the patterns we make with different body parts and implements (e.g., bats and racquets) as they move within our personal space.

Relationship Concepts This is the fourth component of Laban's descriptive analysis and it considers our relationship with the environment, which is composed of people, sounds, and various objects that we can touch, hold, hear, see, and smell (see figure 2.6). We may pay attention to what is in our immediate environment or we may ignore it. Our past experiences influence our perception of the environment, therefore each of us interprets it differently.

In physical education we are particularly concerned with the differing relationships inherent in the various activities that form the basis of the curriculum (see table 2.4).

People in the Environment Dance, games, and gymnastics all provide opportunities for developing relationships with people, but the nature and purpose of the relationships differ considerably. The pleasure we get from the activities is often dependent not so much on our physical skills but from the enjoyment of sharing an experience with others, whether as being one of an eight-some in a square dance, or playing a game of tennis. We need specific skills to be able to relate to the other members in the dance group; we need different skills as we try to outwit and outplay our tennis opponent. This is discussed more fully in chapters 5, 8, and 11, as we examine dance, games, and gymnastics separately.

Objects and Sounds in the Environment Dance provides a rich experience in relating to sounds of many kinds. Music often accompanies movement, especially in folk dance and singing games, and music may

Playing music for a partner to dance.

also be the stimulus for the creation of dances (chapter 7). Sounds produced by percussion instruments, voice and body sounds, nonsense syllables, and words can all be important components of dance lessons.

Objects such as chairs, pieces of material, and balloons may all find their place in dance lessons, either as sources of ideas (i.e., stimuli) or as props.

A very complex environment develops in games playing. Some objects remain stationary, such as boundaries and targets, while others are in a constant state of motion, such as the ball with which the game is played. Therefore, we have to understand how to help children cope with both a static and a dynamic environment. You may have read of closed and open skills, the former occurring in a static environment and the latter in a dynamic one. Games activities require mostly open skills and the learning tasks we set for children must be designed to provide experience and information that will improve the children's ability to *play* games rather than do numerous drills out of the game context.

Staying "in bounds."

In gymnastics, the environment is mainly static as we design various apparatus arrangements to go over, under, along, across, around, etc. There are opportunities for developing skill in a dynamic environment—swinging ropes, seesaw benches, and other unstable (yet safe) structures provide exciting challenges enjoyed by children.

Relationship Words There are two groups of words that describe relationships: the first tells us *what* the positional relationship is, and the second tells us *when* it is occurring (see table 2.5). It is the merging of these ideas that results in a rich and diverse experience in relationships.

Over and under benches.

Table 2.5

▼▼▼▼   ▼

Some useful words for describing and developing relationships

Positional relationships:	*Relationships can occur at different times:*
I can move across	Successively
under	Alternately
along	In canon
over	and may result in question—answer
toward	action—reaction
away from	leading—following
onto	meeting—parting
off	*Relationships can occur at the same time:*
I can be in front	Together
behind	Simultaneously
at the side	and may result in mirroring
near	matching
far	contrasting

▼▼▼▼   ▼

Application of the Four Movement Concepts When Designing Learning Experiences (Tasks)

Every movement we make is composed of elements from the four major concepts, but these elements may be unequal in terms of importance. This is important to grasp as you plan lessons and design tasks in dance, games, and gymnastics. The less experienced and/or less competent learners will initially need challenges that help them understand simple, single movement concepts. As they become more skillful, additional concepts can be added, thus increasing the complexity of the cognitive, psychomotor, and affective aspects of the learning experience. Examples of tasks in dance, games, and gymnastics are given in figure 2.7.

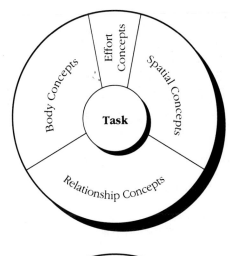

Dance (basic task)
Using a combination of skipping and galloping steps, with your partner design a floor pattern that combines curves and straight lines.

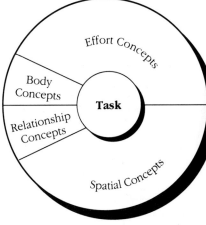

Games (basic task)
Dribble the ball (with hands or feet), changing direction and speed as you go around the markers.

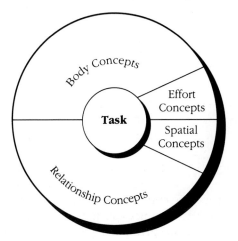

Gymnastics (basic task)
Travel along the bench, alternating being completely on it and being half on the bench and half on the floor.

Figure 2.7 Using the concepts in dance, games, and gymnastics

Skipping, circular pathway.

Acquiring control.

Notice how in the dance task there are three movement aspects stressed with very little emphasis on the effort content of the task. The prime challenge is to apply the already acquired skills of skipping and galloping in a dynamic environment with a partner.

In contrast, the games task emphasizes the effort content of the movement (i.e., change speed). It is complicated further by the spatial focus on changing direction. The environment has static and dynamic components, the markers being static and the ball dynamic.

The gymnastics task is concerned with a change in a relationship with the apparatus, a single bench. Contact with the bench is maintained throughout the traveling, thus eliminating jumping. The children must investigate various weightbearing possibilities and much of their attention will be on exploring what the body can do. As the children work we will observe their ability to apply the specific movement concepts stressed in the task, and design refining tasks that focus attention on concepts, helping them to improve their performance. In the example from games, the children have been allowed to choose whether they control the ball with their hands or feet. A refining task, appropriate for everyone, might include a spatial concept: "As you approach the marker, keep your steps small (spatial concept) so you are better balanced (body concept) and able to change direction (major spatial concept)."

Chapter 3 discusses in detail the structuring of tasks and the kind of information we need to provide for children as they are in the process of learning new skills and improving already known skills. Our aim is to help the children develop a broad base of skills that they can utilize to achieve a product, be it a dance, game, or a gymnastics sequence.

Completely on the bench—Partly on the bench.

Summary

The content of the physical education program is movement, and the educational objective is to help children become skillful in functional and expressive movement forms, especially dance, games, and gymnastics.

   The concepts on which the program is developed are derived from the work of Rudolf Laban, whose descriptive analysis consists of four major concepts: the body, effort, space, and relationships of movement. Each of these has been described and illustrated with examples from everyday activities, as well as from the selected movement forms of dance, games, and gymnastics.

Review Questions

1. Why is it important to distinguish between functional and expressive movements?
2. A physical education program based on Laban's movement concepts has three major long-term objectives. What are they?
3. Laban's descriptive analysis of movement is based on four major concepts; what are they? What does each concept tell us about movement?
4. Three kinds of activities form the core of dance, games, and gymnastics programs; name them and give examples of each.
5. What does Laban mean by **effort?**
6. Name the four motion factors and give the extremes of each.
7. Define (*a*) personal space, and (*b*) general space.
8. Discuss some of the different relationships arising in (*a*) dance, (*b*) games, and (*c*) gymnastics.

(Remember that relationships will be discussed more fully in chapters 5, 8, and 11. At this point we hope you understand the introduction to the concept.)

References

Holbrooke, J. 1973. *Gymnastics: A Movement Activity.* London: Macdonald and Evans, Ltd.

Laban, R. and F. Lawrence. 1947. *Effort.* London: Macdonald and Evans, Ltd.

Logsdon et al. 1984. *Physical Education For Children: A Focus on the Learning Process* 2d ed. Philadelphia: Lea & Febiger.

Mauldon, E. and B. Redfern. 1969. *Games Teaching.* London: Macdonald and Evans, Ltd.

Russell, J. 1975. *Creative Dance in the Primary School* 2d ed. London: Macdonald and Evans, Ltd.

Stanley, S. 1977. *Physical Education: A Movement Approach.* Toronto: McGraw-Hill Ryerson Inc.

Wall, J. 1983. *Beginnings: Movement Education for Kindergarten & Primary Children* 2d ed. Montreal: McGill University.

Related Readings

Barrett, K. 1988. Two Views: The Subject Matter of Children's Physical Education. *JOPERD* 59:2.42–46.

Bean, D. 1985. Movement Education: Potential and Reality. *CAHPER Journal* 51:5.20–24.

CHAPTER

3

The Teaching Process

This chapter will attempt to provide some insight into teacher effectiveness, and will offer guidelines for you to use to monitor your own teaching behavior.

Teaching physical education is both rewarding and demanding. Learning to become an effective teacher is somewhat similar to doing a jigsaw puzzle; there are many pieces that have to interlock, no one piece is more important than another, and different people begin at different places. The similarities end there, as no two teachers are alike. We each take the same pieces of the puzzle, and, because we are individuals, end up with our own "picture" or style of teaching. This style is variable and as we gain experience, or as the situation changes, we become more able to combine the "pieces" in different ways to deal with changing conditions.

What Research Tells Us About Effective Teaching

In physical education lessons, our primary function is to provide learning experiences that lead to achievements in movement skills. To do this, we have to understand the relationship between our teaching behavior, or what we do in lessons, and pupil learning, or the change in the children's behavior and/or performance. What do we know about this relationship? The following discussion introduces you to some of the available information.

A study by Grant and Martens (1982) compared the effectiveness of the teaching skills of elementary education student teachers with physical education student teachers. Both groups were teaching physical education to children.

The three main findings were:

1. No significant differences in behavioral patterns between the physical education and classroom teachers.
2. The most effective teachers displayed more versatile behavioral patterns.
3. The most effective teachers provided each child with approximately three times as much purposeful activity as the least effective teachers.

The finding significant for us is that a classroom teacher can be as effective as a specialist; in other words, a good teacher is a good teacher!

Siedentop (1983) summarized some of the research on teaching behavior and identified five main components of effective teaching:

1. Children spend a high percentage of lesson time engaged in learning and practicing their motor skills.
2. They show high rates of on-task behavior. This includes learning experiences, organizational tasks, and watching demonstrations.

3. The teachers match the lesson content to the students' abilities.
4. The learning environment is warm and positive.
5. The teachers develop class structures that allow for high rates of on-task behavior.

We also know that:

1. There appear to be no differences in student activity whether the teacher is male or female.
2. Experienced teachers appear to give more feedback and the feedback is more specific in nature than that provided by less experienced teachers. Where an experienced teacher will say, "Good bend in your knees as you landed," a less experienced teacher is more likely to say, "Good landing."

The five variables (O'Sullivan 1985) that consistently discriminate between the more and the less effective classroom teachers are:

1. task-oriented behavior
2. opportunities to learn
3. clarity
4. variability
5. enthusiasm

Task-Oriented Behavior

Effective teachers are "achievement oriented," and they develop an environment that encourages children to **learn,** not just "do." Lessons have specific objectives and children should know what they are trying to achieve. Feedback provided during lessons is congruent with the task in hand and children may measure their own success during and after the lesson. This means saying more than "Oh, we played basketball today." It implies the children can and will knowledgeably discuss concepts, skills, and other aspects of the lesson.

Opportunities to Learn

Effective teachers are good managers. Lessons must provide students with the maximum amount of time to be involved in activity. Our management skills are employed here as we minimize time spent waiting for a turn, listening to instructions, and moving and arranging equipment (see chapter 4).

Clarity

This refers to our skill in using language effectively and appropriately for the age, experience, and "know-how" of the students we are teaching. It also refers to our ability to sense whether or not our students are understanding what we are saying. For many children in our multicultural society, the language of instruction may not be their mother tongue, and we need to be able to communicate a message in more than one way.

Blackboards, charts, flash cards, and other interesting, eye-catching visual aids can contribute considerably to lessons. There are some commercially produced aids, but more often than not we need to create our own. Children enjoy creating charts and cards and it is possible to combine a language arts and/or art lesson with the production of charts and flash cards.

Gestures can often clarify meanings and we should practice using them so they become an integral part of our personal "communication system."

Variability

Effective teachers are able to provide a variety of learning challenges. It is a matter of presenting ideas in more than one way so that lessons are nonrepetitive and interesting. The same skills may be the focus of more than one lesson but the tasks should differ. Individual children may respond differently, and therefore we need to react differently to them.

A second dimension of variability is our open-mindedness as we are teaching. Effective teachers are able to make changes as the need arises during lessons.

Enthusiasm

Our enthusiasm is communicated to the students by our verbal and nonverbal behavior. Participation in lessons, the way we move and stand as we observe, and our interaction with the students are indicators of our enthusiasm (Caruso 1982). We need to be "tuned in" kinesthetically to what the children are doing and be ready to join in with them. This is especially important at the beginning of lessons as it helps to motivate the group and also provides a model of the task. The younger the children, the more the teacher may feel the need to participate. When teaching dance to kindergarten children, you may feel you dance more than they!

It is important to show interest in individual students by using their names during lessons. If you teach children in classes other than your own, it may not be easy to remember the names other than those of the obvious few, usually the very able and the troublemakers.

It takes some determination to learn and use three or four new names in each lesson, but it can be done.

The Basis of Concept Teaching

In addition to developing effective teaching behavior, it is important for teachers to present meaningful content to the children. As a teacher your presentation must be accurate and effectual. Chapter 2 outlines the concepts upon which we believe the physical education program should be developed; chapters 5, 8, and 11 give details of how these concepts relate to dance, games, and gymnastics skills.

To Do

Balance on

1. two hands and one foot

2. your head and two hands

3. any three body parts

Notice that one of these movements has a specific name and the others do not. Number 2 is called a *headstand,* while numbers 1 and 3 are called? The concept is weightbearing and it includes all of the above.

▼▼▼▼   ▼

Teachers must have a thorough understanding of the material with which they are working. As our primary task is to expand and improve the students' movement responses, we must be able to select relevant concepts and know how to present, explore, and develop them into skillful dance, games, and gymnastics movements.

Our aim is to encourage versatile movement by increasing students' movement vocabularies and their ability to select appropriate motor responses to the challenges set. We may need to focus on a particular aspect of a movement concept and encourage responses that are not displayed by the children. To develop quality movement, we will refine their responses, decide whether to restrict or keep open the responses, and, in both cases, work on *consistency* and *accuracy* of response through practice. The long-term objective of the physical education program is for the children to be versatile and skillful movers in a variety of movement forms, particularly in dance, games, and gymnastics.

The term *movement concept* is an encompassing one and it does not necessarily refer to a specific movement. The movement concepts discussed in chapter 2, and expanded in chapters 5, 8, and 11, provide the content of dance, games, and gymnastics lessons. *Movement vocabulary* is a phrase that children seem to understand, especially when it is likened to acquiring a language vocabulary.

Dance, games, and gymnastics each has unique content (see chapters 5, 8, and 11, respectively). The idea of expressive (dance) and functional movement (games and gymnastics) helps us define the nature of the movement form and apply the movement concepts appropriately so that the skills indigenous to that form are developed. The lesson plans in chapters 7, 10, and 13 are examples of learning situations designed to do just this.

The Development of Concepts in Physical Education

Teaching Skills

A variety of skills is needed and those common to dance, games, and gymnastics include:

1. communicating with the children,
2. planning learning experiences,
3. organizing children effectively in large and small places,
4. observing accurately, and
5. providing feedback and skill information for the children.

For each movement form our role is many-faceted—we may switch from being the motivator to the organizer, the observer, the comforter, or the participant.

Communicating With the Children

Before we can really deal with the more technical and applied skills of teaching we need to be "at ease" with ourselves in front of other people. As teachers, we are consistently working in front of an audience (as are actors) and we have to make the best use of our personal variables so that we "reach" our audience in the most effective way. On paper we may have an excellent lesson plan, but unless we feel confident in front of the class, can make ourselves heard and seen, can communicate our ideas to the children, and can interact with them as they are working, it is doubtful whether the lesson will be more than marginally successful—and we may feel very uncomfortable during the process of delivering the lesson.

There are some variables brought to the teaching situation with which we must learn to live, as we cannot change them. We need to know ourselves, to identify and be objective about our strengths and weaknesses, so that we can build on the former and try to compensate for the latter.

Feedback and practice are needed here as much as when learning any motor skill and the help of a videotape, peer or experienced observer cannot be underestimated. For some, the development of confidence in front of a class is a gradual process, while others seem to be born with it. Initial levels of confidence are not indicators of teaching abilities. There are many excellent teachers who have overcome "stage fright."

Less experienced teachers may find it beneficial to spend part of each lesson concentrating on how a personal variable affects our teaching.

One example is height. Tall teachers may have an advantage over shorter teachers. It is easier to observe—and be observed—when we are head and shoulders above the children we are teaching. If we are short, we can compensate by being very aware of where we stand when observing the children, and we can organize children into groups, and watch half the class at a time, etc. To help children "find" us we may choose colors in contrast to the school uniform; to help them focus on us when we wish to speak to the whole class, we may have them sit down. Experimenting with different strategies will help us compensate for innate "inadequacies."

We bring many other personal variables to the teaching situation, including our sense of humor, personal likes and dislikes, prejudices we may have about people and/or the activities we are teaching, and the quality and strength of our voices. The more we are aware of these traits, the more we are able to use them to augment learned teaching behavior.

Teaching is an interactive process involving the teacher and the learner(s), a process in which communication skills play a fundamental role. In order to teach effectively we must have an appreciation of the elements of communication and attempt to develop and practice invitational nonverbal and verbal behavior, because students learn best when invited to learn (Turner and Purkey 1983).

Teaching is very similar to acting, as communication is a combination of the use of voice, posture, and gesture.

Communication Skills

Nonverbal Behavior Children receive indications of how we feel about them by our use of gestures, our posture, and our facial expressions. If possible, have someone videotape you when teaching and keep the camera focused on you, regardless of what the children are doing. When reviewing the tape, notice how you stand, how you move among the children, whether you smile as you speak to individuals or groups.

Posture and Movement The way we stand and move among children indicates our attitude, sense of confidence, competence, interest, and concern. Moving with a sense of purpose, changing the speed at which we move, and, when standing still, always exuding energy (albeit "quiet" energy) will have positive effects on the class atmosphere.

The way we move must be appropriate for the movement form we are teaching. This is especially important at the beginning of a lesson when we are trying to establish the mood. In dance this means that our movement must be rhythmical and well-phrased; in games, we need a briskness; in gymnastics, our posture and movement should convey controlled energy. Try to be tuned in kinesthetically with the children, "feel" how they are moving, and be ready to move with them. Appropriate, comfortable clothing helps us feel prepared for activity and at ease as we move.

Facial Expression In general, people are very responsive to facial expression. Young children in particular rate a person based largely on facial expression. A smile, therefore, is a very important invitational technique, whereas a frown is the opposite. We can consciously increase the amount of time we smile—it just takes a little practice.

Making eye contact is another invitational technique that helps the children to feel included. When we are giving instructions, feedback, asking questions, or simply talking to the class it is important to make eye contact with as many children as possible. This applies both when the group is spread out in the space and when it is close together.

To Do

Comment on the teacher's positioning in the following two photographs. Make suggestions for alternative places to stand.

Gestures   These have already been mentioned when we discussed clarity (see page 70). Clear hand and arm gestures animate, amplify, and clarify verbal communication. Some people use gestures quite naturally during conversation; others do not. For teachers, gestures should become a part of the packet of communication skills developed. In large teaching spaces or areas that have poor acoustics (e.g., outside, indoor swimming pools, etc.) they can replace voice commands when combined with established whistle signals.

Positioning   Our positioning in relation to the class indicates our concern for control and safety. The aim is to keep all children in sight during a lesson. They should also be able to see us at all times and "feel" our presence. We must be prepared to change our positioning as the children move around. When our attention is required in one place for an extended period of time, e.g., organizing apparatus or helping an individual, placement must be such that we can give the help needed and still be able to survey the rest of the class. This entails having nobody, or very few people, behind us.

In order to develop and maintain effective nonverbal behavior, we need to know what we are doing. Our behavior must be observed, recorded, and analyzed. This is difficult to do alone; therefore, the use of videotape or a peer observer is recommended. To see ourselves as others see us is a valuable, though sometimes uncomfortable, experience.

Voice Skills   Our voices are very important instruments and we must use them carefully as well as effectively. We need to know the strengths and weaknesses of our "instrument," and learn to use it to its greatest advantage. Unfortunately, many of the places/spaces in which we teach do not have good acoustics. Large gyms are often equivalent to echo chambers, as are many indoor swimming pools. The activities also have their own inherent noise components and we are expected to be able to make ourselves heard at all times. A sense of *what, when, how, to whom,* and *why* the teacher speaks can consciously be developed and practiced.

What
1. Careful choice of words is important. Become aware of the level of comprehension of the different groups of students, and select and phrase your words accordingly.
   a. Being concise will conserve your voice. This means thinking ahead and planning a short statement. Full sentences are often unnecessary as well-chosen key words

can be full of information. If more than two or three words
have to be said, consider bringing the children to you so
that you do not have to shout. This will also help them pay
attention. A disadvantage, of course, is that it takes time.
Children can learn to "come in quickly and not dawdle en
route."

b. Word all tasks in nonconfusing ways, yet in ways that
    motivate, interest, and generally make the children wish to
    participate.

2. Develop an extensive vocabulary and be able to give the same
    information in more than one way. If a new word is essential in
    the lesson, write it clearly on a board or have a flash card, be
    prepared to spend a little time explaining and discussing it
    before using it.

3. Include color, interest, flavor, and humor whenever suitable.
    The more we appeal to the children, the more carefully they
    will listen.

4. Our speech should be grammatically correct. Children are
    exposed to a considerable amount of poor speech on T.V.,
    especially if they listen to sporting events.

5. Avoid *repetition* and *redundancy*—the two Rs. Two common
    examples are "okay" and "What I want you to do is. . . ."
    Neither adds to the clarity of the message it follows or prefaces.
    We all have favorite sayings, and we should become aware of
    them and use them sparingly. By listening to ourselves as we
    speak, listening to a tape recording of our teaching, or having a
    friend write down our particular two Rs, we can monitor
    ourselves. It is not that we advocate eliminating a
    conversational approach as we teach, rather we wish to
    encourage "word efficiency" for two specific reasons: clarity and
    quality.

When

1. Knowing when it is the most appropriate moment to speak is a
    "developed sense." However, it is probably better to say more
    than is necessary than less. Children left on their own without
    any input often lose interest in the task, and learning time is
    lost. When reviewing tape recordings of their teaching, some
    inexperienced teachers are surprised to hear stretches of
    silence.

2. Practice talking to the children while they are working, as well as when they have stopped. In both instances, ensure they are listening and preface your information with comments such as:

   "**L**isten as you work."
   "**S**top and listen."
   "**C**ome here and listen."
   "**S**tay where you are and listen."

How What we say is inextricably entwined with how we say it; it is the combination of the two that results in the message.

Our quality of speech is affected by several variables. Our voices must reach all "receivers" and the children should not have to "concentrate hard" to hear what we are saying.

1. Good breath control is very important; this includes breathing from the diaphragm and controlling the speed at which we exhale. The louder we speak, the more breath we need to carry the sound. When teaching outside, blow a short, sharp blast on your whistle to attract the attention of the entire class. If it is windy, stand with your back to the wind and use it to help carry the sound of your voice.

2. When speaking loudly, lower your pitch. This will help reduce the tightness in the throat that often accompanies shouting—which is to be avoided! "Think low" is advice we often give to female teachers who have difficulty making themselves heard in large spaces. At the other extreme, very low voices can be difficult to hear and some men have to pitch higher.

3. Speech that is slower than the usual conversational speed is easier to hear. Emphasize key words and phrases by isolating them from the rest of the sentence—verbally "underline" them.

4. Vary expressiveness and tone. It is possible to say "What was that?" in at least two ways, one sounds condemning and the other genuinely suggests that we wish to know. The two words "Well done!" can be said so that the meaning conveyed is just the opposite. Awareness of tone must be developed and this is where a tape recorder can be such an asset. To hear ourselves as others hear us can be surprising; we may find we do not "mean what we say and say what we mean."

5. Be articulate; enunciate words carefully. How often do we say/ hear "I'm gonna" instead of "I'm going to"?

Table 3.1 suggests some ways to help develop the above ideas.

Table 3.1

▼▼▼▼   ▼

Voice skills

Dimension	Skill	Helpful Hints
Volume	Able to change according to needs (e.g., large room, poor acoustics, large number of children) against conflicting ambient sounds	Have a peer signal to indicate volume Tape recorder on sideline Converse with peer across empty room
Articulation	Clarity of words Speed of speech Moderate any extremes of accent	Practice specific exercises to make mouth and tongue work Listen to own speech on tape recorder Concentrate on delivery
Expression	Able to combine changes in volume, pitch, speed	Listen to own speech on tape recorder Practice reading stories, poems aloud Think "dramatically" as you speak

▼▼▼▼   ▼

To Do

Try the following tongue twisters.

Tongue twisters twist tongues twisted
Trying to untangle twisted tangles
My tang's tungled now!

She is a thistle sifter and she has a sieve of sifted thistles and a sieve of unsifted thistles because she is a thistle sifter.

Betty Botta bought some butter to make some batter but, she said, this butter's bitter. So she bought a bit of better butter and it made her batter better. So 'twas better Betty Botta bought a bit of better butter.

Mo	Me	Me	Mo
Me	Mo	Mo	Me
Mo	Me	Me	Me
Me	Mo	Mo	Me

▼▼▼▼   ▼

Recorder: _____

Teacher Observed: _____

In the chart below, place an *X* in the appropriate box when the teacher communicates with the entire class, a group, or an individual. Each column represents three minutes. Summarize your findings and recommend any changes you feel might help improve communication between the teacher and the children.

Class

Group

Individual

        Time in minutes

        Totals: **C** _____

                   G _____

                   I _____

        Summary:

        Recommendations:

Figure 3.1
Communication—with whom?

To Whom We may speak to (1) the whole class, (2) a group, or (3) an individual.

Often the answer to a question, words of encouragement, information, etc., given to a small group or an individual will be valuable for the rest of the class. In this case, we can take advantage of the *ripple effect* and speak *publically,* or loud enough for everyone to hear. At other times it is more effective and considerate, to speak *privately,* especially if for any reason our comments have negative overtones. We may also speak privately if the children addressed are at a different stage in the learning sequence and the information we are providing is inappropriate for the majority.

Less experienced teachers are often found to give more information privately, and find they have to repeat the same thing many times. Initially practice speaking to the whole class more than to groups and individuals. A peer may watch and record to whom you speak during a lesson so that you can find out with whom you communicate most, the class, groups, or individuals. Figure 3.1 is a sample recording sheet that you may find useful.

Why We must have a clear reason for everything we say, and our comments should be purposeful and add to the learning climate. We may wish to:

1. create or develop ambiance and rapport;
2. motivate, encourage, praise;
3. control or discipline student behavior;
4. organize equipment or children;
5. present movement tasks; and/or
6. provide feedback.

Evaluating Your Teaching

One of the most useful skills you can develop is the analysis of your own verbal behavior during the teaching process. Besides listening to what you say as you say it, the use of audio tape recordings is recommended. Using systematic coding, verbal behavior can be recorded on paper, and analyzed and evaluated.

You may ask a colleague to evaluate you as you teach, or you may ask your colleague to videotape you so that you can evaluate your own teaching skills. As an example, it is quite easy for someone watching you to record to whom you provide feedback during the lesson. This evaluation may reveal that you spend more time with the boys than the girls, or that you provide general feedback to the less-skilled children and specific feedback to the highly skilled. This kind of information is most useful if you wish to develop and improve your teaching. Over time all teachers form habits, and all too often we are unaware of these habits—we need to take a look at what we are doing.

Lesson Design

The core of our work is the lesson. Everything we learn and practice is to help us function at the highest level possible in the actual teaching situation.

In the simplest form lessons consist of three parts:

Part 1: The Introduction—tasks are basic and refining

Part 2: Concept and Skill Development—tasks are basic, refining, simplifying, and extending

Part 3: Culmination—tasks are applying, refining, and extending

Part 1: The Introduction

Part 1 is designed to introduce the children to the selected movement form, to establish a movement-centered learning environment, and to prepare the body for activity. The tasks chosen vary from movement form to movement form, and from lesson to lesson, depending on the objectives of the specific experience, but in general they are familiar activities that are comparatively energetic.

These often begin with a whole group imitative, rhythmic pattern danced to known and well-liked music. You may play the role of the Pied Piper with the children, or the children may be called upon to provide the motifs for their peers to copy. In singing games and folk dance lessons the children may dance freely around the space, practicing a selected dance step; in creative dance the children may have the choice of responding freely to the music, selecting their own ways of traveling.

Dance Lessons

It is important that a dancelike atmosphere and attitude are established immediately when the lesson begins, and therefore, the choice of task(s) is made with that in mind.

Introductory tasks for the younger children tend to be gross motor, i.e., running, chasing, escaping, and the beginnings of guarding skills. The emphasis is on good footwork and use of the general space. It is important that all the children are very active, therefore any activities that include "freezing" and eliminating players are unsuitable. Small equipment, such as ropes and hoops, encourage jumping and skipping skills, both of which are vigorous actions that permit children to work on their own, which is a time saver. The pace of a lesson can be slow when asking children to find partners or form groups, and valuable time is lost at the beginning of the lesson.

Games Lessons

As an alternative to the above kinds of activities, the older, more skillful children may begin a lesson by practicing manipulative skills, either alone or with a partner. The skills may be of their own choice or selected from the ones included in the previous lesson. We can use this time for free activity to help someone who may find a particular skill difficult, to watch the children to see if there is a common problem, to join in with the activity and relate on a one-to-one basis with the children. This is particularly useful if you reprimanded someone in the previous lesson and you feel the need to establish a more positive relationship.

Familiar gross motor skills—running, rolling, rocking, jumping—are good activities for beginning a lesson. This can be followed by bending, stretching, and twisting selected areas of the body. You may develop a sequence to teach the children, which they can repeat on their own at the beginning of a series of lessons. During the time they are working on warming up, you can give individual feedback and encouragement in much the same way as at the beginning of a games lesson.

Gymnastics Lessons

Part 2 is the time for the introduction of new concepts and skills, the development and reinforcement of known concepts, and the practice and extension of already acquired skills.

Part 2: Concept and Skill Development

Dance Lessons

In creative dance, the divisions between the lesson parts are often barely discernable. Part 1 may lead imperceptibly to the introduction of the movement concept(s) or stimulus, beginning either with discussion or improvisation.

In singing games and folk dance lessons the new step(s), figures, and words are learned, gradually integrated and refined, until the whole dance pattern develops.

Games Lessons

There is a more definite change of focus in games lessons. New manipulative skills or aspects of known skills are introduced, practiced, and combined; strategies and rules are explained and applied in mini-games situations with little or no focus on keeping the score, as the objective is not to play the game but learn *how* to play.

Gymnastics Lessons

As in dance lessons, the students may barely notice a shift in emphasis as the new movement concept(s) may already have been introduced in Part 1. However, you will now include simplifying and extending tasks to meet individual differences in skill performance. Repetition of skills or parts of skills occurs as the children strive to gain and increase control over their actions. The environment will be the floor or arrangements of small apparatus, e.g., mats, hoops, benches. Sequences will be developed with a focus on transitional actions. The resulting sequences may or may not be applied to the apparatus selected for Part 3.

Part 3: Culmination

Part 3 is the time for the children to utilize their newly acquired competence and increased movement vocabulary to accomplish some specific end, so that they leave the lesson with an identifiable product and, we hope, a feeling of achievement.

Dance Lessons

This is the time for dancing—enjoying what one has learned and created in this and previous lessons. Dances can be shared in a mini-performance setting and the performer and spectator roles experienced. (See chapter 5 for more on dance.)

The children's accumulating repertoire can be highlighted, and, in singing games and folk dance lessons, children may be asked which dance(s) they would like to do.

Games Lessons

The skills, strategies, and rules are tried within the context of various games. These games may be (a) created by you, (b) created by the children, or (c) selected from one of the numerous resources of children's games. Groups of children may be playing different games, which may be very simple, utilizing few skills and rules, or comparatively complex (see chapter 8).

During the playing of the games you will reinforce the concepts and skills experienced during Part 2 of the lesson; therefore do not hesitate to stop the games.

A different environment is structured in gymnastics lessons, and apparatus arrangements, maybe combining large and small pieces, provide exciting challenges (see chapter 11). The youngest children will be exploring unfamiliar pieces, while the more experienced and skillful children will be developing sequences which they can repeat, refine, and remember.

Gymnastics Lessons

Table 3.2 is a simplified list of the three parts of a lesson plan and the main objectives of each part.

Designing good lessons requires considerable planning, and planning means decisions have to be made about:

the movement form—dance, games, or gymnastics
(see chapter 4)

the objectives of the lesson

the tasks

organization of the students

organization of the apparatus/equipment (see chapter 4)

"An objective describes an intended result of instruction" (Mager 1975), and each lesson planned must have very specific objectives. These are required to ensure the possibility for:

Objectives of the Lesson

1. progressive lesson planning
2. structuring the tasks
3. observing accurately
4. evaluating the lesson

Your choice of objectives for a lesson depends on the unit focus and, for every lesson after the first one, on the children's responses. They "are useful tools in the design, implementation and evaluation" of each lesson (Mager 1975). As the unit progresses, it may be necessary to change or add an objective.

Objectives should be written in terms of what you expect the children to be able to do as a result of the lesson. If the children know the objectives for a particular unit or lesson, it should help them "organize their own effort toward the accomplishment of those objectives" (Mager 1975). The decision as to whether you tell the children at the beginning

Table 3.2

The parts of a lesson plan

Part 1: The Introduction

The introduction of a lesson plan
—should prepare the body mentally and physically
—should be vigorous
—should serve as a review
—should stress continuity of action
—should stress continuous movement
—should include both movement on the spot and throughout the space
—should be individual

Part 2: Concept and Skill Development

The concept and skill development of a lesson plan
—should introduce/review concept
—should include discussion to clarify concept if it is new
—should involve application of concept
—should stress continuity of action
—should include exploration, discovery, selection
—may include working with others
—may include children observing others

Part 3: Culmination

The culmination of a lesson plan
—should stress consolidation of material covered
In dance and gymnastics, Part 3
—should stress a beginning, continuity of action and an ending in a dance or sequence work
In games, Part 3
—should stress utilization of games skills and concepts
—should include equipment if it was used in concept development portion
—should include working with others if this was in concept development
—may include children observing others
—should include relaxation
—may include putting equipment away

of the lesson, or ask them at the end what they thought were the objectives, is yours to make. The age of the children will be one factor influencing this decision.

The sample lesson plans in chapters 7, 10, and 13 all have specific objectives.

The Tasks

Lesson plans consist of a variety of **tasks** or things to do, the majority of these tasks being designed to meet the objectives of the lesson and improve the motor performance of the children. These are called *movement tasks* (Rink 1979). Another category of tasks is concerned with organizational procedures necessary for the smooth running of the lesson (see chapter 4).

Task Style

We have stated that the physical education program should consider children's capabilities in terms of their cognitive development as well as their physical skills (see chapter 1). We have also stated teaching implies a "marriage" between content (movement concepts) and what is familiarly termed teaching style. This refers to the amount of freedom the children have to make decisions in a lesson. When selecting and wording the tasks for a lesson, be very aware of the kinds of decisions you are making and what decisions are left for the children. The more "closed" a task, the fewer the decisions.
Closed tasks:

1. elicit more uniform responses
2. remove responsibility from the children
3. may save time
4. may focus attention on a specific movement or movement concept

The more "open" a task, the more the decisions. They:

1. elicit individual interpretations of the task,
2. increase children's responsibility for their own learning,
3. may mean the children spend more time thinking before responding,
4. may encourage exploration and discovery of a movement concept,
5. require a flexible approach to skill development,
6. require good observational skills from the teachers.

The kind of decisions that may or may not be left to the children include the following.

1. With whom they will work:
   "**M**ake groups of 4." (open)
   "**C**ount off in 4s." (closed)

To Do

Study the examples of tasks and decide what choices have been given to the children and what decisions have been made by the teacher.

Change each task, first trying to increase the freedom of choice for the children, then reducing it.

▼▼▼▼   ▼

2. Where they will work:

"**M**ove into your own space." (open)
"**S**tand in your lines." (closed)

3. The apparatus they will use:

"**S**elect either a rope or a hoop." (open)
"**E**veryone take a large ball." (closed)

4. Their movement responses:

"**W**hen you hear the music, skip, sometimes going forward, sometimes backward, maybe even trying sideways." (open)
"**S**kip 4 steps forward, 4 steps backward." (closed)

The less experienced teacher, or the teacher meeting a new class, is wise to use more *closed* tasks, until both teacher and children have become accustomed to each other. Some children balk at being required to make decisions, some may lack the confidence to "try their own thing," still others may not have the movement vocabulary or ability to produce their own response. In all of these situations, more closed tasks should be provided.

A lesson usually consists of a mixture of open and closed tasks, with the teacher making the adjustments as the opportunity and need arises. The sample lesson plans in chapters 7, 10, and 13 include a range of closed and open tasks.

Different Tasks

The concept of tasks is being used more widely in physical education literature (Siedentop 1983; Logsdon et al. 1984; Siedentop, Herkowitz and Rink 1984; Rink 1985). In its simplest form, the task concept is a

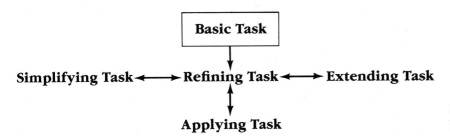

Figure 3.2 Interrelationship between movement tasks

most useful method of monitoring the development of a lesson. Rink (1979) postulates four kinds of movement tasks in a learning sequence, each with a specific function:

1. Basic tasks
2. Refining tasks
3. Extending tasks
4. Applying tasks

We include a fifth:

5. Simplifying tasks

It is the interrelationship between these tasks that allows for "a true progression of activities" (Siedentop, Herkowitz and Rink 1984). (See figure 3.2.)

(Another concept, organizational tasks, will be discussed in chapter 4.)

Basic Tasks Basic tasks are those that begin each learning sequence in a lesson. A lesson will include a limited number of basic tasks, each of which relates to one or more of the objectives of the lesson. As a rule of thumb, each basic task is followed by a refining task, as it is the beginning of a learning sequence and cannot stand on its own. These tasks can range from being *closed* to *open* (see figure 3.3).

Lessons for young or less-skilled children usually include more basic tasks than do lessons for the older, more skillful children. This is because the less-skilled need frequent changes of activity to maintain their interest and level of motivation. Skillful children, because they are more successful, are able to spend more time refining and extending their performance.

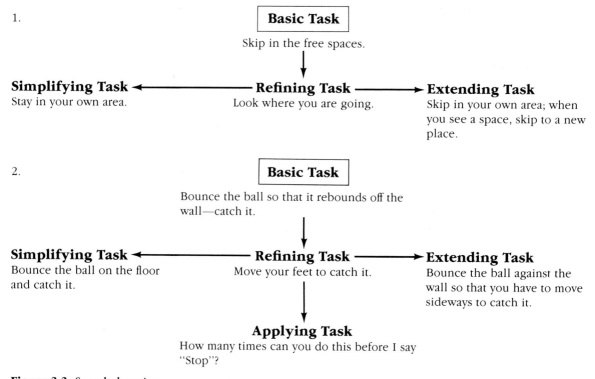

1.

Basic Task

Skip in the free spaces.

Simplifying Task ◄─────────── **Refining Task** ──────────► **Extending Task**
Stay in your own area.   Look where you are going.   Skip in your own area; when
                                                                 you see a space, skip to a new
                                                                 place.

2.

Basic Task

Bounce the ball so that it rebounds off the
wall—catch it.

Simplifying Task ◄─────────── **Refining Task** ──────────► **Extending Task**
Bounce the ball on the floor   Move your feet to catch it.   Bounce the ball against the
and catch it.   wall so that you have to move
                                                                 sideways to catch it.

Applying Task
How many times can you do this before I say
"Stop"?

Figure 3.3 Sample learning
sequences

To Do

Think of different ways of simplifying the following basic tasks.

1. Throw the tennis ball to your partner so that it is caught at different levels.
2. Balance on two body parts.
3. Run quickly and smoothly with small steps, keeping the group close together.

▼▼▼▼   ▼

We receive signals from the children that may indicate when it is time to change to another task. If you notice an increase in off-task behavior, such as an increase in chatter, or a drop in skill performance, it is probably time to change the activity. It is better to change too soon than wait until the children become tired, bored, and frustrated with what they are doing.

To Do

Discuss ways of increasing the difficulty of the following tasks:

1. Rise and sink with your partner.
2. Run, jump, and roll.
3. Play three against three Keep-Away, using a 7-inch playground ball.

▼▼▼▼   ▼

Refining Tasks These tasks tell the children how to improve what they are doing. The information focuses on execution ("I can do a waltz step!") and quality of performance ("My legs are much straighter now when I balance on my hands"). You may recognize them as "teaching cues" or prescriptive feedback. They are the core of the learning sequence. Our ability to provide appropriate refinement in response to children's movement is dependent upon our observation skills, knowledge of movement, and the components of movement. Refining tasks tend to be more *closed*, as the intent is to focus attention on a specific aspect of a concept or movement pattern.

Simplifying Tasks The degree of difficulty of a task may need reducing for some children before any development or improvement will occur. Simplification can be done in many different ways and we must be able to adjust the task to meet the specific needs of the moment. Some of the ways we can do this are by:

1. changing the equipment, as in "We'll take one layer off the box";
2. altering the environment, e.g., "Try it first in this small space";
3. changing one dimension of the previous task, "Instead of running as you bounce the ball, begin by walking."

Extending Tasks These are the opposite of simplifying tasks. The degree of difficulty is being increased in extending tasks to meet the children's new level of competency. It is possible to do this by adjusting similar components, such as equipment, environment, and movement concepts, and by combining skills. Extending tasks also range from *closed* to *open*.

Applying Tasks When a movement concept or specific skill has been explored, expanded, and practiced, it is time to use it, integrate it with other known skills, and enjoy the newfound competency. This may come anywhere in a lesson as mini-culminations of learning sequences. Applying tasks provide children with a focus and measure of what has been

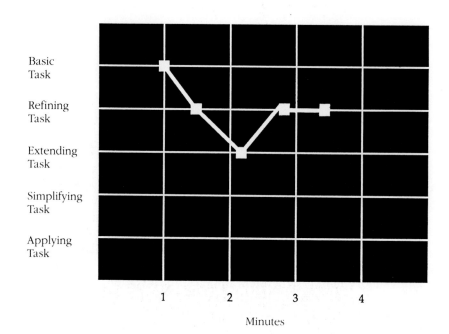

Figure 3.4 Toss and catch learning sequence

learned. Children lose motivation if they do not have the opportunity to use their skills and knowledge to achieve results. Once a movement product has evolved, it should be applied in appropriate situations. These tasks range from closed to open.

Relationships Between the Tasks

Less experienced teachers tend to provide fewer refining and applying tasks than the more experienced. A rule of thumb to remember when planning lessons and teaching is to provide a refinement after each task you set. The following is an example of what we mean by this:

> **B**asic task: Toss and catch your beanbag.
> **R**efining task: Put your hands together under the beanbag to catch it.
> **E**xtending task: Toss the beanbag a little higher.
> **R**efining task: Use a big, smooth arm swing. Let your hand follow the beanbag.

A graphic analysis of the information you provide during a lesson gives a clear picture of the interaction between the tasks you have selected. This analysis is shown in figure 3.4.

To Do

Discuss the following learning sequences in terms of (1) the interrelationship between the tasks and (2) the amount of information provided in five minutes.

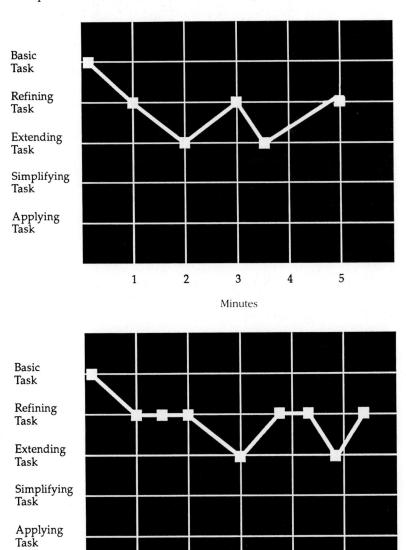

Besides knowing the interaction between the tasks, we should be aware of how much information we provide during a lesson. When the horizontal axis of the graph represents time, an analysis of the graph will provide this information.

Observation Skills

It may seem obvious to say we must be able to observe accurately as we teach. To develop the insight that is essential for creating appropriate tasks and providing helpful (congruent) feedback, we must become skilled observers. We need to play this role constantly if we wish to base our instruction on the current needs of the students. When teaching, we are constantly observing children and perhaps unconsciously, evaluating both the children and our teaching. Our aim should be to make a conscious effort to develop the skills necessary to make objective evaluations and informed decisions.

We are, therefore, challenged to develop objective and reliable observation skills that are process-oriented and directed towards skill development.

Barrett (1981, 1983) has been responsible for defining observation as a concept and a process involving interpretation and decision making (Logsdon et al. 1984). This means we must know clearly what we are looking for as we observe, we must be able to understand and explain what we see, and we must be able to take action based on what we have seen.

Table 3.3 summarizes the **how?, who?,** and **what?** of observing.

How

There are the two observational techniques and during a lesson we must learn to switch constantly between the two. The first observational technique to use is *scanning,* noting if the spacing is adequate/safe, if all the children are on task, who is coping well and who is having difficulties. This is followed by *focusing.* If the children are working in their own space, we select an area and observe the children working in that area. We can move into the group, still keeping the rest of the class in sight, and give individual and/or group feedback. We then move to a new area and repeat the process with a different group of children.

Scanning gives us an overall picture of what is going on. It is used at the very beginning of a lesson, immediately after a new task has been set and after observing something or someone in particular. It provides us with a general impression of the class and helps us to decide (1) on *whom* we need to focus, and (2) on *what* we need to focus.

When focusing, we may pay particular attention to one area of the room, a specific individual, or a small group. We also may look for a specific aspect of the children's responses. For example, if we set the following open-ended task—"Use upper-body parts to keep the ball in the

Table 3.3

The **how?**, **who?**, and **what?** of observation

How Do We Do What We Do?

Scan

Entire class

Focus

Small groups
Individuals

Who Watches Whom?

Teacher

Watches children

Children

Watch other children
Watch teacher

What Are We Looking For?

Teacher

Looks for mood of class
    safety factors
    spacing of children and equipment
    task understanding
    on-task activity
    problems—common and individual

Teacher and children

Look for quality performance
    task interpretation
    application of concepts

air"—considerable variation of response might be expected. From past experience, we know the chances are high that some children will use their heads. If we wish to develop the skill of heading, we will, therefore, watch specifically for this response.

Who

We should be observing the children at all times during the lesson. In order to do this, we must position ourselves in relation to what is happening. This has already been mentioned briefly (see page 75).

If the children are traveling throughout the area, it is advantageous to stand still when observing. When the children are scattered or in formations in their own space, the teacher should travel, moving in and out of the class, maybe zig-zagging down the length of the teaching area, as illustrated in figure 3.5.

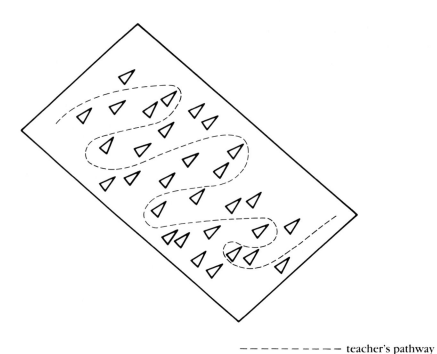

—————————— teacher's pathway

▷ child

Figure 3.5 Positioning

REMEMBER THAT

Children can learn much from observing each other, provided they:

 1. *are positioned to see the movement pattern being shown*
 2. *are given specific elements to observe (e.g., "Watch Bill's stretched feet") or are asked a question that helps them focus (e.g., "Does Sue travel at the same speed all the time?")*
 3. *immediately apply the concept shown to their own work.*

When teachers demonstrate, the children watch the teacher. Teachers may demonstrate (a) to provide a model, (b) to clarify a concept, or (c) to focus attention on a common error and provide the correction. The children must be told what to look for as they watch. The demonstration should be followed by practice or question and discussion, followed by practice of the technique or application of the concept observed.

Peer models are very important and there should be many opportunities for the children to watch and learn from each other. When children are accustomed to demonstrating their work, they will work more diligently to select and refine their movement responses in order to gain approval from their teacher and their peers. This is not meant to imply that only the very skillful are chosen to demonstrate. Because the program is concept-oriented and tasks more likely to be open-ended, allowing for variation for responses, it should be possible for every child to demonstrate during the school year.

In another instance, the teacher may say "Watch your partner as he spins, sinks, and rises. How does the timing of your partner's sequence differ from yours?" In this situation, the children are being asked to discriminate between what they are doing and what they see, which are very different challenges. The continuation may be for the partners to help each other clarify the time element in their sequences.

Children may watch a partner, a small group, half the class, or one child. They should be told what they are looking for and time must be spent after the observation to clarify, reinforce, and apply what has been observed.

Each day we make conclusions regarding the moods of the different groups of students we teach. Often a class reflects the general personality of the teacher with whom they spend the most time, or the teacher who taught them immediately before coming to the physical education lesson. Some groups are naturally energetic, while others are placid. The time of day, day of the week, season of the year, weather, or a special event, such as a school play or class outing, will often affect the mood of the class. A wise teacher will attempt to employ an identifiable mood to the advantage of the lesson. A dance lesson that requires sensitivity and slow movements may have to be modified if the class has witnessed some exciting event at recess (such as a fight on the playground). An energetic games lesson may be unsuitable if taught on a Friday at 3:00 p.m. and if the children seem tired. We must be flexible and adapt according to what we observe, while at the same time safeguarding against the class overruling the planned activities.

We must ensure that the environment is safe as the children participate. Immediate action must be taken if we notice anything that might be hazardous as the children work. Since conditions change during lessons as equipment is brought out and put away and formations change, we must always foresee what hazard might occur and be prepared to interject.

Continuously scan for good spacing before and during an activity; children need space so that they can concentrate on what they are doing, rather than on avoiding others. We must always observe the spacing, changing it if necessary, before beginning a task. Some tasks, particularly those done at speed, need a lot of space, which we may have to create by reducing the number of children on the floor at one time.

We must notice and rearrange gymnastic apparatus that is set too close together. We must notice and move dance groups who are so intent on their own creations that they are unaware of crowding other groups.

When children begin to respond to a task, we immediately look for interpretation to ensure everyone understands the challenge. When the task is closed, e.g., "toss the ball high and catch after it bounces," it is easy to see if anyone catches before it bounces or has some other variation. There are several reasons why responses may be different. The intent here is not to find out why but to notice who has not interpreted the task correctly. A quick word to anyone who has misunderstood should suffice. On the other hand, if the majority of the class interprets the task

What

The Mood of the Class

Safety Factors

Spacing

Task Understanding

incorrectly, there may be a general misunderstanding, in which case stop the class and re-explain the task, maybe with a demonstration by you or one or two children who were doing it correctly.

When tasks are open-ended, it is harder to assess the children's interpretation and understanding. Various interpretations may arise because the instructions were unclear or the children may not fully understand the concept(s). Whichever the case, the result is the same: a confused set of responses. When this occurs, children need assistance in clarifying cognitively and kinesthetically the essence of the task, as in the following example:

> **T**ask: "Add changes of direction to the traveling sequence you have created."
>
> **R**esponse: Some children interpret the concept of direction in terms of the general space and produce zig-zagging and curved pathways.
>
> **R**emedies:
>
> 1. Children who interpreted directions as traveling right, left, forward, and backward, are asked to demonstrate.
> 2. Half of the class watches the other half. The observers are asked to identify children who show clear changes in direction as they travel.

In all tasks there are key elements which are included because they are the focus of the learning experience. Refining tasks emphasize those elements, and focus the children's attention on these aspects of the task. Before teaching a lesson, we must prepare ourselves to watch for these elements. Notes written on the lesson plan, opposite the task, are helpful. You will find some of these in the sample plans in chapters 7, 10, and 13.

On-Task Activity

Some children find it difficult to remain on-task for extended periods of time. Usually we soon know who they are and can be prepared to help them, maybe by standing close by, separating friends (a last resort!), or giving additional encouragement and/or help. Noticing the general level of on-task activity also gives clues as to when the task has been continued long enough and it is time for a change. We may sometimes be surprised to find children absorbed in a task, and we might continue with it, foregoing something else.

Individual and Common Problems

Since it is one of our main objectives, we are always looking for ways to improve the quality of performance. It is not a matter of simply looking for what is wrong, as we are apt to do when we are less experienced, it is more a need to identify and look for problems. Some problems we may be able to anticipate because of the nature of the task. These may

To Do

Remember

your own "gym" days
the importance of the emotional and physical environments
and their effects on the children (Koma 1987).

▼▼▼▼　　　　　　　　　　　　　　　　　　　　　　▼

be encountered by the majority of the children. We should be able to identify these problems by scanning the class as they work. Other problems will be specific to individuals and will be identified by focusing on each child in turn.

Quality Performance

This is always desired. While exploration and discovery are important processes and variety an important product, none should be emphasized at the expense of quality movement. Because the development of physical skill in expressive and functional situations is a major objective of every physical education program, the children should constantly be directed towards efficient and improved movement. Teacher and peer models are important, and when the children know how to observe and relate what they see to their own performance, the quality of movement will be enhanced.

Children will readily learn to recognize quality movement. In a game situation quality may be more easily seen because of the functional nature of the activities. When a goal has been scored, a pass intercepted, or a ball passed sensitively to a teammate, the movement pattern has been successful and quality is implied. In gymnastics, elements of quality are seen in the appropriate effort content of a skill sequence, e.g., the efficiency with which the child jumped over the box, and in the more aesthetic components, such as change of body shape and continuity during a sequence. In dance, the aesthetic elements, such as the pleasing line within the group or the exciting rhythm emerging, may predominate observation.

"**S**ee how tightly Jean curled her body and how smoothly she rolled."

"**W**as Chris fully stretched during the balance part of the sequence?"

"**W**atch this group to see how they move into open spaces as they dribble a ball. Who is using the space well?"

"**N**otice how the dancers arrive at different levels and a strong group focus is developed."

REMEMBER THAT

You should provide a quality learning experience for ALL your students. This may be easier said than done! The following questions may help you monitor your interaction with your different students.
Do you:

1. *smile as frequently at your low-ability students as your high-ability ones? At your least "favorite" as your "favorite"?*
2. *convey negative nonverbal feedback, e.g., frowns, turning away, to your low-ability students?*
3. *give as much prescriptive feedback on skill performance to your low-ability students as your high-ability students?*
4. *praise and respond positively to appropriate behavior and good performance from your low-ability students, or do you consider it a "fluke," and ignore it?*

Based on a class handout prepared by J. Hodge [undated] 434–342 Physical Education Methods. Montreal: McGill University, Department of Physical Education.

Task Interpretation

Many of the tasks set in a physical education program are open-ended and, as such, result in variation of response. This is obviously one of the times when the children learn from observing each other's differences or similarities as the movement concepts are applied.

The children who are observing may be helped to see the differences or similarities between two or more performances. The following statements and questions are examples of how the children can be helped to focus on the critical features of performance.

> "**W**atch Susan's use of time; sometimes she rolls slowly and then she rolls quickly. Now watch Nancy; how does she use time?"

> "**C**arol, Chris, and José, show us how you each trap the ball as it rebounds off the wall. Which different body parts are they using to stop the ball?"

> "**T**his half of the class watch the others as they rise very slowly and collapse very suddenly. Notice how some people come part way up, others all the way up."

Teachers and children gain new ideas from observing other children. A child's unique response may spark ideas not previously considered. Children find unusual ways of working with equipment, which may prompt the teacher to challenge the other children, as in "Watch how John keeps his hoop moving as he jumps; now try to keep your hoop moving."

REMEMBER THAT

When observing, you should:

Decide **what** to observe (safety, use of equipment, response to the task).

Decide **whom** to observe (whole class, a small group, one child, a body part of one child).

Position yourself to observe (from a corner of the room, from the side of the room, standing on a bench, near the child, far from the child).

Look at **whole response** to the task (was the task answered? how could the movement be improved? does it need to be simplified? extended?).

Alternate between **scanning** and **focusing** (are the children being challenged to produce quality responses?).

Adapted from V. J. Wilson, presentation at the Canadian Association for Health, Physical Education and Recreation (CAHPER). 1982, Montreal.

Feedback

Feedback provides us with information on our behavior, which we need in order to learn. It is essential for our development. We need it to improve, adapt, and change our teaching behavior; the children need feedback in order to improve their motor skills. The following discussion is related to this latter aspect.

A search of physical education literature reveals that different authors categorize feedback in different ways, some being quite complex. All of them agree feedback is essential for learning to occur, and the ability to provide feedback is a characteristic of a good teacher.

You can give children *public feedback* as they continue the task: "John, you're keeping the ball close to you, that's good", "Chris, go more slowly and keep the ball in front of you all the time." You can also speak *privately* to an individual. Public feedback has several advantages, as

1. it uses less time,
2. other children hear and may be able to utilize the information, and
3. praised children may gain status within the peer group.

It could be a disadvantage if the feedback is interpreted as being negative or critical in nature. Recipients may feel embarrassed or demeaned in front of their peers.

Two categories of feedback are helpful and easy to understand, use, and monitor when teaching. These categories are *general* feedback and *specific* feedback.

REMEMBER THAT

. . . specific, positive, descriptive feedback can help you let the children know (1) what you expect and (2) that you appreciate good performance. Comments such as,

"I see some beautifully pointed toes"
"There are some good stretches as you jump"
"Listen to those quiet landings—they are good"

help the children understand that "any old response" does not get public recognition. These public comments contribute to a warm and positive learning environment.

Table 3.4

▼▼▼▼   ▼

General feedback

	Verbal	Nonverbal
Positive	That's good! Well done! Good try! Great!	A wink A smile A thumbs-up sign A hug
Negative	No good! That's not right. Poor! Oh dear!	Frowning Shaking the head Pointing a finger Turning away

▼▼▼▼   ▼

General Feedback

General feedback is often our immediate response to a task, as we tell children if they are "on track." It can be *verbal* or *nonverbal* (often called body language), and *positive* or *negative*. Table 3.4 give examples of each type.

Positive feedback provides support and encouragement as the children work. The comments are valuable because they contribute to the learning atmosphere, yet limited in usefulness because they neither specify why something is good nor what has been improved.

Negative feedback should be used sparingly so that the children do not feel incompetent or threatened. Positive effects will arise only if we follow such feedback with help and information so the children can make corrections and improvements to their work. If the rapport between a child and the teacher is "right," occasional negative feedback can be interpreted as friendly and humorous, but we need to be very aware of the signals we send.

Specific Feedback

This is specific information we provide for the students. We can give it to them after they have done something (past), or while they are doing it (during). Table 3.5 gives examples. Specific feedback can be *descriptive* or *prescriptive*. The amount and kind of feedback we provide affects the learning environment. Siedentop (1983) suggests that "In most skill-learning situations, a rate of 4.0 feedbacks per minute is easily attainable." Research has shown that we can significantly increase the amount and kind of feedback we give when teaching (Williamson et al. 1985). To do this, our verbal behavior must be systematically monitored and we must be prepared to change what we do.

Table 3.5

▼▼▼▼   ▼
Specific feedback

	Descriptive	Prescriptive
Positive	Your legs were very straight. (past)	Keep curled. (during)
	You're moving too soon. (during)	Push harder next time. (future)
Negative	You didn't look for the ball. (past)	Don't look at your feet. (during)
	You're not releasing soon enough. (during or past)	Don't hit so hard next time. (future)

▼▼▼▼   ▼

Descriptive feedback tells the students what they have done (past) or are doing (during). What they have done or are doing may or may not be correct; therefore, we need to qualify the description. For example, we might say, "Your hands are shoulder-width apart. Remember where you have them for the next time." This comment reinforces the student's response to the task. It has positive overtones and contributes significantly to a good learning atmosphere.

The descriptive feedback may imply the students need to change something the next time, with the information having a corrective function. "Your base is small and therefore you are finding it difficult to balance." We may assume the student will make the necessary adjustment or we may give them the information, as in "Move your hands further apart." This is particularly important when working with younger or less-capable students. Siedentop (1983) warns that, if overused, an "error-centered climate is created." At all times the positive message should be emphasized. We can do this by prefacing descriptive/corrective feedback with some evaluative comment.

We can be negative and specific as well. It is most important that we are aware of the nature of what we say to our students and that we tell them what *to do* more often than what *not* to do.

Descriptive Feedback

We prefer to call this category of feedback *refining tasks* as information is provided on how to do something or how to improve something. As with descriptive feedback, we can give this information while the students are working (during), or when they finish (past).

Prescriptive Feedback

Lesson: _____

Date: _____

Name of Teacher: _____

Name of Observer: _____

Listen to the teacher (or a tape recording); recognize and record with ✓ the different kinds of feedback given during the lesson.

	General	**Specific**
Positive		
Negative		

Figure 3.6 Feedback recording sheet

Totals:

In a dance lesson we might say, "Open your fingers more as your hands rise." It might be equally appropriate to say it as the students are rising or when they have finished. Your choice will depend on the situation.

When monitoring our teaching we should become very aware of how much feedback we provide our students, and also the kind of feedback (positive or negative) we use. Overall, we should try to score high on providing specific feedback that is both descriptive and prescriptive in nature. We should also be considerably more positive than negative in the tone of our communication. By using a simple recording device we can discover how much feedback, and its nature, we give. Figure 3.6 is easy to complete; ask a colleague to record as you teach one day, or else tape-record yourself as you teach the lesson and complete the chart afterward.

Summary

Teaching is a cyclical process involving the interaction of many components. Our own personal traits, beliefs, and value system form the foundation of our teaching behavior. In addition to this we can develop, and learn to use consistently, some specific, observable, and sometimes measurable skills. We can practice teaching skills in much the same way that we practice other skills. We must be prepared to monitor our teaching and, based on the information generated (the feedback) make decisions about what we can change to improve our teaching behavior. A few suggestions have been made on how to do this, and related readings that suggest many other analytical systems will be found at the end of this chapter.

1. What are some of the characteristics of "good" teachers?
2. Five groups of teaching skills are discussed in this chapter; what are they? Which one(s) do you consider to be your strength(s)? Which one(s) do you think you will (or already do), find difficult?
3. Why is specific feedback a critical component of the learning sequence?
4. Discuss factors influencing your positioning during a lesson.
5. Explain the function of each part of a lesson.
6. What kinds of decisions can children be encouraged to make during their lessons?
7. When will you use (1) scanning and (2) focusing observational techniques?
8. What will you look for when observing your children?

References

Barrett, K. 1981. Observation as a Teaching Behavior. *Quality Programming in H.P.E.R. vol. II.* J. Jackson, D. Turkington, eds. CAHPER Convention Papers. Victoria: Univeristy of Victoria, 103–6.

————. 1983. A Hypothetical Model of Observing as a Teaching Skill. *Journal of Teaching in Physical Education* 3(1).

Caruso, V. 1982. Enthusiastic Teaching. *JOPERD* 53:3.47,48.

Grant, B. and F. Martens. 1982. Teacher Effectiveness in Elementary Physical Education. *CAHPER Journal* 48:4, 7–10.

Koma, C. 1987. *Movement Education Resource File.* Project for 434–324 Movement Education for Early Childhood Teachers, Faculty of Education. Montreal: McGill University.

Logsdon, B., K. Barrett, M. Ammons, M. Broer, L. Halverson, R. McGee and M. A. Roberton. 1984. *Physical Education for Children: A Focus on the Teaching Process,* 2d. ed. Philadelphia: Lea and Febiger.

Mager, R. 1975. *Preparing Instructional Objectives,* 2d ed. Belmont, California: Pitman Learning, Inc.

O'Sullivan, M. 1985. A Descriptive Analytical Study of Student Teacher Effectiveness and Student Behavior in Secondary School Physical Education. *Teaching Effectiveness Research.* B. Howe, J. Jackson, eds. Victoria: University of Victoria.

Rink, J. 1979. *Observation System for Content Development Physical Education—Manual.* The University of South Carolina, Columbia.

————. 1985. *Teaching Physical Education for Learning.* St. Louis: Times Mirror/Mosby College Publishing.

Siedentop, D. 1983. *Developing Teaching Skills in Physical Education,* 2d ed. Palo Alto, California: Mayfield Publishing Co.

Siedentop, D., J. Herkowitz and J. Rink. 1984. *Elementary Physical Education Methods.* Englewood Cliffs, N.J.: Prentice-Hall, Inc.

Turner, R. and W. Purkey. 1983. Teaching Physical Education: An Invitational Approach. *JOPERD* 54:7, 13, 14, 64.

Williamson, K., M. O'Sullivan and J. Jackson. 1985. The Effects of Monitoring on the Verbal Feedback of Student Teachers in Physical Education Lessons. *CAHPER* Sept./Oct.: 8–13.

Related Readings

Allison, P. 1985. Observing for Competence. *JOPERD* 56:6.50,51,54.

———. 1988. Strategies of Observing During Field Experiences. *JOPERD* 59:2.28–30.

Anderson, W. G. 1980. *Analysis of Teaching Physical Education.* St. Louis: C. V. Mosby.

Anderson, W. G. and G. T. Barrette. 1978. What's Going on in Gym: Descriptive Studies of Physical Education Classes. *Monograph 1. Motor Skills: Theory Into Practice.*

Caskey, S. 1981. A Task Analysis Approach to Teaching. *JOPERD* 52:1.59,60.

Darst, P., V. Mancini and D. Zakrajsek. 1983. *Systematic Observation Instrumentation for Physical Education.* New York: Leisure Press.

Grant, B. 1985. The Relationship Between Specialist Training and Effective P.E. Teaching in the Elementary School. *Teaching Effectiveness Research.* B. Howe, J. Jackson, eds. Victoria: University of Victoria; Physical Education Series #6.

Goldberger, M. 1984. Effective Learning Through a Spectrum of Styles. *JOHPERD* 55:8.17–21.

Luke, M. 1983. Professional Preparation of the Elementary School Physical Education Teacher: A National Survey. *CAHPER Journal* 49:5.11–13.

Martinek, T., P. Crowe and W. Rejeski. 1982. *Pygmalion in the Gymnasium: Causes and Effects of Expectations in Teaching and Coaching.* West Point, N.Y.: Leisure Press.

Purkey, W. 1978. *Inviting School Success: A Self-concept Approach to Teaching-Learning.* Bellingham, Calif.: Wadsworth Co.

Scott, E. T. 1976. Humor in Teaching, *JOPER* 47:8.18.

Williamson, K., M. O'Sullivan and J. Jackson. 1985. The Effects of Monitoring on the Verbal Feedback of Student Teachers in Physical Education Classes. *CAHPER Journal* 51:7.8–13.

CHAPTER

4

DEVELOPING
THE YEARLY
PROGRAM

The development of a quality physical education program is dependent upon our knowledge of children and how they most effectively acquire movement skills. A quality program is also dependent upon successful planning and management. Sound planning and management practices will promote efficiency, safety, and a positive learning environment in which children's skill development will occur.

Planning and evaluating are important interrelated facets of teaching. How are they related? Very simply, we could say that planning comes prior to teaching and evaluating occurs after teaching. This may be superficially true, but we need to go further. Both planning and evaluating should be continuous and concurrent within the program. That is, planning should be based upon evaluation, and evaluation based upon careful planning.

Planning

The hallmark of an effective teacher is sound planning (Luke 1987). While at times we may be busy and overcome with new curricula, a problematic child, or the feeling that there is not enough time in the day, planning is essential for good teaching.

Factors Affecting Planning

For the new physical education teacher, planning a program may appear to be a monumental task. You are guided by the children's needs, scheduling and facilities, the season of the year, the class size, and the equipment available for your program.

The Children's Needs

The children's needs consistently influence our planning. We should consider their differing abilities and interests as we strive to enhance their skills and the pleasure they gain in movement activities.

In every classroom there are students who require special attention. For numerous reasons these students may be categorized or labelled "slow learners," "developmentally delayed," "learning disabled," or "gifted." There may be a child who is exceptionally skilled, another who is hyperactive, one who has emotional problems, another with a slight hearing impairment.

Scheduling and Facilities

Our primary concern is to develop the best possible program for the students as we strive toward daily physical education. However, the number and size of classes, and the facilities available may influence the schedule, as demands for appropriate spaces for activity are usually at a premium.

The length of classes is important. Ideally, younger children should be allotted shorter, and perhaps more frequent, periods for physical education, while older children require longer periods of time to engage in increasingly complex activities.

Planning pays off.

REMEMBER THAT

The special needs of some children are more readily apparent and pronounced than others. The enactment of Public Law 94–142 in the United States has made it mandatory for all children, regardless of their handicap or special circumstances, to receive instruction without discrimination. In Canada, "mainstreaming" children with special needs means that they will be scheduled into regular classes of physical education and should participate as fully as possible.

Sometimes two or even three classes of children will be grouped together for physical education lessons. In this case, a large facility or additional spaces and extra equipment are necessary to accommodate all of them.

Many teachers have successful physical education programs that utilize the space of a classroom, library, cafeteria, or staff room. If the area is clear, there may be sufficient space available for activity. In these situations we must utilize our ingenuity and perseverance to cope with a less than desirable situation.

Once gymnasium time is allotted, check the availability of additional facilities, such as the school's playing fields, a nearby swimming pool, a skating rink, or other special activity area. If these facilities can be reserved for appropriate dates, you can begin to plan a monthly and yearly program.

You should consider the climate and weather when planning the physical education program. Most teachers wish to use good weather to the best advantage of the program. For this reason, activities and games are usually played outside during the fall and spring. During the winter, you may have to plan for dance and gymnastic activities indoors.

Weather

Many lessons may be taught effectively outside.

The Outdoors

In some areas, the outdoors is the only space available for physical education experiences. Under these circumstances weather and alternate facilities will largely govern what activities will be most appropriate.

Often we do not use the outdoors as fully as possible. On an unexpected nice day, we should be spontaneous and flexible enough to alter the lesson plan and take advantage of the good weather. Some activities are suitable outside despite inclement weather and the snow and rain it may bring. Often it is the teacher who imposes negative feelings about activity in the rain or snow, while the children would tremendously enjoy the fresh air and open space, provided they have appropriate clothing.

Children will delight in a series of dance or gymnastics lessons normally experienced inside. For these activities, a grassy or cement surface needs to be relatively clean and smooth, and the weather warm enough to permit a minimum of restrictive clothing. Many sports at the adult level are ideally played outside. It is suggested that games activities be taught outside as often as possible.

Also consider the possibility of using both the outdoors and the indoors for a single physical education class. If the two activity areas are relatively close, having the beginning of the lesson outside may be a stimulating experience. The rest of the lesson may be taught inside to provide for the creation of a dance sequence or exploration on large gymnastic apparatus. When this type of flexibility is employed, facility use becomes less of a problem and the children grow accustomed to adapting to various environments.

The type and amount of equipment will influence program planning. A sound physical education program may be taught without extensive and expensive equipment, but there should be enough so that each child may actively participate.

Equipment

> Maximum participation requires appropriate quantities of equipment. Although one ball or bat may be appropriate for game play, individual dribbling practice requires one ball per student. Teachers should provide for maximum use of equipment within the limits of safety and practicality . . . an attempt should be made to decrease the number of participants interacting with a piece of equipment and to increase the number of pieces of equipment (Harrison 1984).

Beanbags, hoops, skipping ropes, paddles, and playground balls of various sizes are some of the essential items for a quality games program. If the largest class in the school has thirty students, then thirty of each piece of equipment should be available for use. For dance, a good record or cassette player is necessary, while in gymnastics a sufficient number of mats, benches, and apparatus for climbing will promote maximum participation. See table 4.1 for a comprehensive list of equipment.

Homemade equipment may be as effective as purchased equipment.

As may be seen from table 4.1, an array of equipment is desirable; however, a sound program may be developed with minimal equipment and ingenuity on the part of the teacher. Equipment may be modified or constructed by parents, teachers, students, or other school personnel.

Ensure that equipment is age-appropriate. Games equipment should be designed for children rather than adults. This implies that it is smaller and lighter than the "sport-specific" balls and sticks, for example, that are used in a formal game. Much gymnastic apparatus has been designed specifically for children; the Olympic gymnastic apparatus is usually too large and heavy to be easily transported by elementary school children.

REMEMBER THAT

Regular physical education lessons should be scheduled.

You should adhere to the schedule as much as possible.

Children need physical education (don't punish children by taking away their physical education lesson!).

The class prior to the physical education lesson should finish on time.

It is wise to schedule physical education lessons after classes that require a high level of concentration, such as math or language arts, and that don't require clean-up.

Table 4.1

▼▼▼▼

Suggested equipment for the elementary physical education program

Equipment	K	1	2	3	4	5	6
Dance							
Percussion instruments	△	△	△	△	△	△	△
*Record, compact disk, or cassette player	△	△	△	△	△	△	△
Games							
Adjustable basketball hoops (7-inch to 8½-inch)					●	●	●
Adjustable nets (badminton, volleyball, tennis)					●	●	●
Badminton rackets				●	△	△	△
Beachballs	△	△	●	●	●	●	●
*Beanbags	△	△	△	●	●	●	●
Bowling pins or small blocks	△	△	△	△	△	△	△
Field or floor hockey sticks				●	△	△	△
Footballs					●	●	●
Frisbees					●	●	●
*Hoops	△	△	△	△	●	●	●
*Large utility balls—playground balls (8–10-inch)	△	△	△	△	●	●	●
Mini basketballs (8–9-inch)					●	●	●
*Paddles			●	●	△	△	△
Pinnies (scrimmage vests) or colored team markers					●	●	△
Pylons or traffic cones	△	△	△	△	△	△	△

▼▼▼▼

We must check equipment availability before the physical education lesson begins. Part of lesson planning includes ensuring that what we want for the lesson is available. "Check the storage room" is a good policy.

Sometimes it is necessary during the lesson for you or the children to venture forth into an untidy storage room to retrieve equipment. It is at these times that the need for planning is paramount. Either set up equipment prior to the lesson, instruct the class to wait patiently as they

Equipment	K	1	2	3	4	5	6
Scoops and whiffle balls				•••	△	△	△
*Skipping ropes	△	△	△	△	△	△	△
*Small utility balls—playground balls (4–6 inch)	•••	•••	•••	•••	△	△	△
Soccer balls				•••	△	△	△
Softball bats, balls (plastic and wood or aluminum)	•••	△	△	△	△	△	△
Softball "tees"	•••	△	△	•••	•••		
*Sponge balls (Nerf)	△	△	△	•••			
Tennis rackets						•••	△
Volleyballs					•••	△	△
Gymnastics							
*Benches	△	△	△	△	△	△	△
*Climbing apparatus	△	△	△	△	△	△	△
Climbing ropes	△	△	△	△	△	△	△
*Mats	△	△	△	△	△	△	△
Springboard and/or beatboard					•••	△	△
Stools	△	△	△	△	△	△	△
Trampette or mini-tramp					•••	△	△
Trestles	△	△	△	△	△	△	△
Vaulting boxes (various heights)	△	△	△	△	△	△	△

Key

••••••• used occasionally

△△△ used often

* essential items

REMEMBER THAT

Equipment should be safe. Children should learn to treat equipment with care, and report splintered bats, paddles, and other unsafe items. Unstable benches, boxes, and other gymnastic apparatus should also be noted by both teacher and child so that the item is discarded or repaired before causing injury.

work on their own, or organize the children to set out their own equipment. It is both extremely frustrating and dangerous for both you and the children to have to stumble over equipment while carrying what you need from the rear of a storage area.

Careful planning is essential for the development of a safe, productive, and pleasant learning environment. Planning benefits children when their individual needs and interests are considered. Heightened efficiency will occur as children participate for the maximum amount of

Objectives of Planning

A tidy storage area makes
teaching easier.

time in each physical education lesson. Research (Howe and Jackson
1985, Verabioff 1987) has shown that time on task is a key discriminator
between effective and ineffective teaching.

Long-term Planning

Your role as a teacher is to facilitate learning by every child in your class.
Because children have a diversity of interests and abilities, the program
should be well-balanced between the functional and the expressive, the
social and solitary, the competitive and the cooperative. Therefore, we
believe in a balanced program that includes equal time spent in dance,
games, and gymnastics.

Planning Appropriate Activities The most important thing to remember when planning an activity in physical education is that it must
be appropriate for the particular age group. Volleyball is as inappropriate for second-grade children as is the game of "Brownies and Fairies"
for sixth-grade children. The teacher must not only consider the children's capabilities in physical skill, but also their cognitive and social
levels. We aim, then, to build increasingly complex skills based upon
what the child can do, rather than "watering down" adult skills.

The material in the dance, games, and gymnastics chapters has been
developed to assist you in developing age-appropriate activities. You may
also refer to table 1.3 in chapter 1 for further guidance.

Fitness Facts

In order to improve cardiovascular fitness, consider:

F = Frequency: we must exercise at least three or four times a week

I = Intensity: movement activities need to be at an intense level so the heart rate increases

T = Time: the activity should be maintained for at least fifteen minutes to improve our cardiovascular condition

T = Type: the type of exercise will influence how fit we are

In order to improve flexibility, a slow, sustained (20-second) stretch is necessary.

▼▼▼▼   ▼

Planning for Fitness The work of the President's Council on Fitness in the United States and of Fitness Canada have served to heighten our awareness of the importance of fitness. A child's level of fitness may be enhanced or maintained through dance, games, and gymnastics. When developing your program, you will need to make decisions regarding what movement form and specifically what skills will benefit the children's level of fitness. If your class is weak in flexibility, for example, you may choose to spend more time on tasks that involve stretching actions in dance or gymnastics.

In May, 1973, at the Child in Sport and Physical Activity Conference held at Queen's University, Kingston, Ontario, it was recommended that there should be thirty minutes of physical education per day (Verabioff 1986). While a primary goal of physical education is to promote skill development, we believe that the more children are skilled, the greater their fitness levels will be challenged. When we are fit and have a positive sense of well-being, it will be easier for us to learn new skills. We will have more energy and stamina, and will find it easier to concentrate. Thus, fitness development will be one result of quality programming.

Planning with Other Teachers You will be wise to consult with other teachers when planning. In this way, specific activities may be coordinated so that common facilities and equipment are available and ready for expedient use.

Maybe all dance classes are programmed for the same day or week so that the floor is kept clean and the record or cassette player remains in the gymnasium. Gymnastic lessons that require the use of heavy mats or large apparatus will benefit from cooperation and joint planning between teachers. One teacher may have the students set up the equipment while another teacher has the class put it away. When games lessons are taught on a particular day, week, or in coordinated units, then all classes can enjoy the benefits of a net previously set up or all the balls being inflated. Coordination of facilities and equipment between teachers will ensure that the time children spend in the gymnasium is of high quality and maximum quantity.

Planning for Special Occasions Children love the anticipation of a special day such as Halloween, Christmas, Valentine's Day, and Easter. Art, music, and social studies often incorporate these special occasions in their subject areas, and physical education can as well. Dance lessons may utilize Christmas music, Easter poetry, or Halloween stories as stimuli for expressive movement. Games that involve "the witches" competing against "the ghosts," or "the hearts" being tagged by "the cupids" may be played. When you are planning to incorporate special days in other classroom subjects, remember to include physical education as well.

Management Skills

Class management refers to the ability of the teacher to organize the elements of the learning environment and to maintain appropriate behavior of pupils (Luke 1987). Good teachers are good managers. Management involves organizing the children, apparatus, and equipment and results in safety, efficient use of time, and good behavior.

Organizing the Children

You will have to decide on the most effective organizational procedure for your lesson and plan tasks for the children in order to implement this. These are called *organizing tasks* (Rink 1979). They tell the children where to stand, with whom to work, what equipment or apparatus to get, where to place it, when to put things away, etc. Some typical organizing tasks are:

"**F**ind a space."
"**F**ind a partner."
"**P**ut the beanbags in the hoops where you found them."
"**Y**our group needs a mat and a bench; remember to lift the apparatus as you move it."

As with basic tasks (discussed in chapter 3) the children may need help to complete organizational tasks, and refining and simplifying tasks should be provided. Each "job" should be carefully thought through when planning the lesson, and some tasks will have to be broken down into parts and presented to the class bit by bit. This is particularly so when introducing a new apparatus arrangement in a gymnastics lesson.

Young children need considerable help with carrying and placing apparatus. If you have four groups working with benches and mats you will probably need to help one group at a time, even though the apparatus is identical. Children waiting should be told to watch carefully so that they will know what to do when their turn comes.

Every subject has its own "hardware" requirements and physical education is no exception. A considerable amount and variety of equipment is needed to provide a diverse and complete movement experience for the children. Equipment has to be selected for each lesson taught and decisions made regarding its placement in the teaching area. Gymnastic lessons make considerable demands on our managerial skills (see chapter 12) as the apparatus is heavy, large, and has to be well-placed in the area. Teaching the children to lift, carry, and arrange the pieces according to a pre-set plan or to their own design is an important part of the learning experience. Children can become good managers, working together with minimal control problems.

Equipment needs in games lessons are different. The equipment is not bulky (unless one has to carry goalposts), but there is usually a quantity to cope with. Tasks often require each child to take one piece of equipment. There is more "taking out and putting away" as children pair up and make larger groups. The equipment should be placed strategically throughout the teaching area so that minimum time is spent getting it, and the children can do so without colliding with each other. Well-spaced equipment usually results in well-spaced children who are able to begin to work safely without waiting for the teacher to space them out.

Safety is always of utmost concern. When children are free to move in open spaces and with equipment, safety factors become increasingly important. We need to establish rules of safety for physical education as soon as possible in the school year.

Children's use of space should be one of the initial concerns in all lessons. When children are working on their own, they should be as far away from others as possible. "Run into the empty spaces" is a good task to promote this, whether the class is in first or sixth grade. After much practice, children will no longer need to focus their attention on this aspect of safety.

Another important skill that is imperative for children to learn is how to stop. While this may appear exceedingly obvious, few teachers spend the time with young children to discuss the importance of a wide base of support (feet spread apart) a lowered center of gravity (knees bent), strong legs, and arms out for balance so that children can readily stop.

While a whistle may be appropriately used in some teaching environments (particularly the outdoors), its shrill sound is usually unnecessary indoors. We must each find an appropriate command or signal in order to gain the children's attention. A raised hand or the commands "freeze" or "stop" must be used with consistency, and obedience must be expected from the children.

Children must learn to stop correctly.

REMEMBER THAT

You should establish a command of "stop," "freeze," or "rest" (depending on the activity) to gain the children's attention.

Children should understand that they should only attempt skills that are within their capabilities.

Children should report damaged equipment to you as soon as it is noticed.

Children should wear appropriate clothing. Baggy sweaters and loose jewelry may get caught on apparatus; too tight pants may restrict movement. Children should never work in socks; bare feet or sneakers are appropriate and safe.

Children should stay as far away from others as possible when they are working on their own.

Children (and teachers!) should not chew gum—it can choke you.

Time Management

Time should always be used efficiently. A quality program maximizes learning time through an effective timetable, established routines, clear-cut behavioral codes, and preventative discipline.

Most children feel secure and enjoy being in a well-organized classroom with established routines. Children should always know what is expected of them so that they may follow rules and work within the guidelines successfully. Many teachers delegate responsibilities to designated "monitors" or groups of children to ensure that particular duties

Children may refer to task cards, charts, or diagrams to begin activity.

are carried out, and children will usually be happy to set up or put away equipment if they are treated as "special workers" for that day or week.

Most children happily anticipate each physical education lesson. Movement should begin as soon as possible, unless safety is of concern. The first task can be set in the classroom or as the children change into gym clothes. Having an interesting task to do reduces dawdling and control problems. When children are unoccupied, they usually find something to do on their own, and time is wasted regaining their attention. "Get a ball and travel with it," "Practice running and jumping," "Repeat the dance sequence you created last lesson" are the kinds of tasks that elicit immediate activity, thus maximizing the use of time. Task cards or charts suggesting possible beginning activities can be posted on the gymnasium wall and the children may be told to select from them.

When dealing with children, you should try to employ preventative discipline. Encourage **good** behavior.

Behavior Management

Be as positive as possible; look for good things to say to every child every day.

Plan to include children in some decisions (e.g., music preference, equipment selection).

Rules should be made only to protect the rights of others. Keep the number of rules at a minimum. The fewer the number of rules, the fewer there are to break. If possible, encourage children to participate in the establishment of rules.

Respond to the child after misbehavior has occurred; talking things out usually helps.

When a child misbehaves tell him what *to* do rather than what *not* to do. Rather than "Don't bounce the ball!", you could say, "Put the ball down."

Employ preventative planning; that is, construct situations that encourage good behavior.

Interfere with the misbehavior so that it does not give the child the public attention that may be sought. Quietly stop the behavior.

Expect the same behavior from children of both sexes and discipline them in the same manner.

Types of Programs

There are an array of excellent physical education programs, each of which differ in design. The type of program you plan as a teacher will reflect your unique interests and abilities, as well as the current interests and abilities of the children you are teaching. Locale, climate, facilities, equipment, and the priority of physical education as viewed by your school and school board will also largely influence the type of program you design.

The specific athletic interests of the local community may be reflected in the program. Some areas in the United States and Canada are known as hotbeds for gymnastics, swimming, track and field, ice hockey, and other sports. For this reason, the wise teacher will ensure that these activities are given ample time within the program. However, a balanced program is of utmost importance and no one activity should be taught at the expense of others. For instance, a games unit consisting entirely of basketball or hockey, or a program that does not include dance is totally unacceptable.

Organizing Your Program

At the beginning of the school year, we suggest that you outline when units of dance, games, and gymnastics will be taught. Other, shorter, units of activities may also be included, depending on your climate and any special facilities available. These may include swimming, roller-skating, ice skating, or other seasonal activities. You may wish to involve parents or local experts to assist in teaching or supervising these activities.

When designing your program you will have to decide how much overlap or continuity you wish to have between the movement form and concept being developed. Samples of program organization are presented for you in table 4.2.

Table 4.2

▼▼▼▼   ▼

Dovetailing plan

	Monday	Tuesday	Wednesday	Thursday	Friday
Week 1					
Dance	X			X	
Games		X			X
Gymnastics			X		
Week 2					
Dance		X			X
Games			X		
Gymnastics	X			X	
Week 3					
Dance			X		
Games	X			X	
Gymnastics		X			X

In this program, lessons are taught daily. The movement form is varied and there is ample opportunity to carry the movement concept from one form to the next.

▼▼▼▼   ▼

Dovetailing Plan

If you are fortunate enough to have daily lessons, dovetailing the activities (as illustrated in table 4.2) allows for a variety of experiences and reinforces the concept approach to physical education. You are able to plan dance, games, and gymnastics lessons around the same concept. This will help children to understand the common basis of movement and how the intention of the movement and the application of the concept results in different movement forms.

Repeating Monthly Plan

Some teachers like to provide continuity through a repeating monthly plan, where the majority of time is spent on one movement form one week, and on another in the next week. While the movement concept remains the same, it is developed through differing activities. For instance, you may work on the concept of body parts in two games lessons and one dance lesson. The next week the concept of body parts is continued with two dance lessons and one gymnastics lesson. The advantage of this plan is that the children are exposed to the same theme through a variety of activities. Its disadvantage is that specific skills are not worked on for a long period of time. Table 4.3 shows a sample repeating monthly plan.

Table 4.3

A repeating monthly plan

	Week 1			Week 2			Week 3			Week 4		
	Mon.	Wed.	Fri.	Mon.	Wed.	Fri.	Mon.	Wed.	Fri.	Mon.	Wed.	Fri.
Dance	✕	✕							✕	✕	✕	
Games			✕	✕	✕							✕
Gymnastics						✕	✕	✕				

In this monthly plan there are two lessons of one movement form in a week, followed by another movement form in that same week. This provides variety. The next week begins with the previous movement form taught. This plan provides for much continuity within movement concepts.

Table 4.4

An overlapping yearly program

	Sept.	Oct.	Nov.	Dec.	Jan.	Feb.	Mar.	Apr.	May	June
Dance				——	——			——	——	
Games	——	——				——	——			
Gymnastics		——	——				——	——		

Within any given month in the overlapping yearly plan, each movement form is taught for a period of time by itself, and other times with a different movement form. This provides for some continuity within both the movement form and movement concepts being developed.

Overlapping Yearly Plan

Another type of plan is the overlapping yearly program, illustrated in table 4.4. Here, one month is spent on dance, games, or gymnastics. In the next month, two of the three (dance, games, or gymnastics) are taught. The advantage of this plan is that there is ample time for skill and theme development while some variety is still employed.

A Yearly Plan with Little or No Overlapping

This plan, illustrated in table 4.5, is designed so that the movement form is taught in lengthy units. This may be appropriate when equipment or facilities are at a premium, and it is a "do it now or never" situation. Here the children have ample opportunity to develop specific skills, but are not afforded any variety. In this type of program, the primary disadvantage is that once the unit is completed, the children may not pursue the activity for another year and the "skill development advantage" is lost.

Table 4.5

A yearly plan with little or no overlapping

	Sept.	Oct.	Nov.	Dec.	Jan.	Feb.	Mar.	Apr.	May	June
Dance				————	————	————	————			
Games	————	————	————	————						
Gymnastics							————	————	————	————

This yearly plan has no overlapping, which provides for much skill development within each movement form. However, the movement concepts will have little obvious correlation from one movement form to another, and the skill development advantage may be lost.

Evaluation

Evaluation is the process of giving meaning to a measurement by judging it against some standard (Baumgartner and Jackson 1982).

Most of us think of evaluation in terms of tests, exams, grades, and the ominous pressures of striving to perform successfully according to the predetermined standards of teachers and parents. Although formal testing and grading are important facets of evaluation in education, they play only one role in the total teaching and learning process. While you may feel somewhat negative toward evaluation from a student's point of view, as a teacher, evaluation is a most helpful, complex, multifaceted teaching aid.

What is Evaluation?

Evaluation is a process by which something or someone is measured and compared with an agreed or established standard. It is intended to enhance both teaching and learning, and result in immediate, continuous, and long-range benefits for children and teachers. Evaluation need be neither formal nor threatening to the child. Fowler (1981) states:

> Evaluation should be a positive process designed to facilitate learning and encourage the development of an awareness of one's own limitations and capabilities.

Thus, it does not necessarily nor merely imply grading. While formal tests may be used sporadically, informal tests and casual observation (of which children may be unaware) are important tools used extensively by the teacher of a quality physical education program.

Why Do We Evaluate?

Evaluation is used to provide guidance for both the teacher and the student. Through this form of analysis we can determine strengths, weaknesses, and possible means for remediation within our physical education program.

Table 4.6

▼▼▼▼   ▼

Why evaluate?

To improve
To motivate
To clarify objectives
To redefine objectives
To discover strengths and weaknesses
To reward achievement
To provide guidance
To revise
To plan and organize
To report to children, parents, administrators
To be accountable
To provide credibility

▼▼▼▼   ▼

Evaluation may motivate you to improve instruction, or it may motivate the child to improve movement responses. It may be used to clarify the objectives of the program. Because planning is necessary for evaluation, it may encourage you to redefine your objectives, and thus indirectly clarify the goals for the child. Strengths and weaknesses of both teaching and learning will emerge in almost every type of evaluation. Whether you are employing a formal fitness test or casually observing children's movement sequences, conclusions may be drawn concerning the quality of responses and those that require additional attention.

Evaluation of the program as a whole may reveal that facilities and equipment are insufficient, or that improved planning and organizing in the scheduling of classes is necessary. An informal chat over coffee by the teachers or a questionnaire issued by the school's principal to the teachers may reveal that a simple thing such as the untidiness of the gymnasium storage area poses a major negative factor affecting the program. Examination of the gymnasium scheduling arrangement may disclose reasons for lack of cooperation between teachers. If teachers' priorities are markedly different because of the interests of their students (i.e., a kindergarten teacher and the school's volleyball coach), then evaluation may be used to revise the timetable.

As parents become increasingly involved, they may demand of administrators concrete evidence of a quality education for their children. This directly affects you, as you may be requested to provide reliable evidence of the credibility of your program. Teachers are usually very aware of the need to be accountable and it is through evaluation that a positive report may result. Table 4.6 summarizes why we evaluate.

To Do

Focus on interpersonal skills. Ask yourself the following questions
or observe another teacher.

Am I warm and friendly?

Do I create situations that will make children feel good about
themselves and others in the class?

Do I spend equal time with all children, regardless of their
skill level?

Am I open to the children's thoughts?

Do I encourage varied ideas and responses from the class?

Do I allow and encourage the children to make their own
decisions for some things?

Do I laugh with the children?

▼▼▼▼   ▼

What Can We Evaluate?

Almost every aspect of both our teaching and the children's learning
may be evaluated in some manner. This, however, does not imply
that formal tests exist for every aspect of the program. It does imply
that the totality of all experiences concerning the children and their
subsequent learning within physical education is worthy of critical in-
vestigation. Thus, we may evaluate by examining the teacher (through
self-evaluation or peer evaluation), the child, and/or the learning experience.

The Teacher

Self-evaluation is extremely important so that we may develop and mature
to become the best teachers we are capable of being. We have all had
bad teachers—why didn't they notice we were falling asleep, skipping
classes, or talking instead of listening during class? These teachers failed
to self-evaluate in order to discover why the students weren't actively
involved in their class. We needn't be like those teachers, if we take the
time for introspection and reflection upon our teaching behaviors.

When students misbehave, fail to understand, or would prefer to sit
on the sidelines of the physical education class, self-examination is vitally important. It is our responsibility to analyze the causes for this behavior starting with ourselves. We can examine one of any number of
influences we have upon the children. We may wish to focus upon our
interpersonal skills, our use of time, or our planning.

Our use of time may also be evaluated in physical education lessons.
Minimal time should be used for organization (changing, taking out
equipment) and directions, allowing for maximum time for activity. While
the amount of time you spend on organization and discussion will
depend upon the objectives of the lesson and the stage in the unit,
movement time should be maximized. In evaluating our planning, we
may focus on a single lesson or the program as a whole. Since we vary

To Do

Focus on your lesson planning and ask yourself:

Are all children participating for a maximum period of time?
Are children developing skill?
Are children thinking and learning?
Are positive attitudes toward activity and others being developed?

▼▼▼▼   ▼

in our priorities as to what is important within a physical education class, those priorities will be revealed in the questions we ask in terms of lesson evaluation.

The Child

Teachers are most commonly concerned with evaluating the child. Formal evaluation has posed problems to most teachers at some point in their career, for it is a complex and often sensitive issue. However, children should always be evaluated according to our instructional objectives.

We all strive for self-improvement. As we gain experience with children, our teaching methods and skills in selection of appropriate content will be refined, and thus will increasingly benefit the children. When an increased skill level is witnessed, we may deem teaching content and/or method to be successful. Children also strive for increased mastery in their movement. As they become accustomed to showing their work so that others may observe, they will become cognizant both of their own increasing skill and of the skill of others. The children's level of enjoyment may be assessed. While enjoyment is not a prerequisite for learning, it should be an outcome, one that certainly will enhance children's attitudes toward the subject and foster an eagerness for participation.

Evaluating Psychomotor Learning Within this domain we may evaluate either the movement *pattern* (how the movement was accomplished) or the movement *skill* (what the movement accomplished). In the nonmanipulative movement forms of dance and gymnastics, we tend to evaluate in terms of the movement pattern. Are the children running with full strides, arms in opposition to their legs, and with all action moving forward and backward? Can the children skip with a smooth step-hop pattern? Can they hold a curled shape when rolling? In the manipulative activities found in games, we most commonly evaluate in terms of movement skill. Can the child catch a ball that has been bounced? Can the child strike the ball? These questions refer to the child's skill as seen by the result or product of the movement. To help clarify these differences, additional questions for evaluating psychomotor learning are given in table 4.7.

Table 4.7

Evaluating psychomotor learning

Movement Concept	Movement Pattern (quality)	Movement Skill (quantity)
Locomotion		
Running	With effective strides?	How fast?
Jumping	With feet together?	How high?
Hopping	Using arms?	How many times?
Body parts	How are they being used?	How many?
Directions	Is it forward, backward, or up and down?	How far up?
Levels	Is it high, medium, or low?	How high? How low?
Time	Is it quick or slow?	How fast?

We may also be concerned with elements of *physical fitness* and *performance fitness,* which are basics for success in all activities (see chapter 1). The components of physical fitness may be measured by evaluating muscular strength, muscular endurance, cardiovascular endurance, and flexibility. This is evaluated in the AAHPERD (American Alliance for Health, Physical Education, Recreation and Dance) and CAHPER (Canadian Association for Health, Physical Education and Recreation) Fitness Tests, which many schools use annually.

Performance fitness may be evaluated by examining the child's capabilities in agility, balance, coordination, posture, power, reaction time, and rhythm. While physical fitness tests evaluate whether or not the body is fit, performance fitness "takes into account efficiency of basic movements" (Johnson and Nelson 1969).

There exists a vast number of psychomotor elements that may be evaluated within the elementary school physical education program. You will have to decide which elements will be formally evaluated. Chapters 6, 9, and 11 will help you make these decisions.

The Program

While frequent self and child evaluation is essential, the component parts of the physical education program discussed in the first section of this chapter should also be assessed. Some possible questions you may ask are outlined in table 4.8.

Almost every factor that affects your physical education program should be evaluated. In all likelihood, you will be able to answer many evaluative questions immediately. Since this is not an easy task for every aspect of your program, the following information on when and how to evaluate will be helpful to you.

Table 4.8

▼▼▼▼   ▼

Assessing the program: sample questions you may ask

Are there unused facilities?

Are facilities available when they are supposed to be?

Is the floor clean and free of equipment not needed?

Are children fresh and awake, ready for physical education when it is scheduled?

Is the outdoors used as much as possible?

Is there enough equipment for every child?

Is the equipment appropriate for the age and size of the children?

Are all children exposed to all of the equipment?

Is some equipment outdated or useless?

Is equipment stored properly?

Is unsafe apparatus repaired immediately?

Do children adhere to rules of safety?

▼▼▼▼   ▼

How Do We Evaluate?

There are probably as many evaluative techniques available in physical education as the total number of tests you have taken in your school career. Evaluating children's knowledge or attitudes in physical education may be accomplished through written tests such as rating scales, checklists, questionnaires, fill in the blank, short answer, true/false, multiple choice, or essay exams. Their movement skill may be evaluated through standardized fitness tests, skill tests, and motor patterns tests. We can measure or evaluate many things through many and varied means!

However, because we believe children's individual differences are important to note and we do not wish all children to perform the same skill in exactly the same way at the same time, observation will most often be employed in order for conclusions to be made about your program, your teaching, and your students. These observations may be recorded in a variety of ways. You will likely spend the most time evaluating the children through observation of their movement, social development, creativity, and attitudes exhibited toward physical education. Points to remember when observing were outlined for you in chapter 3.

Criterion-referenced Evaluation

While we believe that norm-referenced standards may be useful at times, a more effective method of evaluating is through criterion-referenced standards. This method is appropriate in assessing all children. In criterion-referenced evaluation, you first establish the criteria, then decide to what degree each child has met the criteria. One of the strengths of this form of evaluation is that it allows you to consider the child's individual progress. Evaluation is based on current and previous performance, not the achievements of a peer.

Table 4.9

Sample rating scale for evaluating dance sequences

	Agree 1	2	Disagree 3
The movement sequence is demanding of the child's skill.	X	___	___
The movement concept developed is obvious.	X	___	___
Body shapes are clear.	___	___	X
At least two pathways are incorporated.	___	X	___
At least three directions are used.	X	___	___
At least two levels are incorporated.	___	X	___
The child follows the beat of the music.	X	___	___

When evaluating the child, we should be prepared to recognize certain factors that can affect performance, such as the child's confidence level, acceptance among the peer group, our own expectations, previous test situations, and the child's preference for certain activities.

A child may contribute significantly to a program by being a good observer, an initiator of ideas, an analyzer who poses questions (Wall 1981).

Rating Scales

Rating scales are typically used on report cards or progress reports. They are characterized by a quantity that represents the quality of performance. This subjective estimate brings order to the processes of observation and self-appraisal, and provides for degrees of the quality, trait, or factor being examined (Barrow and McGee 1979).

You may wish to utilize standardized rating scales, or you may find it helpful to create your own, based upon the objectives of the program. When devising a rating scale, you must clearly state the performance objectives to be evaluated. Terms used must be specific verbs, nouns, and adjectives that are attainable and indisputable in their meaning. You may develop a scale based on a rating of 1 to 3, 1 to 5, 1 to 10, or any other number that seems appropriate to you. Rating scales may be used to evaluate almost every aspect of the physical education program. Your teaching behavior, aspects of the program, and the children's movement patterns, skills, fitness levels, attitudes, enjoyment, creativity, and application of movement concepts to movement situations may be observed, evaluated, and translated into a numerical system. A sample rating scale is shown in table 4.9.

Table 4.10

Sample checklist for movement concepts developed in the program

	Not Developed	Developed Adequately	Developed Extensively
Locomotor actions			✗
Body shape			✗
Body parts			✗
Levels		✗	
Pathways		✗	
Directions	✗		
Time	✗		
Weight	✗		
Relationship to partner		✗	
Relationship to objects		✗	

Table 4.11

Sample movement pattern checklist

	Child Demonstrates Clearly	Child Demonstrates Somewhat/ Sometimes	Child Does Not Demonstrate
Throwing			
1. Prepares for throw by bringing throwing hand behind head.	✓		
2. Upper body rotates.		✓	
3. Takes a step with opposite leg to throwing arm.			✓
4. Releases ball at appropriate time.		✓	
5. Follows through with throwing arm and upper body.	✓		

Checklists Checklists (illustrated in tables 4.10 and 4.11) are very similar to rating scales in that they also translate quality into some form of quantity. However, checklists are usually constructed with varying numbers of positive or negative categories and the appropriate box is checked off. Like rating scales, the value of this tool is that it takes relatively little

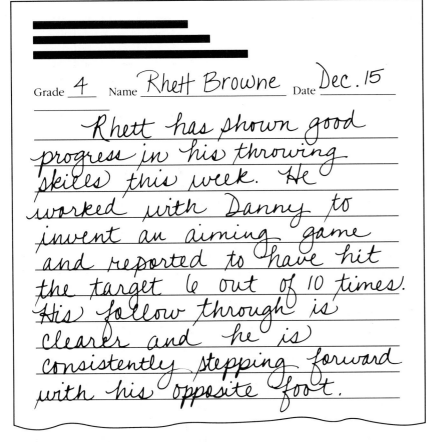

Grade _4_ Name _Rhett Browne_ Date _Dec. 15_

Rhett has shown good progress in his throwing skills this week. He worked with Danny to invent an aiming game and reported to have hit the target 6 out of 10 times. His follow through is clearer and he is consistently stepping forward with his opposite foot.

Figure 4.1 Sample anecdotal record

time to complete, and the results may be readily tabulated. The disadvantage of rating scales and checklists is that the cause for, or remediation of, a problem is not evident. Another problem of checklists having only two categories (i.e., "yes," "no") is that provision is not commonly made for borderline cases, which fall between these categories.

Anecdotal Records Anecdotal records (see figure 4.1) may be written by teachers as an informal method of evaluation. After a number of records are collected, you may then refer to these notes to evaluate each child. Anecdotal records are valuable in that they are candid accounts of useful information. While some teachers find them easy to do, others find them time-consuming. One distinct disadvantage of writing these accounts is that they are subjective and may be biased by the teacher.

Evaluation can be either norm-referenced or criterion-referenced.

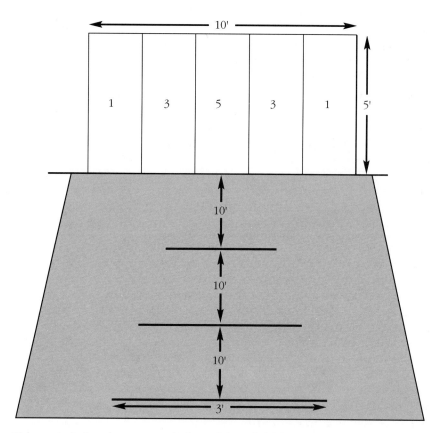

This test is designed to measure kicking ability of children in grades one through six. The child tries to hit the center of the target with nine trials. Score by adding the total number of points; when the ball lands on a line, the higher score is awarded.

This test could be adapted to assess accuracy in throwing, kicking, or striking skills.

(Reprinted by permission of the American Alliance for Health, Physical Education, Recreation and Dance, 1900 Association Drive, Reston, Virginia 22091.)

Figure 4.2 Sample test for kicking skills

Norm-referenced Evaluation

This type of evaluation involves comparing children to others in our class, school, or country. Norm-referenced evaluation focuses upon the product. We might use this form of evaluation to select the fastest runner or the best gymnast. Skill tests and fitness tests are examples of norm-referenced evaluation.

Skill Tests Skill tests (see figure 4.2) rely upon observation but are primarily quantitative, rather than qualitative. These **objective tests** rely minimally upon interpretation by the teacher. Success is most commonly measured in terms of time or distance. Skill tests measure such things as the child's ability to aim at a target, catch a ball from a specified distance, or jump vertically as high as possible. Most of these standardized tests provide the teacher with specific and detailed directions and often include norms or averages for a particular sex and age group. The results are usually easily interpreted.

When you evaluate specific predetermined movement skills, ensure that you have worked with the class on the movement (unless you are testing before the unit begins) and that your test can accommodate even the weakest of children. Very often the child who is the most physically gifted in skill is surpassed by others who are more creative, innovative, or have better "movement intuition"—they are more cooperative or can grasp the movement concepts more readily. We suggest that you praise the children who have these latter talents. You may evaluate each child's progress on these skills.

Fitness Testing Fitness tests (given in tables 4.13 and 4.14) are quantitative and objective, as results are measured in terms of time or distance. Fitness tests evaluate such things as running speed and number of sit-ups or push-ups completed in a specific time. Most of these standardized tests will provide you with detailed instructions and will often include norms or averages for a particular sex and age group.

Fitness tests are often given at the beginning or end of the school year, occasionally both. Ensure that you discuss the tests with the children and that the results are used as an ongoing challenge for the children. Results may be used as a basis for programming throughout the year when completed early in the school year. It is strongly suggested that you explain to the children the significance and meaning of one's fitness level, the components of fitness, and the individual's results. This information may spark discussion and be pursued in other subject areas such as health, science, social studies, arithmetic, and language arts. Some children will enjoy keeping records of their ongoing performance on individual file cards over the duration of the school year (see table 4.12). These activities may spur them on to a heightened awareness of the importance of fitness and encourage them to increase their fitness levels.

The **AAHPERD Youth Fitness Test** and the **Canada Fitness Awards Test** are the two most regularly used fitness tests employed in elementary physical education. While they are somewhat time consuming (they may take two or three classes to complete) and the procedure detailed, you and the children's parents may find the results valuable when compared with the established norms.

The AAHPERD Youth Fitness Test (table 4.13), was originally designed in 1957 by the American Alliance for Health, Physical Education, Recreation and Dance Research Council. Since then, the test has been revised and norms established for students from ages 10 to 17.

Table 4.12

Sample index cards for fitness tests

NAME *Cara Nielsen*   AGE   *8*   TEACHER *Mr. McNiven*

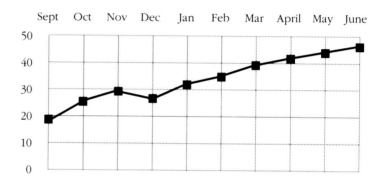

SIT-UPS (in 1 minute)

NAME *Cara Nielsen*   AGE   *8*   TEACHER *Mr. McNiven*

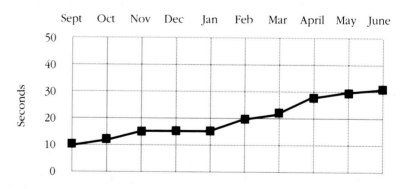

FLEXED ARM HANG

Table 4.13

▼▼▼▼   ▼

AAHPERD Youth Fitness Test

Percentile Rank Norms for Boys on the AAHPERD Sit-ups Test (number)*

					Age			
Percentile	9–10	11	12	13	14	15	16	17+
95	47	48	50	53	55	57	55	54
75	38	40	42	45	47	48	47	46
50	31	34	35	38	41	42	41	41
25	25	26	30	30	34	37	35	35
5	13	15	18	20	24	28	28	26

*Modified from the AAHPERD Youth Fitness Test Manual.

Percentile Rank Norms for Girls on the AAHPERD Sit-ups Test (number)*

					Age			
Percentile	9–10	11	12	13	14	15	16	17+
95	45	43	44	45	45	45	43	45
75	34	35	36	36	37	36	35	35
50	27	29	29	30	30	31	30	30
25	21	22	24	23	24	25	24	25
5	10	9	13	15	16	15	15	14

*Modified from AAHPERD Youth Fitness Test Manual.

Reprinted by permission of the American Alliance for Health, Physical Education, Recreation and Dance, 1900 Association Dr., Reston, VA 22091.

▼▼▼▼   ▼

Test items include both physical and motor fitness items, such as:

pull-ups (boys), modified pull-ups (girls)
sit-ups
600-yard run/walk
30-yard shuttle run
50-yard dash
softball throw for distance
standing long jump

The AAHPERD Physical Best program is a physical fitness education and assessment program intended to encourage students to be physically active. It focuses upon self-competition (improvement) rather than competition with others. The Physical Best test items include:

one mile run/walk
sit and reach
pull-ups
modified sit-ups (60 seconds)
body composition (skin folds with body mass index as alternate)

Table 4.14

▼▼▼▼   ▼

Canada Fitness Awards Test Bronze Level

Test Item		Age						
		6	7	8	9	10	11	12
Shuttle run	girls:	17.2	16.7	15.8	15.2	15.2	14.6	14.3
	boys:	17.2	16.7	15.8	15.2	14.6	14.1	13.7
Standing long jump	girls:	95	100	110	117	123	130	133
(centimeters)	boys:	95	100	110	117	128	135	143
Push-ups	girls:	2	3	6	5	7	4	2
	boys:	2	3	6	5	8	5	9
Partial curl-ups	girls:	6	8	10	11	17	18	19
	boys:	6	8	10	11	12	17	22
50-meter run	girls:	12.9	12.2	11.4	10.8	10.9	10.4	10.2
	boys:	12.9	12.2	11.4	10.8	10.3	10.0	9.7
			800 meters			1600 meters		
Endurance run	girls:	6:50	6:26	6:01	5:41	12:52	12:46	12:46
	boys:	6:50	6:26	6:01	5:41	11:17	10:50	10:31

Source: Canada Fitness Award Program—Leader's Manual, 1984. *This material was developed by, and is reproduced with the permission of, Fitness Canada, Government of Canada.*

▼▼▼▼   ▼

The AAHPERD Youth Fitness and Physical Best tests are available from the American Alliance for Health, Physical Education, Recreation and Dance, 1900 Association Drive, Reston, Virginia 22091.

The Canada Fitness Awards Test (table 4.14) is very similar to the AAHPERD Youth Fitness Test but has the advantage of being appropriate for a wider age range. Norms have been established for children ages 6 to 17. It has been used extensively throughout Canada by general classroom teachers since 1976 and includes the following items:

    shuttle run

    standing long jump

    push-ups

    partial curl-ups

    50-meter run

    endurance run: 800 meters for ages 6 through 9

                       1600 meters for ages 10 through 12

                       2400 meters for ages 13 through 17

When Do We Evaluate?

Due to the type of the physical education program we believe in, evaluation should most often occur informally, through your observations and discussion with the children. Evaluation may occur through summative or formative means.

Table 4.15

▼▼▼▼ ▼

Formative and summative evaluation

	When is it used?	*Who uses it?*	*What is evaluated?*	*Why is it used?*
Formative Evaluation	Continuously	Teacher, student	Process	To remediate
Summative Evaluation	At the end	Teacher	Product	For final evaluation

▼▼▼▼ ▼

Summative evaluation occurs at the **completion** of a lesson, unit, or program. This term implies the sum or totality of learning that has occurred throughout the unit or school year and may be used to evaluate each child or the class in general. Tests may be norm-referenced or criterion-referenced. Summative evaluation may be used effectively when the same test is given both before and after the lesson, unit, or program. This is termed *pre-test/post-test,* and it measures the progress the students have made. While summative evaluation may be valuable at times, it fails to address the process of learning, which we feel is so important.

Summative Evaluation

You should most commonly employ evaluative procedures that occur *during* a lesson, unit, or program. As the term *formative* suggests, your teaching and your student's learning may be formed or changed as a result of this type of evaluation, which is normally criterion-referenced. You may revise your objectives, modify your teaching methods, decide to review previous work, accelerate skills covered, or adapt and modify equipment as a result of your evaluation. Formative evaluation is valued, as it places the focus upon the children's learning and the process of their development. Table 4.15 summarizes these two types of evaluation.

Formative Evaluation

REMEMBER THAT

Since we believe that individual differences are part of being human, the way in which results are handled is important. While some children may benefit from knowledge of the results, for other children, being told once again of their continued failure could be most destructive. Your sensitivity, as the teacher, is crucial.

Selecting and Designing
Appropriate Tests

Selecting and designing an appropriate test may be an ominous chore if you are vague concerning the intent of the evaluation. However, deciding the basic items you wish to test, what the results will be used for, how many students will complete the test, and how much time you wish to spend on evaluation will assist in the process.

REMEMBER THAT

The amount of time in testing should reflect the amount of time you have spent teaching. Don't spend more time evaluating than teaching! Plan how, what, and when you'll test before teaching begins.
The test should directly relate to what you've taught.
Administration of the test should be relatively simple.
Results should be used to motivate and inform, not degrade, children.

Summary

When a yearly program is planned, the factors of patterns of scheduling, facilities, use of the outdoors, weather, equipment, and the children's needs must be considered. Learning should be maximized by planning for children's safety and efficient use of time. There are many ways to organize a program: weekly, monthly, or yearly, and with much, some, or no overlapping of the movement form.

Evaluation is a vital component of the teaching process. You may employ self-evaluation, peer evaluation, or student evaluation to improve the physical education program. Evaluative techniques exist in rating scales, checklists, anecdotal records, skill tests, and fitness tests, and may be formative and/or summative.

Review Questions

1. How may children's needs be met through careful planning?
2. Discuss why you prefer one particular type of program organization over another.
3. What component parts of the child's cognitive domain can we evaluate in physical education?
4. What is the difference between formative and summative evaluation?
5. You administer a fitness test to your class in October. Some children do well and others very poorly. How will you handle the test results?
6. When would you use a skill test?
7. What points would you use as a basis for evaluating children's movement in dance on a rating scale?

References

Barrow, H. M. and R. McGee. 1979. *A Practical Approach to Measurement in Physical Education,* 3d ed. Philadelphia: Lea and Febiger.

Baumgartner, T. and A. Jackson. 1982. *Measurement for Evaluation.* Dubuque: Wm. C. Brown Publishers.

Fowler, J. S. 1981. *Movement Education.* Philadelphia: Saunders College Publishing.

Harrison, J. M. 1984. *Instructional Strategies for Physical Education.* Dubuque: Wm. C. Brown Publishers.

Howe, B. L. and J. J. Jackson. eds. 1985. *Teaching Effectiveness Research Monograph.* Physical Education Series #6. University of Victoria, British Columbia.

Johnson, R. L. and J. K. Nelson. 1969. *Practical Measurements for Evaluation in Physical Education.* Minneapolis: Burgess Publishing Co.

Luke, M. 1987. Analysis of Class Management Physical Education. *Canadian Association of Health, Physical Education and Recreation Journal* vol. 53, no. 3: 10–13.

Rink, J. 1979. Observation System for Content Development Physical Education Manual. University of South Carolina.

Verabioff, L. 1986. Can We Justify Daily Physical Education? *CAHPER Journal* vol. 52, no. 2: 8–11.

Wall, J. 1981. *Beginnings.* Montreal: McGill University.

Related Readings

Farley, M. 1984. Program Evaluation as a Political Tool. *JOPERD* vol. 55, no. 4: 64–67.

Luke, M. 1987. Analysis of Class Management Physical Education. *CAHPER Journal* vol. 53, no. 3: 10–13.

Milverstedt, F. 1988. Are Kids Really So Out of Shape? *Athletic Business* January, 24–29.

Pritchard, J. 1987. Programming for Quality Daily Physical Education. *CAHPER Journal* vol. 53, no. 6: 14–19.

Ratcliffe, T. 1986. Influencing the Principal. What the Physical Educator Can Do. *JOPERD* vol. 57, no. 5: 86–87.

Verabioff, L. 1986. Can We Justify Daily Physical Education? *CAHPER Journal* vol. 52, no. 2: 8–11.

Virgilio, S. and P. Krebs. 1984. Effective Time Management Techniques. *JOPERD* vol. 55, no. 4: 68–73.

SECTION

2

DANCE

One of the best things to be said about dancing is that like all the arts there is really no end to it. Therefore it is always interesting and no sooner has one learnt one thing than one realises how much more there is still to know; and with each lesson a little progress only opens up more possibilities. . . .

. . . Dance is language without words, so there is communication and contact among participants through their relationships in lines, circles or groups.

. . . Dance has always been, and always will be, a very basic form of human expression.

Fonteyn, M. 1978. A Dancer's World *London: W. H. Allen.*

CHAPTER

5

THE DANCE
PROGRAM

Teaching dance is rewarding, exciting, demanding. Lessons are times for sharing and developing ideas as well as becoming more skillful. Dance, probably more than games and gymnastics, offers many opportunities for integrating movement experiences with other aspects of the curriculum. Other art forms, especially music, are quite easily associated with dance, as can be social studies, science, and language arts, especially poetry. Table 5.1 offers examples.

Dance tends to receive less attention in physical education programs than the objective movement forms of games and gymnastics. This may be partly due to the value that society places on dance. "Dance was once an integrated expression of the whole life" (Mettler 1980). Over the centuries, dance and sport have existed in some form in every culture and society. These two movement forms are so interwoven into human behavioral patterns that, although the forms may change according to the practices and values of the particular society, involvement in them is a hallmark of being human (Hill 1982).

The inclusion of dance is certainly due to whether teachers consider it important for children to become skillful in and knowledgeable about expressive movement forms. Sometimes there is the question whether dance is part of the physical education or art education program. On reflection it probably does not matter where dance is in the curriculum; what is important is that children have learning experiences in the expressive form of movement.

Why Should Dance Be Included in School Programs?

This question has been discussed by groups of concerned educators and several definitive statements and resolutions have been made and published. There is no lack of support for teachers who wish to introduce dance into their schools. The National Dance Association of AAHPERD, the Dance Committee of CAHPER, and Dance and the Child: International (daCi) are three associations that exist mainly for the purpose of ensuring that all children have the opportunity to dance and providing help and encouragement for teachers.

Following are statements published by these associations.

National Dance Association of AAHPERD (1976)

Dance education is a medium for enhancing the quality of life for children, youth, and adults. Every human being has the right to move in ways that are primal, expressive, imaginative, and transformational.

Table 5.1

Integrating dance and other subject areas

Subject	Dance Ideas
Music	
Recorded music	Stimulus for dance
Music played by the teacher	Accompaniment for
Music composed by the teacher	singing games
Music played by the children	folk dance
Music composed by the children	creative dance
Instruments	Make and/or play percussion
	instruments for creative dance
Language arts	
Poetry and stories	
Published	Stimulus for dance
Written by the teacher	Written after dance experience(s)
Written by the children	
Verbs, adjectives, adverbs	
	Stimulus for dance
	Describing dances
Art	
Adult art	Stimulus for dance
Children's art	Created after dance experience(s)
Pictures, sculptures	
Social studies	
Costumes	Folk dance
Customs	Creating dances
Festivals	
History	
Science	
Natural phenomena: the sea, storms, weather, birth and death.	Stimulus for dance
Scientific concepts: magnetism, electricity, gravity, crystals	

Therefore, we urge art, civic, and educational groups to support dance programs where they exist and to develop programs where they do not exist that:

foster aesthetic-kinesthetic education;

integrate the human capacity to form and transform, in and through movement;

celebrate the human ability to move with power and expressiveness;

promote movement skills that explore and extend the artistic, cognitive, and psychomotor potentials of the human being;

articulate and verify a commitment to man's heritage of dance forms from all cultures and all races; and

include sequential dance experiences appropriate to the developmental level of the human beings for whom they are designed.

Reprinted by permission of the American Alliance for Health, Physical Education, Recreation and Dance, 1900 Association Drive, Reston, Virginia 22091.

Constitution of Dance and the Child: International (daCi)

Article II (adopted Stockholm, 1982)

Aims and Purposes The aim of Dance and the Child: International is to promote everything that can benefit dance and the child, irrespective of race, color, sex, religion, national or social origin; and that this aim shall be carried in a spirit of peace and universal brotherhood.

Its objectives are to:

recognize the right of every child to dance, including those with special needs, the term "child" covering ages 0–18 years.

promote more opportunities for children throughout the world to experience dance as creators, performers and spectators.

reveal and respect the views and dance interests of the child.

preserve a cultural heritage of all forms of dance for children.

promote the inclusion of dance in general education and stimulate the exchange of ideas on dance programs in schools and in communities.

Reproduced by kind permission of Dance and Child: International, Burlington, Ontario, Canada.

Dance Committee of CAHPER, 1983

Statement of Position

It is recommended that:

dance be a part of the school curriculum at the elementary level.

dance be taught at each grade level as a continuous and developmental program.

children be exposed to a variety of dance forms including creative, folk and square as well as suitable current popular dances, singing games and other rhythmic activities.

dance, where appropriate, be integrated with other subject areas such as drama, language arts, music, social studies, art, etc.

dance experiences be taught using appropriate teaching techniques ranging from exploratory to initiative.

opportunities be given for children to improvise and spontaneously create dance works.

a variety of stimuli be used in conjunction with the dance experience; for example music, words, percussion, imaginative ideas and visual stimuli.

dance experiences allow children to develop an aesthetic awareness through the enjoyment of doing and an ability to view attentively and comment knowledgeably on what they see, feel and hear.

Reproduced by kind permission of the Canadian Association for Health, Physical Education and Recreation.

The Nature of Dance

Experience in one art form does not compensate for lack of experience in the other arts. In school curricula, the tendency has been for children to have some program in art or music and possibly some drama included in English lessons, though probably not from the point of view of providing the children with an artistic experience. Dance is a movement form and some people—parents, administrators, and even teachers—may feel that as long as the children have some activity then it really does not matter whether it is in the form of a game, gymnastics routine, or folk dance. This is not so. It is only when an "arts in education" commitment is made "that the more human purposes of education relating to values and feelings and personal growth and fulfillment of young people" occur (Brinson 1979). Fortunately, there are concerned parents, administrators, and teachers who are aware of an "essentialist shift which emphasises that each art form is unique in its own right and cannot be replaced or supplanted by any other art form or movement form" (Boorman 1980).

Dance is a word that embraces a range of expressive activities and as such:

has unique and significant contributions to make in the total education of the child. Dance and the arts play a large part in the "humanizing" of man by encouraging creativity, discovery, inquiry and the overall process of flexible cognition, in a changing, challenging environment (Dance Committee of CAHPER 1983).

In an educational environment the production of an artistic masterpiece is not the main concern.

Whether the dance meets the criteria of being an important art work, whether the dance of the school child is as enjoyable to observe as that of the student of the National Ballet Company is irrelevant to the teaching situation. The priority is not one of judgment, but of providing the artistic experience (Dewar 1980).

Table 5.2

▼▼▼▼   ▼

Expressive = objective movement experience continuum

Less expressive dance experience		More expressive dance experience
Singing games	Folk dance	Creative dance

▼▼▼▼   ▼

This is not to say that quality work will not result, but that the reason for the experience is the concomitant learning, rather than the products the children create and/or perform.

Dance is varied in nature and the word may have different meanings for each of us. If you stop people at random on the street and ask them what they think of when you say the word "dance" you may be told the name of the latest craze in nightclubs, ballet, jazz, etc. If you then asked these people how many learned to dance as part of their school program, you would probably find that very few had. While the majority of people in the Western world have seen dance (as the television has brought dance in some form into the majority of homes), few have had the opportunity to learn about this activity and art form.

We all use expressive movement many times each day, often without being aware of it. We use gestures and assume postures to indicate how we feel about something or to reinforce what we are saying. Watch the politicians and evangelists on TV and notice how they use movement as they speak. Recognize, too, that we are influenced as much by the movements as by the words. We may feel the speaker is very confident because he stands upright, looks directly at the camera, and uses large, definite hand gestures. Conversely, many small, limp hand movements, or the repetition of the same gesture, may detract from what is being said by suggesting uncertainty or maybe lack of conviction.

The nature of dance is such that we can develop awareness of our unconscious movement patterns, enabling us to bring them under conscious control and develop our range of expressive movement patterns, so that we have a well-developed kinetic mode of communication.

Anthoney (1979) considers that the transformation of everyday movement into an artistic experience occurs at three levels. These levels may provide us with a focus when we plan learning experiences for children.

Level 1: Movement for movement's sake, to develop an awareness of enjoyment in moving. Young children and beginners in dance particularly need this kind of focus in their lessons.

Table 5.3

Suggested appropriateness of dance forms

	K	Grade 1	Grade 2	Grade 3	Grade 4	Grade 5	Grade 6
Singing Games	*	*					
Folk Dance			*	*	*	*	*
Creative Dance	*	*	*	*	*	*	*

Level 2: The concern is with having an aesthetic experience. Our everyday movements are transformed into a form with new meaning. A dance program such as the one we are proposing should give the children this level of dance experience.

Level 3: This completes the transition from the "everyday to artistic." The intention is "to give form . . . to create a structured dance . . . to show someone the dance" (Dewar 1980). An arts program, rather than a physical education program, would aim to reach this level of experience with all of the students.

Each of the three levels is a legitimate dance experience and more or less emphasis will be placed on each of them at different stages of learning and according to the focus of the learning experience. Reference is made again to these three levels of experience in chapter 6.

Dance Forms

The concept of *functional* and *expressive* movement has already been discussed in chapter 2. A dance program for children in elementary schools should consist of a variety of dancelike experiences, some being more expressive than others. Three dance forms are suggested as a minimum, each form challenging the children in specific ways and thus the learning objectives vary (table 5.2).

The stage of the children's development will also guide us in our choice of the form most suitable at a particular time, as illustrated in table 5.3.

The choice of form will also be based on the movement concepts considered appropriate for the children's needs and capabilities at that particular moment. For example, you may decide the children need help in working cooperatively in pairs. You might, therefore, select a simple partner folk dance that demands coordinating with one another, as in a

Table 5.4

▼▼▼▼   ▼

Selected characteristics of the three dance forms

	Singing Games	**Folk Dance**	**Creative Dance**
Relationships	Range from individual to group; single and double circles; simple	Partners, groups; lines, squares, circles; range from simple to complex	Range from individual to group; varied formations; range from simple to complex
Rhythm	Metric; pre-set; simple	Metric; pre-set; simple to complex	Metric, nonmetric, pre-set, or created; simple to complex
Stimulus	Song, music	Music	Infinite possibilities
Accompaniment	Music, voice	Music	Silence, music, voice percussion
Actions	Running, skipping, galloping, clapping, stamping	Combinations of step patterns	Combinations of six basic activities (figure 5.1)
Responses	Imitative, predetermined	Imitative, predetermined	Mainly creative

▼▼▼▼   ▼

clapping dance like the German Clap Dance or a dance in which the partners have to change hold, such as the Gay Gordons. The main focus of your teaching (refining, simplifying, and extending tasks) will be directed toward the skills and awareness necessary for making the partnership function. Comments such as "Have your hands ready as you face your partner," and "Keep level with your partner as you travel," will give the children information they can use to improve their relationship.

The three dance forms suggested as being the most appropriate for inclusion in a school program are:

1. singing games
2. folk dance
3. creative dance

Each one will be discussed separately, and table 5.4 outlines selected characteristics of each one so that it is fairly easy to compare them.

Singing games are a part of children's oral heritage that is closely allied with music and poetry, particularly nursery rhymes. Many singing games are simple coordination exercises while others are little dramatic experiences, for example *The Farmer's in the Dell.* Children often know these songs and action sequences before they come to school; therefore they make a good link between preschool experiences and classroom activities.

Singing Games

Singing games are rhythmic and repetitive in nature. The relationships between the participants are simple, as are the actions. There is little room for individual variations and the teacher's focus will be more on general participation, keeping in time with the music, and knowing the words than on improving motor skills. Singing games that require partners and formations other than scatter and a single circle are closely related to the beginnings of folk dance.

This dance form is really "borrowed" from the adult world. Years before the days of radio and commercial entertainment, folk dances were the social dances of the people. When schooling became compulsory and some form of physical activity was considered essential for the children, adult movement activities were scaled down and included in the curriculum. Folk dance was one of these. Teachers knew the dances, and they were considered easy to teach.

Folk Dance

Over the years, folk dance has become firmly established in many elementary school programs and is probably the most common dance form taught.

> In terms of educational value folk dance is perhaps one of the best examples of integration of subject matter which can be found in the school curriculum. Here it is possible for children to learn about the history and life of people of different ethnic origins: their customs, their music, their celebrations and costumes (Evans 1980).

Children can have very happy learning experiences when folk dance is taught by sensitive and confident teachers who are able to select and maybe adapt the predetermined dances to meet the needs of their particular children.

Creative dance, which offers children a diverse dance experience, demands a disciplined mind and body. The children may dance alone, with a few chosen friends, or with the whole class. In the lessons, dance ideas are explored by discussing, analyzing, improvising with or without any accompaniment, synthesizing, and transforming the ideas into concrete movement patterns or motifs. These motifs are symbolic representations of the original idea or ideas. It is an opportunity for children both to

Creative Dance

express themselves and be themselves. This does not mean there is no direction from the teachers or that neither structure nor limitations are set. In fact, the opposite is necessary. A carefully structured environment has to be designed, one that guides the children (often through the use of problem-solving techniques) to explore, experiment with, and formulate their motifs. Children are helped to evaluate their own work and that of their peers from the point of view of effectiveness. Thus, appreciation and aesthetic judgments are encouraged.

Creators— Performers— Observers

A final comment on the nature of the dance program for children: three very different experiences are possible. As educators we must recognize the importance of each experience and ensure that the children we teach have opportunities to be *creators, performers,* and *observers* of dance, learning to assume different roles that demand different kinds of knowledge and skill. Table 5.4 gives some indication of which dance form probably provides the best learning experiences in these separate roles. When observing others dance, if possible include dance artists as well as other children. Many dance companies and studios have a children's program that they bring to the school. Universities with dance programs sometimes welcome an opportunity for their students to perform. Taking the children to see a performance in a theater is, of course, most valuable, but in days of budget restrictions there often is no money for such field trips.

Rhythmic Activities

Some programs include doing general activities to music. The general objectives are to move in time to the music, adjust to different tempi, and recognize and move to different rhythmic patterns. Children have these experiences when the program includes singing games, folk dance, and creative dance. The addition of another dimension to the dance program reduces the time available for each one. We feel that three dance forms allow for in-depth learning, and provide sufficient variety for the children.

The Material of Dance

All dance forms emphasize the expressive, qualitative elements of movement—the ever-changing dynamics that add "color" and meaning to our actions. When put into spatial and relationship contexts, action becomes a means of communicating and sharing thoughts, ideas, and feelings. Sometimes we are expressing ourselves; at other times, we express other people's ideas and thoughts. In the former situation we are the creators as well as the performers; in the latter, we learn the dance created by another. This may be a folk dance or a creative dance.

As discussed in chapter 2, all human movement can be categorized into four major concepts: body, effort, spatial, and relationships. As our understanding develops of how these concepts relate specifically to dance, and as we become more skilled in producing planned movements at will, our movement vocabulary will increase, and we will become more able to use our bodies as instruments of expression. We will consider each concept separately.

> It goes without saying that teachers of dance, like those of another discipline, should have a total grasp of the basic structure of their subject and the material it contains (Johanna Exiner, speaking at the Dance Education Conference held in Melbourne, Australia, 1977).

Body Concepts

Body concepts are concerned with understanding and developing control of our physical selves; an overview of these concepts was introduced in chapter 2. Here we look at them more specifically as they relate to dance for children.

In the dance context, the body is often called the instrument of our expression, with movement being the medium through which we communicate.

> The body serves the same purpose in dance as, for example, the piano serves in music. The musician uses the piano to create sound. The dancer uses the body to create movement (Mettler 1980).

Dance is a *kinetic art* for the dancer and is, therefore, activity-oriented. Children "come to dance" through activities such as skipping, turning, jumping, lifting their arms in reaching gestures, and being "statues." Each of these belongs to one of the six general categories of activity (see figure 5.1), which can be considered the basic vocabulary of dance. These activities "carry" the dynamics we select and become expressive in nature.

1. Locomotion
2. Stepping
3. Gesturing
4. Jumping
5. Stillness
6. Turning

Locomotion

Locomotion or traveling focuses on all the different ways the body can move through the space to new places. The intention of the dancers is to "go somewhere" and therefore their focus is outward, not on themselves. Examples of locomotor actions are walking, running, rolling, and sliding. An extensive locomotor vocabulary is developed over a period of time and whole dances can be created based on simple locomotor patterns. Many folk dances are composed of various locomotor patterns.

Figure 5.1 Body
concepts—the six basic
activities of dance

To Do

A Stepping Sequence

Begin with weight on two feet, change to one knee and one foot,
one knee alone, finish on one foot.

Repeat on the other side of the body (i.e., if you put weight on your
right knee the first time, use your left knee in the repetition).

Repeat the sequence until you can do it smoothly and seemingly
without exertion.

▼▼▼▼   ▼

Stepping   Stepping refers to changing which parts of the body support the weight.
The focus is not on "going somewhere new," but on shifting the weight
from one part to another, an action requiring considerable strength and
control. Children often understand this idea if the word "stand" is used
in the task, as in "stand on two different parts, then find how you can
change to two new parts."

Interesting positions of stillness may arise, the world can be observed upside-down, or unusual sensations can be experienced as a result of changing from one base to another. When performed on different bases, gestures result in changing visual effects, an important consideration when a dance is to be performed and observed.

Children enjoy simple folk dances.

Balance and strength are two important factors involved in stepping. Coordination is also involved. This is highlighted in some of the complex step patterns that are found in some folk dances.

Gesturing

Movements of the "free" parts of the body, i.e., those not involved in supporting the weight, are called *gestures*. In our daily lives, our hands and arms are probably involved in gesturing more than any other body parts. In dance leg gestures and movements of the head and spine all have important roles to play in clarifying, highlighting, and adding to the aesthetic aspect of the movement.

Changing from standing—
kneeling—sitting—lying.

Gesturing with arms and
legs.

Jumping requires strength.

Table 5.5

The basic jumps

The Basic Jumps	French Term	English Term
Take off and land on same foot	Temps levé	Hop
Take off one, land on the other	Jeté	Leap
Take off one, land on two	Assemblé	Jump
Take off two, land on two	Sauté	Jump
Take off two, land on one	Sissone	Jump

Jumping is the name given to an action in which the body leaves the floor, the person enjoying for a moment the sensation of being unsupported. The focus of attention can be on that moment of freedom from the ground or on the moment of returning to earth.

    There are five possible basic forms of jumping. Each form has a French name because all are in the classical French ballet repertoire. Only two have English names. Table 5.5 lists the five basic jumping forms.

    The possible variations and combinations are numerous, challenging the dancers' stamina, strength, and balance.

Jumping

Going and stopping.

Stillness

Stillness may not be seen as an activity, since there is an absence of movement, but the ability to arrest motion is very important. Stillness may be for only a fleeting moment, as in a pause, but the cessation of movement can be as powerful a statement as movement itself. Phrasing and rhythmic patterns are formed as the dancer combines moving and pausing. Stillness might be considered equivalent to silences in music and punctuation marks in writing.

In photographs, it is just as difficult to give a feeling of stillness as it is to give a feeling of movement.

Turning

Turning is an activity involving the rotation of the body around an axis so that the dancer faces a new direction. The rotation may be small, as in a few degrees only, complete (360 degrees) so that the dancer ends up facing the starting point, or multiple rotations, which can result in dizziness. Dizziness can be resolved by a sudden action of the head in the direction opposite to the turn, or by moving up and down. Dizziness can be prevented by the more technical concept of "spotting;" dancers are taught to fix their eyes on one spot on the wall and keep looking at it for as long as possible during the turn, moving their head last and quickly looking at the same spot again. This reduces eye movement that causes vertigo. Spotting is a technique that is not appropriate or necessary for young children or beginners, but may be introduced when the students are fairly skilled.

Table 5.6 is a list of action words, which are variations of the six basic activities.

Swing your partner!

Table 5.6

▼▼▼▼   ▼

Sample activities from the basic activities vocabulary

Locomotion	Creeping	Running
	Dashing	Rushing
	Fleeing	Skipping
	Galloping	Sliding
	Rolling	Walking
Stepping	Kneeling	Sitting
	Lying	Standing
Gesturing	Bending	Scattering
	Gathering	Stretching
	Reaching	Twisting
Jumping	Bounding	Prancing
	Hopping	Pouncing
	Leaping	
Stillness	Freezing	Pausing
	Hovering	Stopping
Turning	Pivoting	Rotating
	Pirouetting	Spinning
	Revolving	Twirling

▼▼▼▼   ▼

Table 5.7

▼▼▼▼   ▼

Development of the basic activities

Body Parts	Body Shapes
Identification and isolation of parts	Wide
Relationships between parts: meeting	Long
parting	
over	Round
under	Twisted
around	Symmetrical
Stressing different parts during activity	Asymmetrical
Parts leading the activity: away from	
toward	
around	
Parts initiating the activity	

▼▼▼▼   ▼

Experiencing Dance

In the study of dance, the basic actions are explored and expanded by focusing on different bodily aspects, such as stressing a particular part or shape when jumping, turning, or stopping. The actions are combined into sequences that can be repeated and clarified (see table 5.7).

Our basic dance vocabulary develops as we become familiar with and skilled in controlling our bodies. Our enjoyment of dancing increases, sometimes simply because of the sensations we receive from the movement done for its own sake.

> A refreshing swim in the sea is a wonderful and health-giving thing, but no human being could live constantly in the water. It is a very similar case with the occasional swim in the flow of movement which we call dance. Such swimming, refreshing in many respects for the body, the mind and for that dreamy part of our being which has been called the soul, is an exceptional pleasure and stimulation. As water is a widespread means to sustain life, so is the flow of movement (Laban 1948).

Through planned learning experiences based on the above concepts, children's kinesthetic awareness is heightened as they are helped to focus on the relaying of "muscular, articular, cutaneous, vestibular and auditory cues to the brain" (Preston-Dunlop 1980). Interpretation of these cues gives children knowledge of position and movement in space, and thus they become aware of their own artistic instrument.

Effort Concepts

Some of you may already be familiar with the term "dynamics" in the dance context. *Effort* may be considered to have a similar meaning. Both words infer the qualitative dimension of movement, the result of combining different *motion factors:* time, weight, space, and flow.

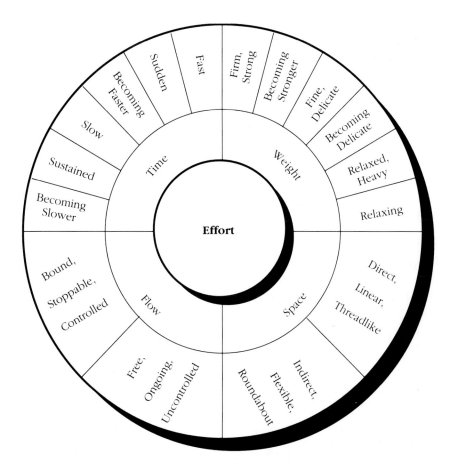

Figure 5.2 Single factor concepts

These factors may be likened to the primary colors, which, when combined in different proportions, produce all the colors known. It is an ability to produce, select, and combine these factors producing varying shades of effort that gives the qualitative dimension to action and results in a rich vocabulary. A jump, for example, can be very strong and explosive, or it can be gentle and appear almost weightless to the observer. Compare the jumps seen in Russian cossack dances with the jumps in a corps de ballet sequence.

Figure 5.2 expands the basic motion factors to show the range of each. In the early learning experiences, tasks are designed to focus attention on contrasting aspects of one factor at a time. An example is a movement phrase, repeated three times, of a fast run and a slow turn.

As the children become more skillful, combinations of the motion factors are explored and dance studies developed so that the children use their growing vocabulary in an artistic way. Table 5.8 shows the combinations possible.

Table 5.8

▼▼▼▼   ▼

Multiple motion factor concepts

Combining Two Motion Factors

Weight	*&*	*time*	Firm + sudden Firm + sustained Fine + sudden Fine + sustained
Weight	*&*	*space*	Firm + direct Firm + flexible Fine + direct Fine + flexible
Weight	*&*	*flow*	Firm + bound Firm + free Fine + bound Fine + free
Time	*&*	*space*	Sudden + direct Sudden + flexible Sustained + direct Sustained + flexible
Time	*&*	*flow*	Sudden + bound Sudden + free Sustained + bound Sustained + free
Space	*&*	*flow*	Direct + bound Direct + free Flexible + bound Flexible + free

Combining Three Motion Factors

Weight & time & space (e.g., firm + sudden + direct)

Weight & time & flow (e.g., fine + sustained + free)

Time & space & flow (e.g., sudden + flexible + bound)

Space & flow & weight (e.g., direct + free + firm)

Note: There are eight possible combinations for each of the above, making a total of 32 combinations!

▼▼▼▼   ▼

Spatial Concepts

Space is a very important element in dance and the idea of general and personal space was introduced in chapter 2 (see figure 2.4). As we dance in and through the space around us, our gestures make three-dimensional shapes in the air and our feet make pathways on the floor. An awareness of the shapes and patterns we are creating helps us design and place our dances in the space, in much the same way artists place images on their canvases.

Many folk dances involve
remembering patterns.

Many folk dances demand a sensitivity to the general space in which
the dance is being performed. Remembering the patterns involved in a
folk dance is a considerable challenge, and it takes time for children to
be able to dance patterns without error. Some children become quite
frustrated when they feel "lost" in the space in which they are dancing.
They are usually easy to identify. If several children give this impression,
it may be that the dance is too complex for them. In this case, either
modify the pattern or find another dance. Figure 5.3 illustrates/defines
general space concepts.

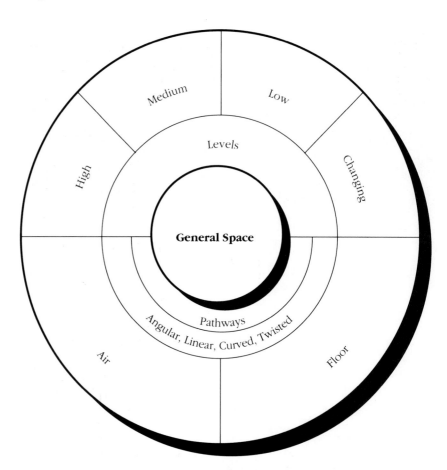

Figure 5.3 Space
concepts—dimensions in
general space

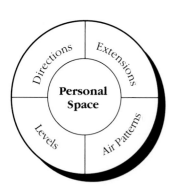

Figure 5.4 Concepts of
personal space

Awareness of space in creative dance is closely connected to expression. The communication resulting from an action placed at a high level changes when the same action is placed at a low level.

Likewise, skipping and traveling forward is very different from skipping and traveling backward. There is a feeling of freedom and openness in the former and a closed, more restricted sensation in the latter. Figure 5.4 and table 5.9 illustrate the concepts of personal space.

The *raison d'etre* for some creative dances is similar to that of abstract sculptures: the enjoyment and appreciation of shapes, sizes, lines, and spaces. Lessons can be developed in which the children transform one art form into the other, the dances being stimulated by a piece of sculpture and vice versa.

Skillful use of space enriches our dances and adds another dimension to our vocabulary.

Traveling high and low.

Table 5.9

▼▼▼▼   ▼

Dimensions of personal space

Directions	Forward—in front
	Backward—behind
	Sideways—left
	Sideways—right
Levels	High—up/above
	Low—down/below
Extensions	Toward—near to the body
	Away—far from the body
	Small—smaller
	Large—larger
Air Patterns	Straight—linear
	Twisted—convoluted
	Angular—zigzag
	Curved—circular

▼▼▼▼   ▼

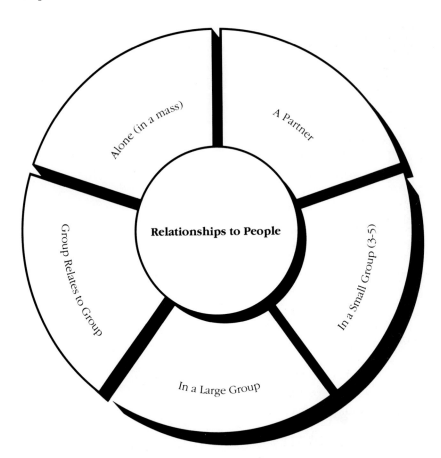

Figure 5.5 Basic
relationship concepts

Relationship Concepts

Laban's fourth movement concept is that of relationships. Relationships
play a key part in the dance program, as much time is spent dancing
together, sharing ideas, watching one another, and discussing what has
been seen. None of this can develop without an awareness and appreciation of the relationships involved. The attitude we have toward the
others with whom we are working is always a cooperative one.

When considering the varied concepts involved, the attention shifts
from actions to people. The following two schema, therefore, have the
individual as the core. Figure 5.5 shows basic relationship concepts, and
table 5.10 develops these ideas.

Much of the enjoyment in dance is obtained from dancing with friends.
Both singing games and folk dance provide opportunities for the children to be with chosen partners, to change partners, and to dance in

Table 5.10

Developing individual and group relationships

People may:
    mingle—separate
    meet—part
    lead—follow
    merge—disperse
    match—contrast
    mirror
    shadow

Spatially, they may move:
    toward—away—around—over—under—between—through

They may be:
    close together—far apart in front—behind—beside—below—above

Temporally, they may move:
    in unison—canon—simultaneously—successively

larger groups. At times, some children wish to create and/or dance alone. Dance allows for this. In such situations the children, like painters, are independent of others for their art experience.

Summary

We have looked at the four major concepts as they relate specifically to dance and we can see that two are concerned with self-understanding and the development of conscious control (skill) over our physical (body concepts) and emotional (effort concepts) selves.

The other two concepts relate to our environment: external factors that influence us and to which we react. First, there is the space, general and personal, in which we move and which we can learn to use effectively. In so doing we develop a different kind of knowledge and skill. Second, we focus on the people around us, learning to adapt to, react to, and work with others in groups of varying sizes, always with the purpose of sharing and always in a cooperative manner.

We also learn to attend and respond to other elements in our environment (music, poetry, props, etc.) to supplement and complement our expressive powers. Reference to these will be made in chapter 7.

Having analyzed some of the multiple strands of human movement, we must attend to the task of interweaving them into the dynamic fabric of **dance.**

Review Questions

1. What are some of the reasons for including dance experiences in physical education programs?
2. Which three dance forms are suggested for inclusion in the program? Discuss the nature of the three dance forms.
3. How should emphasis on the three dance forms change for the different grades?
4. Explain in your own words what Anthoney (1979) means when discussing "the transformation of everyday movement into an artistic experience."
5. Name the six activities that can be considered the basic vocabulary of dance.
6. What are the extremes of the four motion factors?
7. Two of the four major concepts (body, effort, space, relationships) are concerned with developing conscious control of our physical and emotional selves; two are concerned with developing skill in adapting to the environment. Explain.

References

Anthoney, M. 1979. An Introduction and Position Statement. *Values Into Action.* J. Emmel, D. Molyneux, N. Wardrop, eds. Australian Council for H.P.E.R., 171–75.

Boorman, J. 1980. Dance & the Child: Curriculum for the Eighties. *CAHPER Journal* 47:2, 15–17.

Brinson, P. 1979. Dance in Education: An Overview. *Dance in Education Conference Papers.* W. Lett, S. McKechnie, eds. Melbourne, Australia: A.A.D.E. 18, 28.

Dance Committee of CAHPER. 1983. *Dance in Elementary (K–6) Education.* Position Paper. Ottawa: CAHPER.

Dewar, P. 1980. Teaching Creative/ Modern Dance in the Schools. *CAHPER Journal* 46:4, 27–29.

Evans, J. 1980. Movement Education & Folk Dance: A Rationale (Part 1). *CAHPER Journal* 47:2, 42–44.

Hill, R. 1982. Let's Teach Sport and Dance. *CAHPER Journal* 48:6, 13–16.

Laban, R. 1948. *Modern Educational Dance.* London: Macdonald and Evans, Ltd.

Mettler, B. 1980. *The Nature of Dance as a Creative Art Activity.* Tuscon, Arizona: Mettler Studios Inc.

National Dance Association. 1977. *Dance as Education.* Washington, D.C.: AAHPERD.

Preston-Dunlop, V. 1980. *A Handbook for Dance in Education,* 2d ed. London: Macdonald and Evans, Ltd.

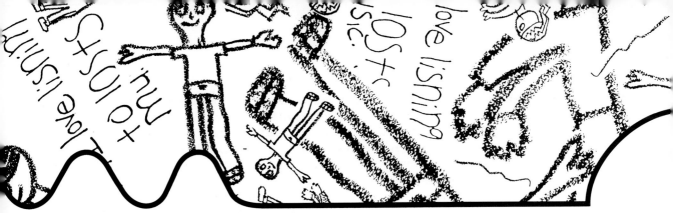

CHAPTER

6

**TEACHING
DANCE**

Dance is an art form arising from the expressive use of movement. Because of this, teaching dance differs considerably from teaching games or gymnastics (discussed in chapters 8 and 11) in that we are involved in artistic and aesthetic endeavors. It is comparatively simple to set dance problems/tasks for children; for example, "combine rising, turning and running into a sequence." The hard part is to guide its development into dance form. Our teaching behavior must be carefully developed and planned so that we help our children make the "transition from generalized movement into movement as an aesthetic experience" (Anthoney 1979).

Anthoney (1979) considers this to be a three-stage process:

1. Movement: awareness of delight in movement
2. Aesthetic experience: transformation of movement and concurrently a new meaning
3. Artistic experience: intention to give form, to create a structured dance, to show/perform the dance

These three stages are useful in two ways. First, we can use them to help us become "better" dance educators, by giving us a point of departure as we begin to teach. Once we know we are providing learning experiences in which the children enjoy moving rhythmically just for the sake of moving, then we are ready to tackle the next hurdle in our development. Likewise, we can assess when we are nearing the third stage in our teaching behavior. At this point, the children will be creating and/or remembering dances that have structure and that they would like to share with others, i.e., perform.

Second, the stages can help us in relation to curriculum development. Younger children will begin at the first stage; as they become more experienced, they will move through the second stage, and then to the third. Beginning units in the dance program will, therefore, concentrate more on global concepts related to body management in general space, with a strong rhythmic stress. Evaluation of the "products" will be tempered by the stage at which the children are working.

Dance lessons can be (indeed, should be) enjoyable for both teachers and children. These lessons are times for sharing, selecting and rejecting ideas, participating in the creativity of others as well as our own, observing dances in the process of development, and when the dances are finished, evaluating what we see with the aim of refining and clarifying the product.

To Do

Which dance form(s) provides opportunities for:

1. exploration?
2. imitation?
3. improvisation?

▼▼▼▼   ▼

We need to be creative teachers and become skillful in providing different kinds of learning experiences for our children. These experiences may be *exploratory, improvisational,* and *imitative* in nature, and through such experiences we hope to "enrich, extend and reinforce the child's total dance experience" (CAHPER position paper 1983).

Dance Experiences

These are learning situations in which teachers must be nonjudgmental yet provide guidance so that the children discover something specific about themselves and dance. It is not an "anything goes" situation (far from it!). The learning environment is quite structured, so that the children are secure and know what they are trying to achieve. Tasks are often structured in the form of problems to be solved and the children may find more than one solution to each problem. They may be asked to select from the various responses, their own and/or others, to sequence, repeat, and refine, the eventual result being a complete dance. Examples of tasks/experiences will be found in the lesson plans in chapter 7.

Exploratory Experiences

Tasks are again set as problems but there is little or no emphasis on reaching a repeatable product. There is more attention to spontaneity of response than "thinking out" and modifying responses, as in exploratory work.

Both exploratory and improvisational learning situations allow for individuality of response, the use of imagination, and acknowledgment of the emotions as a source of ideas.

Improvisational Experiences

Children enjoy copying and much can be learned by doing so. Much of what children learn is copied and many ideas come from "internalized copies," which are eventually adapted to meet a new situation. Initially, attention is on learning predetermined dance steps, patterns, and sequences. Success is often more immediate than with exploration and improvisation, and many children gain confidence as they master and repeat the step, pattern, or sequence.

Imitative Experiences

To Do

Discuss the following and decide what each means to you.

A creative teacher
Teaching creatively
Teaching for creativity

▼▼▼▼▼ ————————————————————————————— ▼

Teaching Skills

Many of the skills we employ when we teach dance are the same ones we use when teaching games and gymnastics. Discussion of these generalized skills is found in chapter 3. The following skills will be discussed in detail, as they apply specifically to the dance situation.

Voice sounds
Vocabulary
Management skills
Observation skills
Evaluation
Questioning
Playing percussion instruments
Listening to music

Voice Sounds

Our voice is a very valuable instrument that can be used most effectively as a motivator and an accompaniment. This idea of the voice as an accompaniment is one that we probably do not consider and employ enough. We need to be able to make many different vocal sounds, both rhythmic and expressive, to accompany whole group activity. There are several advantages. We can produce the sound we feel is appropriate for the task; we do not have to explain it to a pianist or other musician, we do not have to seek it on a record. It is ours; wherever we are in the room, it is with us. We can change it at will as the task is extended; we can produce a portion of it to accompany part of the sequence we wish to repeat and refine.

Practicing humming, lah-lah-ing, *zzzz*ing, *pppp*ing, and other consonant and vowel sounds in repetition at different pitches and volumes is a good exercise. Develop the ability to repeat a phrase of two or three different sounds with changing quality.

Nonsense syllables are useful when a rhythmic pattern is needed; for example, try "dum-di-dum-di-dummmm-di," accenting and drawing out the *m* sound. "Ya-ta-ta, ya-ta-ta, ya-ta-ta-ta" has a different quality. It may

---

To Do

Have a "nonsense conversation" with a friend, varying the volume and pitch of your voice. Try to convey emotion through the sound, rhythm, tone, and volume of your voice. As you become more confident, add movement to enhance the communication, the movement being secondary to the sound. Gradually let the relationship between the sound and the movement change, so that movement is the main mode of communication and sound the secondary.

▼▼▼▼   ▼

take a bit of courage to use your voice in this way, but once you begin you will not stop. The voice is a rich resource, one that needs developing.

A large vocabulary of descriptive words and phrases is a must for dance teachers. We need to be able to arouse visual, kinesthetic, and auditory images in the students as they respond to the tasks. If, for example, the informing task is to raise one arm lightly and with sustainment and lower it strongly and suddenly, what phrases and/or words could we think of as we plan refining tasks that are descriptive? We want to help the students experience the contrasting dynamics and shift from a dreamlike state to a more awake, almost on-guard attitude. Different students will respond to different images, depending on their having (relevant) past experiences to which they can relate this new one.

Vocabulary

The English language is rich in descriptive words, far richer than, for example, the French language, where one often needs several words to convey the approximate meaning of one English word. We are fortunate to have such a resource available, and we should make a conscious effort to extend both our own vocabularies and those of our students. Boorman (1973) indicates that there may be a connection between dance experiences and the development of vocabulary in young children. We should recognize the hidden curriculum components of the dance experience, and if "all teachers are teachers of English" (Russell 1975), we should utilize this knowledge as we design the tasks and select the words we will use. Table 6.1 suggests adjectives, adverbs, and verbs relating to specific motion factors. No attempt has been made to equalize the number of words in each column and you will probably be able to add words. Some of the words are quite complex and suitable for the older, experienced children; use your knowledge of the specific children you will be teaching as you select and plan. Some of the verbs are in more than one row; e.g., "writhe" suggests it is pliable and strong, "drift" suggests it is threadlike and light.

Table 6.1

Descriptive words

Adjectives	Adverbs	Verbs
Roundabout, plastic, indirect, supple, lithe, pliable, flexible	Wavily, pliantly convolutingly	Undulate, meander, fluctuate, squirm, writhe
Direct, linear, threadlike, straight	Unerringly, deliberately, smoothly	Drift, glide, slide, soar, press, pull, heave
Strong, firm, forceful, vigorous, powerful, triumphant	Boldly, resistantly, pressingly, tortuously, aggressively	Writhe, beat, stamp, kick, punch, heave, pierce
Delicate, gentle, fine, light, fragile, frail, subtle	Quietly, softly, daintily, sensitively	Stroke, caress, creep, float, drift
Sudden, abrupt, sharp, staccato, flippant	Hastily, excitedly, precipitatingly, joltingly, urgently, lively, unexpectedly	Quiver, jab, stab, twitch, burst, flee, rush, throb, shimmer
Dilatory, sustained, legato, tardy, casual	Calmly, dreamily, slowly, stealthily	Linger, loiter, meander, creep, drift, stroke
Viscous, resistant, stoppable, hesitate, restricted, uncertain, doubtful	Cautiously, reluctantly, unwillingly, fearfully	Ooze, withhold
Continuous, ongoing, free	Abandonly, uncontrollably, willingly	Stream, flow, gush

Management Skills   Unlike games and gymnastics, little equipment is needed for dance lessons. A good tape recorder and record player, a selection of records, a drum for yourself, and some percussion instruments for the children (a list is given in table 6.2) are the basics. It is a bonus if you are able to play an instrument such as the piano, guitar, or flute, particularly if you can improvise as you accompany the children while they dance.

We recommend taping all music chosen for your dance lessons, for the following reasons:

1. A tape recorder is easy to start and stop in a hurry.
2. It is easy to find and play a specific section of the music.
3. A section of the music may be recorded several times, with a pause between each recording, thus making it possible for you to provide feedback without running to turn off the recorder.

To Do

Find as many synonyms as possible for strong, light, sudden, and sustained, in the following ways:

1. use a dictionary or Roget's *Thesaurus*
2. ask children of different ages

▼▼▼▼   ▼

4. Tapes are small, lightweight, and easy to carry.
5. Tapes are less likely to be damaged than records. If they are damaged, the source of the music is still available.

If the lesson is held in a space other than the gymnasium, you must ensure the floor is clean and the space free from obstructions. Select the position for the tape recorder so that you have a good view of the children. If this means using an extension cord, make sure it is tucked against the wall out of the children's way. Remember, too, that you will need to run to and from the tape recorder as you teach.

If your lesson includes percussion instruments, place them in groups so they are easily accessible, yet out of the way.

Observation Skills

Because dance is expressive and difficult to quantify, our ability to observe, understand, and react to the children's dancelike responses to the tasks that we set is crucial. For some tasks, as in singing games and folk dances, we know there should be uniform responses, and we can be prepared with visual and/or kinesthetic image checklists against which we measure the children's movement patterns. In creative dance, there will be varied responses, and the amount of variation possible and acceptable will depend on the degree of openness of the task.

There are several strategies we can use to help ourselves improve our ability to observe children as they dance and the following ideas may be helpful. It is an organizational progression which may be used in games and gymnastics lessons. Two different tasks are chosen, the first being more closed than the second. The expected responses to the first task are uniform; the responses to the second are expected to differ considerably.

Closed Task—Uniform Response

"Begin facing your partner; stamp right foot three times, left foot three times, turn to your right taking four steps, finish facing your partner, and clap your hands three times." (Four bars 4/4 may be played on a drum, or a piece of marching music can be played.)

What Is Wrong With This Situation?

A first grade class of thirty children are participating in their first dance experience of the year. Until now their physical education lessons have been in the gymnasium, but today it is not available. The lesson is being held on the stage, an activity area new to the children. The stage curtains are closed. A tape recorder is situated at the back of the stage with an extension cord running along the back wall. The movement concepts of locomotion and time are the focus of the lesson. Rock music has been chosen as the stimulus. The teacher puts the record on and tells the children to run to the beat of the music. The children respond by running without control, not to the beat of the music, pushing against the curtains, bumping into each other and giggling as they do so.

In the above situation:

1. The space is too small for thirty children to be able to run safely. Activities such as leaping and running need ample space. When children have been used to working in a large area it is difficult for them to adjust to a more restricted area.

2. Some rules should have been established concerning the potentially dangerous extension cord and the curtains. Young children need time and guidance to adjust to a new space.

3. Moving at a fast speed was not appropriate for this first lesson. The children need help with finding out the size of the new area and adjusting their speed when traveling to that of others. The first task could have been to walk and stop, accompanied by a drum beat played by the teacher. In this way the teacher could control the speed and spacing.

4. Rock music may have been too exciting in this new environment.

5. The task should be given BEFORE the music is turned on. We suggest that you let the children listen to the music, then give the task (or vice versa), say, "Begin as you hear the music," then turn it on.

6. When children do not hear the task they often copy one another. In this situation wild behavior encouraged more wild behavior!

▼▼▼▼   ▼

1. Have the entire class working; focus on one child only. When you have decided whether or not the response is correct, make an appropriate comment to the child, move to a new place and scan the entire group before focusing on a second child. Remember to check off mentally what you have seen; it is no use looking without analyzing.

2. Divide the class into four groups. Have three groups sit down and watch the other group. Tell the children to repeat the pattern twice. Notice and praise the children who are successful; encourage and give refinement to the others. Repeat with the other three groups.

   On the positive side, this system means we are really able to observe each child and give appropriate refinement, thus improving performance. It is also a good system for improving the children's observational skills, and, if used after some very energetic activity, it provides them with a rest while they are still involved. On the negative side, it is a time-consuming method that reduces participation. As we become more skilled at observing, this technique may be replaced by the following one.

3. Move around the room as the children repeat the sequence. Focus your attention on a specific small group of children (maybe three pairs) and give appropriate feedback to those who are performing well and those who are having problems. Move to another area, scanning the entire class as you go, providing feedback to everyone if possible. Then focus on another small group. If you observe a common problem, stop the class, give the necessary refining task, and let them continue to practice as you move to another small group.

4. When you know your class well, you will probably be able to anticipate who may encounter difficulties with a particular task. Immediately focus your attention on these children and help them before observing the remainder.

5. If the children are experienced, used to observing each other, and can work well on their own, you might have three work together in reciprocal teaching situations (Mosston 1981), two dancing and one observing. In this case, the observers should have a checklist (such as the one in figure 6.1) to which they can refer. This is one concrete way the children can take responsibility for their own learning and improve their ability to observe as well as dance. It is successful when the children have some experience in working in small groups without constant supervision. For obvious reasons, this is more appropriate for older children. You have two options: you can visit each group, discuss with the observers what they have seen, and offer refinement and encouragement as necessary to the individuals; or you can stand "outside" the class, alternately scanning and focusing until everyone has had a turn at observing and being observed.

6. Eventually you will be able to scan a whole class accurately and pinpoint who is doing well and who needs extra help. This stage is reached after consciously practicing observing children

SAFETY TIP ///////////

Never allow children to dance in socks alone. On a bare floor there is insufficient friction between the sole of the foot and the floor.

Figure 6.1 Checklist for reciprocal teaching

Observer: _____ Melanie _____

Teacher: _____ Mrs. Roth _____

Children may observe each other to evaluate progress in specific skills. The observer checks the appropriate box if the student demonstrates the skill.

Name:	John	Susan	Chris
Face partner			
Three steps right			
Three steps left			
Turn right			
Four steps			
Face partner			
Clap three times			

moving in different settings. In all settings, the mental checklist is a must. For all previously mentioned organizational procedures, the following progression might be helpful.

a. In the earliest stage, do not try to see the whole pattern; instead, focus specifically on a portion of the pattern, for example, three stamps right foot, three stamps left foot—is everyone doing that? During the next repetition, watch the turning action—does it begin and end facing the partner? Repetition three: are four steps taken, beginning with the right foot? On the fourth repetition, look at the children's hands.

b. In this kind of sequence we should also use our sense of hearing, as stamping and clapping are important actions. We need to listen to the rhythm of the stamps and claps and their relationship to any accompaniment we have provided. Observing means more than just seeing.

c. "Feel" the movement sequence kinesthetically as you observe. This may help you sense when someone is out of tune. Go one stage further and dance the pattern with a small group, giving feedback as you participate.

Open Task—Varied Responses

Suggestions have been made to help you observe a predetermined pattern, one with no variation in response. What can the teacher do when an open task is set and there may be as many answers as children in the class? Even in this case, there will be some commonalities for which we can look, as shown in the following task.

"Choose either a low- or high-level starting position. Change to the opposite level, showing clearly whether you are more involved with leaving the starting level or arriving at the new level."

Clear focus when rising or sinking.

A rather complicated task has been selected, and provided you know kinesthetically what the task is and what experience you wish the children to have, what new movement concepts are being introduced or what known concepts are being applied, learning to observe open tasks is no more difficult than learning to observe closed ones.

Options for organizing the children are the same as before (see the preceding list) and the visual and kinesthetic checklist is just as necessary.

After the children have had a short time to experiment with the idea, you might ask all those who have selected a low starting point to continue to work and the others to sit down. You will then have at least one common factor. The next aspect is the focus of the children: do they clearly show by focus and use of selected body parts whether they are more involved in leaving or arriving? After watching this group and providing refining tasks, encouragement, and praise, change the two groups.

Evaluation

In dance we tend to evaluate in terms of the aesthetics of the movement pattern. Since dance is an art form, as well as a physical activity in which equipment is rarely used, we observe how the body moves and is held in stillness. Questions are asked: was the body shape effective? Was there an appropriate use of tension? Did the children have a clear focus as they traveled? Because dance is a mixture of the physical and the affective instruments designed to evaluate children's skills need to take into account quantitative (how high? how fast? which body parts?) and the qualitative (how softly? how fluidly?) components. In folk dances and singing games, the stress may be more on the quantitative elements; in creative dance the qualitative components may be more important. In your dance program formative techniques are more appropriate than summative ones, and the instruments designed should be criterion-referenced.

Lessons

There is considerable potential for variety of content and experience in dance lessons. Preston (1963) suggests the following six points as a guide to whether we exploit and use this variety as we try to cater for individual needs, likes, and dislikes within our classes.

1. **Methods of presentation:**
   a. imitation
   b. exploration
   c. improvisation
   d. creation (this is equivalent to applying tasks, as discussed in chapter 3. The result is a product that can be shared with others.)
   e. recall an already-known dance.
2. **Movement content:** This refers to which movement concepts have been chosen as the learning focus of the lesson. Over a period of time, we must achieve a balance between body, effort, space, and relationship concepts. As an example, a unit of dance may focus on effort experiences with minimal attention paid to space. This unit should be balanced with another attending to spatial concepts and integrating the children's effort knowledge.
3. **Social aspect:** We can design tasks requiring children to work alone or with others in small or large groups. It is important that we maintain a balance between these possibilities. Over a period of time, we may find that the children have had less time to develop their own ideas than to share ideas. In the latter situation, ideas may be manipulated, changed, and integrated with other ideas. Children may recognize very little of their own contribution to the dance—it is there, but in a different form.

I love the music and I love lisning
to losts of
music.

Heather. Loise.
Fagan.

Age 6

Figure 6.2 Child's response to music

4. **Placement in working space:** This is an organizational aspect of the lesson. We tell children, "Work in your own space," "Use the space freely," "Stay on the spot." Monitoring the amount of a lesson spent in one place and comparing it with the amount for traveling through the space is useful. Young children in particular need to be "off the spot" several times during a lesson. Concentration is assisted by a change of focus and pace and this can partially be achieved by a change in working space.

5. **Accompaniment:** Many people think dance is always accompanied by music. This is far from the case. A balance between accompanied and unaccompanied dance is hoped for.

   Dancing in silence is challenging and should be part of the overall dance experience.

   The range of accompaniment possible is wide and can vary from voice sounds, words, and body sounds to full orchestral sounds, the latest pop music, or the classics. We should take advantage of the wealth of music available and introduce the children to sounds they may not hear on their favorite radio station but may grow to like.

   One of the great "sound experimenters" of the 20th century is the composer Murray Schafer. He has investigated likes and dislikes in sound and the relationship between sound and visual images. He composes music using a tremendous variety of everyday objects as the instruments. He calls some of his compositions "soundscapes" (Menuhin and Davis 1979). Children, too, love experimenting with sounds and creating the accompaniment for their own dances. (See the section on percussion instruments later in this chapter.)

6. **Link with previous lessons:** After the first lesson in a unit, there will be tasks that relate to already familiar concepts, as well as new ones. We should avoid introducing too many new concepts in a lesson and monitor how many lessons are spent on each one. Obviously, the first lesson in a unit will be composed entirely of new concepts, some of which we may include to "get the class going," and others to develop over two or more lessons. A balance between the familiar and the unfamiliar is likely to maintain the interest and motivational levels of the children.

A quick method of monitoring these six aspects of teaching dance, and recording in very general terms the children's responses, is to prepare a page of grids; one grid per lesson in the unit plan. A sample grid is shown in figure 6.3. After reviewing the grids, you will have an overall picture of the concepts taught, the kind of experience, the accompaniment used, and the children's responses to the various tasks. It is a useful means of checking the variety and range of learning experiences provided in a unit (Preston 1963).

Children's Skills

Children who are good at singing games and folk dances are able to imitate steps, remember combinations of steps and the patterns of the singing game or folk dance, and make the transitions between one sequence and the next. They can anticipate what is coming. These are the quantitative elements. "Good" dancers also relate well to their partner or group and produce the particular effort combinations that give the singing game or folk dance its expression/quality. These are the qualitative elements.

Simple checklists such as figure 6.1 can be employed to evaluate the children's dance skills quantitatively. It is doubtful, though, that you will create checklists for each singing game and folk dance you teach. A general checklist including the step and spatial patterns learned in the particular unit is more likely to be useful. Such a checklist is shown in figure 6.4.

Lesson 1

Task	Experience	Concept(s)	Social	Sound	Placing	Link
1	Imitate	Traveling	Alone	Drum	Free	New
2	Explore	Shapes	Partner	Silence	On the spot	New
3	Improvise	Travel, stillness	Alone	Record	Free	New

Comments: Quickly involved task 1; giggled task 2, clearer focus needed, (accompaniment?). Task 3 became imitative—large group unison!

Lesson 2

Task	Experience	Concept(s)	Social	Sound	Placing	Link
1	Recall	Travel, Stillness	Alone	Record	Free	New
2	Respond	Shapes, time	Partner	Drum	On the Spot	Develop
3	Explore	Pathways	Alone	Record	Free	New
4	Create	Combine tasks 2 and 3	Partner	Silence	Free	Develop

Comments: Danced with them task 1, gradually withdrew, individual responses coming. Drum helped task 2, complementary shapes emerging. Class skipped for task 3, poor quality, must work on this. Cue cards for next time. Task 4 surprisingly good.

Figure 6.3 Lesson grids

Evaluating creative dance presents us with a quite different—and difficult—problem. Hawkins (1964) provides some guidelines that we have found useful and which have been modified over a period of time to meet the needs of specific situations.

Unit 1—Singing Game

Name: _____ **Grade:** _____
Date: _____

Criterion for steps: Dances a complete phrase with correct timing.
Criterion for patterns: Changes direction with the phrases.

Steps:	Most of the time	More than half the time	Less than half the time
Skipping			
Running			
Walking			
Galloping			
Patterns: Circles left and right			
Straight lines			
Turning with a partner			
Other: Transitions			

Figure 6.4 Dance unit checklist

General comments:

A simple rating scale (see figure 6.5) for the younger or less experienced dancers is probably the most useful. It gives an assessment of the children's developing dance vocabulary. This kind of recording sheet may be filled in during the dance unit, particularly when a child is responding above your expectations. Decisions regarding children responding below your expectations should be left until toward the end of the unit so that they have the maximum chance of improving their performance. A word of caution: we must be objective, accurate observers when using these scales, and, when using them more than once, we must not allow our objectivity to be influenced by an earlier opinion.

When evaluating the creative work of the older, more experienced children (possibly grade 4, definitely grades 5 and 6) a different format is suggested.

Name: _____ **Grade:** _____
Date: _____

	Below Average	Average	Above Average
Use of Body Parts:			
In Isolation			
Integration			
Use of Body Shape:			
Clarity			
Variation			
Use of Space:			
Levels			
Directions			
Pathways			
Use of Effort Changes:			
Time			
Weight			
Rhythm			
Use of Relationships:			
Partner			
Small Group			
Large Group			
Other:			
Concentration			
Variability of Response			

Above Average: Above that expected for age and experience
Average: What is expected for age and experience
Below Average: Below that expected for age and experience

Figure 6.5 Sample rating scale for dance

The end of a unit might be the sharing of small group dances developed during several lessons. The children may have been working on their own interpretations of a piece of music you selected, because it seems to combine the movement concepts that have been the learning focus of the unit, or you may have challenged them to select their own action words and create a partner dance based on these words. The checklist in figure 6.6 is designed for this situation.

The children should be given the checklist when they are at the refining stage of their creative work. They should be asked to complete part *A*. Seeing the criteria in written form helps some children to clarify their dances. Also, as you discuss the checklist, you will find children who (a) have a good grasp of the concepts they are including in their dance, but have difficulties performing; (b) move well but have little understanding of the concepts; and (c) both understand the concepts and move well. Enough time must be allowed for this "paperwork" so the children feel challenged rather than threatened! You fill in part *B* after each pair dances. A comparison can be made between what the children wanted to include and what you saw.

Videotape and Evaluation

If possible, videotape the children dancing so they can see their own creations and you can discuss the completed checklist with them. Watching videotapes can help them in their creative endeavors only when they get past the "look, there I am!" stage of watching the playback.

Videotapes allow children to try an idea, watch it replayed, and make decisions about the effectiveness of the developing motifs and the actual performance. They can see whether lines are straight, feet are pointed, groups are focused in the same direction, changes in levels are effective.

It is important to be able to stand back and view what one is doing. Painters are able to do this as their creations are separate from themselves. The videotape now makes it possible for dancers to stand back and evaluate themselves.

Questioning

In exploratory and improvisational work we do not always know what the children intended to happen, and therefore we must find a way of helping them perform what they wanted. Skillful questioning is needed. This point will be illustrated with the following open task: "In threes, begin close together, then move away from each other with strong gallops. Return with slow turns." There are specific challenges of beginning together, galloping away, turning, and meeting again. There are, though, many aspects of the sequence to be decided by the children and each threesome will develop different sequences. General questions such as, "When you begin, do you all begin together or does one dancer begin

Date: Nov. 6
Topic: Action words – rush, vibrate
Name of student: Chris

	Not Used	Used Some	Used Extensively
Changes in body shape			
Body parts stressed			
Changes in level			
Specific pathways			
Changes in direction			
Contrasts in time			
Contrasts in weight			
Changing relationships			

Observer: K. Ottawi	Not Seen	Seen	Seen Extensively
Changes in body shape			
Body parts stressed			
Changes in level			
Specific pathways			
Changes in direction			
Contrasts in time			
Contrasts in weight			
Changing relationships			

Comments:

Figure 6.6 Simple checklist for dance sequences

and then the others?'' should help the children clarify their phrase. Some may already have realized there was the possibility of leaving successively or in canon; others may not. Of course, that question must be followed with specific refining tasks for the different groups, and a shift of your focus from the entire class to one trio occurs.

Another question, also dealing with the emerging relationships, might be "Where do you look when you move away?" Keeping in mind Anthoney's concern with transforming every day movement into an art form (Anthoney 1979), attention to this aspect of the sequence will add meaning to the movements. As the relationships develop in each trio, aggression and fear, equality and unity, and domination and submission may be communicated to the observers. The dancers should be aware of the developing expressive aspect of their sequence and the power of their form of communication. This, after all, is what creative dance is about.

When the dance activity is more imitative than exploratory or improvisational, feedback will probably be more in the form of statements than questions. For example, if the imitating/informing task was "gallop four steps to the right, stamp left-right-left-right, gallop four steps to the left, stamp right-left-right-left" you may tell the students, "Your line of travel is too much to the side and not on the diagonal enough." Refinement and maybe a demonstration can then be given, and the children repeat the phrase with, it is hoped, immediate improvement.

Playing Percussion Instruments

There are times when the "right" music is just not available—it hasn't been composed or we just haven't heard it—but we know the kind of accompaniment we would select if we could. This is a time when percussion, perhaps together with voice and/or body sounds, may be the answer. One of the great advantages of selecting percussion for a dance is that the music can be composed along with the dance. We do not have to be musicians to play percussion well. What is meant by "well" in this context? It means that we know and can play a range of sounds that can be produced by each instrument, we can accurately repeat a sound phrase several times, and we can increase and decrease the volume of sound, change the speed at which we can produce it, and combine the two, i.e., play loudly and slowly, quietly and fast. We must also develop the skill of combining playing, dancing, and talking.

Even though percussion instruments have their own particular sound quality, most fit conveniently into one of the three categories in table 6.2.

Table 6.2

▼▼▼▼   ▼

Percussion groups

Rhythmic	Vibratory	Resonant
Drums	Maracas	Cymbals
Tambours	Bells	Chime bars
Claves	Tambourines	Xylophones
Woodblocks		Gongs

▼▼▼▼   ▼

To Do

Practice producing rhythmic phrases to accompany:

1. running
2. skipping
3. walking

For each, know how many steps there are to the phrase so there is "shape" to your playing; e.g., starting in stillness, six running steps, and pause.

How will you change the accompaniment if the children are asked to add a change of level as they run?

▼▼▼▼   ▼

The rhythmic group is useful for accompanying metrically rhythmic phrases of movements, e.g., skipping, galloping, running, and leaping. Loud and soft accents can be highlighted with practice, and it is quite easy to increase and decrease the speed at which the phrase is played.

Vibratory sounds elicit small shaking actions; indeed, one uses a shaking action to produce the vibratory sound. Short phrases of vibration are exciting, lively, and surprising in quality, providing a vivid contrast to the rhythmic and resonant sounds.

The resonant instruments have sounds that begin, continue, and gradually fade, so that an impulsive flowing quality is suggested. The movement fades away.

We can also produce our own accompaniment or stimulus by using body sounds, especially finger snapping and clapping. The advantage of using body sounds is that we can make the sound spontaneously at whatever point in the lesson we feel it is necessary; we do not waste time getting a percussion instrument.

To Do

1. Select one instrument from each of the three percussion groups.
2. How many different sounds can you produce?
3. Try unusual ways of playing the instrument; e.g., if you have a drum, hit it with an open hand, knuckles, cupped hand, wooden stick, spoon.
4. Create a short composition using (a) at least three different sounds from one instrument, (b) a change in speed, (c) a change in volume.
5. Tape-record the composition at least twice. Play it back and listen for variations in sound. Which recording was more pleasing? Can you repeat it accurately?

Sound as Stimulus and Accompaniment

What is the difference between sound as a *stimulus* and as an *accompaniment?* In the former situation, the movement response is elicited by the sound—the musical composition suggests certain actions, spatial ideas, and relationships, and establishes moods that suggest particular qualities of movement. The dance composition develops *because* of the music. In the latter situation, the music is composed to "fit" the movement. Skillful percussion playing and voice sounds, by the children or the teacher, can be great fun and advantageous. Tailor-made music can be modified according to the needs of the dance composition. The music is secondary to the dance, playing a supportive role instead of an initiating one.

Music is an important aspect of the dance program. Listening to and selecting from various recordings should become an integral part of your lesson planning. Over a period of time you should build up a mini-library of pieces for each aspect of your dance program.

Music for Folk Dance

Whenever possible, choose recordings of folk dance musicians of the particular country from which the dance originates. The quality of the music, particularly the rhythm and harmony, is usually quite different from that of educational recordings made especially for children's dances. Some countries have their own particular instruments as well as different combinations of instruments. For example, the Scottish bagpipes are tonally different from Irish bagpipes; French Canadian folk dance bands often include a set of spoons playing exciting rhythms; a Ukranian folk dance ensemble sounds quite different from one from Greece.

 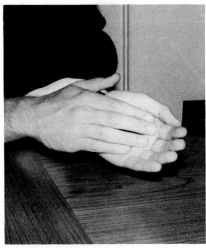

Clapping hands.

To Do

1. Practice clapping, making different sounds by:
    a. relaxing hands "soft hands"
    b. tensing hands "hard hands"
    c. changing relationship of hands
    d. rubbing hands, making a continuous sound. Add accents by changing speed of rubbing every so often.
    e. "bouncing" heels of hands together
2. Practice snapping fingers loudly, softly, alternating left and right, "running" across several fingers.

▼▼▼▼ ▼

If your community is multicultural, you may be able to invite a folk dance band to your school for a special occasion, to accompany dances the children have learned. This could be part of a major social studies project.

Music for Creative Dance

There is a wide variety of music we can use in creative dance lessons. This includes the latest pop, western, jazz, classical, electronic, and film score music (Murray 1984). Many children know what is broadcast by the local radio station, some children will be influenced by older siblings' likes and dislikes, and children without siblings may hear their parents' choice. One of our objectives should be to broaden the children's musical perspective (and, incidentally, broaden our own).

Begin listening for dance music whenever you hear some, which may be in a car or at a party. Begin collecting your own library, remembering that pieces you select must appeal to you as well as the children. You must feel "comfortable" with the music and it must elicit a dance response from you.

When listening to a piece, ask yourself if the music suggests actions: does it sound like spinning or rising or jumping? A series of action words may develop that might suggest a story or a poem, one already written or one you or the children write in a language arts lesson. The resulting poem or story could then become the stimulus for the dance.

Having selected a piece of music, either as the stimulus or the accompaniment for a dance composition, familiarize yourself with it completely, so that you "know where you are" in the music. This means listening to it several times so that you recognize the musical signposts. This will enable you to help the children learn the music and begin associating the sounds with specific motifs or dance ideas. You hope that the children will eventually anticipate what happens next, rather than paying attention to what is happening at the moment. When this stage of awareness is reached, the transitions in the dance will be accomplished more easily.

A visual representation of the music is one method of helping everyone become familiar with the composition. An example is seen in figure 6.7. It can also be a useful reference during the lesson. There are several ways of transferring the sound to paper and each of us may devise our own symbols, adding color to indicate changing dynamics or repetition if we find it aids understanding. The representation can be transferred onto an overhead transparency or a large chart that children can refer to as they compose their dance.

A musical composition is usually divisible into sections, some of which may sound similar, others distinctly different. We need to be able to recognize where one section ends and the next begins, and also whether the musical content of the section is the same as or different from the others. Offenbach's famous "Can-Can" from *Orpheus in the Underworld* is used here as an example. It has a short introduction followed by five sections and a conclusion, which is longer than the introduction. Sections 1, 2, and 4 are musically different. Sections 4 and 5 are repeats of 1 and 3. The conclusion, while maintaining the character of what has gone before, is a new idea.

Musical Form A B C A A

Figure 6.7 Visual analysis
of *Trepak*

To Do

Listen to Offenbach's "Can-Can" from *Orpheus in the Underworld*.

1. Find words to describe sections 1, 2, and 3 of the music (e.g., bouncy, energetic, carefree).
2. Do you recognize some of the instruments being played? If not, ask someone to point out the brass, the strings, and the woodwind instruments. Each group is heard separately at some point in the composition.
3. Does the music increase or decrease in energy?
4. Does the music suggest any change in size or flow of movement?

▼▼▼▼▼   ▼

Each section can be analyzed so that the phrase lengths, dynamics, and rhythmic patterns are recognized. The degree of analysis needed will depend on both the nature of the dance composition being created and the nature of your analytical skill. If you feel your musical knowledge is limited, begin by listening to short pieces; for example, R.C.A. Victor's *Listening Series* productions are very useful, as they have notes to help teachers.

If you have an understanding of basic musical concepts, this will certainly help you. "A teacher with awareness of the elements of both music and movement should be able to enrich and clarify the movement through the music" (Docherty and Churchley 1982). Of equal importance are the abilities to listen, to remember what you have heard, and to be persistent in case you are not immediately successful.

Aerobic Dance

Dancers train very hard to maintain the high level of fitness required in their profession. Hours are spent developing strong and supple bodies and increasing levels of cardiovascular fitness. It is acknowledged that professional dancers are fit people.

In the 1980s, there has been a big fitness boom, and aerobic dance activities have added a new dimension to the whole business of commercial fitness, a dimension which is appealing to people of all ages and both sexes. However, we must recognize that dancelike activities are being used to improve levels of fitness—the intention is not to teach dance. Because of the general appeal of this dancelike approach to fitness, it may be a useful introduction to the art form of dance, especially when beginning a dance program with older students (grades 5, 6, 7).

At these ages children may be reluctant to become involved in an expressive movement form. Boys may feel less threatened when asked to repeat a dancelike movement if the focus is on the physical aspects of the sequence. There will be attendant emotional responses to the movement but attention will not be drawn to them, nor to any aesthetic components of the sequence, until the children are comfortable with themselves and the teacher. Once this stage has been reached, you can gradually make the transition to the involvement of the aesthetic dimension and the intent of the performer in dance, which "leads to a different kind of end product" (Hodge and Farmer 1983). It is important that we understand our intention when setting the tasks in the lesson and that we are aware of when our focus shifts from the so obvious physical aspect of a movement sequence to the emotional, aesthetic aspects. It is at this time that we are concerned with an artistic experience, which is the core of the dance program.

The Influence of Television

It may be helpful to note the influence of television upon children's expectations and attitudes towards physical education in general, and dance in particular. Children regularly have the opportunity to observe professional and other elite athletes, and as a result desire to model the behavior of their idols. You will be faced with young children who wish to learn complex skills and rules of specific sports before they are physically, socially, and emotionally ready for them. To compound the problem, dance programming receives much less attention. Many advertisements include dancelike movements, some very poorly performed, but it is rare to find an entire program on dance. Unless they are taken to the theater children have very little opportunity to see "good" dance and dancers, or to discover the variety of dance forms.

Summary

Teaching dance, while demanding many of the same skills we use for all teaching, does have some special requirements. Our approach to the lessons, the model we set, and our interaction with the children must all have a dancelike quality. By this we mean that artistic elements must be stressed, as one of the objectives is to give the children an aesthetic experience. We hope that they acquire movement skills which allow them to be expressive.

The following guidelines may be of some help.

1. Appeal to the interests of the children; use music, poetry, stories, and ideas that they enjoy.
2. While considering the above, select music that you like.

3. Begin with action words that are concrete and straightforward (examples are given in table 6.1).
4. Avoid asking children to "be" a flower, or to "act out" an idea. Silliness and giggling often ensue as the children feel self-conscious. In dance lessons, the children are themselves. Draw their attention to the movement characteristics of the stimulus you or they have selected.
5. Perhaps most important of all is to make sure you feel comfortable and ready to do whatever it is you have planned. Your feeling at ease gives the children a sense of security, in that no one is trying to make them look foolish.

Your choice of words and speech, how you stand and move, and the tools you use for observation and evaluation must all be qualitatively inclined.

The content of dance lessons is rich and varied and provides the children with opportunity to "be themselves" while performing, creating, and observing. We aim to give them a dance experience—not to turn them into dancers (Laban 1948).

Review Questions

1. Discuss the differences between exploratory, improvisational, and imitative learning experiences for children.
2. It has been suggested that our voices are particularly important when we teach dance. Explain why this may be so.
3. In chapter 3 it was suggested that, as you teach, you should move appropriately for the movement form of the lesson. How will this affect your movement in dance lessons? Will it be different for singing games, folk dances, and creative dance?
4. Management skills may appear to be used minimally when teaching dance lessons. What safety precautions should we consider?
5. What are some factors influencing the observation of dance?
6. Design a criterion-referenced evaluation form for a dance that you have either taught or performed yourself.
7. Why is percussion so useful in creative dance lessons?
8. What is the purpose of aerobic dance activities?

Anthoney, M. 1979. An Introduction & Position Statement. *Values Into Action.* J. Emmel, D. Molyneux, N. Wardrop, eds. Australian Council for H.P.E.R., 171–5.

Boorman, J. 1973. *Dance and Language Experiences With Children.* Toronto: Longman of Canada, Ltd.

Dance Committee of CAHPER. 1983. *Dance in Elementary (K–6) Education.* Ottawa: CAHPER position paper.

Docherty, D. and F. Churchley. 1982. Making the Most of Music in Teaching Movement. *CAHPER Journal* 48:4.15–19.

Hawkins, A. 1964. *Creating Through Dance.* Englewood Cliffs, N.J.: Prentice-Hall.

Hodge, L. and J. Farmer. 1983. Dance Fitness. *CAHPER Journal* 50:1.28.

Laban, R. 1948. *Modern Educational Dance.* London: Macdonald and Evans, Ltd.

Menuhin, Y. and C. Davis. 1979. *The Music of Man.* Toronto: Methuen Publications.

Mosston, M. 1981. *Teaching Physical Education,* 2d ed. Columbus, Ohio: Charles E. Merrill.

Murray, N. 1984. Selecting Music for Educational Dance. *CAHPER Journal* 50:3.34.

Preston, V. 1963. *A Handbook for Modern Educational Dance.* London: Macdonald and Evans, Ltd.

Russell, J. 1975. *Creative Dance in the Primary School,* 2d ed. London: Macdonald and Evans, Ltd.

References

CHAPTER

7

LEARNING
EXPERIENCES IN
DANCE

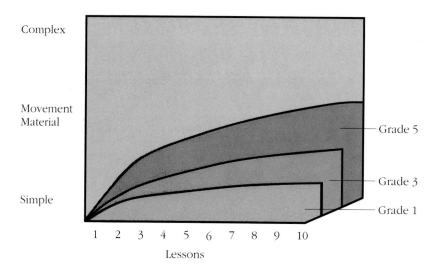

Figure 7.1 Hypothesized differences in progress made by children in grades 1, 3, and 5 with no previous dance experience

In chapter 5 we suggested that some forms of dance appeal to children at certain ages more than at others (see table 5.3). Concurrent with this notion is our concept of *lesson planning,* and being concerned with the children's levels of development and experience. At a school where no dance has been taught previously, we would probably plan the first lesson for grades 1, 3, and 5 around similar movement concepts. However, the objectives and design of the learning experiences for the different grades would not be identical because of the varying needs, interests, abilities, and experiences of the children. Traveling and stopping with changes in speed might be the content for an initial lesson with grade 1, changes of level or direction might be added for grade 3, and the idea of working with a partner added for grade 5. More is expected from the older children, who should progress more rapidly since their learning rate is faster, they are able to grasp more complex ideas, motor development is more advanced, and they are more skillful. Our expectations regarding the outcome or products(s) will be very different for each group. Although each group begins at more or less the same place on a hypothetical dance experience continuum, by the end of a unit of ten lessons, for example, considerable divergence will have occurred (see figure 7.1).

Lesson Design

Laban arranged his movement concepts in a thematic sequence, which progresses from simple to more complex (Preston-Dunlop 1980). In total there are sixteen themes (Laban 1948, Preston-Dunlop 1980) during which the "body, dynamics (effort), space and relationship(s) are gradually studied and trained together. It is impossible to work thoroughly on one aspect irrespective of the other three" (Preston-Dunlop 1980). Table 7.1 shows the first eight of the sixteen themes that form the basis of the dance program for elementary school children (Russell 1975, Logsdon et al. 1984).

Table 7.1

Laban's eight elementary themes

Theme 1: Body Concepts	Awareness of whole body actions. Emphasis on body parts, especially knees, elbows, hands, feet. Going and stopping.
Theme 2: Effort Concepts	Elements of **time** and **weight.** Extremes of each; i.e., fast-slow; strong-light. Getting faster-slower, stronger-lighter. Rhythmic patterns.
Theme 3: Spatial Concepts	Use of general space. Spatial words; e.g., toward, away, big, small, high, low.
Theme 4: Integrating Ideas From Above Three Themes.	Emphasis on **flow,** linking movements to make sequences; transitions.
Theme 5: Relationship Concepts	Beginning to work with a partner, the development of roles (e.g., leader, follower).
Theme 6: Body Concepts	Isolation and integration of body parts during specific actions; skillful movement is stressed as the body is used as an expressive instrument.
Theme 7: Effort Concepts	Expansion of themes 2 and 4 into eight basic effort actions, combining three motion factors: weight, time, space.
Theme 8: Integrating Ideas From Themes 5, 6, and 7.	Dances created that focus on work rhythms and actions.

Table 7.2

Progression through the themes

Theme	Grade K	1	2	3	4	5	6	
1	*	*	*					
2	*	*						
3	*	*	*	*				
4			*	*	*			Integrating themes 1, 2, 3
5		*	*	*	*	*	*	
6			*	*	*	*		
7				*	*	*		
8						*	*	Integrating themes 5, 6, 7

Table 7.2 shows the shift in learning focus over a seven-year period. It should help you select movement material, which provides the ideas and stimuli for your dance program. Notice the overlapping and extending of the movement concepts as the children gain experience and become more skillful, knowledgeable, and independent movers.

REMEMBER THAT

Dance involves expression. When you create a dance, it is a sharing experience for all (Koma 1987).

In the sample lesson plans that follow, the movement concepts are diagrammed at the beginning of each plan. These concepts are common to each kind of dance experience. The difference is seen in the development and application of the movement skills, which, when put together in the culmination of the lesson, will result in a singing game, a folk dance, or a creative dance. Always remember, along with the development of motor competency, your concern for the "whole child" when planning each learning experience. In dance, the unique contribution to education is the aesthetic experience. The lessons should reflect this.

You will find sample lesson plans in singing games, folk dance, and creative dance. The lessons are not designed for a specific group of children but are based on our own teaching experience and accumulated knowledge. If you wish to use the sample plans you will probably have to make some adjustments so that they are appropriate for your children. There is no guarantee they will work for you exactly as they are!

For the sake of simplification we have decided that the first year of the dance program is for kindergarten children aged 5–6 years, and that the dance program extends over the seven years in elementary school.

Singing Games

Singing games, a minor part of the dance program, are excellent activities to do in a classroom where space is limited. These games include activities familiar to many children, as some have been learned before starting school, and are therefore great confidence boosters. They can be learned easily, and the focus can be more on participation rather than execution. Singing games belong equally in music, language, and dance lessons, with the learning focus shifting from one dimension to another. In dance lessons they are analyzed for the movement content, and the learning focus is on the improvement of motor skills and the development of expression through movement.

We have suggested singing games are appropriate activities for kindergarten and grade 1 children in table 5.3. Some with more structure may appeal to older children and they can be an excellent lead-in to simple folk dances. It is sometimes difficult to tell when a singing game becomes a folk dance, as is seen with *Annie Goes to the Cabbage Patch* in lesson plan 2.

The general format of a lesson in which the movement material is derived from singing games is as follows:

1. Vigorous, whole body activities focusing more on being involved than on quality or standard of performance.
2. Specific tasks improving and extending known skills (e.g., skipping in different directions, "high" skips, introducing new skills) relating to the chosen singing game.

3. Learning the words and tune of the new song. If this has been done during last week's lesson or in the classroom before this lesson, sit and practice.

4. a. The new singing game.
   b. When it is the second or later lesson in the unit, recall and repeat the singing game(s) learned previously.

This format may be varied to be more appropriate and enjoyable for your children. For example, you may wish to begin the lesson with a well-known and fairly vigorous singing game. You may wish to combine stages 2 and 3, perhaps learning the chorus of a singing game and its actions before adding the verses.

The two lesson plans that follow are considered to have fifteen to twenty minutes of content. Each singing game has been analyzed to pinpoint the relevant movement concepts and the tasks are based on the concepts.

The second lesson plan demands considerably more from the children than the first and it assumes previous knowledge of singing games. It is not a progression of the first lesson. Suggestions for possible movement concepts to include in the following lesson are found at the end of each plan.

Lesson Plan 1

Dance Form: Singing Games

Grade: Kindergarten

Length: 15–20 minutes

Equipment: Drum

                  Flash cards

Objectives: The children will be able to:

1. travel in the general space without colliding
2. sequence travel, stop, collapse, rise
3. sing and dance at the same time

Movement Concepts: See figure 7.2.

Tasks	Teaching Aids
Basic	
Follow me around the room, copy what I do.	Walk, run, skip, weaving throughout the space. Watch the children carefully; adjust your speed to theirs.

American Version

Ring around the rosey
A pocket full of posies
Ashes, ashes,
We all fall down.

British Version

Ring-a-ring of roses
A pocket full of roses
Atishoo! Atishoo!
We all fall down.

Ring Around the Rosey		
Body Concepts Activities: Walk, skip, collapse, rise, stop, "sneeze"		
Effort Concept	Spatial Concepts	Relationship Concepts
Phrasing	Moving freely in the general space. Progress to traveling in a circle.	Unison with the teacher. Alone in a group. Progress to holding hands in a circle.

Music:

Figure 7.2 Movement concepts—*Ring Around the Rosey*

Refining

Let's have quiet bouncy feet.	Always stress quality of action.

Organizing

Spread out so that you can all see me. Look toward me.	The children may need constant reminders to use their own space.

Extending

Copy me and when I stop, stop very still.	Begin with equal length phrases of going and stopping so the stop is predictable and the children can anticipate the change.

Extending

Do the same thing without me. Find your own space to travel in. I will play on the drum so listen very carefully.	Make sure the children are well-spaced apart before they begin. Repeat the same phrasing on the tambour.

Refining

When you stop, look for a new space to go to. Watch other people as you go. Go on your own "journey." "Grip" the floor when you stop. Strong legs.	If necessary, re-position the children after a stop. Make sure the stop is long enough for the children to feel the position.

Basic

Kneel in your own space. S-l-o-w-l-y collapse onto the floor.	Do it with the children, stressing slow collapse. Your voice will help here.

Refining

Let your seat/hips touch the floor, then let your trunk touch the floor. Collapse slowly so there are no bumps.	Move to another place in the room and do it again with the children. You set a model without giving a demonstration.

Extending

Collapse to the other side. Collapse and stand up. Now let's try collapsing s-l-o-w-l-y! Stand up.	Children will have a preference and probably will have practiced on one side only.

Refining

Bend those knees. Keep your head up.	Control the speed with your voice. Repeat collapse and stand several times.

Extending

Put together phrase of skip and stop, collapse and stand.	Remind children of the phrasing previously established. Repeat several times giving refining tasks as necessary.

Basic

Come and sit down near me, listen to me singing, if you know the words, join in.	Have the words written on the blackboard or flash cards.

Extending

Sing again without me.	

Refining

Take a big breath before you begin. Sit up tall as you sing.	Gently beat on the drum to keep the children in unison.

Applying

Sing, skip and stop.
"Ring-a-round-a-rosy, a pocket full of posies."
Choose where you go.

Begin children in spaces; eight skips and a stop. Travel freely in the space. Repeat two or three times before adding next part.

Extending

Two sneezes, "Ashes! Ashes! We all fall down."

Refining

Travel and find the spaces.
Slow, gentle collapse; remember no bumps.

Extending

Now all the way through.

The children should be able to recall the entire sequence without your participation.

▼▼▼▼   ▼

SAFETY TIP //////////

When children are skipping or running, watch for their concentration to decrease, and for them to begin to "cluster" and collide. Develop phrases of "going and stopping," for example, by using a drum or dancing to music that has clear phrasing so that they skip/run for two phrases and pause and clap for two. Being "on the spot" helps young children refocus.

Possible Progressions

Skipping was chosen as the form of locomotion in the applying task. An alternative is to give the children the choice of running, walking, or skipping. If this is done you must ensure equal emphasis is placed on these activities earlier in the lesson and that the children have developed their own sequences of TRAVEL, STOP, COLLAPSE, and RISE.

Another variation is to repeat the singing game three times, the task being "the first time we all walk, the second time we all run and the third time we all skip"—or the children could choose their own order. How much freedom you give the children to make their own decisions will depend on how well you feel they can manage to (a) make their own decisions and (b) remember which activity they have already used and which one(s) to do next.

Relationship concepts can also be developed in a follow-up lesson. Some of the possibilities are listed below. Your choice will depend on how well the children can relate to each other.

1. Alone in a mass (as in the sample lesson plan).
2. In twos, follow-the-leader relationship, no contact. Take turns to lead.

3. As above, hold hands for traveling.

4. In fours, linear formation for traveling, no contact.

5. As above, hold hands.

Similar Singing Games   Many singing games stress body awareness; particularly skipping and running, identification of body parts, turning, rising, and sinking. Some examples follow, together with the country of origin (White and White 1982).

Singing Games	Movement Concepts
Go round and round the village (England)	Skipping
Garden game (France)	Walking, different body parts
Bean porridge hot (England)	Hands, clapping sequence
Sing a song of sixpence (England)	Skipping, arm gestures

Some singing games include role playing and tell a story as in *The Farmer in the Dell* (England, United States). In these games, the actions usually have an effort focus, as in *The Gallant Ship;* therefore the lessons must include learning experiences to help the children produce the appropriate effort.

Lesson Plan 2

The singing game in this lesson is beginning to show some folk dance form and "folk quality" (Fleming 1976). The form (spatial and relationship concepts) has been simplified considerably for this lesson. You may need two lessons to attain the objectives and an asterisk(*) is placed at the point where the first lesson might end. An applying task for the end of that lesson is included.

Dance Form: Singing Games

Grade: 1

Length: 20 minutes

Equipment: Drum and beater

Stick castanets

Record or tape of "Annie Goes to the Cabbage Patch."

Record player or tape recorder.

Song	**Action**
Annie goes to the cabbage patch	Skipping
Cabbage patch, cabbage patch	
Annie goes to the cabbage patch	
To pick the fresh green leaves	
Johnny sees her	Stand
Ha, Ha, Ha	Clap three times
Now I'll catch you	Stand
Tra, la, la	Stamp three times
No! No! No!	Shake head
Go away	Shake finger
I'll not play with you today.	Skip

Annie Goes to the Cabbage Patch		
Body Concepts		

Activity: Skipping
Body Parts: Feet   (stamping)
             Head   (shaking)
             Hands (clapping, finger shaking)		

Effort Concepts	Spatial Concepts	Relationship Concepts
Rhythmic phrases	Specific pathways to travel 1] 2]	With a partner in a group: 8–12 children

Figure 7.3 Movement concepts—*Annie Goes to the Cabbage Patch*

Objectives: The children will be able to:

1. skip sixteen steps in sequence
2. sequence skip, stop, clap, stop, stamp, stop
3. remember the dance sequence well enough to repeat the singing game twice without prompting

Movement Concepts: See figures 7.3 and 7.4.

Annie Goes to the Cabbage Patch

An - nie goes to the cab - bage patch, cab - bage patch cab - bage patch,

An - nie goes to the cab - bage patch, to pick the fresh green leaves.

John - ny sees her ha ha ha. Now I'll catch you Tra la la.

No No No go a - way, I'll not play with you to - day.

Figure 7.4 Music notation for *Annie Goes to the Cabbage Patch*

Tasks	**Teaching Aids**
Basic	
Skip freely, on drum beat, freeze!	Make sure the children are spaced apart well before beginning. Double beat on drum for stop, accent second beat.
Refining	
Keep steps fairly small. Select speed so that you can stop. Push against the floor on hop. Feel "lift" in upper body on hop. Listen carefully for stop signal. Watch for the spaces.	Keep phrases fairly short so excitement of unexpected "stop" is maintained. This also helps with spacing; remember to praise good spacing.

Basic

Drum feet on floor, stop.	Use stick castanets to accompany "drumming." Repeat phrase several times. Stress alert stillness and anticipation to begin next phrase.

Refining

Keep body strong when still.
Bend knees to help drumming
  action.

Extending

Skip lightly, freeze; drum feet, freeze.	Accompany running with quick, light beats on drum, two stronger, abrupt beats for freeze, castanets for feet. When beating drum, hold castanets in same hand as the drum, change to the other hand when playing.

Organizing

Sit down near me.

Basic

Shake your hands; stop. Shake one hand; stop. Shake the other hand; stop. Clench your hands, spread your fingers slowly, curl them again. Shake them again. Clap your hands in time with me. Tap your feet on the floor in time with me. Alternate: claps, pause, floor taps with feet, pause.	Always phrase the actions, shake and freeze! This aids development of hearing and moving to phrases. Begin to introduce the clapping pattern 2/4 clap-clap-clap-pause. Repeat several times to establish rhythm.

Refining

Loose hands!
Watch your hands as you curl and
  uncurl the fingers.
Watch me as you clap so that you
  know when to stop.

Continue to participate. Stress
  slow curling and uncurling so
  that there is time to feel the
  difference.

Extending

Three claps—and stop!
Three taps—and stop!

Do this standing so that the
  children can add skipping.
  Equal-length phrases as in the
  dance.

Applying

Join together, skip, pause, clap,
  pause, stamp, pause.
Copy me.

Suggested pattern: eight skips,
  three claps, pause, three stamps,
  pause.
Repeat several times.

Refining

Use small steps.
Lift free knee in skip.
Arms slightly spread will help
  balance and body lift in hop.
Make "up" important in skip.
Look for the spaces.
Be ready to change direction to
  avoid others.

Remember you know the music
  and are able to structure the
  sequence accordingly. Gradually
  withdraw from participating, but
  continue to give verbal cues;
  gentle beats on drum may also
  help. (Note: "Advanced"
  skippers will swing arms as
  when walking. Encourage
  opposition as you see it
  developing.)*

Basic

Sit down and listen to this song.
Follow the words on the board.

Sing with the record.
Have words on blackboard or
  flash cards.

Extending

Begin to sing.	Repeat first verse ("Annie . . .
Skip and sing to the first verse.	leaves") alone. Stress the pause
	at the end of the verse. Repeat
	two or three times.

Refining

Take a breath before beginning.
Repeat refining tasks related to
  skipping.

Organizing

Find a partner and stand in a big	This presupposes the children are
space.	able to find their own partners.

Extending

Skip and sing, going with your	If children cannot find their own
partner, hold inside hands, and	partners, put them in twos (no
travel side-by-side.	attempt to have boy and girl,
	unless it happens that the two
	are good friends and wish to be
	together). If there is an uneven
	number of children, a
	threesome will work.

Refining

Keep level with your partner.	If you find a pair coping well,
Stay fairly close together so	have them demonstrate and
there's no pull between you.	point out what is good.
Remember to keep steps fairly	
small.	

If you use an extension cord, make sure it is placed very close to the wall, and taped down if possible, so that it is well away from feet.

Basic (performed to the words of the song)

Stand facing partner. "Johnny sees her."	Do this sequence with verbal guidance then with the music.
Clap hands three times. "Ha. Ha. Ha."	Repeat two or three times and give specific help to any pair who is having difficulty.
Stand. "Now I'll catch you."	
Stamp three times. "Tra-la-la."	
Shake head and forefinger at partner. "No, no, no, go away."	
Join hands and skip in place. "I'll not play with you today."	

Applying

Sit and listen to the complete song.	This is to refocus attention on the first part of the sequence. It may help if you dance with an imaginary (or real) partner. Dance through once, stop and give feedback. Then dance twice through.
Now begin with skipping then add the clapping and stamping.	

▼▼▼▼   ▼

Possible Progressions

You will remember that the formations and relationships in this singing game have been simplified. Figure 7.5 shows the "true" set pattern of *Annie Goes to the Cabbage Patch,* which is danced in small groups of four to six pairs (eight to twelve children).

Another possible formation is a large double circle, where the couples skip counterclockwise, shown in figure 7.6.

When selecting singing games and folk dances that have set formations, always look for other ways to structure them. Remember it works both ways—you may either simplify or make more complex, according to the needs and capabilities of your children. Some patterns become firmly established as favorites and children derive great pleasure from repeating the familiar. Other patterns are not particularly interesting but may appeal greatly with some well thought-out changes. Be prepared to experiment! Always remember what you wish the children to learn in the lesson and plan with a clear focus of what the children should be able to achieve at the end of the particular lesson. You should be able to tell them at the end what they accomplished; better still, *ask* them what they accomplished. You may be surprised at their perception of what the lesson was about.

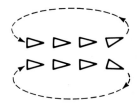

Part 1

Begin facing front. Leaders turn outward. Skip to bottom of set, others follow in line. Meet partners and skip to place. Finish facing partner.

Part 2

Face partner. Begin clapping and stamping in place. Join both hands and skip around in place. Drop hands and finish facing front.

Figure 7.5 Formation of *Annie Goes to the Cabbage Patch*

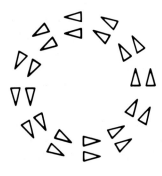

Part 1

Begin facing counterclockwise. Skip alongside partner, holding hands. Finish facing partner.

Part 2

Face partner. Begin clapping and stamping in place. Join both hands and skip around in place. Keep holding hands. Finish facing counterclockwise.

Figure 7.6 Alternative formation for *Annie Goes to the Cabbage Patch*

Fitness Facts

Folk dances that:

1. last a minimum of three minutes,
2. include repetitions of galloping, skipping, and running steps, and
3. have little "standing-still" time;

increase the heart rate (cardiovascular fitness) of the dancers.

▼▼▼▼   ▼

Similar Singing Games

There are a few singing games with a likeness to folk dance, and, as has been mentioned in chapter 5, it is sometimes difficult to decide which they are! The distinguishing factors include the relationships (partners), and formations (linear, single or double circles). The following exhibit characteristics of singing games (i.e., all have a song) and of folk dances (dancing with a partner or changing partners).

Song and Origin	Formation
The German Clap Dance (Germany)	Double circle
Skip to my Lou (United States)	Double circle
Bingo (United States)	Single circle

Folk Dance

This form of dance is enjoyed by many children because it provides plenty of opportunity for skipping, running, and jumping combined to form step patterns. It is the patterning and repetition that seems to appeal to all ages, but because of the social nature of folk dance and the more complicated spatial patterns, it is more appropriate for children in grade 3 and above (Evans 1981).

The teaching of folk dance closely parallels that of singing games. Each dance is analyzed in terms of the movement concepts and a lesson plan is developed providing the relevant learning experiences so that the children can dance with enjoyment.

For the folk dance experience to be authentic, the dances should not be modified to meet the needs and abilities of the children. There are plenty of very simple dances from a wide range of countries from which to choose. Your ability to select appropriately depends on your understanding of the movement content and learning challenge inherent in each dance.

The social dimension (relationships) in folk dancing must be emphasized, and if the children are not ready to work in groups, both with and without partners, then omit folk dance for the time being.

Fitness Facts

Step patterns will increase leg strength, especially when they include jumping variations and resiliency is stressed.

Jumping, with clear leg gestures during the flight portion of the jump, requires strong muscles around the pelvis. Strength is also required when landing.

▼▼▼▼   ▼

Learning how to select a partner is so much part of a folk dance lesson that it merits special mention. Young children like to work with their friends and they usually work better when with people they like. We suggest they are allowed to choose with whom to dance. This may be time consuming, but since social interaction is part of the folk dance experience then time must be allowed for it. Do not be concerned if initially you have mixed groupings in your class with boys partnering boys, girls with girls, and maybe a few mixed pairs. In many simple partner and line dances (e.g., "The Shoemaker" and "The Noble Duke of York" [CAHPER 1980]), there is no differentiation of roles. In dances where sets are formed and partners are exchanged, complications can arise. Even this situation can be coped with if one partner wears some color identification, and, instead of referring to boys and girls, the teacher says "reds to the right."

Activities challenging children to find partners or make groups quickly without being concerned with the "who" element are useful at the beginning of a lesson. One example is to play a piece of "skipping" music, or music to accompany any step pattern the children know. The children skip freely about the space until the music stops. The teacher says "Form groups of three and sit." Other groupings ("Find a partner and face each other") are used and the children are praised for completing the challenge quickly. The last challenge can be the formation needed for the dance, e.g., "circles of six." Of course there is the perpetual problem of dealing with incomplete numbers but if we know how many children are present we can be prepared to deal with it.

While the dances are worth learning for the satisfaction of mastering the various step patterns, remembering the formations, and dancing with friends, even more pleasure is possible when they are learned in the broader context of social studies. We are suggesting the folk dance unit be closely linked with the classroom study of a particular culture and that, whenever possible, the music used to accompany the dances should be played by folk musicians. The quality of sound produced by an Austrian dance band is very different from that of an Israeli music group.

The combination of instruments is often specific to a country; harmonies and subtle rhythmic patterns differ considerably from country to country and we should encourage the children to listen with discrimination. In North America we are fortunate to have so many cultures forming our continental fabric. In most large cities (indeed, in many small communities), there are centers where musicians of various ethnic groups play for dance. It may be possible for them to visit the school and play for the children.

Each country has its own style or quality of movement, and for the dances to be more than exercise, attention must be paid to this. It is important for the children to recognize, understand, and appreciate ethnic characteristics. This is one way in which respect for differing cultures may develop.

Dances that utilize known skills, such as walking, running, skipping, and hopping, should be selected for the introductory unit of folk dance. Attention can then be paid to the style and ethnic character of the dance. Formations should be simple so the children can pay more attention to what they are doing than where they are going. To illustrate this, *Syvspring* ("Seven Jumps") from Denmark is chosen as the first dance (CAHPER 1980, Evans 1981).

Lesson Plan 3

Syvspring is a cumulative dance in that each figure is a repeat of the previous one with the addition of a new action. Originally danced by young men, it is a dance to show agility, strength, and stamina. The focus is on the awareness of specific body parts, being able to change the base of support, and producing vigorous, controlled movement.

Dance Form: Folk Dance: *Syvspring* (Denmark)

Grade: 3

Length: 30 minutes

Equipment: Tape recorder or record player, and record EMI RLS 720

European National Dances

Objectives: The children will be able to:
1. dance with an upright posture
2. change direction of the circle on first count of the phrase
3. use strong gestures

Movement Concepts: See figure 7.7.

Syvspring
Body Concepts Activities: Walk, step-hop (similar to skip but even rhythm) Body Parts: Elbows, feet, head, knees

Effort Concepts	Spatial Concepts	Relationship Concepts
Strong, vibrant quality	Traveling in a circle, first counterclockwise then clockwise	Stage 1: Alone Stage 2: Circle, hands joined at shoulder level

Figure 7.7 Movement concepts—*Syvspring* (Seven Jumps)

Tasks	Teaching Aids
Basic	
Free skipping.	Use a known skipping tune (e.g., *Pop Goes the Weasel, Virginia Reel*).
Refining	
Strong upper body, upright posture. Head held high. Look ahead.	
Extending	
Hold arms shoulder height. Skip eight steps to left, then eight to right.	Have all children face same direction. Count 1–8 then all begin together. This will assist your observation as well as begin to develop a feeling for group rhythm.
Refining	
Make last skip small, on the spot. Turn head to face new direction on count of eight. Last hop 1/2 turn to face new direction.	Practice this pattern about three times, with a pause in between so you can give a refining task.

Extending

Use even step-hop, eight to left, eight to right as before.	Play the music *Syvspring;* make sure children hear the even beat. Demonstrate the step so they see and listen before they try.

Refining

Strong leg lift, on hop. Knee bent, low lift. Ankles should be at right angles.	Reinforce 1/2 turn on last hop. Attention to head position will aid upright posture.

Extending

Listen to music. There are thirty-two counts for the chorus. Begin the step-hops with a stamp-hop. Chorus is: eight step-hops to left eight step-hops to right eight walks to left eight walks to right	Accentuate first step-hop with a stronger step. Feet are fairly flat throughout the step-hop (i.e., no pointed toes). Show this as you demonstrate. Let them dance the chorus once before forming groups.

Organizing

Form circles of 10–15. Join hands, keep hands at shoulder level, elbows slightly bent.	

Applying

Dance the chorus, finish with left foot forward and a strong gesture.	Repeat two or three times. Use above refining tasks.

Extending

Repeat chorus, finish left foot forward, change to right foot.	You can now begin to call the sequence—the cumulative aspect of the dance has begun.

Refining

Make strong leg gestures, place heel on ground somewhat proudly, look across circle, keep hands high. (Note: When the kneeling sequence begins, drop hands; rejoin for chorus.)

The sequence is:

figure 1: left foot forward.

figure 2: figure 1 plus right foot.

figure 3: figure 2 plus kneel on left knee.

figure 4: figure 3 plus kneel on both knees.

figure 5: figure 4 plus place left elbow on ground.

figure 6: figure 5 plus place right elbow on ground.

figure 7: figure 6 plus place forehead on ground.

Applying

Repeat entire dance in two circles.

▼▼▼▼   ▼

Possible Progressions

The following lesson could begin in different ways. The first task might be to practice the step-hop to a piece of Scandinavian folk music such as *The Ace of Diamonds* (EMI Records Ltd. RLS 720) or, if the children learned *Syvspring* very easily and they have good movement memories, they could dance the entire dance. This could be followed by spending some time refining the transitions and repeating the dance before introducing a new one for them to learn. The selection of a dance can be based on different criteria. You might decide to introduce:

1. a new step pattern
2. a different formation
3. partners, keeping the same formation (i.e., circle).

Whichever you decide, there should be enough difference between the dances that the children do not confuse them.

"The Shoemaker's Dance" is a very popular Danish partner dance, similar to a singing game in that the actions mime the work done by a shoemaker. It is very suitable for introducing relationships in folk dance, as there is no distinction between male/female roles and much of the dance takes place on the spot, so children do not get "lost." The dance

Shoemaker's Dance		
Body Concepts Activities: Clapping, skipping, gesturing Body Parts: Fists, elbows		
Effort Concepts	Spatial Concepts	Relationship Concepts
Strong, direct quality with bound flow	Scattered in the general space	Partners

Figure 7.8 Movement concepts—Shoemaker's Dance

can be in a circle of scatter formation. The movement concepts in the dance are shown in figure 7.8, but no lesson plan is given. We hope you will use Lesson Plan 3 as a model and design your own. Once you have highlighted the important movement concepts, design the tasks, remembering those directed toward quality performance of the dance.

Other Folk Dances

There are many dances appropriate for the elementary school program. Which ones you select will depend on whether you integrate them into other subject areas or consider them as one aspect of the dance program. When integrating dance into another subject area, you will be choosing dances because of their relevance in another context. As an example, with a fifth grade class you might be discussing which ethnic groups form the core of the community in which your school is situated. Folk dances from these countries could be learned. You may choose dances because of the

1. step patterns
2. rhythm
3. formations

Because we do not know the rational behind your selection, the dances are grouped according to each dance's formation. Figure 7.9 shows three general folk dance formations.

Dances that are appropriate for grades 3–6 include:

1. Longways
   Virginia Reel (United States)
   The Grand Old Duke of York (England)
   Gigue aux Six (Canada)
2. Square
   Carding the Wool (Canada)
   Cumberland Square Eight (England)

1. LONGWAYS

2. SQUARE

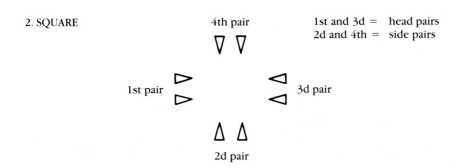

3. CIRCLES

a) single

b) double   or

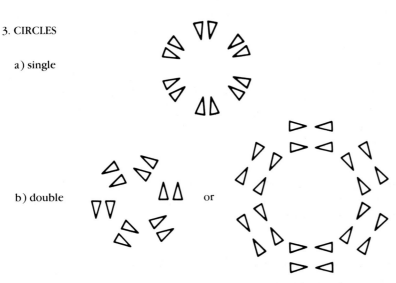

pair faces pair

Figure 7.9 Folk dance formations

▷ = child

There are numerous figures that can be combined to make up square dances for your children.

3. Circles
   single
      Hokey-Pokey (United States)
      Peasants' Dance (France)
      Dance of Greeting (Denmark)
      La Raspa (Mexico)
   double
      Lot is Dead (Danish)
      Clap Dance (Germany)
      Chimes of Dunkirk (Belgium)
      Bridge of Avignon (France)

Creative Dance

This dance form is included for children of all ages. There is the potential for a varied range of movement experiences together with plenty of opportunity for children to use their own ideas as they create dances. Lessons may center on selected movement concepts that are new to the children, so they will need considerable guidance as the lesson progresses. Such a lesson may end with an improvisation to a piece of music, during which the children use their new movement ideas (Lesson Plan 4). At other times, the children will develop *motifs,* which are repeatable phrases of movement that they can combine into a dance form. Some of the dances will be very short, lasting less than one minute, while others may last five to ten minutes and consist of several scenes, as do dance dramas like "The Pied Piper" (see page 241).

Stimuli

What do we "dance about" in creative dance lessons? When teaching folk dance and singing games, the material and structure are there—we know what should happen at the end of the lesson and therefore can plan how to begin and develop the lesson. This is not so in creative dance.

Laban wrote (somewhat esoterically): "The subject matter of dance lies within the verbally almost inaccessible field of vital experiences and qualitative thought" (quoted in Russell 1975). By this he meant that, when the "subject matter" of a dance lesson is other than a movement concept, it must be something the children have experienced. They must be able to transpose their images and understanding of the stimulus into movement concepts, which can then be changed into action.

Lessons for young children are often "about" movement, as they need little urging to move. Older children may need the security of a comparatively concrete stimulus. As maturity and experience increase, children are able to return to more abstract ideas. The same applies to us as teachers. When first teaching creative dance, lessons may be more of a creative experience for us than for the children. This is natural.

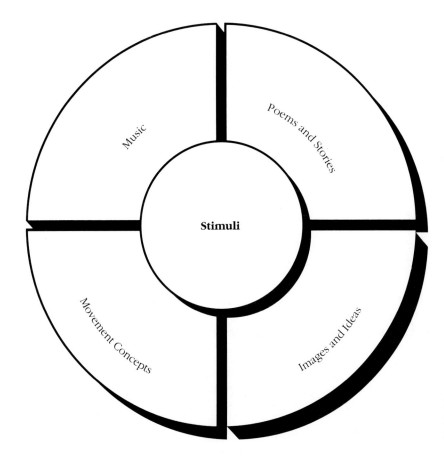

Figure 7.10 Main sources of ideas for creative dance lessons

Fitness Fact

Large, slow gestures of the limbs encourage flexibility, especially when the movement is in different spatial areas (planes) around the body.

Much of the success of a creative dance lesson depends on the stimulus chosen. Stimuli come from various sources (some are listed in figure 7.10) and are often interrelated.

When "searching for ideas that can be worked out in a dance" (Boorman 1969), be sensitive as to whether they will appeal to the children with whom you are working, and that various movement images

---

Fitness Fact

Curving, stretching, and twisting the trunk, as when exploring different body shapes, encourage flexibility in the spine. Remember the head is part of the spine—all too often it is "left out" of the shape.

▼▼▼▼   ▼

---

spring to mind when you and the children think about them. Boorman talks about the "movement potential" of stimuli and poses four questions which are useful guides as we make our selection.

1. What various activities are suggested by the stimulus?
2. How can the stimulus be made "alive" by changing dynamics?
3. Does the stimulus suggest a varied use of space?
4. Does the stimulus suggest we dance alone, with others or something?

To illustrate lesson development, there are sample lesson plans in this chapter for grades 1, 2, 3, and 5/6. Notice (1) the increasing complexity and number of concepts, (2) the abstraction of ideas, and (3) the length of the final dance.

Movement Concepts This is the most abstract form of creative dance—the stimulus comes from movement itself. Maybe it can be likened to a piece of art in which the artist selects particular colors and blends, contrasts, and/or highlights them so the painting is "about" color. The product may evoke emotional responses in some; others may look at it from a more analytical point of view and wonder "What colors did the artist mix to get that shade?"

Lessons may introduce children to new concepts and skills, ask children to show their understanding of particular concepts or be a combination of both, as in the following lesson plan. Therefore, it is for children with some experience. It begins with fairly vigorous movements, focussing attention on hands and feet. This focus gradually changes to movement of the whole body and changes in level.

Lesson Plan 4

Dance Form: Creative Dance

Grade: 2

Length: 30 minutes

Equipment: A variety of rhythmic and vibratory percussion instruments

A Movement Conversation		
Body Concepts Activities: Skipping, rising, sinking, stopping		
Effort Concepts	Spatial Concepts	Relationship Concepts
Children's choice	Contrasting high and low levels	Conversation in twos

Figure 7.11 Lesson Plan 4: Movement concepts

Objectives: The children will be able to:
1. improvise with a partner, having a "movement conversation"
2. identify the different levels seen as their peers dance
3. show clear focus

Movement Concepts: See figure 7.11.

Tasks	Teaching Aids
Basic	
Copy me! Shake your hands: up above your head, down by your feet, now in two places. Now shake one hand and stop! Shake the other and stop! Quick runs on the spot—stop! Now hands—now feet.	Shake hands in different areas around the body. Initially keep the hands fairly close together, then separate. Begin phrasing the sequence. Establish a pattern.
Refining	
Loose hands. Hold your arms lightly. Little steps, on your toes. "Bright" feet.	
Extending	
Now without me, make your own pattern of hands and feet.	Watch for the phrasing chosen. If any children show marked changes in level, select them to demonstrate. Draw attention to these changes.
Repeat your pattern and notice if you include changes in level.	

Basic

Skip, keeping the body as low to the ground as you can.	Accompany the children on a drum.

Refining

Feet apart may help you keep low. Let your arms swing loosely. Bend your knees and lift them to the side of your body.	The skips may look ungainly due to the unusual posture. Stress resilient foot work.

Extending

Now skip and keep high.	Tap the metal rim of the drum and produce a "bright" sound.

Refining

Feel the lift in your body. Push away from the floor.	

Extending

Listen to the drum; change the level of your skipping as the sound changes.	Play equal length phrases. The tempo may need to be slightly slower for the low level skips.

Basic

Start close to the floor, then look up high. Begin to rise, keeping your eyes on that high point. Stop for a moment, then begin to sink, still looking at the high point.	The focus helps concentration and helps clarify the actions, rather than just "being" low or high.

Refining

Push against the floor with your feet.
Feel the strength in your legs.
Keep moving in a straight line toward your spot.

Watch the tension in the bodies; encourage an alertness in the action. Some children may need help with their starting position—it should be stable.

Extending

Start close to the ground again. This time look at a low spot—it may be quite close to you or a little distance away.
Now begin to rise, while still looking.

If the spot is too far away, the up-down dimension is lost and a more appropriate action might be to approach it.

Organizing

Find a partner.

Make sure everyone has a partner before giving the next task.
A group of three may be needed.

Choose a percussion instrument different from your partner's.

The instruments should be placed in small groups around the area. Allow the children some time to make their choices.

Applying

You are going to have a movement conversation with your partner.
The conversation is about different levels, getting there and being there.
Play your instrument as you dance, as it is part of your conversation.
People having a conversation take turns to talk, so one dances and the other is still.

Discuss with them the ideas already experienced, especially skipping, focusing, rising, sinking.

The assumption is being made that the children have experience in playing.
Help them understand the relationship involved.
Let them try before giving any more guidelines.

Refining

Show very clearly which level you are when still; plus where do you focus.

Your movements may say "I am skipping at a high level, then looking high, sinking low."
Your partner's reply might be "I'm starting low, focusing low, skipping low, changing my focus to high and stopping low."
Finish your conversation.

They may wish to focus on their partner, or they may decide on an external focus. Help them clarify which they prefer.
The ability to respond to one another with spontaneity and skill is being developed.
There are many variations possible, some conversations will be longer than others.

Organizing

Half the class sit at the side, the others spread out in the space.

Set the observers something specific to notice (e.g., do the partners change over quickly?)
Is one person "saying" a lot more than the other?
Did you find a pair who showed the levels very clearly?

Applying

Show your conversations.

Do people "speak" in short or long sentences?
Does one person "say" more than the other?
Find a pair who shows the levels very clearly.

The groups change places so everyone has improvised and observed. Some discussion may end the lesson, reinforcing the movement concepts experienced.

Movement Concepts		
Body Concepts Activities: Stopping, jumping, gesturing (pointing), skipping, turning		
Effort Concepts	Spatial Concepts	Relationship Concepts
Contrasting fast and slow turns Sudden stops ("freezing"), sudden gestures ("pointing")	Skipping forward/ backward Changes of level Clear focus when pointing	In twos, question and answer form

Figure 7.12 Lesson Plan 5: Movement concepts

Music A piece of music may elicit comments from the children indicating they have transposed what they heard into something they have experienced. After listening to unfamiliar music, comments such as "that sounds like rushing water" or "that was spooky" tell you immediately that the children can relate to the piece you have chosen.

Music associated with a popular film or character will greatly influence the children's interpretations, so be prepared for common reactions. Very thorough preparation is needed to help the children make the experience "theirs" rather than trying to simply recall what they saw.

If the title of the music is descriptive or narrative (e.g., *Danse Macabre* or *In the Hall of the Mountain King*), you may decide not to tell the children until the dance has been finished. Knowing what the composer felt or visualized can affect our perception of the music. Music without a title allows the listener's imagination complete freedom. Another time, you may decide selected information will help the children focus on relevant aspects of the music, and therefore you will tell them something of the composer's ideas or the title of the music.

In some lessons, you may wish to remind the children of a previous dance experience and relate what they did then to what they will hear. For example, figure 7.12 shows the content of a lesson based on contrasting activities that were developed into a short dance form.

For the next lesson, "Trepak," from *The Nutcracker Suite* by Tchaikovsky, has been chosen as the stimulus for the dance. This music suggests the same actions shown in figure 7.12, though not necessarily in

Movement Concepts

Body Concepts
Activities: Jumping, pointing, running, skipping, stopping, turning
Body Shapes: Asymmetric jumps, stops

Effort Concepts	Spatial Concepts	Relationship Concepts
Sudden quality Strong quality Contrasting free and bound flow	Curving pathways when running Skipping forward and backward High, middle, and low focus	Four groups merging and separating Canon in small and large group(s)

Figure 7.13 Movement concepts for Lesson Plan 5: "Trepak" from Tchaikovsky's *Nutcracker Suite*

the same order. Figure 7.13 details the movement concepts to be developed into motifs. This is one of the occasions when we do not tell the children the title of the piece until after they have created their own dance. Many children have preconceived ideas about ballet, which may interfere with the development of their dance.

The lesson is written out to give you a feeling for the kind of information and guidance that is necessary. The movement concepts are well within the capabilities of a third grade class but the relationships make it challenging, and the children should be an experienced group. The plan has been presented as one lesson; however, it is more likely that two to three lessons will be needed to complete the dance and the children can perform it with confidence. It is quite easy to divide the plan.

Lesson Plan 5

Dance Form: Creative Dance

Grade: 3

Length: 60–90 minutes

Equipment: Tambourine

Record player or tape recorder and record/tape of "Trepak," from *The Nutcracker Suite* by Tchaikovsky

Objectives: At the end of this lesson, the children will be able to:

1. dance in unison in small groups
2. dance in canon and unison in a large group
3. relate and modify motifs developed in the previous lesson (see figure 7.12) into a group dance

Movement Concepts: See figure 7.13.

Tasks	Teaching Aids
Organizing	
Make a loose group in center of space.	
Basic	
Run lightly in the open spaces. Stop suddenly on loud beat of the tambourine.	Accompany with shaking a tambourine.
Refining	
Keep weight on your toes. Take small steps so that you can change direction easily. Place feet apart for the stop; stay and look alert.	Watch to see if the group becomes too compact; stop and spread them apart if you see this happening. Vary the length of the phrases so there is a sense of excitement and anticipation.
Extending	
When you hear a double beat on the tambourine stop and point strongly in any direction.	Introduce this idea when they can intermingle without colliding.
Refining	
A sudden, strong gesture of the arm. Look intently where you point. Very strong position of legs; wide base.	Encourage complete stillness.
Basic	
Where you are, practice big jumps, landing, and being strong and still.	If necessary, spread the children apart; they need space for this.

Refining

Bend your knees before pushing off. Lift in upper body; heads up. Remember, your arms will help your take-off. Bend knees when landing—land quietly. Land one foot after the other, feet apart.	Descriptive words such as "explode," "powerful," and "surprising," may help the children understand the strong, sudden quality of the jumps.

Extending

Make the jump asymmetrical.	If necessary, clarify the meaning of asymmetry.

Refining

Keep your body firm in the air. Hold the shape.	Pay attention to bent/straight arms/legs; "tip" of the body will help asymmetry.

Extending

Listen to this music. "Feel" the jumps and firm landings, the traveling and intermingling, and the sudden stops. This happens four times. We call this *A* music.	Play "Trepak," finishing after four repeats of the first musical idea. Have a visual representation of the music available and help the children follow it as they listen.
Now begin as a loose group; decide if you will jump first or second, intermingle, stop, and point. This happens four times.	The two basic tasks are combined but in reverse order. Verbal cueing may be needed the first time they try. Encourage them to listen to the music and stop cueing as soon as possible.

Refining

Select from the previous ones.	Reminders will be needed as the children focus on remembering the sequence rather than performing.

Organizing

Divide into four numbered groups, each in own area of room.	Consider the effect when placing the groups, see the applying task that follows.

Applying

Group 1 dances to first section, points at group 2, which begins to dance and points at group 3, etc. Design own starting position.	Repeat this part two or three times so that the sequence becomes firmly established. It is now that attention can shift to quality performance.

Refining

Remain very still when waiting to
  begin and after pointing.
Strong arm action so that the
  pointing toward the next group
  is very noticeable.

Basic

a) Listen to next part of the music. "Feel" the skipping: large skips then small, quick skips. At the end of this part, be ready to jump. b) Now try it.	Remind them of the skipping sequence done in previous lesson: big skips traveling forward, small skips traveling backward.

Refining

Lift arms and free knee for big
  forward skips.
Slight crouch for backward skips.
Tuck arms close to side.

Extending

Finish as a loose group ready to jump. There are several, so you decide when to jump.	The group should "pop" at different times so the effect is somewhat unpredictable.

Refining

Keep "pops" strong. Be very still when not jumping.	Children should be encouraged to jump to same music each time. Some groups need considerable help to establish the pattern.

Applying

Put the skipping and the "pops" together. Listen to the music first, then dance.	Begin again from the previous applying task, which ends first part of the dance.

Refining

Watch the other dancers carefully, so that the loose group forms.	

Extending

Dance from the beginning.	Help may be needed to link the two parts together. Use refining tasks already listed to help with quality of performance. Verbal cues should help, remove as soon as possible.

Basic

The group begins to disintegrate; follow a leader out of the group and into the general space. Run swiftly and make curving pathways.	A music repeated; ignore the jumps.

Organizing

Decide whom you will follow. Lines of 3–5 dancers.	Depending on number in class, have several lines emerge, with not more than five children per line.

Refining

Smooth running.
Leaders: watch the other lines
  carefully and avoid them.

Extending

As the music builds to its climax, begin to return to one group, spin, suddenly stop, and make a strong pointing gesture.

The final group must still be fairly loose, yet be a whole. The group must decide on where the focus will be for the final gesture.

Refining

Listen carefully to find notes so that everyone stops at the same time.
Very strong final position.
Consider different levels of stopping to clarify group focus.

There are several options; e.g.,
1. All focus high to same point (this may be above group or outside the group).
2. Some focus high, some medium, some low.
3. All face same direction.
4. All face outward from group and in different directions.

Applying

Dance from the beginning.

The dance has been built up in three parts; help the children make the transition from one part to the next. Select refining tasks already used as you see the need.

▼▼▼▼ ▼

Images When an image is selected as the "dance idea," the lesson often begins with the children being asked questions about the image. Their answers and ideas are collected on a board. The children may need some guidance with carefully designed questions in order to elicit information that can be used during the creation of the dance. The image may be strengthened by pictures, poems, films, or even a field trip, so that the children can extract the essence of the image.

Movement Concepts		
Body Concepts		
Activities: Drift, fall, spin, sweep* Body Parts: Hands, feet		
Effort Concepts	Spatial Concepts	Relationship Concepts
Fine touch, light quality Changes in speed	In the general space	Alone (in a group)

Figure 7.14 Lesson Plan 6: Movement concepts arising from the stimulus **snow**

*Travel with a horizontal emphasis as if blown by a strong wind.

The image of snow is taken as an illustration of this stimulus form. The idea is presented for two different levels of experience, beginning with a very simple dance lesson. The children might be asked questions about what the snow "does" (e.g., it falls, spins, drifts, etc.) and how it does these actions (e.g., softly, slowly, gustily, etc.). Two groups of words will result—verbs and adverbs—and the lesson is developed around these body and effort concepts. For the culmination of the lesson, some music may be played, for example Debussy's *Snowflakes Are Dancing* as interpreted by Tomita (*The Newest Sound of Debussy*, RCA ARL 1— 0488) and the children set the applying task of improvising, or dancing freely, to the music and incorporating the ideas experienced during the lesson.

Figure 7.14 shows the movement concepts around which a lesson could be developed. The lesson might be of twenty minutes duration and would be most appropriate during the winter months, especially if it were taught during or just after a snowstorm.

If the children live in an area without snow, they will need some help understanding what snow is and how it "behaves." Films, photographs, and poems may help. It may be an unsuitable stimulus for your children and you may wish to replace it with another weather element—the sun for example, or rain—that suggests specific movement ideas.

Lesson Plan 6

Dance Form: Creative Dance
Stimulus: Image of snow
Grade: 1
Length: 30 minutes

Equipment: Cymbal
             Castanets
             Record or tape: "Snowflakes Are Dancing"
             (Debussy, arranged by Tomita)
             Record player or tape recorder
Objectives: At the end of this lesson the children will be able to:

1. change speed of actions
2. move with lightness
3. relate movement ideas to music and dance freely

Movement Concepts: See figure 7.14.

Tasks	Teaching Aids
Basic	
Shake hands and stop suddenly.	Play short phrase on stick castanets. Repeat.
Refining	
Loose, floppy hands. Strong fingers when stopping.	
Extending	
Shake hands high, low, around the body.	Encourage children to use all space around their bodies. You might do it with them (i.e., omit percussion and provide ideas visually).
Refining	
Elbows slightly bent, watch your hands. On "stop" keep whole body still.	
Basic	
Travel with quick, light feet and stop.	Castanet accompaniment, short phrases, maybe uneven lengths to encourage listening skills.

Refining

Take small steps. Run on your toes. Look for the spaces. Strong bodies when stopping.	Dance with the children. Provide feedback during the task.

Extending

Alternate phrase of 1. shaking hands, stop 2. quick traveling, stop	Verbal cues may be needed, but eliminate as soon as possible.

Refining

Hands ready to begin! Keep movements small.

▼▼▼▼   ▼

Bring children in and sit down with them. Discuss the stimulus (snow). Write their words on a board so they can see them. Select three or four words that will allow for the development of a movement sequence, for example, turning, stopping, traveling and sinking. Begin working on sequencing two actions, e.g., travel and sink. No tasks are suggested here as they will depend on the children's responses. The refining task should focus on quality inherent in the actions; the extending tasks on adding another action to a sequence *or* changing the speed and direction of an action.

Tasks   **Teaching Aids**

Basic

Listen to this music.	Play *Snowflakes Are Dancing* and fade at an appropriate moment.

Extending

Listen again and imagine dancing your sequences.	Fade the music at the same moment so the children know how much music they have for their dance.

Applying

Move into your own big space and show me how you wish to begin; be very still. Ready and. . . .	You may need to provide verbal cues this first time, small reminders of actions, quality, and listening to the music.

Refining

Listen carefully to what the music tells you. Watch for the spaces. Light feet as you travel. When still, make it important.	Stillness is very difficult; give plenty of feedback on stillness as an action.

Applying

Now you've tried your dance once, think about what you did; keep what you liked, find your space, and dance it once more.	Repetition is important even though this is an improvisation. Only give help if it really is necessary; otherwise, permit the children to focus entirely on their movement and the music.

▼▼▼▼   ▼

A more complex idea for the upper elementary grades, possibly grade 4, still based on the stimulus of snow is suggested in figure 7.15. In this instance, the dance has four distinct parts—*A, B, C, D*—which are patterned according to the wishes of the class; for example, *A-B-C-B-D-C-B*. This may be too long, in which case *A-B-D-C-B* has good potential. Notice that both dance forms finish with group shapes and stillness. This is very important. Dances where everyone finishes in a relaxed shapeless heap on the floor—as could happen with "melt" as the stimulus—are visually boring.

The accompaniment to the dance could be voice sounds, appropriate words, percussion instruments, or any combination of the three. Much experimenting will be done to find the "right sound" the children want as they create their "music." They may wish to tape-record their composition or they may prefer to have "live" music, playing and dancing

A. Falling Snow		
Body Concepts Activities: Sinking, rising, spinning, hovering Body Parts: Upper body parts leading activities		
Effort Concepts	Spatial Concepts	Relationship Concepts
Changes in speed Sustainment Light quality	Changes in level, stressing high and low Air patterns	Alone (in a group)

B. Snowflakes Falling on the Ground		
Body Concepts Activities: Jumping, rolling, stopping Body Parts: Different body parts taking weight Body Shapes: Different body shapes		
Effort Concepts	Spatial Concepts	Relationship Concepts
Contrasting strong and light qualities Sudden and slow "arrivals"		Small groups forming and dispersing

C. Snowflakes Drifting and Freezing Into Shapes		
Body Concepts Activities: Travelling, turning, stopping Body Shapes: Shaping of the body in groups		
Effort Concepts	Spatial Concepts	Relationship Concepts
Contrasting free and bound flow Firm body shapes Fine touch when travelling Sustained quality		Small groups, 3's 5's Group shapes

Figure 7.15 Development of a "snow dance"

D. Melting Snow		
Body Concepts		
Activities: Gesturing Body Parts: Isolation of parts Body Shapes: Asymmetric shapes		
Effort Concepts	Spatial Concepts	Relationship Concepts
Fine touch, changing to heavy (relaxation) Contrasting slow and sudden (dripping) qualities		Alone or in small groups

at the same time. This is one of the many situations when roles can be found for the children who, for various reasons, are not able to take part in the dance itself. They can be part of the "orchestra" and thereby share totally in the creation of the dance.

Poems and Stories Boorman (1973) writes of the close links between our verbal and motor languages, and there are several publications that help with the development of lessons using words as stimuli (Shreeves 1979, Wall 1983).

When selecting a poem or a story as a stimulus for a dance, the most important element is its movement potential. The following characteristics can be used as criteria. Two or more should be present in order for there to be sufficient movement content for the development of a dance:

1. a clearly defined story line
2. plenty of activity
3. well-developed characters
4. a series of events so that the poem or story can be divided into scenes or acts
5. contrasts of moods, characters
6. strong imagery
7. onomatopeia
8. words and/or phrases with strong rhythmic content

The kind of dance developed will depend on the combination of the above characteristics. The dance could be completely nonliteral, its ideas having been abstracted for their own worth and the story or poem almost disregarded. Other dances will have closer alignment with the original source of the movement ideas. The resulting dance may be:

1. A dramatic dance, developed around effort and relationship concepts. The dance is an abstraction of moods and does not tell any story. If told the original idea, observers may see no connection between it and the finished dance.

2. A lyrical dance, developed around space and effort concepts. This dance is also an abstraction, but of shapes and sensations of flow, rather than specific moods. This kind of dance is often accompanied by music with a strong melodic line.

3. A rhythmic dance, developed around body awareness and effort concepts. This is also abstraction, with the interest and excitement coming from the ability to "play" with different rhythms. Children may create their dance around words taken out of the context of the poem or story, the words making no verbal sense on their own but the resulting dance being totally logical. Nonsense poems such as "The Jumblies" by Edward Lear and "Jabberwocky" by Lewis Carroll are wonderful for boh rhythm and onomatopoeia.

4. A dance drama, developed around effort and relationship concepts. This is the most concrete dance form as it includes characterization and a fairly clear story line.

When selecting a poem or story, do not feel you have to follow it word for word. If two or three dance ideas are suggested by parts of the poem or story, and these ideas make sense on their own, then discard the remainder. Remember it is a dance that is being created, and the focus is on conveying the essence of the poem, or parts of the poem, rather than its literal translation into another medium.

The poem chosen for a series of lessons is the "Pied Piper of Hamelin" by Robert Browning. This is a long narrative poem that has elements of both stories and poems. The resulting dance is a dance drama, which means that the movement ideas are developed into motifs and mimetic action is minimized. This is very important to remember; otherwise, the result is neither dance nor drama.

In this example, the characters of the poem are the main source of ideas, the story line being hinted at by the order in which the characters appear and what they do. The characteristics of each person chosen are discussed with the children and the ideas noted on a board, as they must be kept in mind as the motifs are developed. Some suggestions are shown in table 7.3; your children may have other thoughts and those are the ones that should be kept.

A dance drama unit of fourteen lessons is probably required: three lessons per scene, plus another two to put the dance drama together. If it is not possible to spend fourteen or so lessons with one group of children, scenes can be given to different classes to work on separately. Time then has to be made available to bring the different groups together to share their dances and rehearse putting the scenes together. As this is a

Table 7.3

Ideas upon which the dance drama "The Pied Piper of Hamelin" is based

The rats	Mischievousness "Popping" out of spaces Highlighting long tails, which can be used to hang onto, jump over, etc.
Mayor and corporation	Ceremonial in style Pompous "Thinking" motifs Posing Procession and grand entry before council meeting
The Pied Piper	Playing of pipe, wooden stick about 30 cm long and held either as a flute or a recorder Dancing through the space and around people
The children	Playing games of tag, leap-frog, hide and seek, jumping rope, throw and catch, on a seesaw and other activities that can be developed into motifs

major unit with a very definite product orientation, it follows that a performance with an audience is appropriate.

A synopsis of each scene follows with task ideas. We hope this model will help you plan similar dance experiences for your children.

Scene 1 If possible, structure an environment that provides holes to creep in and pop out from; objects to hide behind, peer over, jump off, scurry around.

Dance Drama: The Pied Piper of Hamelin

Synopsis

1. Groups of "rats," some hiding, others peering, listening intently. Dancers have tails consisting of ropes tied around their waists.
2. Rats scurry, stop, appear, disappear, listen, always "on guard."

Task Ideas

Mingle freely, then freeze. Select interesting positions that result and practice them.

Short phrases of quick, small running steps and stops at different levels; appearing and disappearing behind and into; jumping on and off obstacles. Stress stillness at different levels with hands, heads; alert bodies are important.

The Rats		
Body Concepts		
Activities: Hiding, peering, scurrying, jumping, stopping Body Parts: Emphasis on hands, heads, tails (skipping ropes)		
Effort Concepts	Spatial Concepts	Relationship Concepts
Sudden and light Fast and light Free flow	Changing from high to low	Pairs; groups of 5–7

Figure 7.16 Scene 1: The Rats

Music: "The Fossils," from *The Carnival of Animals* by Saint Saens

3. Rats play with tails: use as skipping ropes; hold onto as in a line dance; wrap and unwrap each other, etc.

Practice rhythmic swinging of tails, dancers in small groups of 3–5. Each group develops its own motifs based on play actions.

4. "On guard" motifs repeated. Finish dance with scurrying, hiding, and peering.

Traveling in small groups, stopping, hiding behind each other, peering out from behind another, etc.

Scene 2 Chairs or a platform of different levels to represent steps to a council house.

Synopsis

1. Procession appears very stately, slow march, unison action.

2. Procession approaches the steps or chairs; half of the group sits and other half stands. Everyone is thinking. Groups change over, (the number of times this happens will depend on the counting of beats).

3. Grand entry of Mayor. If children are strong enough the Mayor can be carried on a chair; if not, the Mayor walks ahead of a small procession acknowledging the onlookers. Mayor sits or stands in a highly visible place.

Task Ideas

Develop a step pattern with very definite leg gestures. Arms carried pompously. Group processes in unison.

Develop "thinking" poses, stress posture and gesture of upper body, especially arms and heads. Change over must be counted so there is either action or stillness. Suggest four counts for each idea.

A new step pattern is needed for the Mayor. If the Mayor is carried, much practice of slow, unison lifting, carrying, and lowering is needed.

Mayor and Corporation		
Body Concepts		
Activities: Walking, sitting, gesturing, stopping Body Parts: Stressing trunk, arms, head		
Effort Concepts	Spatial Concepts	Relationship Concepts
Strong, direct Sustained Bound flow		Unison walking Two groups alternating sitting and walking

Figure 7.17 Scene 2: The Mayor and Corporation

Music: March from *The Love of Three Oranges* by Prokofiev

4. Angry citizens surround the Mayor, who is protected by his councilors.

   Action-reaction motifs developed in twos, one councilor and one citizen.

5. Everyone becomes aware of a strange sound from far off. The group becomes less hostile, more fearful, and gradually retreats.

   Change of focus, from one-on-one to outside the group. Actions are more flexible, hesitant; gestures are protective.

Scene 3 The Piper's Dance is a dance for many pipers, depending on the number of students in the class. Dancers create their own step patterns and style of playing a pipe, which may be a piece of dowling 30–40 cm. (12–14 inches) long.

Synopsis

1. The pipers enter and dance in general space.

2. Half the group poses on steps used in scene 2 and play their pipes, other half dances. Change over.

3. Whole group dances and exits (a line dance).

Task Ideas

Individual or small groups (2–3), unison step patterns, hands and arms important as they hold pipes.

Dancers: line dances, circles, unison step patterns. Players: accentuate upper body gestures and fingers on pipes.

Scene 4
Synopsis

1. Four groups of children enter one at a time, and pose.

2. Each group plays its own game(s).

Task Ideas

Traveling motifs developed with skipping, hopping, and galloping steps.

Enlarge mimetic actions, stress rhythm and shape, and variety.

The Piper		
Body Concepts Activities: Skipping, turning, various step patterns Body Parts: Stressing feet, arms, hands (holding the pipe)		
Effort Concepts	Spatial Concepts	Relationship Concepts
Light touch Rhythmic Free flow	Pathways	Alone (in a group)

Figure 7.18 Scene 3: The Pied Piper

Music: *Tambourin,* by Hasse, arranged by James Galway

The Children		
Body Concepts Activities: Skipping, jumping, running, dodging, throwing		
Effort Concepts	Spatial Concepts	Relationship Concepts
Working activities with appropriate effort content	Large movements Each group in its own space	Small groups Unison for conclusion

Figure 7.19 Scene 4: The Children

Music: *Ruralia Hungarica Suite,* by Dohnany

3. Piper enters, children stop playing and watch as each group is visited by the Piper.

4. Piper sits on steps and watches the children who begin to play again.

5. The children gradually form a circle around the Piper, as if mesmerized by his presence. They are drawn toward him.

6. The Piper dances down from the steps and the children follow him from the dance area.

Develop interesting group shapes for stillness, heads and eyes to follow Piper everywhere.
Repetition or development of motifs previously created.

Unison advancing and retreating (wavelike) motif develops with two circles (inner and outer) changing places.
The Piper selects one of the step patterns used previously.
Children skip, gallop, etc., after him, with no attempt at unison.

An Important Difference

How do dance and drama differ? In the former, the focus is on developing motifs that are representational of a situation or character. The essence of a situation or character is abstracted and transformed into a new form—a dance form. In the latter, a more literal reproduction of the stimulus is sought. It may be in the realm of fantasy rather than of our concrete world, but the children, for that moment, enter into that world and "become" some one or thing other than they are.

In dance, children are not asked to "be" anything other than themselves; neither are they asked to act out a story. Both suggest a somewhat literal interpretation of the stimulus. The process of abstraction is less obvious.

If animals are used as stimuli the children's attention is drawn to the qualities of the stimuli and their own movements modified, so that the quality is highlighted. Phrases such as "ponderous as an elephant" or "hovering like a hummingbird" help clarify the quality of movement being developed.

Summary

Three dance forms are suggested as being appropriate for the dance program: singing games, folk dance, and creative dance. Each dance form provides different learning opportunities and challenges for the seven-year span of the elementary school. The ideas presented in this chapter have been chosen to give a feeling for the diversity of the dance program, which can be as exciting for the teacher planning it as it is for the children who will share it.

Overall, the dance program should provide rich and varied experiences for your children, reinforcing their innate impulse to move expressively and helping them to enjoy the worlds of imagination and fantasy with a disciplined and artistic communicative focus. Laban's words (1948) concisely state the objective of such a program:

It is not the creation of sensational dances which is aimed at, but the beneficial effect of the creative activity of dancing upon the personality of the pupil.

Review Questions

1. Why is it important to consider both age and experience when beginning a dance program with children? How will these factors influence your (a) planning and (b) expectations?
2. Why are singing games considered to be an important, yet minor, part of the program?
3. Discuss possible lesson formats for singing games and folk dances. Why may they be considered together?
4. Select a singing game and extract the movement concepts. Design tasks that could be used in a lesson.
5. Discuss different ways of finding partners for folk dancing. Why is it important to understand the difficulties children sometimes have when selecting partners?
6. Select a stimulus from nature and analyze it so that the movement concepts could be translated into tasks for an age group of your choice.
7. Discuss how creative dance differs from drama.

References

Boorman, J. 1969. *Creative Dance in the First Three Grades.* Toronto: Longmans of Canada, Ltd.

——— 1973. *Creative Dance and Language Experiences For Children.* Toronto: Longmans of Canada, Ltd.

CAHPER 1980. *Folk Dance in the Elementary School.* Ottawa: Canadian Association for Health, Physical Education and Recreation.

Evans, J. 1981. *Let's Dance.* Toronto: Can-Ed Media Ltd.

Fleming, G. 1976. *Creative Rhythmic Movement: Boys and Girls Dancing.* Englewood Cliffs, N.J.: Prentice-Hall Inc.

Koma, C. 1987. *Movement Education Resource File.* Montreal: Project for 434-324 Movement Education for Early Childhood Teachers, Faculty of Education, McGill University.

Laban, R. 1948. *Modern Educational Dance.* London: Macdonald and Evans, Ltd.

Logsdon, B., K. Barrett, M. Ammons, M. Broer, L. Halverson, R. McGee and M. Roberton. 1984. *Physical Education to Children: A Focus on the Teaching Process,* 2d ed. Philadelphia: Lea & Febiger.

Preston-Dunlop, V. 1980. *A Handbook for Dance in Education.* 2d ed. London: Macdonald and Evans, Ltd.

Russell, J. 1975. *Creative Dance in the Primary School,* 2d ed. London: Macdonald and Evans, Ltd.

Shreeves, R. 1979. *Children Dancing.* London: Ward Lock Educational Books.

Wall, J. 1983. *Beginnings: Movement Education For Kindergarten to Grades Three,* 2d ed. Montreal: McGill University.

Recording

White, R. and D. White. 1982. Singing Games. Los Angeles: Rhythm Productions; Tom Thumb Music (ASCAP) T321.

Related Readings

Carlisle, C. 1986. Dance Curriculum for Elementary Children Using a Scientific Approach. *JOPERD* 57:67-72, 78.

Cote-Laurence, P. 1987. Dance and Music: A Look at an Old Alliance. *CAHPER Journal* 53:4.16-20.

Hill, R. 1986. Tribute to Lisa Ullmann: A Shining Star in the Dance World. *CAHPER Journal* 52:6.13-15.

Jensen, M. 1983. Composing and Guiding Creative Movement. *JOPERD* 54:1.85-87.

Lynch-Fraser, D. 1982. *Dance Play: Creative Movement for Very Young Children.* New York: Walker & Co.

Macdonald, C. J. 1986. Yes, You Can Teach Creative Dance. *CAHPER Journal* 52:3.17-22.

Riley, A. 1987. Can Dance Break the Sex Barrier? *CAHPER Journal* 53:3.14-18.

Van Gyn, G. and D. Docherty. 1985. Skill Acquisition and Creative Dance: A Conflict in Goals? *CAHPER Journal* 51:6.9-12.

3

Games are fun, challenging, meaningful and uniquely satisfying to everyone. People like to play games whether they are skilled, unskilled, adults or children.

Schurr, E. 1980. Movement Experiences for Children, *3d. ed. Englewood Cliffs, N.J.: Prentice-Hall Inc.*

GAMES

CHAPTER

8

THE GAMES
PROGRAM

Sports, games—these are words with which we are very familiar and may be used interchangeably. In this book, however, they are considered to be different. *Sports* is a generic term meaning any activity in which there is an element of competition, either direct or indirect. Gymnastics, swimming, cross-country skiing, track and field (indirect competition), and games (direct competition) are sports. This chapter discusses games.

Probably more has been written on games for children than on other aspects of the physical education program. Playing and watching games are important aspects of North American society; indeed, of many societies around the world. Concern has arisen because, in many instances, the *intrinsic value of playing* has been lost. Scores, standings, and medals and other awards have become more important, the playing being a means to an end rather than being sufficient in itself.

> Ideally the objective of the game is non-productive in that the value of the game is intrinsic, not dependent on external award. When this equilibrium is disturbed, through infusion of rewards external to the game, play loses its character and takes on the character of work (Saunders 1969).

Why Should Games Be Included in the School Program?

> People of all ages play games—many of us play games our entire lives while others of us feel that games are played only by the young (Morris 1980).

Children begin to play games at a very early age. Many of the activities, in their unsophisticated stages of development, arise quite naturally to become part of the children's movement vocabulary. How many of us have played "peek-a-boo" with a baby? Probably all of us have. Preschool children play games of hide-and-seek, and enjoy the excitement of being chased by friendly older siblings or parents. Here are the beginnings of role playing and offensive and defensive strategies, which are important aspects of conventional games in our society.

Objects fascinate children. They pick them up, shake them, and often drop them. Initially, the children are exploring the nature of the object, but soon their attention transfers to controlling the object and the dropping becomes deliberate. Adults' reactions reinforce their activities and so manipulative skills are developed. Many toys are designed to develop manipulative skills and fortunate children are given balls, skipping ropes, hoops, bats—the paraphernalia of games playing.

Games provide children with opportunities to be in control of themselves and the environment. When allowed to design their own play, they often surprise adults with their ability to create situations that are self-testing, have structure, and a code to which the players are expected to adhere. They also sensibly adapt the game to meet their own needs as they play: if it doesn't work, is too easy, too difficult, not interesting—change it!

As our lifestyles change, playing spaces diminish and children are bused considerable distances to school, which means their chances to indulge in play are reduced. It becomes more important for the school program to provide children with games experiences. We must ensure that their perspective of "playing a game" is preserved and fostered, and the adult achievement-oriented attitude is avoided.

The Nature of Games

What are games? Is there an idea common to the simple chasing games so enjoyed by five-year-olds and a game of basketball? We might say, "Oh yes; in both of them players are being chased." This cannot be correct as there are other games in which players are not chased (tennis for example), and we must look for something else. A more complete definition might read like this:

Games are competitive activities in which the individual or group objective is to score more points than the opposition (offensive play), at the same time using skills to prevent the opposing individual or group from scoring (defensive play) (Saunders 1969, Stanley 1977).

If you recall your own games experience in elementary and secondary school, you may remember lessons in which the focus was on the development of individual skills (e.g., the basketball chest pass) that were eventually used to play a game. Unfortunately, games playing is not that simple. Games are unpredictable and the context in which the skills are used varies each time the game is played. Skills used in these conditions are called *open skills.* Children who are taught skills out of the context of a game environment have little understanding of *why* or *when* to use them. Too much time has been spent on specific motor responses or techniques, and insufficient time has been spent understanding "the contextual nature of games" (Bunker and Thorpe 1982). As "much of the pleasure involved in games playing lies in making correct decisions in the light of tactical awareness" (Bunker and Thorpe 1982), lessons must help children understand the nature of games playing so they can make decisions and use their specific skills appropriately.

We suggest the games program should focus on developing general games knowledge and appreciation through games playing (see figure 8.1). Common to all games is the concept of *fundamental games knowledge,* and we wish to underscore that this is what should be paramount in games teaching. The belief is that knowledge and appreciation are transferrable from one games situation to another (Piggott 1982). Our responsibility is to help children develop an understanding and appreciation of the interrelatedness of rules, strategies, players' roles, and specific skills or techniques. In other words, children should have the opportunity to learn to play and to enjoy playing.

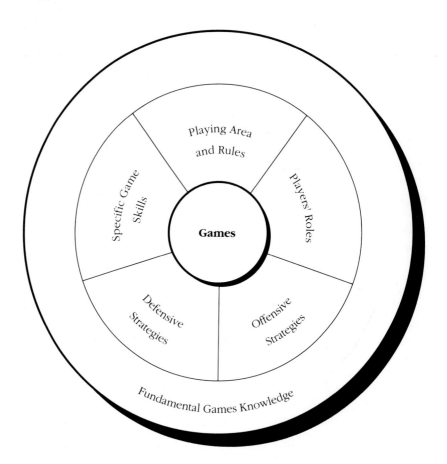

Figure 8.1 Games
understanding

Game Forms

games involve
  equip handling

Each game, however simple, has its own *form,* consisting of players' roles
and responsibilities, selected skills, playing area, and rules. One-on-one
tag illustrates this.

Roles: Player *A*: to touch player *B*.
Player *B*: to escape from player *A*.

Skills: Player *A*: To run and follow player *B*; to anticipate where
player *B* may go; to be able to change speed and direction according to player *B*'s actions.

Player *B*: To run, changing speed and direction so that player
A is unable to follow.

Playing Areas: May or may not be designated.

Rules: Player *A* to touch player *B* with hand only. When caught,
players change roles. Game is over when players decide.

Table 8.1

A comparison of low-organization, lead-up, and formal games

Simple elements found in many games; no game form specified ──────────→ Low-organization games

Combination of elements found in a selected formal games form ──────────→ Lead-up games

Combination of elements found in a specific formal game ──────────→ Formal games

(handwritten margin note: — roles — rules — created by participants ie) teacher parent)

It may be useful to sort into categories the many games that exist. We propose three, which provide:

1. a framework for progression, from simple to more complex game forms.
2. a comparison of the fundamental skills of similar games, target, net, batting, and running games.

These three categories are low-organization, lead-up, and formal games.

Low-organization and lead-up games focus on the fundamentals of games playing, and are therefore the core of the elementary school games program. These games may already exist or may be created by teachers and/or the children. (See the related readings in chapter 10 for more information.)

Many low-organization games include only nonmanipulative skills, providing the opportunity for applying the body management skills of running, dodging, swerving, guarding, and avoiding. These games make little demand on the players in terms of roles, strategy, and rules, so they can concentrate on individual skills or skills in simple combinations, such as running, stopping, and turning. The games bear little resemblance to formal games (see table 8.1 for a comparison).

Group games place little or no emphasis on cooperation. All have introductory elements of competition, such as chasing and being chased, as in tag, or comparing scores, as in Danish Rounders, a game in which running is "matched" against accurate throwing and catching. The game is described in table 8.2.

Categorization of Games

Low-organization Games

To Do

Observe children playing in their school yard. If possible, do this at a school where you are teaching and you know some of the children.

Notice:

1. What games activities they use in their play.
2. The size of group preferred by children of different ages.
3. Any children who appear to be excluded from playing. What do you know about their skill level?

▼▼▼▼   ▼

Table 8.2

▼▼▼▼   ▼

Danish Rounders

Two groups of players, 8–12 players per group.

Objectives:

Group *A* passes a ball around the circle and keeps account of how many times the ball is successfully caught. If the ball is dropped, return to zero.

Group *B* runs around the circle ("follow the leader") as the ball is being passed. On crossing a designated mark, the last runner calls "Stop!"

Groups *A* and *B* change over. Group *B* tries for more passes than *A*; group *A* tries to run the circuit faster than *B*.

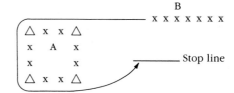

△ Pylons to establish size of circle

x Players

──────→ Running track

▼▼▼▼   ▼

Lead-up Games

These games are becoming more complex and a greater resemblance to formal games is apparent. The games are designed to

1. combine selected nonmanipulative and manipulative skills in a game structure;
2. include role playing, i.e., introduce the concept of offensive (attacking) players, defensive (guarding and goalkeeping) players;

3. require an understanding of strategy fundamental to the related formal game form.

At times, gamelike tasks will be set with the objective of developing cooperative play, for example, "keep the pot boiling" or "how many can we do?" when alternating with a partner to bat a ball against a wall. In such a situation, the players strive to send the ball so that their partners can also bat it. Other cooperative relationships important in team play, such as "where do I go when I don't have the ball?" can be addressed in situations involving three players, in either a cooperative or a two against one situation.

Both low-organization and lead-up games can be adapted, simplified, or complicated to meet the skills of the children and to relate to the learning objectives of the lesson. There are numerous games from which to select, and often children and/or teachers can make them up (see the related readings at the end of chapter 10 for sources of games).

Formal Games

These games are "grown into" gradually as children's nonmanipulative and manipulative skills develop along with their knowledge of game concepts. A considerable amount of learning precedes the playing of formal games with any degree of satisfaction. The structure is such that the players have to adapt to the demands of that game. There are specific skills to be learned for each game, the rules are established and have to be understood, the number of players is predetermined, the equipment and playing area are standardized—each time the game is played the structure remains the same. However, the game is never played the same way twice. (If it were the pleasure of playing games would be lost!)

As players become more skillful they tend to select and concentrate on one game. Their enjoyment increases as their competency increases. To play formal games with any degree of satisfaction, the players, teammates, and opposition need levels of competency that are roughly equal. Unequal skills result in some players dominating play while others are almost left out.

As teachers of games skills, we need to understand the continuum of games playing from the simple to the complex. What follows is a brief look at the structure and demands of formal games.

We have indicated there is a progression from low-organization games to formal games and that the objective of the games program is for children to learn the fundamentals of games playing rather than isolated skills.

In 1969, a book on games in education was published in England. The book, *Games Teaching: A New Approach for the Primary School,* by E. Mauldon and B. Redfern, has had a considerable influence on the way games are understood and taught. Many of the concepts presented in this chapter were developed around their ideas.

Mauldon and Redfern put formal games into three categories according to:

1. the skills employed;
2. the playing area; and
3. the roles of the players.

By doing this, they hoped teachers would develop an appreciation of "the factors common to a number of games rather than view each game as an isolated unit" (Mauldon and Redfern 1981).

However, not all formal games will fit into these categories; therefore, we have added a fourth. The three suggested by Mauldon and Redfern are numbered 2, 3, and 4.

1. Target games
2. Net games
3. Batting games
4. Running games

Target Games These are either small team games, four players per team as in lawn bowling and curling; or individual games, where one plays against oneself and the environment, as in golf and ten-pin bowling. In these games, the scores of different players are compared and it may be the one with the lowest score (e.g., golf) or the highest score (e.g., bowling) who wins. Figure 8.2 lists common target games.

These games are often enjoyed as recreational pursuits and are played by a wide age group. Many seniors enjoy and are able to continue to play them for many years. Curlers and lawn bowlers in their 70s and 80s are not unusual.

Most of these games need special facilities and are therefore too expensive to be part of the regular school program, although some secondary schools do include them as lifetime sports for their older students.

In these games, the main skill focus is on sending away a variety of objects, ranging from an arrow approximately 55 inches (141.4 cm) long that weighs a few grams to a curling stone, 36 inches (91.44 cm) in circumference, 4.5 inches (11.43 cm) high, and weighing a maximum of 44 lbs. (19.96 kilograms) (according to the *Curling Rule Book,* Canadian Curling Association, 1979). No other category of games is so diversified as far as equipment, environment, playing area, rules, and skills are concerned.

Another characteristic of target games is the small range of body management skills. Great control is needed for sending, and, besides curling, where the players have to learn to sweep, no other specific game skills are involved.

Common Aspects		Variations
Playing area shared; players take turns.	**Playing Areas**	Great variation, ranging from 18-hole golf courses to sheets of ice, as for curling.
Same skill for all players; no interaction.	**Players' Roles**	In team games, role differentiation is strategic rather than skill-oriented (e.g., skip in curling).
Sending-away category.	**Specific Game Skills**	Great variation in skills (e.g., drive, release, deliver).
To "hit" a target.	**Offensive Strategies**	Hole—golf Button—curling Gold—archery Jack—lawn bowling
To put up obstacles to prevent opponents from hitting target.	**Defensive Strategies**	No defensive strategy in individual games; i.e., archery, 10-pin, bowling, golf.

Handwritten margin notes:
→ little if any locomotion
→ taking turns
→ defensive strategies
→ opused target game
unipozed target game
→

Figure 8.2 Target games

Examples: Archery, bowling (10-pin, lawn), curling, golf

Low-organization games based on target game concepts are very appropriate when developing the fundamental skill of sending away (illustrated in figure 8.7). Young children gain much enjoyment and satisfaction from hitting a target, especially if it is one that falls over on impact.

Goalkeeping skills found in running games (listed in figure 8.5) are developed when the target is guarded or defended. These are the beginnings of role playing and offensive and defensive strategy. Target games are used in the elementary school program as means to other ends. It is at a much later stage the children may turn to "pure" target games for recreational pleasure.

Net Games These games also include sending-away skills, all being various striking skills. The main intention in all the games is to return the object, ball, or badminton bird to the opponent or opponents. The only time the object may be held is when being put into play or served. Figure 8.3 lists aspects of net games.

— Court games
— Sending away /
* receiving category*
* " always sending "*

Common Aspects		Variations
Area divided by a net; opposing players separated.	**Playing Areas**	Squash, racquetball where area is shared; ball rebounds off wall.
All players require same skills as they rotate after a point has been scored.	**Players' Roles**	In volleyball, some specialization at elitist level of play (e.g., spikers).
Sending-away category—striking with an implement.	**Specific Game Skills**	No implement in volleyball.
Place object so that opponents are unable to return it.	**Offensive Strategies**	The size, weight, shape of the object varies from badminton bird to volleyball.
Return object and keep it "in bounds."	**Defensive Strategies**	In squash and racquetball, return ball above designated line on front wall.

Figure 8.3 Net games

Examples: Badminton, racquetball, squash, tennis, volleyball

The fundamental manipulative and nonmanipulative skills and playing concepts common to net games are:

1. hit an object to a space (body and spatial concepts)
2. cover the playing area and anticipate where the opponent(s) will send the object (relationship concept)
3. move quickly in all directions (effort and spatial concepts)
4. change direction suddenly (effort and spatial concepts)
5. strike the object at a variety of levels (in some games, the ball may bounce before it is struck [e.g., tennis, squash] in others, the object is counted out of play when it touches the ground [e.g., badminton, volleyball]) (spatial concept)
6. send the object over a net, or, in the case of squash and racquetball, make the object hit a wall above a designated line (spatial concept)
7. strike the object when close to and far away from the body (spatial concept)

Common Aspects		Variations
Area shared; offensive team has designated track to run.	**Playing Area**	Shape of running track differs for some games.
Variations in roles for defensive team (e.g., pitcher, catcher).	**Players' Roles**	
Sending-away (throwing, striking). Receiving (catch, collect).	**Specific Game Skills**	Special gloves used to receive ball in baseball and softball. In cricket, the wicketkeeper wears gloves to receive. Implements used for striking vary in shape and size.
Related to scoring runs; therefore, batting-oriented.	**Offensive Strategies**	Each team stays on offense—defense until designated number of batters have a turn.
Fielding team tries to prevent runs from being scored. Skills of receiving and sending quickly and accurately are important defensively.	**Defensive Strategies**	

often implements are involved!

Examples: Baseball, cricket, softball

Figure 8.4 Batting games *field games!*

Batting Games These games use sending-away and receiving skills. The sending-away skills are throwing and striking in different ways, the receiving skills are catching and collecting, often in combination (i.e., players intercept the ball by placing their bodies to stop it, then they pick it up and throw). Figure 8.4 lists common aspects and variations of batting games.

The games are characterized by each team having two distinct roles to play. Team *A* bats and team *B* fields; after so many players have been at bat, the teams change over. Only the batting team can score, and the fielding team tries to prevent scoring.

The fundamental skills and movement concepts common to all batting games are

1. for players at bat to
   a. strike the ball a considerable distance and to specific areas (body, effort, and spatial concepts)
   b. sprint a specific pathway, with or without stopping (body and effort concepts)
2. for players in the field to
   a. receive the ball at various levels (body and spatial concepts)
   b. throw accurately (body, effort, and spatial concepts)
   c. cover a designated area (body and spatial concepts)

Some minor role differentiation occurs when players are fielding. The catchers (baseball) and wicket-keepers (cricket) develop specialized receiving skills, while pitchers (baseball) and bowlers (cricket) develop specialized throwing skills. (Note: When bowling, the wrist action is restricted and the action is not considered to be a throw. In the categorization system used here it is considered to be a throw, as the bowler has possession of the ball.) All other players use the same skills, even though there are specific positions when fielding.

Batting games were originally played outdoors, and all need comparatively large areas. Boundaries may vary according to the space available but the running track for the batters is standardized.

Running Games These energetic games include all three categories of manipulative skills: sending away, receiving and retaining, and traveling. Historically, all except basketball were played outside but now there are indoor versions of several of them. Figure 8.5 lists common aspects and variations of running games.

The fundamental skills and movement concepts of running games are to:

1. run a considerable distance at speed with and without the games object (body and effort concepts)
2. swerve, dodge, fake to avoid opposing players (body, effort, and relationship concepts)
3. guard an opposing player (relationship concept)
4. guard/protect a space (body and spatial concepts)
5. change swiftly from offensive to defensive play (relationship concept)
6. intercept the game object (body, spatial, and relationship concepts)

Common Aspects		Variations
Rectangular, mostly outdoors, with standardized boundaries. Area shared by all players.	**Playing Areas**	Great variation in size of area, shape, size and position of goals, shape of implements and balls.
Designated goalkeeper, other players need same skills; gradual emergence of offensive and defensive players.	**Players' Roles**	Football has many specific roles requiring specialized skills.
Sending-away (throwing, striking). Receiving (catching, collecting). Traveling (carrying, propelling).	**Specific Game Skills**	In hockey, the running has become skating.
To hit, carry, throw ball into specified area, goal, basket, or end-zone.	**Offensive Strategies**	Rapid and frequent shifts from offensive to defensive play (except in football).
Intercept ball/puck before it goes into goal or over line.	**Defensive Strategies**	

Figure 8.5 Running games

Most of these games need a large number of players, the smallest being basketball which has ten players in action. In contrast there are 30 rugby players on a field at one time. Considerable understanding of and skill in playing cooperative and competitive roles are needed.

Strategy can become very complicated and the players have to be able to pay attention to numerous simultaneous happenings, sifting out the relevant from the irrelevant and making split second decisions. The players' intellects and memories are involved when practiced patterns and sequences are put into play. For these reasons alone, formal running games are more suitable for the more mature students.

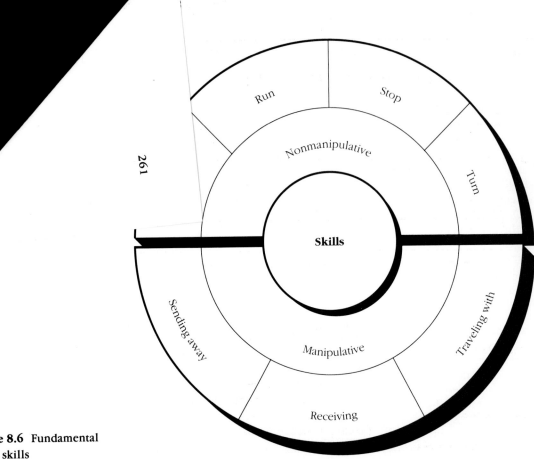

Skills

Nonmanipulative

Run

Stop

Turn

Manipulative

Sending away

Receiving

Traveling with

Figure 8.6 Fundamental games skills

Children in elementary school play their own versions of running games and are adept at modifying the demands of the formal game to meet their own capabilities. Improvised equipment is often used and, regardless of how many players there are, there is often a goalkeeper. Children see that as a very important role and we suggest that they all learn some of the skills specific to it. Goalkeeping skills should be developed alongside the other fundamental skills of games playing and all children should have a turn playing that role.

The Material of Games

The games program differs considerably from dance and gymnastics programs in that a major focus is on developing a variety of manipulative skills. However, these can be used successfully only if the players have control over their nonmanipulative or general body management skills. Figure 8.6 shows these fundamental games skills.

To Do

List the nonmanipulative skills that players need for the following games:

   a. baseball
   b. tennis
   c. hockey

Table 8.3

Nonmanipulative skills

Body Concepts	Actions—bending, stretching, twisting
	Activities—run, jump, turn, stop
	Shapes—changing from stretched to curled, to wide to twisted
	Parts—recognition of the roles played by different parts during activity
Effort Concepts	Time—changes of speed, suddenness, fast
	Weight—resiliency
	Space—direct and flexible
	Flow—control, continuity, go and stop
Spatial Concepts	Changes in direction, extension
	Traveling different pathways
Relationship Concepts	To team members, opposition, boundaries, goals

Nonmanipulative and manipulative skills can be practiced separately in the early stages of learning but should be integrated as soon as a reasonable degree of competency is achieved. Lessons may begin with practicing individual or combined nonmanipulative skills, followed by integrating them with manipulative skills.

Nonmanipulative Skills

Observation of skilled games players reveals they have excellent nonmanipulative skills. They can dodge out of another player's way, turn quickly to run in a different direction, run fast into open spaces, stop suddenly. These players can skillfully integrate nonmanipulative and manipulative skills such as jumping to catch a ball, dribbling a ball in the playing area, or turning to throw a ball.

Body Concepts

The fundamental vocabulary (listed in table 8.3) is small. As selected movement concepts are added, the vocabulary becomes diverse and yet more specialized (e.g., run becomes swerve, break, dodge).

REMEMBER THAT

Direction is in relation to the body (personal space). **Pathways** are related to where you travel (general space).

Therefore, you can travel **sideways, backward, forward** in a **circular, straight, zigzag,** or **angular** pathway.

Effort Concepts

Activities All games players need to be able to run, jump, turn, and stop. Sequences such as running-jumping with a turn, and running-stopping—turning, help develop skillful body management, especially when a "surprise" element is introduced, perhaps by the teacher signalling (a whistle?) to indicate a change of activity.

Shape Players need to be able to change their body shape according to the role they are playing. When on the offense, players may need to travel through small spaces, and thus may need to narrow the body (elongated shape). In contrast, defensive players broaden the body to block an opponent (wide shape). When jumping to receive a ball, the player with the most elongated shape is often the one who reaches it first. In games that involve a lot of running (basketball, lacrosse, soccer), players may have to twist as they run and avoid other players (dodge), and they may also twist as they prepare to receive or throw the ball.

Body Parts The hands and arms become very important when facing and shadowing an oncoming opponent; the head is important when faking and dodging; the shift of weight from one foot to the other is facilitated by movement initiated by the upper body. It is when all parts work harmoniously that efficiency and control result.

All functional movements involve very complicated effort changes, and it is the ability to combine appropriate effort elements that produces efficiency. The children need to be able to produce the right amount of each element at the right moment. What follows is a simplified analysis of the effort content of the fundamental nonmanipulative skills.

Weight Most games activities require firmness rather than fine touch and it is the interplay between increase and decrease in tension (muscle power) that produces the power and resiliency for running, jumping, stopping, and turning.

Time Different games have different time elements. Some are played at a constant pace (basketball, hockey), others have bursts of speed followed by a rest (badminton, squash, tennis, volleyball), or fluctuations of speed (soccer). Fundamental to all games is the ability to move suddenly, change speed, and maintain a certain speed.

Space Flexible movements assist all activities requiring a change of direction, so turning and twisting are assisted by the flexibility of body parts initiating the action. Other skills are helped by a more direct movement quality, such as when planting a foot in preparation for a jump.

Flow Functional movement tends toward bound flow, and efficient movement is often termed "controlled," which means it is predictable.

Free flow activities tend to be unpredictable as they are ongoing and "unstoppable." Players who collide with others, fall over, and generally appear uncontrolled in their actions may require help with binding the flow of their activities.

Flow may also refer to continuity of action, and in order to produce continuity, the action must be under control or bound to a degree. It is the interplay between withholding and freeing the movement that results in control.

Considerable emphasis should be placed on this concept as all strategic decisions require spatial knowledge and skill. Understanding of space is fundamental to games playing.

Spatial Concepts

General Space The general space is usually defined by boundaries. The players have to be able to move efficiently within this restricted area, finding and creating spaces.

Pathways Many different pathways are traveled as players move around the playing area. In games such as softball and football, some pathways are predetermined and time is spent running and rerunning precise patterns. In other games the pathways are determined by where the other players are in the designated area.

Children should learn to run zigzag, hairpin, curving, right-angled, and other pathways. It may help to have markers for the children to run around. As proficiency increases, remove the markers.

Extensions The pathways will vary in size. A small zigzag pattern may result in swerving around a defender; an uneven hairpin (one long arm and one short) may create a space and free the player to receive a pass. Being able to decide what size pathway to run is one of the fundamental skills.

Personal Space Skillful use of personal space is demonstrated magnificently by the Harlem Globetrotters. As they play basketball, the players swerve to avoid others, run backward as well as forward and sideways, and change direction at a moment's notice without the opposition realizing what is happening. The members of the opposing team are "teased" and often seem to end up running chaotically in the playing area.

Directions All games players need to be able to run in different directions. In the personal space this means being able to run forward, backward, and sideways, changing from one direction to another. If you hear the phrase "good footwork" used to describe a player, it implies the ability to run and change direction swiftly. Each game has its own specific footwork demands and you must be able to determine what they

---

To Do

Play tag in twos, gradually reducing the space in which you run. How does your running change? Does anything else change?

▼▼▼▼   ▼

are. Compare, for example, the footwork required when playing games in small areas, such as badminton, with those in large spaces, such as soccer. Compare games that require the players' feet to be "in bounds" when receiving a ball, such as football and basketball, with games like tennis and volleyball.

Extensions Good footwork is also being able to change the size of your running steps. It is only when the feet are in contact with the floor that the force can be produced for stopping and changing direction. Small steps are required when increasing and decreasing speed, changing direction, and stopping. When running at a constant speed, steps are usually larger.

Relationships

Figure 2.11 introduced the concept of relationships to games playing. The games environment consists of people and objects that are both moving and static. It is the interaction between the objects and the players that makes each game, and all strategic decisions are made in relation to these objects and people.

Objects Nonmanipulated objects are the boundaries, zones, and targets needed for the game being played. Many chasing games, such as "What's the time, Mr. Wolf?" and "Crusts and Crumbs" have zones designated as being "safe," and it is by playing such games that children begin to learn about boundaries. Boundaries may also indicate certain zones of the playing space that are reserved for a particular aspect of a game, such as the service zone in tennis, for example. There is a close connection between boundaries, rules, and the beginning of strategy.

Targets are part of the games environment, but because they are so closely allied with manipulative skills, they will be discussed in that part of the chapter.

People Two different relationships arise with people when playing games, *cooperative* and *competitive*.

Cooperative Relationships These are relationships in which a group (a minimum of two people) works together to achieve a *common* objective. To do this, the group members may play similar or very different roles. Words used when referring to cooperative relationships are: with, partner, or team.

Games in which the players have similar roles include volleyball and tennis; games in which players have different roles include football and baseball.

Each member has to be aware of all the other players all the time. The more participants there are in the group, the more complex the situation and the greater the demand on each member.

To make the group "work" means having to watch carefully, adjust speed, change direction, anticipate, modify decisions, and sometimes lead and sometimes follow. Challenging tasks can be set to help children understand how to make a group "work." Two examples are given:

1. Groups of three to five children hold hands and form a line. One end of the line (the head) is the leader, who runs with the group around the space in such a way that the chain remains intact. This sounds very easy but children who are still mostly egocentric find it difficult to lead and be sensitive to the speed at which the others can run. The more curvy the pathway chosen, the harder it becomes to remain intact, as a whiplike effect arises for the "tail."

2. Groups are formed as above, running in the space. On a given signal the "tail" of the line becomes the leader, i.e., the group focus shifts from one end of the line to the other. This demands a major group adjustment if the line is to remain intact!

Competitive Relationships In this situation, the participants try to achieve *opposing* objectives, and, therefore, play different roles. In a simple situation such as one-on-one tag, participant *A* tries to avoid being touched by *B,* and simultaneously participant *B* is trying to touch *A.* The running skills each employs are similar, but they are used to achieve different results. Words that are used when referring to competitive relationships are: against, opponent, or opposition.

There are many group chasing games that provide plenty of practice for fundamental footwork skills (dodging, swerving, faking) and the beginnings of offensive and defensive strategy. These skills can be developed only if the players assume the roles that arise from competition, as in "you against me."

Examples of group chasing games are "What's the time, Mr. Wolf?" and "Crusts and Crumbs."

In these games the groups are not teams—the players are independent of each other. They have to be able to keep out of one another's way when trying to escape being tagged, but that is the only cooperative skill needed.

Tag games that begin to include a degree of cooperation are the tag and release variety. The "free" players have to judge when it is a good time to release a team member and therefore have to be able to assess

Table 8.4

▼▼▼▼   ▼

Progressions for developing cooperative and competitive skills

Relationship	Example
Stage 1: alone	
Alone	Running and stopping on signal
Alone in a group	Avoiding being caught in a group tag game
1 vs. group	Being the catcher in a group tag game
Stage 2: in twos	
With a partner (cooperation)	Holding hands, running, and changing the leader on signal
	Throwing and catching
1 vs. 1 (competition)	Tag
	Child *A* kicks ball at designated target (e.g., a pylon); child *B* defends target, using any body part to stop the ball
Stage 3: in threes	
Group (cooperation)	Keep the ball in the air (volley) using hands
2 vs. 1 (cooperation and competition)	"Monkey in the middle"
Stage 4: in fours	
3 vs. 1 (cooperation and competition)	Child *A* defends a designated goal; other players pass and shoot
2 vs. 2 (cooperation and competition)	Keep-away-type games, tennis-like games
Stage 5: in sixes	
3 vs. 3 (cooperation and competition)	Keep-away games
	Volleyball-like games
Stage 6: in eights	
4 vs. 4	
Stage 7: in tens	
5 vs. 5	

▼▼▼▼   ▼

where the taggers are and act accordingly. Elementary strategy is employed, both offensive and defensive, and the children should be helped to understand these fundamental elements of games playing. These games can be played with varying degrees of skill and many children find them challenging, satisfying, and fun.

Table 8.4 suggests progressions for developing cooperative and competitive skills, integrating the nonmanipulative and manipulative skills of games playing. As soon as stage 3 has been reached, cooperative and competitive skills are always present and the playing situations become more similar to formal games.

Table 8.5

Grade level and group size

Grade	Stages						
	1	2	3	4	5	6	7
K	*	*					
1	*	*	*				
2		*	*				
3		*	*	*			
4		*	*	*			
5		*	*	*	*		
6		*	*	*	*	*	*

When stage 3 has been reached, gradually increase the group size so that the players have the challenge of relating to more team members and more opponents. By the time the children have reached grade 6, they may be playing in groups of ten (five against five). Table 8.5 suggests the progression in terms of grade levels.

Manipulative Skills

These fall into categories (listed in figure 8.6) determined by our intentions as we relate to the game object involved, which is usually a ball of some kind (Mauldon and Redfern 1981). We have three broad options:

1. Get rid of the object—*sending-away skills*
2. Gain control of the object—*receiving skills*
3. Retain and take it with us—*traveling and propelling skills*

Within each category there are two subdivisions, as follows:

Sending-away skills:
   a. throwing
   b. striking
Receiving skills:
   a. catching
   b. collecting
Traveling skills:
   a. carrying
   b. propelling

In subdivision *a,* the object is held in some way; it becomes part of the player. In subdivision *b,* the object remains separate from the player, who has to be able to "find" it in the space.

Table 8.6

▼▼▼▼   ▼

Manipulative skills

Body Concepts	Activities—sending away an object receiving an object retaining and traveling with an object
	Shapes—awareness of shape during the activity
	Parts—awareness of different parts used during the activity
Effort Concepts	Weight—variations in strength required to send, receive, retain, and propel the object
	Time—timing of contact/release of object speed of arm/leg swing
	Space—direct/flexible use of arm/leg during activity
	Flow—change from going to stopping; continuity; control
Spatial Concepts	Judgment of distances; height and size of targets, sending/receiving objects from different directions, retaining and traveling different pathways, sending/receiving at different levels
Relationship Concepts	To other players, team members, and opposition To implements and/or balls To targets

▼▼▼▼   ▼

Attention to specific movement concepts increases skill efficiency and versatility. For each group, there are fundamental components, which must be the focus of the earliest learning experiences. It is through a variety of tasks and the use of different implements (bats, sticks) and objects (beanbags, balls, Frisbees) that efficient, fundamental manipulative skills (listed in detail in table 8.6) are developed. The development of this kind of generalized games vocabulary equips the children for specialization in the upper elementary grades and in the secondary school.

Body Concepts

In all manipulative skills the body is being used as a tool that controls an object in a variety of ways. The object may become "part" of the body for a short period of time or it may remain separate from the body.

Activities Each category of manipulative skills has its own vocabulary. Children soon learn the terms for the skills found in the games related to their culture. During the baseball season in North America, children talk about pitching. The comparable game in Australia and England is cricket, and the children talk about bowling.

Wide shapes are often used
in defensive patterns.

Long, arrow-like shapes
pierce the air.

To Do

For each category of manipulative skills, list verbs that are variations of the same skill (e.g., throw, pitch, and bowl are all forms of throwing).

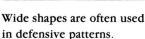

Shape Changes in body shape occur when catching an object and absorbing its impact. The body curves as the limbs move toward the center of the body. Rounding of the body also happens when trying to protect the object from other players.

Goalkeepers have to be able to make very quick changes of body shape to block off the space they are defending. When goal spaces are comparatively small, as in hockey and European handball, wide and rounded shapes are most often used. Defending a soccer goal also requires elongated shapes as the goalkeeper strives to catch or tip the ball over the top of the goal.

To Do

Observe a skilled outfielder in a baseball game and a receiver in football.

Notice the continuity of action as the players

1. prepare to receive the ball
2. receive it; then either
3. throw it to a base player or
4. run across the goal line

▼▼▼▼▼   ▼

Body Parts The most obvious body parts used to manipulate objects are hands and feet. While other parts may block or stop oncoming objects, the hands or feet are then used to pick up the object, or throw it, or kick it away. Soccer players, for example, can block the pathway of a ball with any part of their body except their hands, and then kick the ball to another player. Only the goalkeepers may use their hands.

Lessons should include tasks that give experience in using different parts of the hands and feet to control objects when sending, receiving, and traveling with them.

The addition of implements such as bats and sticks increases the complexity of the skill. The implements become extensions of the hands and attention has to be paid to how to grip these implements.

Effort Concepts

Weight Variations in strength are needed when controlling objects. Tasks that challenge the children to throw different distances, receive fast-moving objects, and run at different speeds while keeping an object close to the body all demand being able to adjust the amount of force produced.

Time Timing is important: knowing when to release the ball, swing the bat, "give" with the hands. A second aspect of time, perhaps the more obvious one, is the *speed* of action. How fast should the arm move when throwing, or the bat swing when hitting? Efficient movement has a rhythm of execution, which can be seen when watching good players. Try to repeat the pattern. The rhythms will be nonmetric and no two players will move with the same rhythm or tempo.

Coordination problems include mistiming actions. Children can be helped to develop a sense of "when" by beginning with slow movements, which allow more time for them to react to what they see. When trying to kick a ball, for example, begin with the ball stationary so that the chances of success are high. Then roll the ball slowly toward the child. Gradually increase the speed at which the ball travels, all the time reinforcing the idea of the "feel" of the pattern.

Flow One aspect of efficient action is being able to combine several skills, or repeat the same skill in fluid succession. This can only be done when movement is controlled and the players anticipate the sequence of events.

Tasks that challenge children to

1. strike a ball continuously against a wall (use a paddle bat and 4-inch plastic ball) or
2. roll a ball against the wall so that it rebounds to a partner, who collects it and throws it back,

are examples of tasks requiring control of the flow factor and anticipation. The end of one action becomes the preparation for the following action.

Considerable spatial judgment, both general and personal, is required when playing games. Many spatial words are used when tactics are discussed, which happens as soon as the children begin playing in groups and the learning focus is on games playing rather than isolated skills. Questions such as, "Who is in a free space and ready to receive the ball?", "Who is closer to you?", and "Which way do you think the opponent will go?", help the children understand the factors that have to be considered when making strategic decisions.

Spatial Concepts

General Space The spatial concepts discussed below relate to specific manipulative skills, not games playing. As soon as the children use these manipulative skills in a playing situation, the tactical aspects have to be added.

Floor Pathways Carrying and propelling skills imply that the players are traveling, combining running, turning, and stopping. Being able to travel different pathways with and without an object is a fundamental skill of games playing. It has been introduced in the section on non-manipulative skills (page 263) and also on page 265.

Air Pathways Objects that are thrown or struck make pathways as they travel through the air. Objects thrown or hit with equal amounts of force will travel along different pathways according to the position of the hand or implement when the object is released or struck. The pathway affects the distance an object will travel. Children need to experiment with "early" and "late" moments of release, and to discover what happens to the object. Some young children seem to generate considerable power when "winding up" to throw . . . only to have the ball land near their feet! This is because they hold on to it too long and the angle of release is wrong. When striking a ball, it is the angle of contact between the object and the implement that determines the pathway.

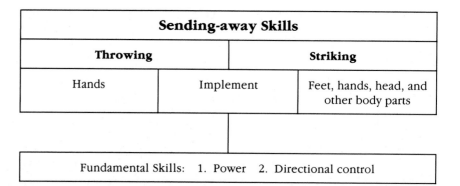

Sending-away Skills		
Throwing		**Striking**
Hands	Implement	Feet, hands, head, and other body parts

Fundamental Skills: 1. Power   2. Directional control

Figure 8.7 Sending-away skills

Personal Space In some games the players have to be able to receive objects coming to them from the front, the side, and sometimes from behind the body. The body may have to twist so that hands, feet, or implement are placed in direct line with the approaching object.

The player to whom an object is being sent may be in front of, at the side of, or even behind the sender, and again the body may have to twist. Tasks with such challenges have to be included.

Extensions This concept is about how near to or far from the body the object is. We sometimes have to reach out to catch a ball. Watch basketball and football players reach up to intercept balls intended for another player. Notice, too, how quickly they bring the ball close to the body to protect it from other players. When practicing soccer or basketball dribbling, the closeness to the body will change as the speed changes.

"Throw the ball so that your partner has to reach to the side to catch it." "In threes, *A* throws to *B*; *C* tries to intercept." These are examples of tasks related to the concept of extensions.

Levels Players have to be ready and able to receive objects at different levels. Even in games where the object, usually a puck or ball, is played on the ground (low level) for most of the time, the players may be required to deal with a rising object. In baseball and basketball, considerable versatility in coping with balls at different levels is required.

Sending-away Skills

This is the first group of skills that children learn. The beginning stages are seen at an early age, as the grasp reflex becomes inhibited. (Everyone has probably been with a child who persistently drops a toy!) There is little "sending" in the action; that comes later.

Design tasks for your lessons that help the children develop the fundamental skills of producing the right amount of force to send the object the required distance, plus the positioning to send it to the desired place (see figure 8.7).

Target practice.

Targets of some kind are essential. There is no game situation where the object is intentionally thrown haphazardly! Targets may be markings on a wall, wastepaper baskets, hoops, partners; they may be still or moving, high or low, horizontal or vertical. Children can monitor their own achievements because there is instant feetback—the object either hit or missed the target. This may help them modify their actions as well as set their own challenges.

The two ways of sending away objects are:

1. **throwing,** using hands or an implement (such as a scoop)
2. **striking,** with hands, feet, head, or implement

Table 8.7 suggests the components of a learning program from which tasks can be developed with specific objectives. Variety is stressed so that the children develop versatility and an understanding of the fundamental skills related to all sending-away skills. Through this generalized approach we also hope they maintain open minds toward games playing.

The smaller the child, the bigger the bat.

Table 8.7

▼▼▼▼   ▼

Sending-away skills

Throwing	Striking
Hands	Specified body parts (hands, head, feet)
Implements:* Scoops Lacrosse sticks	Bats: long, short, flat, rounded (table tennis) Sticks: broom handles, hockey sticks, field hockey sticks, small golf clubs Racquets: badminton, racquetball, squash, tennis
Objects:* Whiffle balls Frisbees Rubber rings Beanbags Playground balls Nerf balls Fluff balls	Fluff balls Nerf balls Whiffle balls Shuttlecocks Playground balls Tennis balls Beach balls

Setting: Air—self receive
               partner receive
               small group activity

      Against wall—self receive
                   partner receive
                   small group cooperative activity

          To specific targets—unguarded
                      guarded

Hit off batting tee or other support.

Vary size, weight, shape, texture, and color.

▼▼▼▼   ▼

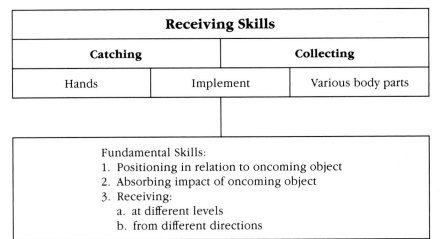

Receiving Skills		
Catching		**Collecting**
Hands	Implement	Various body parts

Fundamental Skills:
1. Positioning in relation to oncoming object
2. Absorbing impact of oncoming object
3. Receiving:
   a. at different levels
   b. from different directions

Figure 8.8 Receiving skills

Variety also allows for greater chances of success. It is important to give the children opportunities to select their own equipment. Some will choose equipment with which they have previously been successful, others will experiment with new combinations. Both situations are important aspects of the learning process.

There are many different kinds of implements available in toy shops as well as through sports manufacturers and suppliers, some of whom specialize in equipment that is appropriate in weight and size for children. At no time should seven-year-olds be struggling with a regulation baseball bat when a fatter plastic one would provide them with success and enjoyment.

These skills are soon linked with sending skills and the two become inseparable. Children begin to play "toss and catch" alone or in small groups and we should recognize the importance of combining the two skills early in the program.

Receiving Skills

The fundamental aspects of receiving skills are: being in the right place at the right time, and being able to absorb or cushion the impact of the object as it arrives (see figure 8.8).

The teacher should design tasks that develop a sense of positioning in relation to objects moving in the air and on the floor. Initially the children send and receive on their own by tossing the object (such as beanbag or ball) into the air or against a wall and then moving to catch it. When they do this, their success depends on themselves, rather than on the throwing expertise of a friend. As with sending-away skills, there is instant feedback, which helps maintain motivation. However, if any children are unsuccessful more often than successful, intervene quickly and change the conditions, e.g., increase the size of the object. It is most important that the children wish to remain on task.

Table 8.8

▼▼▼▼   ▼

Receiving skills

Catching	Collecting
Hands	Specified body parts
Implements:* Scoops	Sticks: Ice hockey
Fielder's mitts	Field hockey
Lacrosse sticks	Broom handles
Objects:* Frisbees	Beanbags
Rubber rings	Rubber rings
Beanbags	Playground balls
Playground balls	Whiffle balls
Nerf balls	Tennis balls
Fluff balls	Solid rubber balls
	Pucks

Setting: Air—Self-send and receive
        Partner send and receive
        Small group activity sending and receiving

Rebounding off wall, ground—self
                partner
                small group activity

Skill variations: Use dominant/nondominant side of body when
      standing
      kneeling
      running
      jumping
      diving/sliding

      Receive at different levels from different directions
        in front
        behind
        the side

      Receive when object travels toward/away from, with varying
        extensions:
        near to the body
        far from the body

      Receive fast/slow oncoming object; judge speed

      Add obstruction (e.g., opponent)

      Change implement and/or object

      Receive objects traveling different trajectories (straight, curved)

      Receive thrown/struck object

      Intercept an object sent to another player

*Vary size, weight, shape, texture, and color of objects and implements.

▼▼▼▼   ▼

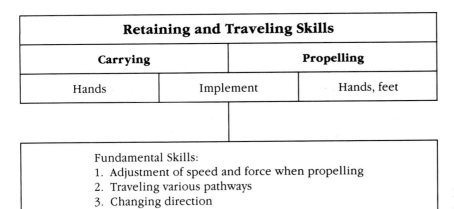

Retaining and Traveling Skills		
Carrying		**Propelling**
Hands	Implement	Hands, feet

Fundamental Skills:
1. Adjustment of speed and force when propelling
2. Traveling various pathways
3. Changing direction

Figure 8.9 Retaining and traveling skills

The two ways of receiving an object are:

1. **catching** it as it travels through the air, either before or after it rebounds off the ground or wall (or even off another player, as happens in basketball and football).
2. **trapping, collecting,** or **blocking** the ball as it travels along the ground (toward and away from the body) or through the air.

Table 8.8 suggests the components of a receiving skills learning program. Again, variety is essential when designing tasks so that the children become versatile and understand the fundamental skills.

When children show some competency at catching and using different parts of their bodies to block oncoming objects, the tasks should require them to travel to meet the ball. The use of a stick to receive the object increases the difficulty; it has already been mentioned that the size and weight of implements must be suitable for the children.

These skills (see figure 8.9) are often the link between receiving and sending skills. In some games, the sequence of events is receive—travel—send. In others the sequence is receive—travel, such as football, because one way of scoring is to carry the object over a line.

Retaining and Traveling Skills

The two ways of traveling with an object are:

1. **carrying** the object, with hands or an implement
2. **propelling** the object

Carrying an object requires being able to hold it firmly and shift it from one side of the body to the other according to where the opponent is. Tag situations, in which the player with the object tries to avoid being caught by swerving or passing the object to another player, are examples of learning experiences.

Negotiating uneven spaces.

More time is spent on propelling skills because games requiring this are more common in our society.

The fundamental skill components of propelling balls, whether with hands, feet, or an implement, include being able to

1. produce the appropriate amount of force to propel the ball and yet keep it reasonably close to the body ("under control");
2. adjust the running speed in relation to the moving ball.

Beginning tasks should focus on adjusting to the implement and/or object being used. Pay little attention to where the children are going beyond reminding them to avoid other people. When watching less-skilled children, notice how they either overrun the ball or send it too far ahead and temporarily "lose it." The secret is to be able to keep the ball close enough to the body so that no one else can get it and be able to travel at various speeds throughout the playing area.

Attention to changing direction and traveling different pathways entails taking the eyes off the object, lifting the head, and looking around the space. As skill increases, the children should be able to look at where they are going more and at the object less. "Heads up as you travel" is a useful refining task to include in learning sequences. As skill increases, children can be helped to use peripheral vision to monitor the object, other players, and the general space simultaneously—no easy achievement!

Various pathways to travel can be designed by using highway markers (pylons) to show the route; spaces may be even or uneven.

Table 8.9 lists other aspects of a learning program designed to develop the fundamentals of and versatility in retaining and traveling skills.

Table 8.9

Retaining and traveling skills

Retaining	Traveling
Hands, feet	Hands
Implements:* Broom handles Hockey Field hockey	Scoops Lacrosse sticks
Objects:* Hoops Nerf balls Tennis balls Solid rubber balls Playground balls Plastic soccer balls Mini-basket balls	Nerf balls Tennis balls Solid rubber balls Plastic footballs Whiffle balls
Setting: In open space Around, between obstacles Stationary: pylons beanbags hoops Moving: people	
Skill Variations: Use dominant/nondominant hand/foot Alternate between dominant/nondominant feet/hands Change grip on implement when walking/running/being chased Add a "chaser" who tries to touch the object	

*Vary size, weight, texture, and color of objects.

It is possible to devise many interesting traveling and propelling tasks that encourage the development of the fundamental skills leading to manipulative control.

Some tag games, used in the development of nonmanipulative skills and the introduction of roles in games playing, can be adapted to include traveling and propelling skills. These games give children game-like experiences that encourage good footwork, which is an essential aspect of this group of skills.

Summary

Games are exciting, complex activities. A wide range of skills is required by all children so that they can make informed choices about which games they wish to play in a recreational setting. We advocate teaching variety to children from the beginning of the educational experience with games. Remember, it is games knowledge and competency in the widest sense that are the basis of an educational program.

The playing of games requires that the players be able to make motor adjustments as they interact with other players, game conditions and games equipment (Morris 1980).

Children may choose to attend an afterschool program that focuses on a specific game. The community and sports associations may also provide training opportunities for a child interested in becoming, for example, a tennis player. The desire to become involved in such a program, which may make great demands on a young child's free time, should be a result of an enjoyable educational experience in school.

Review Questions

1. Differentiate between sport and games.
2. What is the relationship between low-organization, lead-up, and formal games? How does the emphasis on these games change throughout the school years?
3. What is meant by "fundamental games knowledge"?
4. Name the three categories of manipulative skills that form the basic vocabulary for games playing.
5. What are the four categories of formal games? What factors determine these categories?
6. What games situations can you think of that require considerable change(s) in body shape?

References

Bunker, D. and R. Thorpe. 1982. A Model for the Teaching of Games in Secondary Schools. *Bulletin of Physical Education.* 18:1, 5–8.

Mauldon, E. and B. Redfern. 1981. *Games Teaching,* 2d. ed. London: Macdonald and Evans, Ltd.

Morris, G. 1980. *How to Change the Games Children Play,* 2d ed. Minneapolis: Burgess Publishing Co.

Piggott, B. 1982. A Psychological Basis for New Trends in Games Teaching. *Bulletin of Physical Education.* 18:1, 17–22.

Saunders, E. 1969. Some Sociological Aspects of Rugby Union Football. *Physical Education Journal.* 61:182.

Stanley, S. 1977. *Physical Education: A Movement Orientation,* 2d. ed. Toronto: McGraw-Hill Ryerson Ltd.

CHAPTER

TEACHING
GAMES

Playing games is an important aspect of our lifestyle. Skilled games players are valued in our society, as can be seen by the high salaries paid to professional athletes and the correspondingly high ticket prices we pay to watch baseball, football, hockey, tennis, and other sporting events. At an early age, many children have a favorite team game and are familiar with the skills and rules of this game. These children are often "hungry" for games skills and opportunities to play.

School programs often place a greater emphasis on games than on dance and gymnastics. If our backgrounds are stronger in this area, we may feel more confident when teaching. The material of games is concrete; most games have specific forms; the products are easy to understand and there is comparatively little freedom for individual variation of response: these factors also contribute to our feeling of confidence.

Some teachers feel games lessons are comparatively easy to teach, since "unlike dance and gymnastics games are self-propelling. Once students grasp the basic concepts of a game, they require little intervention" (Graham et al. 1980).

Learning to play games well requires more than having the opportunity to play. Our task is no different from that in dance and gymnastics, as we still have the responsibilities of designing the appropriate learning sequences, observing individual progress, and providing feedback so that all children "reach their full potential as skillful games players" (Logsdon et al. 1984). As for other movement forms, this is a large mandate. It means meeting the needs of everyone who comes to our lessons, "the gifted and talented, the slow learner, the less mature, the handicapped, the motivated, the disinterested and the average" (Logsdon et al. 1984). The big advantage when teaching games lessons is that many children come with more knowledge and personal experience.

Myths About Games Experiences

Games have been taught for many years because of their educational value: sportsmanship, honesty, conformity, loyalty, coping with defeat, as well as graciously and humbly accepting the laurels of success. Experience has led us to examine some of these tenets and to question the hidden curriculum that accompanies the teaching of games in school programs.

> What the relationship is between rules in games and moral rules and principles of everyday life is a complex aspect of what is itself a highly controversial matter, namely how morality—and hence moral education—is to be characterized (Mauldon and Redfern 1981).

The implied transfer of training does not occur. Because we may obey a referee it does not follow that we will obey the law of the land. Notice how some professional athletes respond to referees. Willingly? Courteously?

To Do

In small groups, recall your own experiences in elementary school. List the kinds of activities you did and then find out what percentage of your learning experience has been games-oriented.

As an educator, how do you feel about an imbalance between the three movement forms?

▼▼▼▼   ▼

To Do

1. Discuss with a friend what you learned from playing games in school.
2. Has acquiring games skills/learning games influenced your behavior as a member of society as a whole?
3. Read chapters 1 and 2 in Mauldon's and Redfern's book *Games Teaching* (1981, London: Macdonald and Evans, Ltd.) and compare your discussion with their ideas.

▼▼▼▼   ▼

Teaching Skills

A variety of skills is needed to teach games and many of them are discussed in chapters 3 and 6.

Here we wish to emphasize some skills that relate more specifically to the teaching of games.

Movement and Positioning

Games are often taught in large spaces and so we must be able to move swiftly from one area to another, visiting the various groups of students as they practice and play. When children are spread out—and one of the joys of being outside is using the large space—walk briskly or jog between groups (the exercise will be beneficial too!).

When teaching outside, we can help the whole class attend to what we are saying and/or showing by positioning ourselves so that we face the sunshine. We want the children to see us clearly as we talk to them and maybe demonstrate an aspect of the task.

Young children are easily distracted. When playing in an area shared with other children, or an area with a street running alongside, they may be more interested in watching the others or the cars than in the task. If possible, place them with their backs to any distraction and make sure that, when you speak to them, you face the distraction. If something exciting happens on the street (a fire engine races by, for example), it is better to allow the children to look and talk about it rather than attempt to ignore it. The children's curiosity will be satisfied and they will be more willing to return to the lesson.

Vocabulary

REMEMBER THAT

In large spaces,

1. *the combination of a whistle and clear gestures can be very effective,*
2. *there will be more occasions to bring the children in close to you when you wish to provide public feedback and/or give a new task.*

Whistles and Gestures

There is a specific vocabulary related to the playing of games. We should know and use the correct terminology. There are many words that mean to hit a ball, for example, bat, kick, tap, volley, putt, punt, bunt, strike. Variations in meaning may be subtle and children may need help to discriminate between them. The following situation illustrates the confusion that can result from the use of nonspecific words: third-grade children were playing in twos, each pair with a 7-inch playground ball. The task was to use their feet to send the ball to their partner. The children were fairly close together so strength was not a factor. The teacher told the children, "Pass the ball to your partner." All of the children kicked the ball; some used too much strength and the ball went far beyond their partners. The teacher stopped the class and said, "Pass the ball, don't kick it." This had little effect on performance.

When we wish to refine the children's skills, we must be able to state the specific modification unambiguously so that the children know what is expected from them. If there is a choice of response involved, "pass the ball" may be correct; the children have the freedom to kick, bounce, throw, or employ any other sending-away skill. We must decide very carefully what responses are acceptable and how open the task is, and then word the task so that the children know the amount of freedom they have.

Teaching games demands much from our voices. Many of the activities are inherently noisy (e.g., balls bouncing on a hard floor), while others are played in spaces with poor acoustics (e.g., large gymnasia, or the outdoors). Some of us have a hard time making ourselves heard. Two tools we can use to supplement our voices are whistles and gestures.

A good whistle is an essential piece of equipment and skillful use of it is a great asset when teaching games. Learn to use it sparingly and appropriately. Like any instrument, there is a technique involved and this means practice is needed. Always take a deep breath before blowing and control the expiration by using the tip of your tongue against the roof of your mouth.

To Do

Based on the above situation:

1. What did the teacher wish to change?
2. Phrase the refining task so the children would have known how to modify their response.

Of course, a whistle is often required when games are refereed; indeed, you will need several whistles when the children are learning to play the role of referee. Our discussion here is centered on using a whistle to help us communicate, rather than arbitrate.

Establish a system of signals gradually, beginning the first time you teach games activities to a class. A single, short, sharp blast usually means "stop immediately"—this is probably the most important signal to establish. Two or three quick, short blasts may mean "come here." You can play "how quickly can you run to me" with kindergarten and first-grade children, praising the children who respond immediately to the sound. With older children, use the same signal several times in a lesson, praising the children when they respond quickly.

It is important not to overuse the whistle and yet have distinct signals for different responses. Children become confused when the same signal means "stop" and "go."

Gestures and mimetic actions can be used effectively to communicate ideas when outside or in a large gymnasium. If, for example, you wish the children to change from tossing and catching a ball to bouncing it at a low level, attract their attention (whistle?) and mime or demonstrate the action—no words are needed. If you wish them to run to you, use large beckoning gestures and run in place. The children may be able to help you create your own gesture vocabulary.

A considerable amount of equipment is often required for games lessons and you must plan ahead how the children will manage it. Storing balls, beanbags, ropes, etc., in portable boxes facilitates the carrying of equipment from one area to another.

REMEMBER THAT

Children involved in playing together may take more time to be aware of your "stop" signal; ensure it is "big" enough to attract their attention.

Management Skills

To Do

How many synonyms can you find for the following games skills?

1. Running
2. Jumping
3. Avoiding an opponent
4. Sending away a ball
5. Receiving a ball
6. Traveling with a ball

▼▼▼▼   ▼

The lesson includes using floor hockey sticks, plastic pucks, and ropes. The children begin the lesson working on their own, then they form groups of three. These groups of three combine for Part 3, the culmination of the lesson.

Behind each bench (turned on its side) there are six sticks, six ropes, and six pucks.

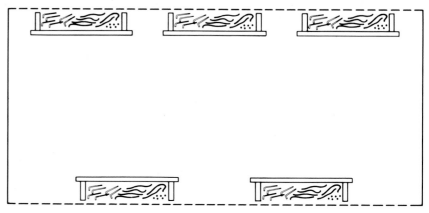

Figure 9.1 Equipment arrangement for a sixth-grade class of 30 children

⌐ hockey stick
〜 rope
• puck

Equipment

Once in the area where the lesson is to be held, have the children place the equipment in dispersed groups, so when given an organizing task to get an object, the class spreads out in the area (see figure 9.1).

When children finish using equipment, they should learn to replace it where they found it. In this way, unused balls will not roll across the playing area; ropes are not left on the floor to trip unsuspecting feet. Time is saved at the end of lessons because the children know where to find everything when putting the equipment away.

Using the Space

When the lesson is outside, it may be necessary to establish boundaries, especially if there is more than one class sharing the space. With older children, the boundaries can be described; younger children will need visible reminders, such as highway markers, of their designated area.

Pathways in the general space may need specifying for safety reasons. The following two examples illustrate this.

1. The basic task is to roll a hoop and run around it. All children run in the same direction (see figure 9.2).
2. The organizing task has the children in groups of three, each with a pylon, batting tee, plastic softball bat, and Nerf ball.

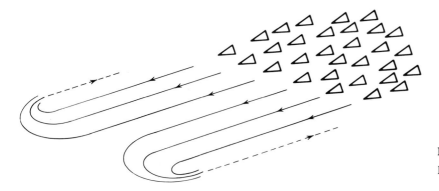

Figure 9.2 Specified pathways for a running task

What's Wrong with This Situation?

In a sixth-grade games lesson, the children form groups of six to play floor hockey, with no goals. The task is to pass the puck between team members and prevent the opposition from intercepting it. The number of successful passes is to be counted; when 5 is reached, the other team begins with the puck.

Some children are in socks only, some are barefoot, and the remainder are in sneakers. Hockey sticks and pucks are stacked in one corner of the room. The teacher tells them to collect their equipment and begin their games.

What is wrong?

1. Children must wear sneakers for games activities. They are needed for protection from being stepped on, to cushion any kind of impact, and to provide a grip on the floor.
2. The equipment should be placed around the area for easy access, preferably one set for each group. Doing so is safer, increases the children's playing time, and spaces the children apart in the playing area.
3. The teacher should tell the children to keep their games within their own area.

SAFETY TIP ///////////

Children learning to control an object are less able to pay attention to where they are in space. It may, therefore, be necessary to designate the specific pathways or areas for them.

The applying task is for child *A* to hit the ball off the tee, and children *B* and *C* to field it and return it to the tee before *A* runs around the pylon (see figure 9.3). All groups are placed so that the batter hits away from the center of the space.

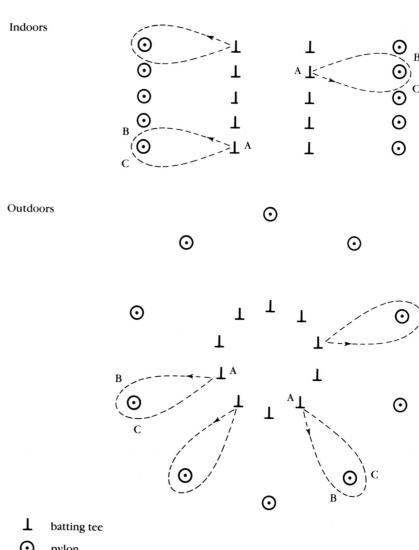

Indoors

Outdoors

⊥ batting tee

⊙ pylon

-- ▸-- pathway

Figure 9.3 Placement of batting tees

Grouping the Children   Find a variety of ways to group the children during the lesson, especially for tasks where the children perceive scores to be important. At no time should children be put in the situation where they feel unwanted, as when captains are designated to choose teams. The least able or popular children are made to feel unwanted by being chosen last. Some ways to divide the class into groups include:

1. Count off in the number of groups needed. For example, a class of thirty children playing three against three floor hockey results in there being five games. Give each child a number one to five and have all children of same number collect in a designated area. You now have five groups of six children. Have pinnies for three children so that each subgroup of three is identified.
2. Divide the class according to alphabetical order, by first or last name. This can be done before the lesson begins.
3. Group the class according to ability or height.

It is important that you use a variety of methods so that the children expect to play with different people and, we hope, learn to accept players of differing abilities.

In many lesson plans, groups for Part 3 (Culmination) will evolve gradually, as in the following situations:

1. Children work individually
2. Children find partners or form groups of three
3. Pairs combine to play two vs. two or trios combine to play three vs. three

Once children have formed their groups, do not split them (e.g., change from working with a partner to groups of three) as friction often arises.

Observational Skills

Whatever games skill you are observing, watch the children's feet. Give plenty of refinement directed toward improving footwork as all games skills depend on the players being in the right place at the right time. Begin encouraging "moving feet" with your kindergarten children and continue to stress its importance at all levels of performance. In every lesson, some time should be spent on improving footwork by itself as well as in combination with specific manipulative skills. Tag games are excellent "trainers of feet," but simply participating in such games is insufficient. It's possible to practice poor footwork!

Table 9.1 has been developed to help you observe the children as they practice games skills (Stanley 1977). The table has two components, questions to ask yourself about the movement concepts/demands of the task and questions to ask about the children's responses. All the movement concepts will not apply to every task or game; therefore, you must select what is relevant.

Table 9.1

Observing game skills

Skills	Questions to Ask Yourself Before You Observe (A) and As You Observe (B)		
Body management	**A** What are the GAME DEMANDS on the player's ability to: 1. Shift weight? 2. Balance? 3. Use different actions? 4. Use specific body parts? 5. Bend, stretch, twist? 6. Change body shape?		**B** Responses observed
Effort	**A** 1. a. Change speed? b. Move at constant speed? 2. a. Use force? b. Change the degree of force? 3. a. Move with flexibility? b. Move in a direct manner? 4. a. Move continuously? (free flow) b. Stop and start? (bound flow)		**B**
Spatial	**A** 1. Change direction a. alone? b. with the ball? 2. Change level? 3. Travel in specific pathways a. alone? b. with a ball? c. with someone else? 4. Send ball along a specific pathway? 5. Receive a ball from different directions?		**B**
Relationship	**A** 1. Relate to the playing area? 2. Relate to the equipment? 3. Relate to team members? 4. Relate to the opposition? 5. Relate to the referee?		**B**

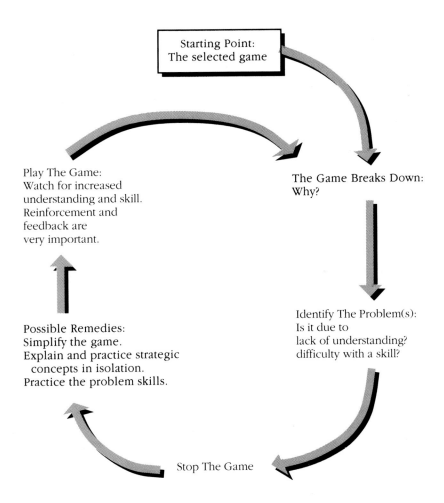

Starting Point:
The selected game

The Game Breaks Down:
Why?

Play The Game:
Watch for increased
understanding and skill.
Reinforcement and
feedback are
very important.

Identify The Problem(s):
Is it due to
lack of understanding?
difficulty with a skill?

Possible Remedies:
Simplify the game.
Explain and practice strategic
  concepts in isolation.
Practice the problem skills.

Stop The Game

Modified from Jones, D. 1982. Teaching for Understanding in Tennis.
Bulletin of Physical Education 18: 1, 29–31.

Figure 9.4 Observation
cycle

Observing Games Playing

It is quite difficult to observe children playing complex games, to decide what is needed now to improve the playing and what action to take if you decide to stop the game. Since we are suggesting the children spend more of their lesson time playing games, it follows that more teaching must be done in the context of the game. This means being able to identify a skill or strategy that needs improving, stop the game, devise a practice or simplified game, give the players information in the form of refining tasks, provide descriptive feedback, and, when you feel the children are ready, return them to the original, more complex situation. This sequence of observation is shown in figure 9.4.

Teaching open skills demands a lot from us. The situation changes so quickly and sometimes it is difficult to recall exactly what happened. Try to reconstruct the situation so the children can examine what they did and suggest what changes are necessary.

Participation

Participating in children's games is a useful and enjoyable teaching technique. When doing so, remember to adapt to the skill level of the children with whom you are playing. This means you should show good performance of the skills involved, but be careful not to dominate the game. Our aim is to act as a *catalyst,* not to demonstrate our prowess.

When playing with the children you can help to distribute the play. You can provide encouragement for all players and can possibly stretch the children beyond their normal standard of play. Even when not playing all the time, by being inside the game you can redistribute the flow of the game and maybe involve some of the less-able players. Do not hesitate to stop the game, reposition the players, give a tactical task, ask a player to repeat a skill (and improve it!) and then continue the game, as is suggested in figure 9.4.

Scoring

The score is an important part of any game; indeed, it is the raison d'etre for the activity. However, the actual score achieved is relatively unimportant. What is important is the combination of skills culminating in the *act* of scoring. Concurrent with that is the combination of skills that may prevent the act of scoring. One of our roles in teaching games is to help children appreciate skillful plays, both offensive and defensive, and help them derive satisfaction and pleasure from their participation in the game itself, rather than in the outcome.

REMEMBER THAT

It is easier to catch a ball you have bounced off the wall or floor than one thrown by a peer.
A small object that you can grip firmly is easier to throw than a large object.
The color of a ball affects skill development.
Young children find it difficult to track a green ball on grass—it is camouflaged!

We have a responsibility to "help children understand philosophical differences between the games they play and professional games shown on television. The professional is an entertainer and a wage earner whose play often reflects these facts" (National Task Force on Children's Play 1979). Other responsibilities include

1. teaching a variety of basic skills
2. changing the positional roles children play in a game; avoiding specialization
3. praising skill improvement and reflecting this in grading (anecdotal reporting may be appropriate here)
4. emphasizing *learning* skills and *playing* games rather than the final result
5. preparing the children for competition at intramural and interscholastic levels by providing good learning experiences so they have the necessary skills and appropriate attitudes that will permit them to enjoy the competition (National Task Force on Children's Play 1979)

Movement Pattern
Was the movement executed as planned?

Movement Skill

		Yes	No
	Yes	Everything's right!	Surprise!
Was the result the expected one?	**No**	What's wrong?	Everything's wrong!

Figure 9.5 Relationship between movement pattern and movement skill

These five "nutshell statements" may help us to focus on the children, so that the play aspect of games remains important. The inherent competition should extend the children as they utilize their skills; it should not be used as a measure of their performance. We hope that children's enthusiasm for active participation in games activities remains with them throughout their lives.

Evaluation

Games, being so functional in their intent, may be easier to evaluate than dance and gymnastics. It is, for example, comparatively easy to evaluate individual games skills from the quantitative point of view. The number of successful attempts at hitting a prescribed target, or the speed at which a child can dribble a ball around markers is easily tallied. In a community, a team is often evaluated on its win–loss record. This may give an inaccurate picture of the individuals making up the team, and, therefore, is an inappropriate evaluation technique in an educational program. When designing tools for evaluation we should consider the means (movement patterns) of achieving functional results (movement skills). We need to attend to action with and without equipment, and with and without other players.

Games are functional activities. Efficiency or the quantitative aspects of movement are important. In addition, however, games involve the understanding, development and implementation of various strategies, the understanding and following of rules, and, in the large majority of games played, the ability to be a member of a team. Evaluation methods should reflect these components.

Individual Skills

Young children should be evaluated on their performance of individual skills, with more attention paid to movement pattern (the qualitative aspect of the skills) than the movement skill or result (the quantitative aspect of the skill). As the children mature, more attention is paid to the relationship between the movement pattern and the movement skill. Gentile (1972) produced a model that helps us understand the relationship between movement pattern and movement skill (see figure 9.5).

Grade: _3_

Skill Observed: _Aiming at target; paddle_ _bat & ball_

Name: _Chris Martin_

Date: _Feb. 6 1990_

Movement Pattern

Movement Skill	Expected	Unexpected
	Box 1	**Box 2**
Expected Result	XXXX 4	XXX 3
	Box 3	**Box 4**
Unexpected Result	XXXXXXX 7	XX 2

% Scores   Box 1: 4/16 (25%)   Box 2: 3/16 (18.75%)
                    Box 3: 7/16 (43.75%)   Box 4: 2/16 (12.5%)

Comments: Chris' movement pattern is consistent and has improved during the unit on net games. Attention needed on consistency of result.

Movement Pattern Consistency = 68.75% (Boxes 1 and 3)

Movement Skill   = 43.75% (Boxes 1 and 2)

Figure 9.6 Evaluation of games skills

This model has been translated into a form that may be used for evaluating children's performance, illustrated in figure 9.6. A simple tallying system will give you a percentage score.

The student, Chris, shows "skilled responses" 25 percent of the time; i.e., both movement pattern and movement skill coincide, yet the movement pattern is consistent 68.75 percent of the time (boxes 1 and 3). Careful observation will be needed to make the necessary adjustments to this child's performance.

Grade: _____   Date: _____

Skill: _____

Names	Movement Skill: Hits the Target			Movement Pattern			Comments
	1.5m	2.0m	3.0m	1	2	3	
1. _____							
2. _____							
3. _____							
4. _____							
5. _____							
6. _____							
7. _____							
8. _____							
9. _____							
10. _____							

1—below what is expected for age and experience.

2—what is expected for age and experience.

3—above what is expected for age and experience.

Figure 9.7 Group evaluation

It is also possible to evaluate several children at the same time, as is shown in figure 9.7, which was developed to evaluate the aiming skills of a class of first graders. Lines are set 4, 6, and 9 feet (1.5, 2.0, and 3.0 meters) from the wall, on which there are clearly marked targets. Groups of four to five children work at this while the others in the class are given different tasks, working on a rotational system at stations.

When watching the children, you might first notice the children who stand close to the wall in order to be successful. Others may begin too far away and will miss the target every time. You will need to help everyone make a wise decision regarding where to stand. It is important that each child hits a target several times so that the movement pattern can be observed in a "successful" situation. They can then be encouraged to have several tries at a greater distance.

Games Playing Knowledge

Strategy and rules can be evaluated by asking questions and some teachers decide to test the children's knowledge by giving mini-tests at the end of a unit. Children's understanding of rules can also be determined by having them referee situations within class and/or in the intramural program. Some children thoroughly enjoy being involved in games while not actually playing the game. Children who have difficulties with ball handling may find great satisfaction in refereeing. You may establish a unit on selected refereeing skills and the children can be evaluated on their ability to apply the rules and control a game. This is appropriate for fifth- and sixth-grade children. Because they may find it difficult to take charge of a game played by their peers, it is suggested that they begin helping with games played by grades 3 and 4.

Summary

A game is a complex movement form that demands quality teaching if the children are to become skilled and knowledgeable. One must be able to analyze the intracacies of strategy, as well as help the children acquire efficient movement patterns.

The environment is not always sympathetic, and teachers have to be able to communicate well when outside, sometimes under very windy conditions. Develop and use a variety of skills that differ from those employed when teaching dance and gymnastics.

The quantitative aspect of games playing sometimes takes precedence over those less easily quantified. An evaluation system should reflect the multifaceted nature of the program.

Review Questions

1. Discuss management skills specific to the teaching of games.
2. When teaching outdoors, how can you attract the children's attention?
3. Why is it important to observe children's feet when they are playing games?
4. It is suggested that whistles are important when teaching games, yet inappropriate for dance and gymnastics lessons. Why?
5. Why do we evaluate movement pattern rather than skill (result) when working with young children?
6. When we participate in children's games, it is to act as a "catalyst." What is meant by this?

Gentile, A. 1972. A Working Model of Skill Acquisition with Application to Teaching. *Quest.* 27: 3–23.

Graham, G., S. Holt-Hale, T. McEwen and M. Parker. 1980. *Children Moving: A Reflective Approach to Teaching Physical Education.* Palo Alto, Calif.: Mayfield Publishing Co.

Jones, D. 1982. Teaching for Understanding in Tennis. *Bulletin of Physical Education.* 18:1, 29–31.

Logsdon, B., K. Barrett, M. Ammons, M. Broer, L. Halverson, R. McGee and M. Roberton. 1984. *Physical Education for Children: A Focus on the Teaching Process,* 2d. ed. Philadelphia: Lea & Febiger.

Mauldon, E. and B. Redfern. 198[ ] *Games Teaching,* 2d ed. London: Macdonald and Evans, Ltd.

National Task Force on Childr[en] Play. 1979. *Fair Play Codes for [ ] in Sports.* Ottawa: Canadian Cou[ncil] Children and Youth.

Stanley, S. 1977. *Physical Educa[tion:] Movement Orientation,* 2d. ed. [ ] McGraw-Hill Ryerson Ltd.

CHAPTER

10

LEARNING EXPERIENCES IN GAMES

REMEMBER THAT

Young children sometimes feel "lost" in large spaces. Physical boundaries (e.g., benches, pylons) that identify the playing area help them "know where they are."

Recently, considerable attention has been paid to the teaching of games, in both school and community settings (Bunker and Thorpe 1982, Piggott 1982, Riley 1977). Concern has been with the games being presented to the children "as more or less complete discrete entities" (Piggott 1982) and a general games sense being ignored, or maybe unrecognized and therefore undeveloped.

We have already indicated we consider the development of this *general games sense* to be the major objective of games teaching (see figure 8.1) and that it is through the playing of different games, related or not, that children learn about and understand the nature of *games playing*. This means that when new games are introduced the players quickly perceive the strategies and roles of the players involved. The acquisition of specific manipulative skills (techniques) and learning the rules of the specific game are the missing links (see table 10.1).

To develop the concept of games playing, we propose a departure from the usual games pattern established in many elementary and secondary schools. We suggest the following programming to be used throughout the school years, as shown in table 10.2.

Kindergarten–Grade 2: Selected games and activities focus on

a. the fundamental skills of games playing
b. generalized knowledge of manipulative and nonmanipulative skills

This is achieved by learning and playing a wide variety of low-organization games, which include simple offensive and defensive strategies.

Grades 2–4: This is a transition period as skill learning becomes more specific. Simple lead-up games, which require the application of combined games concepts, are introduced.

Grades 4–6: The sense of games playing is further developed by playing lead-up games related to the three most common kinds of formal games: net, batting, running (see chapter 8). Equal emphasis on the three game forms is needed to develop an all-round playing sense.

Grades 6–8: We recommend selecting and focusing on ONE formal game from each game category (i.e., a net game, a batting game, a running game), with the possible exclusion of target games (for the reasons stated in chapter 8). This programming allows enough time for the children to become competent in the selected games, and also develop understanding and appreciation of all parameters of each game form. Which three games are selected will depend on your own experience and knowledge, the facilities and equipment available, and also the interests of the community.

Table 10.1

▼▼▼▼

Skill specificity and game form

Combinations of elements in many games (fundamental game skills)	Low-organiza games
Combination of elements in a selected game form (e.g., net games)	Lead-up game
Combination of elements in a specific game (e.g., tennis)	Formal games

▼▼▼▼

Table 10.2

▼▼▼▼▼

Game type selection for the elementary school program and the link with the secondary school program

Grade	Emphasis on Low-organization Games	Emphasis on Lead-up Games	Emphasis on Formal Games
K	Major		
1	Major		
2	Major	Minor	
3	Equal	Equal	
4	Minor	Major	
5	*	Major	Minor
6	*	Equal	Equal
7	*	*	Major
8	*	*	Major
9	*	*	Major

*Denotes the game type is used to practice and reinforce specific game concepts related to the formal game selected.

▼▼▼▼▼

If possible, program parallel learning so that reference can be made to each game form. The focus of learning shifts from the more general parameters of lead-up games to the specifics of the selected formal game. Children in this age group are able to deal with the formal equipment, but the rules, size of playing area, number of players, and length of the game may still need modifying.

Fitness Fact

Tag games increase the heart rate, as does continuous jumping rope. To affect cardiovascular fitness, the activity should last for a minimum of three minutes.

▼▼▼▼   ▼

Experience has now shown that a modified game promotes more efficient learning of skills, allows a more fluent pattern of play and, perhaps most important of all, provides more involvement and enjoyment for children of all abilities (Sleap 1985).

Grade 9 and above: Increase the students' repertoire by introducing additional games. A special focus on lifetime games is recommended; therefore, target games may be possible. Attention to individual talents and interests is paramount at this stage, and, whenever possible, the children should be encouraged to select games they have a chance of playing after leaving school.

Many children are introduced to formal games too soon, well before they have the necessary physical, cognitive, and social maturity to be successful and have enjoyment. When there is little attempt to highlight the elements common to games playing, the specificity of focus minimizes the children's perception of games playing.

Lesson Design

For lessons to be both related to the needs of the children for whom you are planning and progressive, there must be realistic expectations, based on your observation of the children in the games situation. As with the other areas of the program, it is highly unlikely that the same plan will be appropriate for any two classes or different grade levels. We have already indicated a sequence for the selection of game type in table 10.2. Now we will look at some of the other factors that should be considered when designing tasks and selecting games for your lessons.

Relationships and Roles

The complexity of the relationships and roles must be appropriate for the developmental and experiential stages of the children's development. Remember that children gradually learn the skills required for cooperating and competing, and therefore, we must structure tasks accordingly. Table 10.3 shows increasing complexity of relationships and how the environment changes from being more closed to more open as the number of players increases and both cooperation and competition are involved.

Table 10.3

Games-playing progression

Group Size	Relationship(s)	Environment Closed ← → Open	
Alone	—	←	
In twos	a. Cooperative	←	
	b. Competitive: 1 vs. 1	→	
In threes	a. Cooperative	←	
	b. Cooperative and competitive: 2 vs. 1	→	
In fours	Cooperative and competitive: 2 vs. 2	→	
In sixes	Cooperative and competitive: 3 vs. 3	→	

Movement Content

There are three points to remember:

1. The movement content of all lessons must contribute to the objective(s) selected.
2. The movement content of the game(s) you select for the lesson must utilize the skills taught in the lesson. This suggests that you decide on specific aspects of games playing as the focus of your lesson and then find or create a game that utilizes them. This form of planning is most appropriate when the games are low-organization and lead-up, and children are learning the fundamentals of games playing.
3. The skills taught in a lesson must relate to the game selected for Part 3 of the lesson plan (see chapter 3). When children are reaching the transition between lead-up and formal games, it is the game itself that directs the selection of content for Parts 1 and 2 of the lesson.

In both the first and second points above, you will need to analyze the game so that you know the prerequisite skills and why you have chosen it. This may be done in different ways; an example is given in table 10.4 analyzing "Juggle a Number" (from Kirchner 1985), a challenging low-organization game requiring quick reactions for throwing and catching, and a memory for a sequence.

REMEMBER THAT

Games activities provide plenty of opportunities for the children to make their own decisions regarding task and equipment. The following list shows the range from the teacher deciding on the equipment and task to the children making their own decisions.

Equipment	Task
1. *Teacher selects (e.g., a rope)*	*Teacher specifies (e.g., "Jump rope staying in your own area.")*
2. *Teacher selects (e.g., a ball)*	*Children's choice (e.g., free play with the ball)*
3. *Children select (e.g., choose either a stick and ball or a ball alone)*	*Teacher specifies (e.g., "Dribble the ball.")*
4. *Children select (e.g., ropes, bats, sticks, balls, hoops available)*	*Children's choice (e.g., free play with the equipment)*

To Do

Discuss the other decisions that can be made by the children in their games lessons.

▼▼▼▼   ▼

Participation

Select games that allow for maximum participation for all—children should not be spectators during lessons. Ask yourself if all participants have an equal opportunity to play. There are some situations when you may wish to group the children according to ability or height.

Four ideas to maximize participation are:

1. Have several small groups/teams instead of one large group.
2. Use maximum equipment, improvising if necessary, so that children do not have to wait for a turn. Also use maximum space.
3. Avoid elimination games; many can be modified by counting negative points and playing to a predetermined score or time limit, at which point the slate is wiped clean.
4. Plan stations, each one with different equipment. The children rotate and use each station either in one lesson or over several. This is a system found in gymnastics.

Complexity

Select games that are easily explained and organized. Ask yourself how long it will take to get the game or activity started. If a lengthy explanation is needed, the game or activity is probably not appropriate. You

Table 10.4

Game analysis

Game: Juggle a Number	*Simplify*	*Extend*
Game Focus: Keep balls in play		
Skill Objectives:		
a. Receive from and send to different players		
b. Speedy reactions		
c. Remember numerical sequence		
Skill Focus: Throwing and catching		Add traveling
Number of Players: 5	Reduce to three	
Organizational Pattern: Circle; players numbered at random	Numbered in sequence	Random formation
Equipment: Two 7-inch playground balls	Reduce to one ball	Smaller balls; increase group size by one
Rules/Limitations: If ball is dropped, continue with the one(s) in play. Game over when all are dropped.		

Organizational Pattern diagram (random):
```
      1
   4
3
   5
  2
```

Organizational Pattern diagram (numbered in sequence):
```
    1
2       5
    4
  3
```

After E. Schurr, Movement Experiences of Children, 3d ed. Copyright © 1980 Prentice-Hall, Inc., Englewood Cliffs, NJ.

Fitness Fact

Games played in small areas, needing quick footwork, many changes in direction, and the ability to stop and start suddenly, require leg strength and muscle endurance.

may be able to simplify the game or activity considerably when first introducing it, adding a complication or two as the children become familiar with its structure.

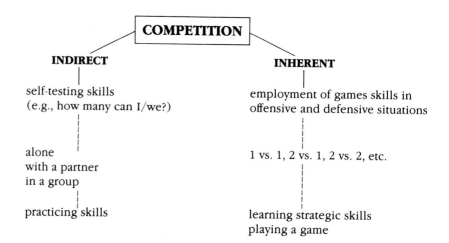

Figure 10.1 Inherent and indirect competition

Competition

Be aware of the kind of competitive challenges you are setting. There are two kinds possible during games lessons: inherent and indirect (see figure 10.1). *Inherent Competition* is part of the activity. A few target games, such as curling and lawn bowling, and all net, batting, and running games are inherently competitive.

Most target games are *indirectly competitive:* individuals play against themselves, as in golf. The scores may be compared with those of others; at times they are compared with the player's previous score. Some tasks designed for skill improvement may include indirect competition. The competitive element should be added with discretion because, if introduced too early, the children become concerned about the result, and the execution of the skills deteriorates. Indirect competition may be introduced to add a challenge, provide the children with some knowledge of their skill level, and maybe encourage a little risk-taking and add excitement.

The following examples underline the fact that a degree of efficiency must be present or else the tasks will not be possible or enjoyable. Applying tasks, such as "Can you keep the ball in the air until I count to ten?", include competition between the students and the teacher. A basic task designed to practice running around a designated track (game form—batting games) challenges the children to outrun the ball as it is thrown around the bases (see figure 10.2). The fielders are also challenged to throw accurately and catch well. The inclusion of indirect competition makes the learning situation more gamelike.

Indoors or Outdoors?

Whenever possible, teach games lessons outdoors. Historically, most games were designed to be played outdoors and it is only recently that indoor facilities have been available for the majority of games.

Needed: one ball, three pylons, four players (*A, B, C, D*). Players *A, B,* and *C* stand by a pylon, placed as in the diagram. Player *D* stands near player *A*.

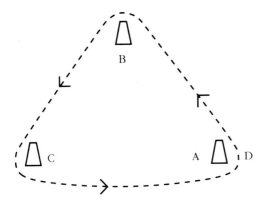

When player *A* calls "go!" the ball is thrown from *A* to *B* to *C* to *A*. Player *D* runs around the pylons from *A* to *B* to *C* to *A*, trying to reach "home" before the ball gets back to *A*. Players should rotate so that everyone has a turn running.

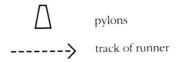

(pylon symbol)	pylons
------->	track of runner

Figure 10.2 Indirect competition—Running task

Fitness Facts
Throwing overarm requires flexibility in the upper body.

▼▼▼▼ ▼

Factors influencing your decision to play outdoors include the size of the outside space available, the kind of surface (grass, concrete, loose gravel), whether it is free from litter (especially broken glass), is fairly level, without potholes or other obstructions, and is well fenced, so that equipment does not "escape" onto any nearby road.

The amount of distraction from pedestrians, dogs, and traffic may make you decide to teach indoors, although you may be more affected by the distractions than the children.

The weather, of course, is a major factor in your decision. There are many sunny, cooler days in the fall when outside play would be very enjoyable if the children have warm clothing to put on; maybe also a pair of gloves or mittens. The lesson content may have to be adjusted as catching balls can be difficult when small hands are hidden in gloves, but striking is possible and balls can be controlled by feet. Plenty of

SAFETY TIP ///////////

Keep boundaries for games well away from walls.

Fitness Fact

Throwing for distance requires strength and flexibility. Children may be given a choice of ball size and weight as their strength increases.

▼▼▼▼   ▼

vigorous activity for everyone and short rests should be included, with minimal time spent giving instruction and the lesson cut short if any children appear cold.

Extra care will be needed to organize the carrying and collecting of equipment; specific children can be responsible for helping you do this. When taking kindergarten and first-grade children outside, it is a great help to have an older child to assist you. Some schools have leadership groups for grades 5 and 6 and one of their learning experiences could be to assist with the physical education lessons for the lower grades.

The game form may also dictate whether the lesson is inside or out. Some schools have fixed basketball goals in the playground, others may have portable goals. Few schools have portable fixtures for nets needed in net games (volleyball, tennis, badminton) and therefore the use of improvised equipment is needed whether teaching inside or out. Do not be restricted by the existing conditions or what has been done before. If you wish to have your lessons outside and there is a suitable area, you can find the means to do so.

Sometimes a lesson plan is appropriate for either an indoor or an outdoor setting. When planning to teach outside, it is advisable to have an alternative plan in case the weather is unsuitable. A minor adjustment may be all that is needed, but it is better to have thought it out beforehand. The sample lessons in this chapter state whether they are designed for indoors or outdoors. It is mainly the organizational procedures that will have to be changed; the tasks should need very little adaptation.

Enjoyment

Finally, and just as important as the previous factors, the tasks and games should be enjoyable and fun for the children. Remember, not all children enjoy the same game and it may be possible to select two or three games with similar skill objectives and focus and allow the children to choose which game they play. An alternative is to ask the children to design their own game(s).

Created Games

Children should be given the opportunity to create their own games or maybe to modify a game they already know. They will need some help so that the game or modification is developed around the selected skills.

Table 10.5

▼▼▼▼

Creating a game

Game Form:	Running games
	  soccer
	  hockey (ice or field)

Skill Objectives:	To send the ball ahead of the receiver Players to be on the move
Skill Focus:	Running Striking Your choice
Number of Players:	3
Organizational Pattern:	Your choice

Equipment:	Either: a. 7-inch playground ball or
	         b. 3 plastic hockey sticks and a
	            3-inch plastic ball

Rules/Limitations:	Your choice

After E. Schurr, Movement Experiences of Children, *3d ed. Copyright © 1980 Prentice-Hall, Inc., Englewood Cliffs, NJ.*

▼▼▼▼

SAFETY TIP ///////////

Outdoor playing areas often have two or more different surfaces. Place your lesson away from the junction of different surfaces.

This is done by providing limitations or setting a problem for them to solve. The complexity of the problem, of course, depends on the capabilities of the children.

Table 10.5 is an example of a problem set for a fourth-grade class that has an understanding of running games. Schurr (1980) points out that it is when children have an understanding of games playing and "experience in variations of each component, and opportunities to make variations of known games" that they are able to create new games.

Progressions

Long-term schemes are needed to ensure the kind of progressive teaching that leads to competency in games playing. You must recognize the children's past learning; to do this, you need to know the content of games lessons in previous years. If there are several teachers responsible for physical education in your school, it will be helpful for you—and beneficial for the children—to coordinate your long-term planning. Table 10.6 is an example of a scheme developed for a seven-year program leading to the selected formal games that the children will begin in grade 5 and continue in the first years of the secondary school. It should be easy to make adjustments to the scheme and substitute other formal games.

Table 10.6

▼▼▼▼

Progression to formal games: A seven-year plan

K–Grade 2

Net Games: Volleyball	Generalized nonmanipulative skills.
	Variations in striking with no differentiation of game form (i.e., use hands, feet, implements).
	When striking with hands, use fairly large, lightweight balls such as balloons, beach balls, bladders of volleyballs. Bright colors are enjoyed by children.
	Cooperative play and low-organization games in twos and threes.
Batting Games: Softball	Generalized nonmanipulative skills.
	Striking, throwing, and catching skills using a variety of implements and objects.
	Use hands, or an implement to strike stationary ball off a support or tee.
	Low-organization games in groups of three: one batter, two fielders. Change places after x turns; individual or no scoring.
Running Games: Soccer	Generalized and nonmanipulative skills.
	Use of feet to strike, stop, travel with, and propel a ball.
	Use targets for aiming and obstacle courses for propelling.
	Sending and receiving in groups of two or three.
	Tag-like games that include balls.
	Develop the ability to run with the ball, stop, change direction and speed, and make floor patterns.

Grades 2–4

Net Games: Volleyball	Low-organization and lead-up games, which emphasize striking objects with hands; still use lightweight balls.
	Introduce indirect competition, e.g., "How many times can you 1. hit the ball against the wall, 2. keep the ball going over a net to your partner?"

	Develop
	1. fundamental skills of run, jump, hit up, hit down.
	2. basic strategies of:
	  a. hitting to a space
	  b. positioning in relation to the ball.

	Games of two vs. two and three vs. three, to maximize participation and teach cooperative and competitive skills.

▼▼▼▼

Batting Games: Softball	Low-organization and lead-up games, which include running, striking, throwing, and catching skills.
	When introducing pitching in a game, begin with cooperative pitching; i.e., have a member of the batting team pitch. Include batting off a tee when you wish to focus on running and fielding skills.
Running Games: Soccer	Low-organization and lead-up games, which require skilled footwork and controlling a ball with feet.
	Aim ball at either undefended or defended targets/spaces.
	Begin goalkeeping skills in one vs. one and two vs. one situations.
	Use playground and large plastic balls that "run" easily on the playing surface.

Grades 4–6

Net Games: Volleyball	Lead-up and modified formal games with boundaries, scoring, and selected rules of volleyball.
	Increase the size of the playing group as the skills develop. Be prepared to decrease if the game breaks down or you introduce a new element.
	Slightly underinflated volleyballs can be introduced as the hands (particularly the fingers) become larger and stronger.
Batting Games: Softball	Play lead-up games that include running around a diamond, which is considerably reduced in size.
	Introduce selected softball rules and team scoring.
	Groups of eight or ten (four vs. four, five vs. five) are probably the maximum for participation to remain high.

	If batting skills are weak,
	  a. hit off tee
	  b. change the bat
	  c. have fungo batting—the players toss the ball for themselves to hit.
	  d. continue with cooperative pitching.

Running Games: Soccer	Groups of six–ten players (three vs. three, four vs. four, five vs. five).
	Lead-up and modified versions of soccer.
	Games with boundaries, reduced playing area, small goals, selected soccer rules.
	Introduce regulation soccer balls when strength and skill level warrant it. Until then, give children a choice of balls when playing.

The lesson plans that follow are designed to show these changing expectations and skill progressions. One game form, net games, has been selected and three lessons are planned, one for each stage of the games program. You will notice how the tasks in the lessons gradually become more volleyball-like.

Lesson Plan 1

This is for children in grade 1 who have minimal experience in striking a ball with their hands. Consequently, the children work alone. Cooperative tasks in pairs should be introduced as soon as ball control is such that pair work is appropriate. In the early learning stages, joining with a partner is an extending task. As ball control increases, basic tasks in pairs are appropriate. This will be seen in Lesson Plan 2.

Topic: Games

Skill Focus: Striking skills, running, jumping

Grade: 1

Length: 20 minutes

Equipment: 1 rope per child
8-inch ball per child
(plastic or foam)
10 hoops

Place hoops around edge of area, three ropes and three balls in each hoop.

Lesson held outside.

Objectives: The children will be able to
 1. strike a ball using different body parts
 2. position themselves in relation to returning ball

Movement Concepts: See figure 10.3.

Tasks	Teaching Aids
Organizing	
Get a rope and find a space.	Praise quickness and good spacing if you see them.
Basic	
Free activity with a skipping rope each.	Look for three different jumps with: both feet, one foot to the same, one foot to the other foot. Maybe select one for demonstration as in the following extending task.

A.

Manipulative Skills: Striking		
Body Concepts Body Parts: Hands and feet to strike the ball		
Effort Concepts	Spatial Concepts	Relationship Concepts
Changing amount of force	Up	Alone

B.

Nonmanipulative Skills: Running, jumping		
Body Concepts Activities: Running, jumping		
Effort Concepts	Spatial Concepts	Relationship Concepts
Resiliency	Change of direction	Alone Large group

Figure 10.3 Movement concepts—Lesson Plan 1

Refining

If traveling, look for the spaces.
  Bouncy jumps.
Strong push off with feet.
Bend knees when landing.
Keep arms away from the body
  when turning the rope.

Extending

(After having watched a student who was hopping) Hop three times on one foot and three on the other.

The children may tire quickly; therefore, give them a rest, some feedback (encouragement, praise) and maybe do it with them.

Simplifying

Without your rope, hop three times on one foot, three on the other. Then add the rope.	If some children find the hop difficult, simplify by removing the rope.

Refining

Hold free leg bent. Make it a "strong" leg. "Big" turn of the rope.	

Extending

Travel throughout the space.	Concentration shifts from self to the general space; this is relaxing.

Refining

Run on toes. Springy run.	Stop and respace the children if they crowd together.

Organizing

Fold rope in half, place on the floor, and sit at one end.	Ensure ropes are spaced apart well.

Basic

On "go," run around rope and sit down.	Comment on those "home" quickly. Notice (without comment) who is last, watch to see if he or she is faster next time; if so, give praise.

Refining

Small running steps. Keep close to rope. Strong "brake" leg when changing direction.	Repeat the task three or four times before telling the children to put the ropes away.

Organizing

Put your rope away in a hoop and take a ball; find your own space.	The equipment should be arranged around the space. The children exchange the rope for a ball.

Basic

Use hands to hit ball into the air; catch it.	Good spacing is essential because they will be watching the ball, not each other.

Refining

Be ready to run to the ball. Watch it and keep "under" it as it returns to you. Have your hands ready to catch ball.	If the balls are hit with abandonment, then restrict the height. As control improves, move to extending tasks.

Extending

Either small, continuous hits or hit ball as high as you can, let bounce, then catch.	Each of these tasks demands control of force. Select one according to the general response to the basic task.

Refining

Hit under the ball. "Easy" arm swing when hitting high. Firm hand/fist to hit ball.	

Extending

Use other body parts to hit ball up. Catch or allow ball to bounce before striking again.	Encourage use of large surfaces; e.g., elbow angle, thigh.

SAFETY TIP ///////////

1. **Check that all shoelaces are tied tightly.**
2. **Children who wear glasses should be encouraged to wear safety straps. If you wear glasses, help by wearing one when teaching games (and gymnastics).**

Refining

Move to the ball as it returns.
Use smaller hits if the ball is not
  under control.

Applying

Strike ball continuously (with or without a bounce) using one body part. Can you hit it 3–4 times?

Help the children with their spacing as full attention should be on the ball, not on where they are going. Circulate and ask the children their scores. Set the challenge of either "repeat the same number" or "add one more."

Refining

Select from those suggested previously.

Reinforce skilled performance and good attempts at keeping the ball going.

▼▼▼▼   ▼

Possible Progressions

The skill level achieved at the end of this lesson will determine the content of the next lesson. You may decide to repeat it in almost the same form, perhaps finishing with a low-organization game that utilizes some of the running skills practiced, or you may decide to challenge the children a little more by designing basic tasks from the extending tasks.
An alternative is to design new basic tasks by changing the equipment, adding a partner, or changing the conditions (such as striking against a wall, etc.).

In your long-term plan, you may have decided to rotate the three game forms, in which case the next lesson would include completely different content. Whichever plan you select, over a period of time make sure that the fundamental skills and the three game forms receive equal emphasis. To help you do this, a record chart might be a useful addition to your plan book. If you teach more than one grade, it becomes a necessity. Figures 10.4 and 10.5 are two such charts; however, you may design whatever meets your need.

Grade: 2
Teacher: Mr. Chen
Date: Sept. - Dec. 1989

Skills	Net Games	Batting Games	Running Games
Striking			
Throwing			
Trapping			
Catching			
Propelling			
Carrying			

Figure 10.4 Record chart 1—Manipulative skills

Comments:

Grade: 1
Teacher: Mrs. Aguirre
Date: Sept. - Dec. 1989

Lesson	SENDING AWAY			RECEIVING		TRAVELING
	Net	Batting	Running	Batting	Running	Running
1	Volleying hands					Bounce ball and walk
2	Paddle bats	✓		✓		
3		Throw at wall		Toss and catch in twos.		
4			Kick ball at wall		Kick ball and run after it; trap it with feet	
5						

Figure 10.5 Record chart 2—Manipulative skills

REMEMBER THAT

Once children have formed groups, they will be reluctant to split and reform groups with different people. Keep this in mind when planning your organization. We recommend grouping in multiples of two or three as follows:

alone—with a partner—in fours or sixes.

alone—in threes—in sixes.

Lesson Plan 2

This content is designed for a third-grade class; again, it is planned for outside but can easily be transferred to an indoor setting. The one outdoor requirement is a wall, against which balls can be hit. Many gymnasia have uncluttered wall space, but it may be difficult if your lesson is held in another area of the school, in which case a substitute task will be needed.

All the tasks require the children to work with others. Initially they work with partners, then two groups combine and small groups of four are formed. Usually, children should choose with whom they work; however, in this lesson, height is a factor in the second basic task. When the children choose their partners, you may wish to explain the nature of the second task and suggest that they choose a partner who is of similar height. An alternative is to ask the children to line up in order of height and pair them off yourself.

Topic: Games

Skill Focus: Striking, quick footwork

Grade: 3

Length: 40 minutes

Equipment: 7-inch plastic ball for each pair of children.

Objectives: The children will be able to

    1. volley continuously with a partner; in groups of 4

    2. bounce ball so that it rebounds high

    3. jump for a ball; move to a ball

Movement Concepts: See figure 10.6.

Tasks	Teaching Aids
Basic	
In pairs: *A* runs and tries to lose *B,* who is the "shadow." On signal, stop.	Encourage the children to stay in a small area. Have short bursts at this activity; stop and give some refinement. Change roles after 2–3 practices at same role.
Refining	
A: Swerve, change pathways often. Quick feet, small steps. Use upper body when swerving.	Refinement is needed for both players.

A.

Manipulative Skills: Striking		
Body Concepts Activities: Volleying, bouncing Body Parts: Hands, fingers		
Effort Concepts	Spatial Concepts	Relationship Concepts
Strong actions Sudden accent when striking	Up Down Forward	Over/under the ball

B.

Nonmanipulative Skills: Running, jumping		
Body Concepts Body Parts: Feet, legs Actions: Bending/stretching when jumping		
Effort Concepts	Spatial Concepts	Relationship Concepts
Explosive action	Small steps Change of direction in personal space; i.e., forward, backward, sideways	Cooperation in twos, fours Taking turns/rotating

Figure 10.6 Movement concepts—Lesson Plan 2

B: Use arms to help you
  balance.
  Watch *A* and try to anticipate
  changes.
  Quick feet, small steps.

Basic

Both children face each other; *A* jumps and tries to see over *B*'s head.

Encourage children to be with someone of similar height. Some may need to change partners. Children should not touch each other and may need help with distance between each other.

Refining

Bend knees before taking off. Upward arm swing will help jump. Take off with both feet. Firm, straight body in air.	Bent arms, which thrust upward at moment of take-off, will add to "lift" in body.

Organizing

One player gets a ball.	Balls are distributed around the area for easy access.

Basic

A tosses ball and volleys it high for *B* to catch above head. *B* volleys for *A* to catch.	At this stage, encourage the children to hit the ball when it is above the head, palms turned up and wrists extended. Some children will be ready for this before others. Have a demonstration and suggest the others try the same.

Refining

Toss ball up straight before volleying. Hands underneath ball for strike. Strong, upward push on the ball. Keep close to the ball.	In the beginning stages, fingers will point forward when volleying. As the ball is volleyed at a higher level the fingers point backward.

Extending

Volley continuously.	When the children are able to volley the ball straight up, eliminate catching.

Refining

"Lively" feet ready to move under the ball.
Volley the ball up.
Move away when you have volleyed; be prepared to move under the ball.

Applying

How many times can you volley? Try to repeat same number or try to increase.

The focus is on consistency of response. You might find one pair that achieved five volleys and set that as the challenge for the class.

Refining

Same as above.

It is important to recognize verbally:
consistency
improvement in performance

Organizing

Find your own space along a wall.

Space children apart along the wall. If there is insufficient space have half the class rebounding and the other half bouncing into a hoop (see figure 10.7).

Basic

A bounces ball so that it rebounds high off the wall for *B* to bounce it so that it rebounds.

Try to keep the ball in the same place so the children are in front of each other rather than side by side (see figure 10.8).

Refining

Use fingers to push ball down.
"Bouncy" arms as you push.
Push ball firmly toward area at foot of the wall.
Move away after bouncing; be ready to move into place for turn.
Jump for ball if necessary.

Organizing

Join with another pair; put one ball away.

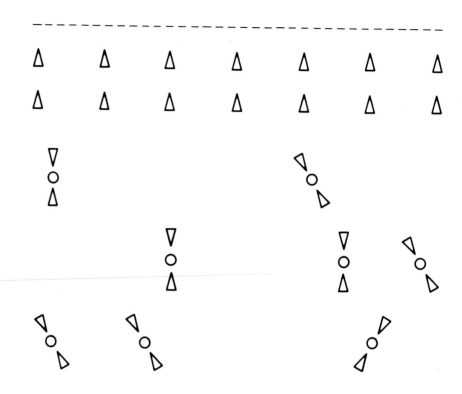

Figure 10.7 Organization of
a class of 30 children

○ hoop

▷ child

Extending

Continuous bounce-rebound.
  "Keep the kettle boiling."

Refining

As above with particular emphasis   Praise jumping and bouncing ball
  on numbers 4 and 5.   from a height. The task leads to
                                     spiking.

Bird's-eye View of Pathway of Ball

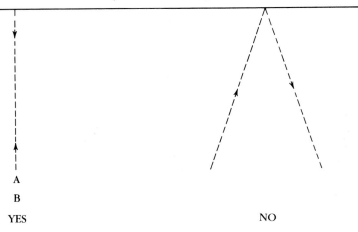

A

B

YES   NO

Side View of Pathway of Ball

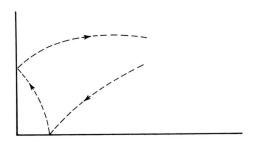

– – –►– pathway of ball

Figure 10.8 Relationships of players

Applying

In your groups of four either see how many times you can bounce-rebound or volley the ball high and see how many times your group can pass the ball.

Observe agility; praise good footwork even if the volley/bounce was inaccurate. If any group is unable to cope, split into pairs and do task.

Ask scores as you visit each group and help the children monitor their own achievements.

Avoid comparisons with other groups. You might give each task a name or ask the children to think of a name.

Possible
Progressions

A follow-up lesson might include the addition of a net of some form so that the volleying is over a barrier separating the partners. The barrier could be a lowered volleyball net, badminton net, or ropes between jumping standards. Some objects must be hung from a single rope so that it is easily visible.

When the children can volley continuously, they are ready for an element of competition. The task "volley 4 times and then make your partner run for the ball" shifts from indirect to direct competition. This is repeated several times with little or no attention paid to a score, just to the successful completion of the task. Making the partner run may involve placing the ball well to one side or hitting it higher and harder so that it goes behind the player.

As skill level increases, all tasks become more gamelike, as several skills are combined and simple rules are introduced. More time will be spent on applying tasks. This is shown in Lesson Plan 3.

Lesson Plan 3

The formal game of volleyball is easily identifiable in this lesson. The organization involved is considerable as it involves the erection of a volleyball or badminton net and jumping standards and ropes. If the playing space is large enough, it may be possible to do some of the preparation before the lesson begins (see figure 10.9). Having the volleyball/badminton net in place is a great help. Remember to adjust the height of the net according to the height of the children. The net must be high enough to encourage an upward, rather than forward, flight of the ball. A rough measure is the fingertips when the arms are fully extended.

As in the previous two lessons, the focus here is on skill development and cooperation in small groups. The tasks themselves are sufficiently challenging and any added competitive factor might detract from skilled performance. The children are set tasks in which they utilize their skills and can monitor success through indirect competition ("How many can I/we. . . . ?" situations). Satisfaction, achievement, enjoyment, and fun are some of the feelings that should result. Direct competition can be added in the follow-up lesson using the same skills in a different applying task. In this forty-minute lesson, a minimum of fifteen minutes should be spent on the final applying task. This should increase in subsequent lessons that focus on the same formal game.

Game Form: Net Games (indoor)
Grade: 5
Length: 40 minutes

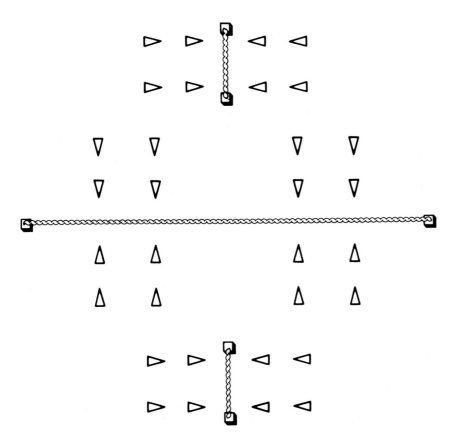

net or rope

child

Figure 10.9 Organization of
equipment for 32 children

Equipment: One volleyball or similar ball for each student.
Volleyball or badminton net, four jumping standards,
two long ropes.

Objectives: The children will be able to

1. volley and bump the ball continuously, both alone and in
groups
2. position themselves in relation to the oncoming ball
3. rotate the playing sequence in a group of four players

Movement Concepts: See figure 10.10.

A.

Manipulative Skills: Striking		
Body Concepts Activities: Volleying, bumping Body Parts: Forearms, fingers		
Effort Concepts	Spatial Concepts	Relationship Concepts
Strong actions Continuity	Up Down	Under the ball Over the ball

B.

Nonmanipulative Skills: Running		
Body Concepts Actions: Crouching, extending Body Parts: Awareness of feet (footwork)		
Effort Concepts	Spatial Concepts	Relationship Concepts
Strong take-off Fast running	Specific pathways	Cooperation Partners Groups of four Rotation within the group

Figure 10.10 Movement concepts—Lesson Plan 3

Tasks	Teaching Aids
Organizing	
Find a partner; one get a ball.	
Basic	
Run and bounce ball to each other. Only one bounce each is allowed.	A demonstration may be needed if this is the first time this task has been set. One bounce each is allowed, so one student will probably be using the left hand, while the other uses the right.

Refining

Adjust running speed to that of your partner.
Keep level with each other.
Keep fairly close together.
Use fingers to push ball.
Slight twist in upper body to face ball.
Bounce ball slightly ahead of your partner.

Stress that this is not a race; the challenge is to keep the ball under control.
Some "traffic control" may be needed; e.g., pairs traveling in same direction length of area; maybe in a wavelike formation (as shown in figure 9.2).

Extending

Change sides and use the other hand.
Increase speed when you feel ready.

Refining

As before.

Organizing

Get another ball. Find a good space together and face each other.

Basic

Bounce your own ball.
Change places and catch partner's ball.

The students must make it possible for their partners to catch the ball; i.e., the bounce must be of reasonable height. Once they do this, the "teasing" or competitive element can be added.

Refining

Bounce ball vertically.
Begin fairly close together.
As the distance increases, prepare your feet for a sudden start.

Extending

Increase the distance you run. Vary the height of bounce.	Remember it must be possible to catch the ball.

Refining

Position of readiness; i.e., feet apart, one in front of the other. Watch your partner. Reach for bouncing ball. If close together, smaller bounces; further apart, higher bounces.	One player may need to say "Go" so that both players bounce their balls at the same time. Suggest this only if you find a problem with the timing.

Extending

If bouncing with left hand, change to right.	Help players realize the change in footwork, i.e., push-off foot in "sprint start."

Organizing

Move into your own space.

Basic

Toss ball in air, volley with both hands and catch.	You may wish to use volleyball terminology; i.e., two-hand overhand pass or set shot.

Refining

Position yourself under the falling ball.
Bend knees.
Feet astride.
Hands above head.
Hands together and fingers flexed and spread.

Extending

Volley once . . . twice . . .
  before catching.
Toss high and slightly to side or
  in front so you have to move
  your feet and reposition.

Applying

How many volleys can you do?   Have three or four turns at this
                                    and encourage the children to
                                    "beat their own records."
                                    Always praise achievement and
                                    improvement.

Organizing

Find some wall space.   If there is insufficient wall space,
                                    have half the class toss in air
                                    and bump. Have several turns
                                    then change over.

Basic

Toss ball against wall so that it
  rebounds and you hit it off your
  forearms.

Refining

Hit ball when just above waist
  height. Crouch and get arms
  underneath the ball so that you
  "bump" it and it bounces off
  your arms.
Keep arms straight and strong.
If using both arms, clasp one
  hand in the other.

Organizing

Make groups of four; put three
  balls away.

Extending

Forearm volley around the group.	The students may decide on a specific sequence or it can be random. If they are successful, encourage the random sequence.
	If the ball is dropped, begin with a player tossing and volleying him/herself.

Refining

Anticipate the ball's movement. Move to the ball as it comes. Crouch and get forearms under the ball. Follow through in an upward direction. Hit ball strongly/firmly.	Encourage high flight of the ball.

Organizing

Join another group and put one ball away; one group each side of the net (as shown in figure 10.9).	A diagram on the board or a large card will help clarify the organization. One group may also demonstrate.

Applying

Volley or bump the ball over the net and try to keep it going. After a few turns, rotate places.	Select one rotation for this lesson. The pattern may be changed in the follow-up lesson. The children may also design/choose their own system. See figure 10.11 for rotation variations for this task.

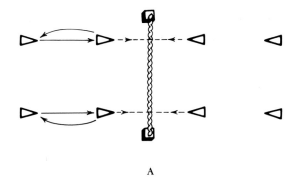

A

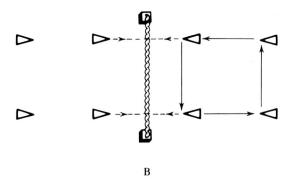

B

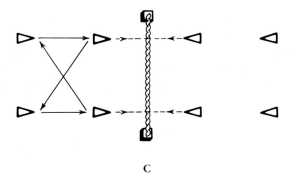

C

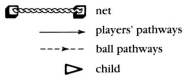 net

——————▶ players' pathways

---▶--- ball pathways

▷ child

Figure 10.11 Rotation variations and the pathway of the ball

Refining

Anticipate when to move and in
  which direction.
Keep knees slightly bent so that
  you can easily move in any
  direction.
Hit underneath the ball and
  follow through in an upward
  direction.
Watch the ball all the time.

Extending

If rotation *B* or *C* is chosen,
  reverse the route.
Count the number of times the
  balls are kept going.
Can you complete three, four, or
  more rotations without dropping
  a ball? A second ball can be
  added.

Help the players understand what
  happens to the feet when
  direction is changed—the push-
  off foot becomes the "brake,"
  the body shifts, etc. This idea
  may be reserved for the
  following lesson.

Refining

Select from the earlier ones.

▼▼▼▼━━━━━━━━━━━━━━━━━━━━━━━━━━━━━━▼

Possible Progressions

Some variations in basic tasks might be introduced together with another skill, maybe serving, or another dimension to setting and bumping,
such as hitting a specific target or sending the ball so that the receiver
has difficulty either in catching the ball or volleying a return.

A different lead-up game can be chosen for the final applying task.
"Newcomb," with four players per team, or volleyball "Keep-Away"
(Kirchner 1985) both utilize the movement concepts around which
Lesson Plan 3 is developed. Scoring can be introduced into this lesson's
final applying task, the simplest way probably being to score a point if
an opposite player fails to return the ball. Decisions have to be made
about restarting the game. If two balls are used, maybe toss the balls
from opposite sides of the net (see figure 10.12). This initial toss must
be cooperative so that the balls can be played; placing the ball in non-
playable areas comes next.

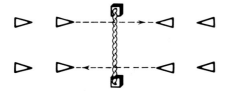

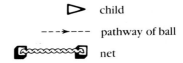

▷   child

- - -▶- - -   pathway of ball

net

Figure 10.12 Restarting head-up games

Whenever a game breaks down, employ the observation cycle (see figure 9.2). Your decision may be for the children to return to cooperative play in which continuity is stressed. You may remove one ball and maintain scoring. Whatever decision you make, provide the children with the encouragement and the information they need as they strive to improve their skills.

Summary

Planning games lessons demands a very clear focus of intent. Your understanding of the nature of games playing, the different game types and forms, the categories of skills, and indirect and inherent competition are some of the prerequisites for developing plans that meet individual needs and provide progressive learning experiences for your children.

Because of the diversity of the content, a careful record of the concepts and skills taught should become part of your plan book. It is exciting to observe the children's increase in competency over the seven years. We hope both they and you will have enjoyment when playing and that many of the children will develop a lifelong interest in games playing, both as participants and spectators.

Review Questions

1. Differentiate between inherent and indirect competition.
2. What factors will help you decide to hold your games lesson outdoors? Give some of the advantages of playing outdoors.
3. What progression/programming of games playing is suggested throughout the school years?
4. How does adding additional players affect a game?
5. Four ideas are provided to help maximize participation in games playing. What are they?
6. What factors influence the selection of a game or design of an applying task for Part 3 of a games lesson?

References

Bunker D. and R. Thorpe. 1982. A Model for the Teaching of Games in Secondary Schools. *Bulletin of Physical Education,* 18:1, 5–9.

Kirchner, G. 1985. *Physical Education for Elementary School Children,* 6th ed. Dubuque, Iowa: Wm. C. Brown Publishers.

Piggott, R. 1982. A Psychological Basis for New Trends in Games Teaching. *Bulletin of Physical Education.* 18:1, 17–22.

Riley, M., editor. 1977. Games Teaching. *JOPER.* 48:7, 17–35.

Schurr, E. 1980. *Movement Experiences for Children,* 3d ed. Englewood Cliffs, N.J.: Prentice-Hall, Inc.

Sleap, M. 1985. Mini-sport; State of the Art. *British Journal of Physical Education.* 16:2, 68–69.

Related Readings

CAHPER 1980. *Basic Skills Series.* Ottawa: CAHPER.

Capel, S. 1986. Games and Sports Offering Social, Competitive and Functional Purpose. *JOPERD* 57:2.29–33, 45.

Docherty, D. 1980. Effective Development of Games Skills for Elementary School Children. *CAHPER Journal* 46:6.30–36.

Docherty, D. and D. Turkington. 1986. A Model for the Sequential Development of Sports Skills. *CAHPER Journal* 52:2.16–19.

Evans, J. 1986. A Look at the Team Selection Process. *CAHPER Journal* 52:5.5–9.

Johns, D. 1987. Persistent Problems Related to Adult Intervention on Children's Sport. *CAHPER Journal* 53:1.19–24.

Sakola, S. 1982. A K–6 Progression Built on Organizing Concepts. *JOPERD* 53:7.38, 39.

Zakrajsek, D. 1986. Premeditated Murder. Let's "Bump-Off" Killer Ball. *JOPERD* 57:7.49–51.

SECTION

4

GYMNASTICS

Within most of us lies a sense of adventure and a strong desire to defy the laws of gravity. We are all enthralled with flight and the unique sensation of being suspended in air. Mary Poppins captured this magical sense for children when she slowly descended, umbrella in hand. The myth and wonder of superhumans who defy gravity in comic strips and television shows has been evidenced in the popularity of "Superman," "Wonder Woman," "Batman," and the "Bionic Man." We have a strong desire to control our environment, to find reassurance that we are king of our castle.

Gymnastic movement is unique in that the focus is upon the body and how and where it moves in relation to the floor or apparatus. Whereas dance is expressive, gymnastic movement is functional, like games, but is not performed to manipulate equipment. Stanley (1969) describes gymnastics as:

Activities which arise when the performer strives to test his ability to control his body movements in relation to the force of gravity in deliberately selected circumstances of difficulty.

The acquisition of (gymnastic) skill is not an end in itself, but the means by which children can experience and understand movement in a variety of situations (Williams 1974).

CHAPTER

11

THE
GYMNASTICS
PROGRAM

Because children naturally delight in running, jumping, rolling, and climbing, the gymnastic experience should be a positive one for all, where movement exploration and refinement result in gymnastic skill. It is our responsibility to foster children's love of gymnastics and channel it into worthwhile learning experiences.

Why Should Gymnastics Be Included in School Programs?

Gymnastic movement is worthy of equal emphasis within the physical education program due to the physical demands it requires. Muscles of the arms, legs, and trunk are taxed as children balance, spring, climb, and hang. Experience with large climbing apparatus provides excitement and challenge. Gymnastics also contributes to the development of fundamental movements necessary for other physical activities. Controlling the body effectively and efficiently is extremely desirable whether one is rushing down a crowded street, throwing a Frisbee, or competing in the Olympics. Since the skills of running, jumping, and rolling are used in every sport, they may be developed in gymnastics and applied to all activities. If the child gains effective body control early in life, certainly this is sound preparation for whatever movement activities will be pursued later.

Body control is the major objective of gymnastics; efficient movement is necessary in a variety of situations, both on the floor and on apparatus. Body awareness is heightened through a focus on the body's shape in jumping, landing, rolling, balancing, hanging, swinging, and climbing. Children learn to control body parts and use them effectively to receive and support their weight as they perform various activities. They will discover that sudden, forceful movement is necessary at times, while at others, energy must be harnessed to create an effective movement. They will grow to realize the importance of timing and rhythm so that movements may progress smoothly from one to the next in sequence. Spatial dimensions will be explored so that height and distance are judged accurately in relation to the body's activities.

The Nature of Gymnastics

For many people, the term "gymnastics" elicits images of thin and muscular adolescents whirling through the air, twisting and turning with great speed and strength, or delicately balancing in contorted positions upon the smallest of surfaces. These images are those of the elite few who choose to compete in gymnastics at the highest level.

Let us look at the other side of the coin at those of us who are "average." If you can, recall your childhood and a carefree summer day with nothing in particular to do. A grassy surface and a clear blue sky may create images and sensations of rolling down a hill, climbing a tree, or gleefully viewing the world upside down. Children find tremendous joy in climbing, swinging, hanging, rolling, and lifting their feet to the sky!

Gymnastics is physically demanding.

The infant's first "gymnastic" skill is that of rolling. Standing, balancing, walking, climbing, hanging, and jumping follow later in the hierarchy of skill acquisition. These fundamental movements, which develop so naturally in the healthy child, form the basis of gymnastics.

Parents who have the luxury of a backyard may purchase swing sets for their children. The neighborhood park and school playgrounds sometimes provide children with similar, but larger, apparatus for gymnastic play. While these structures seem a natural part of the landscape to most of us, they are designed to promote children's innate urge to test their skills in new and challenging ways.

Children delight in testing their physical abilities. The thrill of climbing a tree, walking along a skinny fence, and jumping from a high place are movement sensations most of us can recall.

> Climbing seems to satisfy a desire to be high up, a vivid experience in itself, and little children will often climb to the top of a piece of apparatus for the satisfaction of sitting high up and looking at the familiar environment from a new angle (Jordan 1970).

Children enjoy the sense of vertigo, produced by swinging as high as possible, or watching the world speed by when on a merry-go-round. The speed and motion are delightful kinesthetic sensations. The "Tarzan" exists in each one of us. It is gymnastics that employs this delight and fosters a love for movement in relation to a challenging and exciting environment.

Playgrounds offer a
gymnastic challenge.

Gymnastics is concerned with movement itself, the focus being how and where the body moves in relation to the floor and obstacles. What the action is and how it is performed is the essence of gymnastics, not the result of the action, nor the effect of the action. At all times you are trying to prove that you can defy gravity in a variety of specially constructed situations. Finding out what your body can do and bringing it under conscious control when interacting with the special gymnastics environment is the challenge of gymnastics.

Gymnastic Forms

The challenge of controlling the body in new and efficient ways has long lured humans.

We can deduce that the term gymnastics has for 2000 years been synonymous with physical exercise and indeed was the embryo of our contemporary physical education (Russell 1980).

Table 11.1

▼▼▼▼   ▼

Variations in gymnastic forms

Educational Gymnastics	Artistic Gymnastics	Modern Rhythmic Gymnastics
Functional	Functional, minimally expressive	Functional and minimally expressive
Educational	Educational but performance-oriented	May be educational but performance-oriented
Noncompetitive	Usually competitive	Usually competitive
Process-oriented	Product-oriented	Product-oriented
Movement skills are predetermined by teacher and student	Movement skills are predetermined by teacher or coach	Movement skills are predetermined by teacher or coach
Performed alone or in small groups	Performed individually	Performed alone, in small or large groups
Appropriate for both males and females	Females have four events; males have six events in competition	Only females may take part in competition
Small equipment is used	No small equipment is used	Small equipment is used
Apparatus is not standardized	Apparatus is standardized	No apparatus is used

▼▼▼▼   ▼

Through the centuries, many variations in gymnastic forms have evolved. The three most common forms of gymnastics taught in schools today are: modern rhythmic gymnastics, artistic gymnastics, and educational gymnastics. The basic similarities and differences between these forms are outlined in table 11.1.

Modern rhythmic gymnastics originated in Europe and has spread in popularity primarily in the private gymnastic clubs and studios of North America. A dancelike movement form, modern rhythmic gymnastics was first included in the Olympic Games in 1984. In this form of gymnastics, elements from dance and games are utilized to create a floor routine in which a ball, rope, hoop, ribbon, or club is manipulated in time to the music. A dancelike quality pervades all movements as rhythm, flow, dynamic contrasts, and aesthetic appeal are essential elements in a quality performance.

Elementary school children greatly enjoy the rhythmic elements of movement, and when they can catch, bounce, and throw balls with a high degree of skill they will react positively to the challenge of doing these skills to music. They will also enjoy the challenge of composing a simple gymnastic routine to popular music. Challenges such as these

Modern Rhythmic Gymnastics

may be included in the games and gymnastic lessons at appropriate times. However, due to the complexity of rhythmic gymnastics per se, we do not consider it to be an appropriate movement form to include in the elementary school program.

Artistic Gymnastics

Artistic gymnastics (Olympic) is the form in which a high degree of proficiency in established movement skills is developed. While movements may be simplified for the beginner, the ultimate goal is to perfect predetermined routines on set pieces of apparatus. These routines are then judged. Because the focus of this gymnastic form is upon the movement product rather than the process (how we learn to move), we suggest it is inappropriate in elementary physical education.

> Formal or traditional gymnastics . . . consists of learning numerous, though often unrelated, skills on the various apparatuses of artistic gymnastics. These skills can be very difficult and sometimes risky. Thus, little thought is normally given as to whether the student is receiving well-rounded physical development or is merely performing set gymnastic skills because they are supposed to be "good" for the student (Russell 1980).

Educational Gymnastics

Educational gymnastics is aptly termed, and its major goal is that of education. This implies that the child is most important, as opposed to the activity or movement skill. This is the form we believe should be included in elementary school physical education programs.

In educational gymnastics, children work at their own level on tasks structured to develop understanding and skill in applying selected movement concepts. While each child is responding to the same task, the theoretical framework allows for skill progression appropriate for every child. Your role as the teacher is to encourage the child to think and solve movement problems through gymnastic activity. When competitive gymnastics was taught in schools, the premise was that each child was to learn a specific skill on a specific day. In contrast, educational gymnastics is founded upon the premise that children learn at different rates and the discovery of how and why a movement is appropriate is valuable during the process of skill acquisition (see table 11.2).

You will rarely need to demonstrate specific skills or products. Instead, you will pose tasks such as, "Find different ways of taking weight on your hands," "Find a way to take weight on your hands only, stretching your feet to the ceiling," or "Take weight on your hands only with a wide body shape and place your feet in a different spot from where they began." A cartwheel may result with students showing variation in degree of stretch and control. From here, you would refine the responses so that more stretch, control, and effective body alignment develops. The educational aspect of this gymnastic form is that all children may succeed and acquire movement skills as they discover their levels of competence.

Table 11.2

Teaching styles of gymnastic forms

Competitive Gymnastic Forms	Result	Movement Product
Teacher: "Do a cartwheel." (Children practice)	→ Some succeed, some fail →	Range from poor to excellent cartwheels
Educational Gymnastics		
Teacher: "Transfer your weight onto your hands." (Children practice)	→ All succeed →	With variation in body shape, result is handstands, headstands, frog stand, cartwheels, back arch
"Take weight on your hands and stretch your feet to the ceiling." (Children practice)	→ All succeed →	With variation in degree of stretch, result is handstands, headstands, cartwheels
"Take weight on one hand at a time and place your feet in a different spot from where they began." (Children practice)	→ All succeed →	Variations of the cartwheel

New movements may also be discovered, as the children are required to use movement knowledge as well as ingenuity and creativity to seek an appropriate response. A task that requires the students to alternate stretching and curling while traveling may result in a simple jump, a front walkover, or a dive roll.

Unlike other forms of gymnastics which require precise actions to be done for specific activity or stunt, educational gymnastics uses the dynamics of movement to create new activities and movement sequences. Many variations of known stunts and vaults are produced, as well as activities and sequences which have no known names (Wilson 1979).

Even though each child within the class may respond to a task in a different manner, skill development will result if the teacher provides simplifying, extending, and refining tasks that encourage children to challenge themselves. Students need time to explore, discover, consolidate, and refine new movement as each movement concept is studied.

The concepts of what the body is doing, where the body is moving, and how the body is moving in relation to the floor or apparatus are constantly being explored. Small apparatus, such as small mats and hoops, as well as large apparatus serve as additional stimuli for the child.

Educational gymnastics
should be included in
elementary physical
education programs.

Children may work together. A partner may contribute to the movement sequence as an obstacle, a leader or follower, one who matches
the movements, or as one who assists a partner's movement.

To summarize, educational gymnastics holds tremendous value in the
elementary physical education program for numerous reasons. Morrison
(1969) reinforces this by stating:

> The functional, objective side of movement can best be served by
> educational gymnastics which can be freely adapted to the skill,
> spirit and needs of any group.

The Material of Gymnastics

In chapter 2, movement concepts are presented in a general way to provide the foundation for the elementary school physical education program. While chapters 5 and 8 present the material of dance and games,
respectively, this section concentrates on the material of gymnastics. You
may already be familiar with some of the terminology of gymnastics, as
presented in figure 11.1.

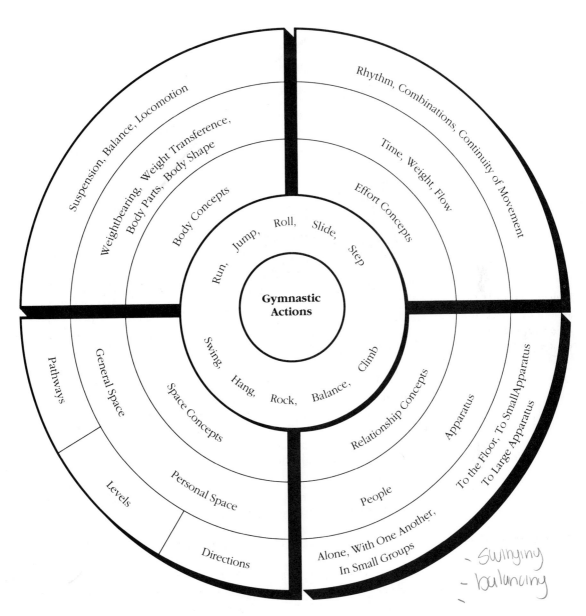

Figure 11.1 Movement concepts in gymnastics

Table 11.3

▼▼▼▼   ▼

Gymnastic actions

Weight Transference		Weightbearing	
On the floor	*With apparatus*	*Balance*	*Suspend*
Run	Climb	Balance (static)	Balance
Jump	Jump	Rock	Rock
Roll	Roll		Hang
Slide	Slide		Swing
Step	Step		
	Swing		

Each of the above may be developed through focus on:

Body concepts	*Space concepts*	*Effort concepts*	*Relationship concepts*
Stressing specific body parts	Direction	Time	Partner work
Stretching and curling	Level	Weight	In small groups
Changing or maintaining a body shape	Pathway		
Flight			

▼▼▼▼   ▼

Movement concepts are developed through a number of specific gymnastic activities. These are presented for reference in table 11.3.

Body Concepts

Body concepts fall into two groups, each with a specific antigravity challenge, on the floor and on the apparatus (see figure 11.2).

1. Weightbearing, in which various skills of balance and suspension are developed.
2. Transference of weight, in which locomotor skills are developed. These include jumping, rolling, and stepping activities.

Weightbearing

Weightbearing is one of the most simple body concepts because it only deals with **how** we are supporting our weight. When you first introduce this concept, focus on which body parts may take the body's weight (points of support). Children will find that in combination, almost all body parts may take weight in some way. We may bear weight on our stomachs, holding our ankles with our hands arching backwards, or take weight on our back, tucking into a ball shape. We may take weight on the shoulders, and place the feet behind our head or supporting our

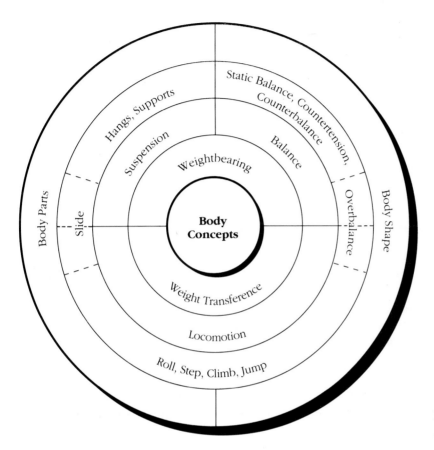

Figure 11.2 Body concepts in gymnastics

body on shoulders only. Weight may be taken in totally inverted positions where the hands solely bear weight, hands and head only, or forearms only. Combinations of body parts and numbers of body parts make this work challenging for children as they learn how to support their weight. They will find that the fewer the number of body parts, the smaller the surface of the body parts, or the smaller the base makes it difficult to maintain the balance and shape being held.

Large apparatus introduced in the theme of weightbearing provides a world of new possibilities. When a child is offered the potential of hanging, gripping, or holding on ropes, bars, rings, and ladders, suspension is possible. The hips, backs of knees, crooks of elbows, hands, ankles, and neck in isolation or combination may provide sufficient support to take the body's weight.

We may bear weight on various body parts.

Balance Balance requires muscular control—a sense of equilibrium as well as a sound kinesthetic sense (see table 11.4). Balance includes static or stationary shapes when the center of gravity is above the base of support and is held for a period of time. Examples of static balance include standing on the ball of one foot, balancing on the hands only, or sitting with legs and arms outstretched off the floor (V-sit).

Static Balance Static balance involves balancing on specific body parts. Common static balances include the headstand, handstand, frog stand (where the hands provide the base of support and the body is in a curled shape, knees resting on elbows), and back arch.

Children will initially practice balancing on various body parts and then may be guided to create various shapes on selected body parts. The teacher may provide such tasks as, "Balance on one foot creating a wide shape," "Find a twisted shape and balance on shoulders only," or "Create a sequence of balance in a stretched shape; roll and balance in another stretched shape." A difficult task that children enjoy is "Run, leap, and balance on the foot you landed upon."

Developing the concept of balance may also be accomplished through partner work. Partial and total weightbearing may be studied both in dance and gymnastics. However, in gymnastics the movements will be functional rather than expressive, and will occur as an outgrowth of partner work sequences and exploration of shape and balance. Children in grade 4 will likely be mature enough to take each other's weight as they balance together. They will enjoy some of the typical ways of taking the weight of another; for example: child *A* crouching in a ball shape to provide partial support for child *B* in a back arch; child *A* on all fours

Table 11.4

▼▼▼▼   ▼

Factors that influence balance

Principle	Interpretation	Gymnastic Implication
Base of support	The wider the base of support, the more stable the balance.	In a headstand, the head and hands should form a triangle to create a wide base of support.
		Palms and fingers should be placed flat on floor to increase the size of the base of support.
Center of gravity	The center of gravity must be above the base of support. If it is not, the person will fall over.	Hips should be above the hands in a handstand.
	The lower the center of gravity, the more stable the balance.	Begin teaching balance with curled shapes; progress to stretched shapes.
Law of inertia	An object continues in a state of rest (or uniform motion) unless it is compelled by some external force to change that state.	"Tight" muscles will hold a balance. Relaxing the muscles will cause the body to fall.
Segmented body	Stability is greatest when each segment of the body is vertically above the center of gravity of the segment below.	In a handstand or headstand, the body should be as straight as possible.
Supporting surface area	The more stable the supporting surface area, the more stable the balance.	A firm, flat, and slightly textured surface is easier to balance on than a bar, mat, or slippery floor.
Absorption of force	Force needs to be absorbed in order to balance.	If jumping and balancing, the force first needs to be absorbed by bending the knees and then balancing.

▼▼▼▼   ▼

while child *B* puts his arms around *A*'s stomach to balance vertically; or child *A* lying on his back, supporting the weight of *B* by extending his arms and feet to contact *B*'s hips and hands.

Overbalance Balance with overbalance is an enjoyable concept to explore with older children. It is not physically difficult, but the basic mechanics of balance must be applied. Overbalance involves balancing and then slightly shifting the weight (center of gravity) outside of the base

Counterbalance involves pushing in order to achieve stability.

of support in order for a transference of weight to occur. A common example of overbalance is a handstand or headstand into a forward roll. However, the balances created to explore overbalance need not be this difficult or established. Children will enjoy simply balancing in shapes they have created, adjusting their center of gravity (usually the hips), and allowing gravity to pull them into a transfer of weight, usually a rolling action. In rolling, the teacher must stress that the soft body parts should receive the weight and a round body shape is necessary to prevent injury.

Counterbalance Counterbalance and countertension are also challenging concepts apppropriate for older children who work well with partners. Counterbalance involves two people pushing against one another in order to achieve stability. A typical example of this is two people leaning into each other, shoulders contacting to create an inverted V.

Countertension Countertension involves pulling away from the partner to achieve balance. A typical example of this is two people locking hands and leaning backward, creating the shape of a V. Initial attempts at both counterbalance and countertension will probably involve contact with hands while feet provide the base of support. Symmetrical shapes will be attempted first but children should be encouraged to progress to asymmetrical shapes and contact made with different body parts. An ankle may pull away from a partner's bent knee, one person's head may push against the hips of a partner, and the base of support may be hips, shoulders or feet, and hands. In both countertension and counterbalance, children will need guidance to ensure that one child is not carrying the weight of another, but both are actually pushing or pulling so that balance is maintained.

Counter tension involves
pulling to achieve stability.

Suspension Balance on apparatus takes the form of supports or hangs.
In supports, the head is above the base of support (e.g., gripping on a
horizontal bar, hips resting on the bar). In hangs, the head is below the
base of support (e.g., hanging inverted by the knees on a horizontal bar).
Apparatus such as ropes, ladders, bars, hanging rings, and vertical poles
encourage suspension.

Weight transference implies a change in base of support, whether it is
on the spot or is intended to take the body to a new place. Whether the
concept is studied with or without apparatus, it will be of value for children to explore the range of ways in which their weight may be transferred. In this theme, the focus is upon the action—what the movement
is—rather than which body parts are taking the weight, or the body shape
employed.

Weight Transference

Much gymnastic sequence work will involve some transference of
weight with the exception of a series of shapes being consistently supported by a few body parts (balance, suspension). For instance, if a child
creates a pin shape, supported by the feet, and then curls to create a ball
shape, still supported by the feet, weight transference has not occurred.
In this case, the movement may become quite expressive, tending toward
dancelike movement rather than gymnastic-like movement. (The only
exception to this is work on the hanging rings when the hands always
support the body as it rotates or holds various body shapes.) The point
to be stressed is that in skill development, which focuses upon weight
transference, the children's movement responses may be similar to those
found in other themes, but their concentration will be directed toward
the action of the movement rather than where the action travels, how it
travels, or with whom it travels.

Weight transference may be accomplished in various ways. The body may stay on the spot merely changing shape as new body parts take the weight. Examples include the headstand, handstand, and shoulder stand. Here the base of support changes and a transference of weight results.

Weight may be transferred from one body part to the same body part, not traveling to a new spot but employing flight. In jumping actions there is no change in parts bearing the weight. However, the weight is taken off the feet and then returns to the feet, implying weight transference.

Weight transference may also serve to take the body to a new space, or may take it away and back again. One may use stepping actions, rolling actions, or jumping actions to initiate momentum for transference of weight. One may transfer weight to and from the feet while jumping on, off, or over apparatus.

When apparatus is used, there is even greater potential for weight transference because new body parts may support weight. The child may hang from knees and elbows while other body parts, such as the head, neck, shoulders, back, hips, legs, ankles, and hands may assist in taking weight or allow for a smooth transference of weight.

Sample Tasks for Weight Transference:

a. Transfer your weight onto your hands in different ways.
b. Take your weight on your shoulders and transfer it onto your feet.
c. Travel over the bench, transferring your weight from one body part to another.
d. Transfer your weight from feet to hands to feet suddenly.
e. With your weight on your stomach, transfer your weight onto your hips.

Locomotion Locomotion implies traveling to a new place. Common types of locomotion used in gymnastics activities focus upon the feet (e.g., running and jumping), feet and hands (e.g., cartwheeling), and rolling.

Rolling A skill children usually bring to the program is rolling. Rolling provides for the child's safety while forming the basis for rotation in gymnastic movement. When a program involves children climbing heights, traveling in unconventional ways, springing off apparatus into the air, and traveling backward where the eyes are not there to guide, the teacher must provide a safety mechanism to prevent injury. The ability to tuck the body in a curled shape and continue moving until the momentum is dissipated prevents injury. If a child happens to fall either from a balance on the floor or off apparatus, injury may be prevented by rolling rather than extending the arms to "catch" the fall or slamming an isolated body part (such as the back) against the floor. Because of this, the sequence of **run, jump, land, and roll** must be learned early in the gymnastic program.

In initial gymnastic lessons, rocking, which leads to various types of rolling, will establish a sound movement basis. Rolling has tremendous value for the child, not only as a form of safety but also because it necessitates focus upon the use of body parts, body shape, weightbearing, and transference of weight. Unlimited potential exists in rolling movements, as the child may be encouraged to perform symmetrical and asymmetrical rolls, backward, forward, sideways, and diagonal rolls, shoulder rolls, chest rolls, rolls with straight legs, rolls with no use of arms, and rolls that link other movements. Rolling may also be performed in relation to apparatus as well as other children. Children may work on their own, rolling along, over, under, around, and through various pieces of apparatus such as hoops, ropes, benches, boxes, and beams. They will enjoy the challenge of mirroring, matching, leading, following, or meeting and parting with a friend as they refine sequences that involve rolling. Partners may also be used as stationary obstacles to be rolled over, under, or through (separated legs). Great challenge is provided when the partner moves and timing is essential in the rolling actions.

Rolling should be taught in the early stages by having children create curled shapes to rock back and forth. Because children are so flexible, many curled shapes, including ones where the back is arched, are possible. The next step in this sequence is to rock and roll in all directions. Teaching points at this stage should include keeping the head, elbows, knees, and feet tucked in, and allowing the body to be taken in whatever direction momentum will take it.

Once children are adept at rocking and rolling, you may ask them to create a sequence of a stretched shape and a curled shape that will roll. These shapes should be joined together in a continuous fashion so that movement is not jerky and the rolling appears to grow naturally out of the curled shape. Stretched shapes may then be required to be vertical—or mostly vertical—so that the child must tuck and roll, taking downward momentum into sideways, forward, or backward movement. This stage provides the basis for the absorption of downward force.

When children can perform these actions with relative ease they may progress to tasks such as:

> "**B**egin with your weight on your knees, tuck and roll sideways and take your weight on your knees again."
>
> "**F**rom a standing position, tuck and roll in any way you like."
>
> "**J**ump very lightly, landing on your feet and roll forward, backward, or sideways."

At this point in children's skill development you may urge students to explore different ways of jumping, landing, and rolling. While jumping on the spot will be explored and refined initially, jumping in different

SAFETY TIP ///////////

Teaching points at this stage should stress the importance of bony body parts being tucked in and the fatty, more muscular body parts taking the weight. Body parts that may take weight include the side of the leg (rather than knees), the shoulders (rather than the elbows), and the lower back, hips, or upper back (rather than the head).

directions should soon be attempted so that the children not only learn to deal with movement down, but also with movement down and forward, down and backward, or sideways.

Once children have mastered rolling these round shapes and can precede them with jumping and landing, they are ready to provide further momentum with running. Thus, the sequence of **run, jump, land, and roll** should be attempted. When children have practiced this sequence sufficiently and are adept at handling the momentum of their body weight as it travels in various directions, they have acquired the basic safety skills necessary for work with apparatus.

Stepping   Stepping actions are a form of locomotion involving either the feet, hands, or both feet and hands to travel. Walking on both hands, traveling along a bar while hanging, cartwheeling, and "scampering with feet and hands" all involve "stepping."

Climbing   Traveling up hanging ropes, vertical ladders or poles, and climbing frames promote climbing. These actions promote upper body strength and require gripping with hands, ankles, and/or feet. Children will enjoy the sense of accomplishment that climbing activities bring, especially when significant heights are achieved.

Jumping   Jumping may take the form of a transfer of weight from two feet to two feet, one foot to two feet, two feet to one foot, one foot to the other (leaping), and one foot to the same foot (hopping).

Jumping is first experienced by the preschooler in stepping down from a minimal height. As the preschooler matures, jumping will be gained in activities such as running and jumping. Later, the skill of jumping onto a height will be mastered. For this reason, the progression of jumping down, then up, over, and later onto apparatus should be employed.

Jumping is normally initiated by a springing action, which is essentially a curling and sudden stretching action. To gain as much spring as possible, all force must be projected in the desired direction of the spring. In the take-off, joints compress in order for the greatest extension of trunk, legs, and arms to occur in flight. While the body is in the air, muscles must be firm and the body "tight," especially in the lower trunk area.

Flight   Flight is produced when we are without support, totally off the ground. Flight is a product of jumping but may also be achieved by releasing our base of support from large apparatus. Children may experience flight by letting go of swinging ropes or hanging rings, or by jumping off a high box, or springing off a springboard.

When children enter grade 4, they should have sufficient physical and mental maturity to experience the joy of flight. It is at this stage that the teacher may introduce flight-assisting apparatus such as springboards, beatboards (reuther boards), and trampettes. These pieces of apparatus require good bodily control, strength, balance, and the ability to land

REMEMBER THAT

The following suggestions may be of value in helping students maintain the necessary round shape when rolling forward or backward.

1. *Bring into a class a box (a shoe box is fine) and a ball. Discuss the shape of each object; push the box and then the ball. Which one rolls? Stress that round shapes roll, square ones do not. Therefore, we need to maintain a round shape to roll.*

2. *Students should start a rolling action with their hips off the ground.*

3. *When rolling backward, students should start with the palms of their hands facing forward near their ears. (We call this "Mickey Mouse Ears" with young children.)*

4. *Place a beanbag in between the student's chin and chest to ensure that the head is tucked in as much as possible during rolling. (The forehead should not contact the ground during rolling forward. Rather, it is the back of the head that should contact the ground in the forward roll.)*

5. *Ensure that children roll in the direction that their momentum is carrying them. For instance, if a child jumps up and forward, the roll should continue to travel forward. Children should also be able to twist and roll sideways as sometimes it is difficult to control forward momentum (see figure 11.3). Many children have difficulty with this concept as they attempt to change the direction of the force.*

correctly. When flight-assisting apparatus is used initially, it must be used in isolation, without boxes or horses adjacent. In this way children will be free to explore various types of take-offs, create shapes in the air, or attempt to rotate in flight, as well as land in various ways. Only when children are adept at using flight-assisting apparatus should it be used as a means for getting onto or over other apparatus.

Flight may also be developed as a minor concept with older children through partner work. This requires physical skill and cooperation between children. Flight may be gained as child *A* supports the weight of *B* as he gains flight, *A* may push off *B* to gain flight, or *A* may prolong the flight of *B* by establishing contact while *B* is in the air.

> If this type of partner work is to be of value the child who is in some way assisted in flight must himself be able to take-off effectively, land safely and control his body in the air (Mauldon and Layson 1965).

Because flight is difficult and potentially dangerous, some elementary school children may never acquire the skill necessary for this concept.

Sliding Sliding is unique in that it is a form of locomotion but does not involve a transference of weight. Sliding requires tension as the body shape is held while traveling. We may slide along the floor or bench, slide up or down an inclined bench on body parts such as our bottom, stomach, or back.

SAFETY TIP ///////////

Apparatus that assists in flight or is used with flight-assisting apparatus demands much bodily control and a sound sense of balance. For this very reason it is suggested that springboards, trampettes, beatboards, and trampolines not be used with children under age 8 as they don't possess the dynamic balance required to safely use them without assistance.

Flight requires much
control.

Body parts may be used in numerous ways. As stated in chapter 2, body parts may lead or initiate action as well as support or receive weight. You or the children may point out which body parts are being used in locomotor and nonlocomotor actions. In stillness and motion, parts may lead or initiate an action as do the hands in a cartwheel or handstand, the head and shoulders in a forward roll, the hips in a swinging action, the hands in rope climbing, or the stomach facing upward in a back arch. When children are developing and refining newly acquired movements you will inevitably provide guidance with reference to specific body parts. Comments such as "Place your hands further apart," "Kick your feet higher," and "Tuck your head in as you roll" illustrate the importance of specific body parts. In most gymnastic movements the feet and knees, as well as hands and elbows, are of particular significance in rotating actions and their positioning and role will be stressed to achieve quality.

Young children will enjoy discovering new movements through exploration of leading with different body parts. Leading tasks include, "Travel leading with your knees," "Lead with your head as you find a twisted shape," and "Transfer your weight with hips leading the action and then roll." When children are working on such movements, the body parts will need emphasis for skill development and sound kinesthetic awareness to ensue.

Use of Hands Because our hands are used so extensively in gymnastics, children should learn to always place their *whole palm* on the floor when taking weight on their hands. Some children will tend to place only their fingers on the floor, lifting the palm, while others may contact the floor only with the fingertips. When we are using a base of support as small as the hands, we want to make it as big as possible. Thus, fingers should be spread apart so that we have "big hands."

Use of Feet, Ankles, and Knees Feet, ankles, and knees are the body parts that not only provide tremendous force when they are suddenly stretched, but also effectively absorb force when they bend. Dancers, divers, and gymnasts are the few athletes who use their lower legs effectively to jump or spring as most other athletes tend to rely more heavily on the quadriceps (thigh muscles) to produce force. Thus, the teacher may find it worthwhile to stress full extension of the feet, ankles, and knees in springing actions. When landing on the feet, the toes, balls of the feet, then heels should strike the ground to absorb force effectively and without injury.

Use of Arms and Shoulders At some point in the children's skill development, springing actions with weight on the hands will be covered. The teacher may pose the task, "Transfer your weight from feet to hands to feet with a springing action." This task may be answered in an array of ways. One child may attempt a type of bear-walk, where hands and

To Do

Try standing with your palms touching a wall, arms outstretched. Push your body away from the wall without bending your arms. It is possible to produce momentum in this manner without bending your arms because of the mobility in the shoulder girdle.

▼▼▼▼   ▼

feet spring from one to the other. Another child may attempt a handstand and attempt to spring back onto his feet. A truly skilled child may attempt a back handspring or a cartwheel with flight (called a round-off).

We know that spring is produced by bending or curling a joint and then suddenly extending it. In the case of arms producing spring, the arms bend, then stretch to create force. The shoulders can also produce spring because of the structure of the joints in the shoulder girdle. Thus, one may produce spring from a handstand without bending the arms.

The Head Head placement is extremely important in games activities because it provides us with the direction of our vision. In dance and gymnastic activities, the head serves this function as well, but may also provide an aesthetic appeal due to the focus on the body shape. In a leap for instance, the eyes should focus upward to provide the appearance of greater height and lightness. Head placement is also important for continuity of line in body shape. The head sometimes serves a functional purpose in dance and gymnastics because it can initiate a turning action.

Body Shapes

Body shape refers to the lines or forms that the body creates in motion and in stillness (see figure 11.3). This is a direct result of the bending, curling, stretching, and twisting actions of the body.

Round Shapes When the joints of the elbows, knees, hips, and spine are primarily bent or curled, the result is a curled or ball shape, where the extremities give the impression of meeting at the body's center. Round shapes may also be achieved by curling sideways or backward (as in a back arch). These shapes rotate most efficiently, as this tucked position provides a curved surface on which to rock and roll. In preparation for take-off and in landing, the body tucks and assumes this round shape as well. Round shapes are easier to hold in balancing activities, as the center of gravity tends to be lower and above the center of gravity due to the compactness of the extremities.

Stretched Shapes When the body is stretched, the direction of the reach may either be vertical or horizontal. A *long* shape is achieved when the hands and head are as far away from the feet as possible. The body may be lying prone on the floor or on a piece of equipment such as a box,

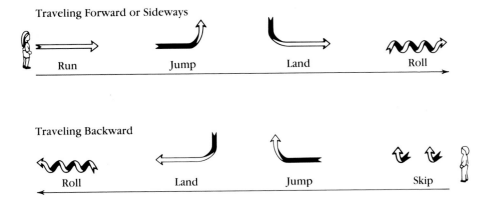

Traveling Forward or Sideways

Run   Jump   Land   Roll

Traveling Backward

Roll   Land   Jump   Skip

horse, bench, or beam. The shape may be supported by one leg as in a "scale," creating a *T* shape. The long shape is used in diving actions where the body stretches in flight as much as possible to achieve height and/or distance. The headstand and handstand are examples of long shapes in balance.

A *wide* shape is also a stretched shape but the body is stretched sideways rather than up. The wide shape in its extreme form takes the shape of an *X*. The most common example of the wide shape is the cartwheel, where the motion is sideways in a foot-hand-hand-foot sequence. Static and dynamic wide shapes are easily balanced on two feet due to the wide base of support. However, when other bases are used, balance is difficult, due to the raised center of gravity caused by the stretched extremities. Wide shapes are most commonly employed with other shapes in gymnastic movement. A straddle jump in which the feet meet the hands in flight is a combination of a round and wide shape. A static balance on the hands or head and hands where the legs form a *V* will combine a long and wide shape. Many wide shapes may also be twisted so that a roll or new balance may result.

Twisted Shapes The twisted shape involves rotation of the trunk with the hips and shoulders facing different directions. Twisted shapes are always asymmetrical, usually facilitate change in direction, and most commonly join movements together. Like wide shapes, twisted shapes are often created in combination with other shapes. Figure 11.4 illustrates various body shapes.

The proportions of time, weight, and flow are the factors that directly influence bodily control in gymnastics (see figure 11.5).

> . . . skill is acquired through the gradual refinement of the feel of the movement and any training has indeed to promote this feel which, in its essence in the awakening of the sense for the proportions of motion factors (Laban and Lawrence 1948).

Figure 11.3 Children should roll in the direction of the force

Effort Concepts

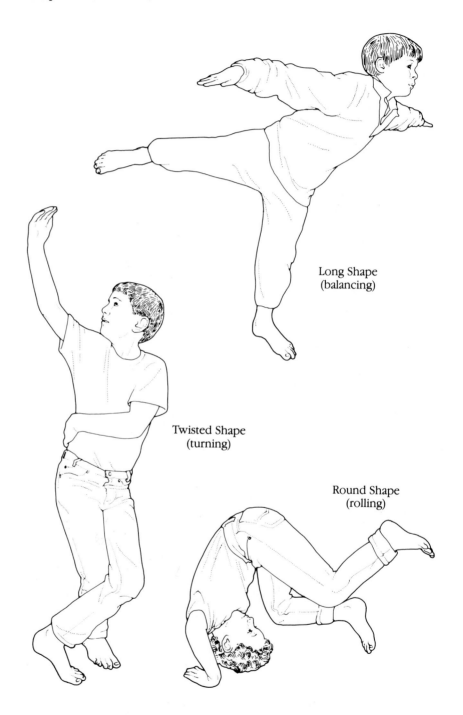

Long Shape
(balancing)

Twisted Shape
(turning)

Round Shape
(rolling)

Wide Shape
(cartwheeling)

Combination Round
and Wide Shape
(jumping)

Figure 11.4 Body shapes in
gymnastics

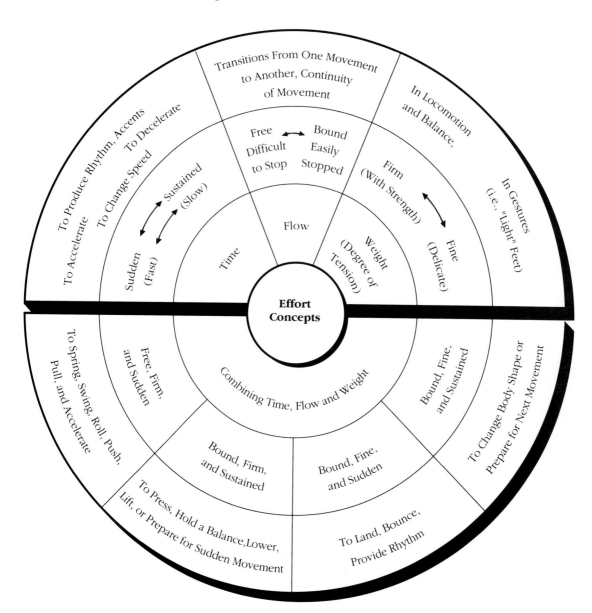

Figure 11.5 Effort concepts

The concepts of time and weight should be introduced separately so that children become aware of the range of movements possible within sudden and sustained time and firm and fine weight. Young children are capable of rather superficial movement exploration of the effort concepts, as they tend toward firm and sudden actions in their everyday lives. However, familiar locomotor movements of running, skipping, galloping, jumping, and hopping may be performed with emphasis on "light" or "strong" feet. Balancing activities that focus upon changing shape in a slow, sustained manner are within the capabilities of young children. Because their muscular control is limited and they are only beginning to appreciate time and flow, movements will tend to go and stop, go and stop. Continuity of movement, which is so necessary for quality sequence work, will develop as the child matures both physically and cognitively.

Time

Sudden movement is necessary to achieve force for springing, swinging, sliding, and many rotating actions and forms of transferring weight. Older elementary school children will enjoy "playing" with the factor of time. Once they are adept at rolling, taking weight on their hands, and transferring their weight in various ways, the teacher may introduce performing these actions in a sustained way. Rolls, handstands, headstands, cartwheels, and variations of all of these will provide tremendous challenge when attempted slowly with unexpected changes in time, or sequenced rhythmically.

Weight

Firm movement is required in almost all gymnastic activities and children must learn to gauge how strong the action needs to be in order not to provide too much force for the action. However,

> If adequate tension is not retained heaviness will result and the body will become inert and unready for action. Overtension is a waste of energy, cramps the body and causes it to be unprepared to move readily (Stanley 1969).

Flow

Flow relates to the degree of control one has over the action. In most sustained movements, such as slowly lifting or lowering the legs or arms in hanging or balancing activities, the flow will be bound. In actions that involve flight, the flow will be primarily free; that is, the movement will be difficult to stop, as in springing, leaping, and jumping. It is the interplay between releasing and binding flow that results in control. While we often discuss flow with respect only to the extremes of bound and free flow, the child will experience and utilize varying degrees of flow within particular movements.

Once children have focused their action on weight and time, combinations of time and weight may be attempted. Phrasing, rhythm, and accents will provide the "final touch" to gymnastic sequence work.

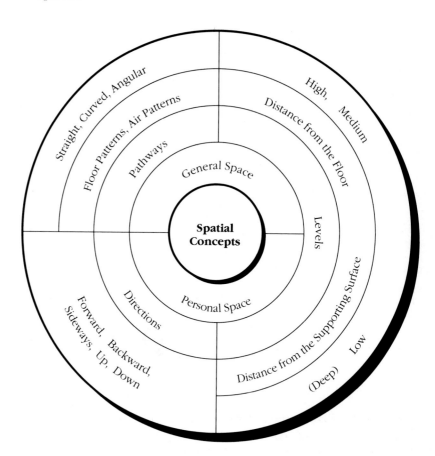

Figure 11.6 Spatial
concepts

Spatial Concepts

As stated in chapter 2, spatial concepts deal with where the body moves
(see figure 11.6). The body may move on the spot within personal space,
or it may travel into open spaces, called general space. We may travel
near the ground as we roll, or reach high in the air as we leap. The distance we have from the floor or apparatus determines our *level,* which
can be low (close to the floor or base), medium, or high (far away from
the floor or base). When we travel from one spot to another we will produce a *pathway.* A floor pattern may take the most direct route possible
to our destination (straight pathway), or an indirect, circuitous route
(curved or zigzag). We may also create an air pattern as the extremities
fill space or as the body travels through the air in flight. When we travel,
we have options as to which direction we choose to move. Each of these
spatial dimensions (personal space, general space, levels, pathways, and
directions) will be discussed with direct reference to gymnastic movement.

A pathway may be seen when one leaves tracks.

Personal Space

Personal space is the space around the body that may be filled without traveling. We may think of our personal space as a bubble or balloon in which we create shapes. We may reach up into space as we stretch high in preparation for a handstand, or tuck our bodies as we land from jumping. We take the "balloon" of personal space with us wherever we travel. When our body parts are stretched to their limits inside this "balloon" of personal space, a transfer of weight occurs and we will probably travel to a new spot in the general space.

General Space

General space refers to all the area into which we may travel. It includes any empty space not filled by people, objects, or structures. When we run, jump, swing, or climb we fill general space.

Pathways

One may illustrate the concept of pathway to children by providing the simple analogy of walking on a clean floor with muddy feet or making tracks in freshly fallen snow. When one turns around to look at the footprints made, the pathway will be evident.

Gymnastics apparatus arrangements promote various pathways. Generally speaking, when we travel on the floor, the accent is on the *floor* pathway. When we employ flight on travel through the air (as we do on hanging ropes), the accent is on the *air* pathway. When the teacher asks children to travel around their hoop on the floor they will follow a circular pathway. The air pathway that one will take while swinging on a hanging rope or bar will be curved. While the design of a long skipping rope may be manipulated by the child, various floor pathways may result as the child travels along the rope. When benches, beams, and planks are used, the teacher may request the child to travel along the apparatus. Here the pathway would be straight. However, the teacher may say, "Travel the length of the apparatus touching it only with your hands." In response to this task, many children will travel from one side to the other over a bench, creating a zigzag pathway.

When children work with mats only, their tendency will be to create sequences that travel only in a straight line. Thus, you will need to encourage various pathways when transference of weight is covered. "Imagine that you can write your name with your feet on the floor as you travel," and "Repeat your sequence, making sure that corners are sharp if you turn," are examples of tasks that direct the child's concentration to the pathway. Once children have explored various movements and the type of pathway these movements tend to create, you may then introduce letters, numbers, geometrical shapes, and other simple forms as impetus for new pathways.

When planning apparatus arrangements, you will need to consider pathway. If the apparatus is set up in a line, then you can assume children will use a straight pathway. Leaving spaces between large pieces of apparatus, or setting up apparatus in specific designs (e.g., circle) will elicit variety in pathways.

Directions

The concept of direction relates to one's personal space. Direction is relatively simple to children. In early childhood they learn the concepts of front, back, beside, up, down, forward, backward, and sideways. They will readily understand that they may travel forward (toward their front), backward (toward their back), sideways (to their right or left side), up (toward their head), down (toward their feet), or diagonally, combining three directions that are not opposites (e.g., sideways, up, right).

Some confusion does exist however with respect to the difference between change of direction and change of pathway. A child may perform a forward roll, turn 90 degrees, and perform another forward roll. In this situation the child is consistently traveling forward into general space and thus is not changing direction, but creating a zigzag pathway. When you ask children to change direction, where they are facing does not matter but *where the action travels in relation to themselves* is significant.

For further clarification, more examples are provided. A log roll travels to the side of the body, as does a cartwheel. A walkover travels forward. A back arch may be created only by moving down and back or forward and downward.

Children will enjoy discovering which activities are restricted to particular directions and which are flexible in direction. You may be specific in providing guidelines for sequence work: "Create a sequence of traveling forward, traveling up and down, balancing, then traveling sideways." This type of guidance will encourage a great range of possibilities. Older children may be challenged further by guidelines that involve the two spatial concepts of direction and pathway. "Create a sequence of a straight pathway where you travel forward, a curved pathway where you travel diagonally, and finally, in a zigzag pathway, travel backward" is an example of such a task.

Levels will probably be one of the first spatial concepts you may develop to some degree with children. Children soon learn that flight and instability occur at a high level, speed and mobility are gained at a medium level, and stability is most effective at a low level. *Levels*

In gymnastics you will probably begin with familiar traveling actions such as running, stopping, hopping, and leaping without apparatus. While these actions are performed at a medium to high level, young children will find gaining height difficult and will perform them at a medium level, while older children will employ flight and will utilize a high level.

Rolling actions occur at a low level. Once children are adept at various types of rolls, the teacher may introduce initiating rolls from various levels. The children may balance at high or medium levels and transfer weight in order to roll. The dive roll is an excellent example of attempting to gain height and flight before one tucks to roll. Children may then explore rolling over objects, rolling from apparatus, and rolling onto apparatus, all of which promote change of level.

As apparatus is introduced, the concept of levels may take on new meaning. A child can create a shape at a high level while balancing on a high box. If the child lies down on the box, he has created a low shape but is still "high" in relation to the ground. Thus, we may take level to mean both the distance from the ground and the distance from the apparatus that supports our weight.

The concept of relationships is comprised of two subdivisions—relationships to apparatus and relationships to people (see figure 11.7). While the former serves as a concept appropriate for gymnastic work with young or inexperienced children, relationships to people is a complex theme appropriate for older children who are socially capable of cooperation with others and have sufficiently developed body management skills. ***Relationship Concepts***

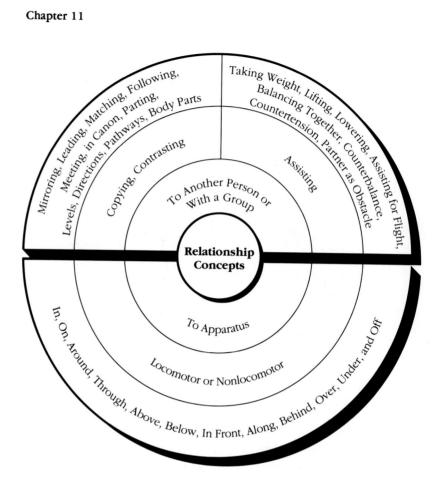

Figure 11.7 Relationship
concepts

Relationships to
Apparatus

This is an appropriate movement concept for children in kindergarten
and first grade, as they are at the stage of grasping spatially oriented words.
Such prepositions as in, out, on, off, around, along, through, above, below,
in front, behind, beside, over, and under may be explored in relation to
small and large apparatus. Tasks such as "Travel over and under the
bench," and "Jump in and out of the hoop, then travel through it," are
simple, yet will challenge young children and provide them with freedom
and structure.

Older children in the upper elementary grades should also explore
this theme if they are relatively inexperienced. Complex apparatus arrangements demand the ability to relate to it, to "see" the possibilities
for action. The tasks you give to these older children should be more
complex and physically demanding and may involve a combination of
spatial prepositions with other concepts such as pathway, level, body
parts, body shape, or time. For example, you may say, "Travel along the
bench backward," "Balance on the box at a high level," or "Try different
ways of traveling quickly around your apparatus with emphasis on hands
taking the weight."

Matching movements are exactly the same.

Relationships to People

Children will find it helpful, encouraging, and satisfying to develop gymnastic skill with others. They may work with partners or small groups effectively as long as their social ability is sufficient to allow them to co-operate, respect others, solve problems, and safely move in harmony together. (The concepts of counterbalance and countertension previously discussed involve relationships to people.)

Initial skill development with a partner or small group will focus upon copying another's movements. Children may combine the best work of their partner with their own to create identical sequences or they may prefer simply to incorporate one or two movements of their partner's into their own sequence. When children are at different levels of skill, it is important for the teacher to stress that at times the more-skilled child should copy the lesser-skilled, and at others the lesser-skilled child should copy the more-skilled.

Matching Matching means that children perform exactly the same movements. It is most easily practiced when children face the same way: if A points her right foot, B must do so as well. However, matching may also be accomplished when A travels in front of B (leading and following, cannon) or A and B face different directions. The latter is difficult, since timing may be "off" without one child seeing to the other.

Mirroring Mirroring implies that children face each other, creating a "mirror image"—if A reaches to the right, B will have to reach to the left to create the correct image. Children may need clarification once they begin traveling forward and backward in mirroring. If one travels

When mirroring, children face each other to create a "mirror" image.

back, the other must do so as well. If one travels forward, the other travels forward, exactly as a mirror image does. Children may also mirror each other while side by side or back to back; however, this is more difficult because they cannot see each other as easily. A glass mirror may help here.

Meeting and Parting Meeting and parting may be performed either in copying or contrasting movements. When children meet, they come together in space. When they part, they move away from one another in space. This concept may be quite challenging if children incorporate apparatus within their sequences as it increases the complexity of the relationship.

Leading and Following Leading and following, like meeting and parting, may be performed either with similar or differing movements. Here the focus is upon the spatial relationship between the two individuals as they follow the same pathway. Children will need to be reminded that once the leader turns 180 degrees, the follower will do so as well and thus will no longer be in the "following" position. It may also be pointed out that traveling in a backward direction is difficult unless preplanned carefully, for the leader may bump into the follower.

Symmetry and Asymmetry Symmetry and asymmetry is a body concept as it relates to body shape. However, when two or more people work to form one shape, it may be viewed as a relationship concept. Children will need much cooperation and the ability to visualize what they look like from the "outside" to create symmetrical shapes. If mirrors are not

A symmetrical shape is the same on both sides. These boys have made one shape.

available, the teacher may demonstrate with a child or use pictures to help the children grasp this concept. Asymmetry is much easier as one child will create a different shape from the other.

Canon Movement in canon implies that a particular movement is repeatedly performed by two or more individuals following the same pathway. A typical example of movement in canon is found in classical ballet, where a number of dancers leap across the stage, one after another. In gymnastics, canon may be developed as children roll or transfer their weight in the same way, one after the other (see chapter 5).

Contrasting Children may also contrast in their sequence work. This contrast may be found in level (one travels high while another travels low), in directions used while transferring weight, in body parts used, or in pathway employed. While the movement one observes in the theme of contrasting with another person may not significantly differ from other themes, it will serve to focus the child's attention upon the relationship one may have to another.

Assisting In partner work, children assist each other in performing gymnastic actions. These were discussed in the section of this chapter that dealt with weightbearing, balance, and flight. However, it may be useful to state that children may take partial or total weight of a partner, lift or lower their partner, or assist in creating an extended period of flight.

Table 11.5

▼▼▼▼   ▼

Selecting appropriate apparatus for gymnastic actions

Gymnastic Activity	Possible Apparatus
Jumping over	Hoops, skipping ropes, horizontal sticks, benches, low beams, low boxes, planks
From/off	Benches, beams, boxes, horses, planks, trestles, rings, ladder, cargo net, vertical ropes, climber
On	Benches, beams, boxes, horses, planks, trestles, springboard, reuther board, trampette, rings, ladder, vertical ropes, climber, cargo net
Rocking and rolling: under, through	Hoops, horizontal sticks, benches, trestles
over, on	Benches, trestles, boxes, horses, planks, beams
Sliding	Inclined plank, inclined bench
Stepping actions	Hoops, ropes, horizontal sticks, stools, benches, trestles, horses, boxes, rings, ladders, planks, climbers, ropes, cargo net, beam
Climbing	Stools, trestles, ladders, horses, boxes, ladders, planks, climbers, vertical ropes, cargo net
Balancing	Hoops, ropes, stools, benches, trestles, horses, boxes, rings, ladders, planks, climbers, nets, beams
Hanging	Trestles, horses, boxes, rings, ladders, climbers, vertical ropes, nets, high beams
Swinging	Rings, vertical ropes, horizontal ladders, saddle on bars, climber, cargo net

▼▼▼▼   ▼

Summary

Gymnastics plays a vital role in physical education. The focus is on the body and how and where it moves in relation to the floor or apparatus. The movement concepts of the body, effort, space, and relationships are applied similarly in dance, games, and gymnastics with very different results. In gymnastics the body concepts of weightbearing and weight transference will be stressed more due to the functional, yet aesthetic, nature of gymnastics. Large apparatus will provide exciting possibilities for various actions. Table 11.5 lists appropriate apparatus for gymnastic activities.

1. Discuss the similarities and differences between modern rhythmic gymnastics and educational gymnastics.
2. What are the four body concepts studied in gymnastics?
3. What is the difference between balance and suspension?
4. How are weightbearing, weight transference, and body parts interrelated?
5. How does body shape affect balance?
6. How may effort qualities be developed with children in grades 1 through 3?
7. What is the difference between direction and pathway?
8. Older children may enjoy working in pairs. What concepts may be developed?

References

Jordan, D. 1970. *Childhood and Movement.* Oxford: Basil Blackwell.

Laban, R. and F. C. Lawrence. 1948. *Effort.* London: Macdonald and Evans, Ltd.

Mauldon, E. and J. Layson. 1965. *Teaching Gymnastics.* London: Macdonald and Evans, Ltd.

Morison, R. 1969. *A Movement Approach to Educational Gymnastics.* London: Dent and Sons.

Russell, K. 1980. *Gymnastics—Why is it in School Curricula.* Journal of the Saskatchewan Physical Education Association. 6:1, 17–19.

Stanley, S. 1969. *Physical Education: A Movement Orientation.* Toronto: McGraw-Hill Ryerson Ltd.

Williams, J. 1974. *Themes for Educational Gymnastics.* London: Lepus Books.

Wilson, V. J. 1979. *Turn On Turn Off.* Canadian Association of Health, Physical Education and Recreation Journal. 46:1, 39–41.

C H A P T E R

12

TEACHING GYMNASTICS

> The teacher of educational gymnastics (also) aims to teach bodily skills, but he is equally concerned with knowledge, for his business is education (Williams 1974).

As in dance and games, teaching gymnastics is complex and constantly demanding. The tone that you set and the creation of a safe, yet exciting, and positive learning environment is essential for children to feel both secure and challenged in gymnastics.

Gymnastic Experiences

Gymnastics offers opportunities for exciting movement challenges. As children are introduced to jumping, landing, rotating, and balancing on the floor, the addition of apparatus provides new experiences. Children will delight in the adventure that apparatus provides for balancing, climbing, hanging, and swinging.

While there may be a strong tendency to let the children play freely on all apparatus available, you will need to select apparatus that is appropriate for the lesson's objectives and plan tasks that provide a focus for the range of movements from which the child may choose. This does not imply that free play is worthless, it simply means that the child must be taken beyond the stage of free play to that of skill development. If free exploration were the only gymnastic experience offered within the school program, it would be no different from the child's play in the schoolyard.

Because we all enjoy that which we do well, chances are that the children who dislike gymnastics are weak in skill and those who enjoy it have natural skill. In every class, there will be children who have tremendous difficulty with even the simplest rolls and others who cartwheel or walk on their hands at every possible moment. It is likely that these two groups of children may initially pose concern for the beginning teacher, for how is it possible to cater to the needs of such a diverse group? While one child may require special coaxing merely to get off the bench and participate in the class, another child may seemingly show off by climbing the ropes and perching near the ceiling of the gymnasium. It is only through sensitive guidance in instruction and an environment that caters to the needs of all children that every child will progress in the gymnastic program.

When children are provided with the stimulus of apparatus, open tasks will allow them to discover some of the limitations and potential of that piece. Once children have familiarized themselves with the possibilities, then closed tasks will provide additional challenges. Children may be asked to select one or two movements that they enjoy and then repeat and refine them. In sequence development the next stage will be to find ways of approaching the apparatus, getting on the apparatus, or traveling away from it. Finally, the aim is to join movements together in a continuous manner so that the movements flow smoothly from start to finish.

Table 12.1

The gymnastic experience

The Physical Experience Must Be:	The Social Experience Must Be:		The Learning Experience Must Promote:
Child-oriented	Positive	Encouraging	Concentration
Challenging	Cooperative	Pleasant	Memory
Safe	Helpful	Accepting	Creativity
Clean	Observant	Reinforcing	Inventiveness
Tidy	Supportive	Guiding	Problem-solving
Predictable	Advising	Sincere	Analysis
			Observation

In this way children will have created a movement sequence that is indicative of their gymnastic ability, and something of which they are proud. Table 12.1 lists the aspects of a successful gymnastic experience.

Teaching Skills

Whatever the children's level of skill, purposeful activity should be maximized. The tasks set and the type of apparatus chosen must be within the children's capabilities. Lessons should occur in sequence, each one building upon the previous one. **Progression from simple to complex both in tasks and apparatus is vitally important.**

You should initially explore the children's abilities in the area of locomotion on the feet. Traveling and stopping in various body shapes, and traveling while changing directions, pathways, and speed will be developed to improve agility and control in running, jumping, hopping, and leaping activities.

New movement concepts are usually introduced on the floor (e.g., body shapes, body parts, time) before small or large apparatus is introduced. With each new movement concept presented, it is suggested that you provide progressive tasks for the children without apparatus so that the basics of the concepts are mentally appreciated and kinesthetically experienced. Initial exploration and later skill refinement will occur as the children experience balance in relation to the floor. Children should learn to roll immediately upon landing to avoid injury. Discovering effective means of gaining height and appropriate ways to recover upon landing are important. Once you have covered the basic movements required for safety (landing and rolling) and have an appreciation of the movement concept, then apparatus may effectively be introduced.

The arrangement of large and small apparatus will determine the kinds of challenges offered the child. The juxtaposition of pieces should be

REMEMBER THAT

It is only when the task requires skill that the child feels is unattainable or when the child deems the skill to be useless that children will not participate as fully as possible. When children know that they can succeed in pleasurable activities, all will participate.

To Do

How would you react if your teacher said, "Do a back handspring"? How would you react if the teacher said, "Travel backward using hands and feet"?

▼▼▼▼   ▼

determined by the movement concept and the tasks you pose. Children may be offered the freedom of repositioning small apparatus to suit their needs or be purposely restricted to a particular arrangement.

It is the design, spacing, and stability of apparatus that will determine its usefulness. Different ways of associating separate elements are required, with each arrangement offering particular and distinct opportunities (Department of Education and Science 1972).

The way in which tasks are worded is extremely important. They must allow for skill development within the movement concept at all skill levels. For instance, less-skilled children may respond to the task "Travel along the bench at a low level" by walking on hands and feet in a crouched position. The highly skilled child may roll forward on the bench, while a child with a lower limb disability may pull himself forward with his arms as he slides on his stomach. All children are gaining experience and developing skill no matter what their capabilities.

Children should be encouraged to help one another if the opportunity arises. They may offer friendly advice, provide reinforcement for one another, or show their newly acquired skills without apprehension. When children are rewarded for their efforts, the vital support so paramount in skill acquisition will provide tremendous reinforcement.

Safety

Some teachers are hesitant to teach gymnastics for fear of children injuring themselves. Lawsuits resulting from tragic accidents in competitive artistic gymnastics classes have compounded the problem.

Let's examine the cause of such injuries. We know that all children are different. In a class there may be a child who finds gymnastics very difficult and another who finds it very easy. If we expect all children to perform exactly the same movement in exactly the same manner, children will suffer in different ways; those who have not mastered the prerequisite skills will not be able to perform as expected while those who are capable of learning a much more difficult skill will not be challenged. What will the "slow" group gain by trying to replicate movements too difficult for them? They will gain a sense of failure from practicing the movement incorrectly, and incorrect use of the body may result in injury. The advanced group may become bored and lose concentration when performing the skill. Because concentration is essential for all gymnastic movements, injury may also result if the child is not

What Is Wrong with This Situation?

The fourth grade class is participating in the third class of a two month-long unit of gymnastics. The teacher has chosen the movement concept of flight for the lesson, as he believes that this is an essential skill to be developed in children with relative inability. After a brief gymnastic warm-up, the teacher gives instructions for the children to set up specific gymnastic stations. A group of six children set up, in a line, a mat, a beatboard, a vault (four feet high), and another mat. The wall prevents the children from placing two mats in a row.

The problems with the above situation are:

1. The movement concept of flight is appropriate only with gymnastically experienced and skilled children. The movement concept of locomotion, balance, body shape, body parts, transference of weight, levels, time (changes in speed), and weight should precede the concept of flight.

2. Every movement concept should be developed on the floor or mats before apparatus is used to challenge the children further. Because the basic principles or ideas pertinent to every theme are applicable both with and without apparatus, the child should be provided the opportunity to develop skill first in its simplest form (without apparatus) then in increasingly complex situations that involve a variety of small, and then large apparatus or with partners or in small groups.

3. Groups of six children will work well if each child is constantly moving and not standing in line. The problem with this apparatus set-up is that it is in a straight pathway where the flow of traffic will progress from one end to the other. Apparatus should be arranged so that children may use any combination of the apparatus and can approach it from a variety of angles.

4. The beatboard should initially be used by itself so that children kinesthetically experience the feeling of flight, landing, and rolling. Because the theme of flight is a difficult, advanced theme, it is very dangerous to have a large obstacle placed near it. If a child lacks control in assisted flight, the chances of him or her striking the vault are quite likely and will undoubtedly cause injury.

5. One of the most dangerous aspects of this situation is that the vault is too close to the wall. When a child is flying through the air after take-off from the beatboard, a wall that may stop the motion is certainly not desirable!

What is wrong with this
apparatus arrangement?

SAFETY TIP

**If you were to
introduce the theme of
balance and
immediately allow
children to climb to
the highest point on
apparatus, or hold a
shape after jumping off
a springboard, injuries
may result due to
children's lack of
control. Teach them
first to run, jump, land,
and roll.**

completely involved. Thus, it is imperative that the activity is structured
around the needs of every child within the class. The teaching philoso-
phy of structuring the class to meet the needs of the activity is not only
erroneous, it fosters the opportunity for injury.

Apparatus

Regardless of your preferred style of instruction and the age and experience of the children, the physical environment must be safe and non-
threatening. Apparatus that is broken or worn to the point of being unsafe
must be repaired. It should also be suitable in size for the children to
be safe. Trestles, stools, and vaulting boxes should be small enough for
children to feel secure, yet large enough to be challenging. Placement
of apparatus should be considered so that children's pathways are not
"crisscrossing" and there is ample space between pieces of apparatus
and the apparatus and the wall.

Procedures

Children must be taught how to lift and carry apparatus so that no injuries occur, either to the floor or the students. Procedures of taking out,
setting up, and putting away apparatus should be clearly established and
closely followed.

Concentration

Safety also implies a level of concentration by each child. The noise level
should be kept at a minimum, though productive chatting is often necessary. Children must be made aware of the importance of concentration
when attempting a new movement, refining a previously acquired skill,
or joining movements together in a sequence. It is important to establish

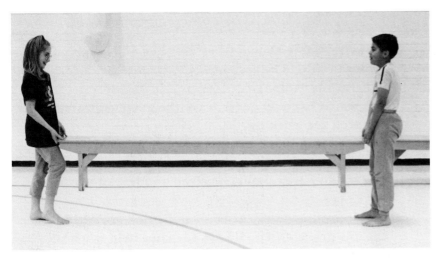

Children should be taught to carry apparatus properly.

that children should decide what movement will be attempted before it is begun, as there are times when children change their minds in mid-action. When the difficult concept of flight is being developed, concentration is paramount for children's safety. It is not acceptable to begin one movement and attempt to finish with another! For example, children should not decide to jump onto a box and then after taking off a spring-board, decide to jump over the box. Very likely, feet would "catch" on the box and injury could result.

One of the basic premises we believe in is that children are aware of their own limits. It is only when the teacher's expectations are too high or the element of competition is introduced that children go beyond their limits. Thus, spotting (manually helping someone perform an action) should be necessary only when children are attempting actions somewhat beyond their limits. We believe that the onus should be placed upon children for their personal safety when they decide what movements will be attempted. You may encourage children to try new and more difficult maneuvers, but children should rarely be forced or manually assisted to perform. The only time that spotting may be helpful is when a child needs assistance to kinesthetically "feel" a new movement. The teacher should be the spotter. For instance, a child may wish to try a back handspring but have no idea where the movement should "go."

Spotting

> Spotting techniques require an understanding of the stunt being performed, knowing how to assist the movement and some degree of strength. . . . The teacher invariably provides the spotting for gymnastics stunts which limits the amount of activity. . . . (Docherty and Morton 1982).

SAFETY TIP ///

1. Rules for safety should be established and enforced.
2. Children should be responsive to the teacher's command of "rest" or "stop."
3. The teacher should never leave the gymnastic area while children are working.
4. Children should use gymnastic apparatus only when a teacher is present.
5. The activity area should be clean and free of apparatus not in use.
6. Children should only attempt skills that are within their capabilities. They should ask for your help when they plan to do something "scary."
7. Children should never touch one another unless instructed to do so.
8. Children should wear appropriate clothing. Bare feet are most safe as they grip the floor or supporting surface well; socks or sneakers tend to slip on climbing apparatus. When children are hanging by their knees, bare legs should be exposed so that the skin is in contact with the bar. Jewelry should be removed.
9. Mats should be used when children take weight on body parts other than feet in locomotor and nonlocomotor activities. However, children should realize that mats do not prevent injury.
10. Children must lift, carry, and place apparatus as instructed.
11. Wear on apparatus should be monitored by both the teacher and children. Damaged apparatus should be reported immediately.
12. Establish and adhere to a maximum number of children allowed on the climbing frame and other larger apparatus.

The vocabulary you use and the energy with which you speak are important. You should convey some of the feeling of the action to the children. Words such as "spring," "tuck tight," and "lift" need to be said with conviction and strength. The timing of your verbal guidance may also be crucial to how quickly a child learns a new skill. Phrases such as "Push NOW," "Tuck NOW," "Let go NOW," and "Now LIFT" require sensitivity to give help at the appropriate moment.

The way in which the class is managed and organized will depend upon the age and gymnastic experience of the children, the apparatus available, and your preferred style of teaching. Whatever the situation, good management is imperative for expediency and safety of the children.

In the gymnastic lesson it should be possible for all of the children to be working at the same time. While line-ups and regimented formations may be pleasing to the eye, they do little to promote maximum activity and maximum skill development. When apparatus is arranged effectively and groups are kept small, waiting will be minimized. The more a child engages in productive movement activities, the more movement skill will result. However, children may also need short periods of rest.

Just as children appreciate the predictability of routine in the classroom, routine in the gymnasium is necessary as well. How you organize the children is up to you, but it is suggested that responsibility is delegated even with the youngest of children. When children are given a regular task to perform, such as taking out and setting up a particular piece of apparatus, they will become quite reliable and adept at carrying it out.

In initial gymnastic lessons, you will find it most helpful to spend a good deal of time reinforcing the importance of safety, care of the apparatus, and how to set up and dismantle specific pieces. Children should be taught always to lift apparatus when carrying it in order to avoid injuring themselves, the apparatus, or the floor. You will need to establish that two, three, or four children (depending on their age) should always carry larger pieces such as benches, boxes, ladders, and planks. The way that children set up large apparatus should also be checked so that bolts are placed in their designated holes, and clamps, wires, chains, and other interlocking devices are effectively secured. Since apparatus differs considerably from manufacturer to manufacturer, you will need to find out how to safely secure each piece.

When various types of large and small apparatus are used repeatedly, there are various ways in which the children may be organized to retrieve and set it up. Individuals or small groups of children may be responsible for the same apparatus each day. Once it is carried onto the gymnasium floor, you may direct which pieces will be arranged together.

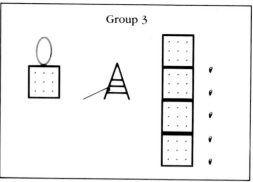

One card per group.

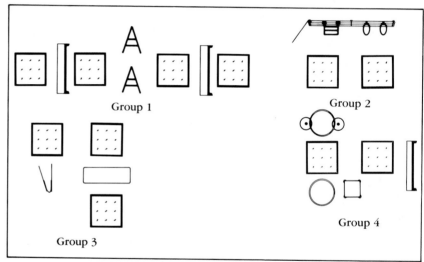

Figure 12.1 Visual aids may
be used to illustrate
apparatus arrangement

One illustration for the entire class.

You may be specific as to how the arrangement will be set, or the children may be allowed to arrange it as they wish. Visual aids such as diagrams or posters tacked on the gymnasium wall, or cards given to leaders of small groups may be used to indicate apparatus arrangements for specific stations (see figure 12.1).

If light and easily portable apparatus such as ropes, beanbags, or hoops are used you may merely tell the children, "Come and get the apparatus and take it into an empty space." In this situation, all children work with the same apparatus. When there is not enough of one kind for each child, then different ones may be used and children switch apparatus halfway through the class. Stations of various pieces of apparatus will facilitate

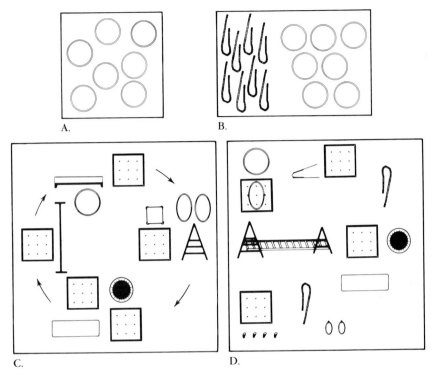

Figure 12.2

A. Everyone works with the same apparatus

B. Half the class works with one type of apparatus; half works with another. The two groups later exchange

C. Children move from station to station as they wish, or when the teacher tells them to move

D. Children take out and set up the apparatus with which they want to work

all children working all of the time. In this type of arrangement, you may choose to allow children to go on to another station when desired or you may indicate to children when it is time to rotate onto the next area (see figure 12.2).

Whether you or the children decide upon the precise spatial arrangement of the apparatus, the setting must always be surveyed to ensure that adequate space is available for the approach to and travel away from, the apparatus. Approaches from various angles should be available so that one particular piece of apparatus is not overcrowded. Mats should be considered apparatus as well, so that children practice the full range of their skills in one area. Because children find greatest enjoyment in apparatus that moves, hanging ropes, hanging ladders and bars, springboards, mini-tramps, and trampettes should be placed at different stations for all to experience. Overcrowding should not be a problem if enough attractive pieces are situated in various spots throughout the gymnasium.

Space is essential if vigorous flight and traveling are to be attempted just as stable and firm surfaces are necessary to support robust take-offs and landings (Department of Education and Science 1972).

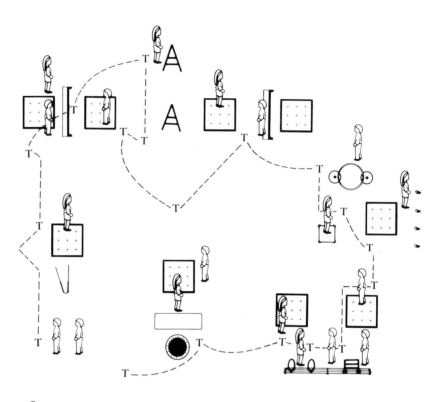

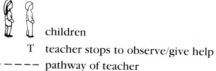

Figure 12.3 The teacher observing the children's movement

children

T   teacher stops to observe/give help

– – – – pathway of teacher

Observational Skills

Being a good observer takes time and experience as a teacher. It is not a skill that can be easily learned overnight or from a book. However, chapters 3, 6, and 9 provide useful information. Some guidelines specific to gymnastics are presented here to help you be a better observer.

The Teacher Observing

Our first concern as we observe children is their safety. If they are carrying, setting up, or putting away apparatus, we should scan the area to ensure that no one is bumping a peer, that apparatus is being lifted and carried properly, and that it is set up in the appropriate place. Once we scan, we should focus on smaller details to further check safety. To focus, we may have to move closer to get a better look at such things as:

> **S**herry's dangling earrings
> **t**he way that Joey is holding the bench
> **h**ow far the springboard is from the wall
> **i**f the bolt on the climber is secured properly

Table 12.2

Observing children's gymnastic movements

You Ask	You See	You Respond
1. Is each child trying to answer the task?(on-task behavior)	No; Robbie is playing with his mat.	May I help you fix your mat, Robbie?
2. Is each child answering the task?	No; Susan must have misunderstood the task. She is stretching-curling-stretching. I asked for curl-stretch-curl.	Susan, can you change the order of your sequence to two curls and one stretch?
3. How could the responses be improved?	The children have a lack of focus; they tend to continually look at the floor.	Public feedback: Meredith, you and Jason both have good focus in your movements. Well done!

We also observe to check the apparatus arrangement. This will involve both scanning and focusing. You may ask yourself such questions as:

Does each child have a hoop?

Have the children interpreted the diagram of the apparatus arrangement correctly?

Is the arrangement that the children created safe?

Is the apparatus appropriate for the theme of the lesson?

Is it appropriate for the children's level of skill?

When you consider these questions, you will likely visit each station/apparatus arrangement to find the answer (see figure 12.3).

Once you are satisfied that the environment is safe and the apparatus appropriate, you will want to observe the children's movement and how they respond to your tasks. Table 12.2 outlines a simple progression of what you should look for, what you may see, and how you could react.

As you observe the children you will need to travel throughout the space. Position yourself far enough away from whomever you are observing—it's similar to "missing the forest for the trees." Stand at least ten feet away so you can see the entire picture and watch the entire movement or movement sequence from start to finish. When you focus on one child, you will likely concentrate on specific body parts, such as knees when landing, the head in balancing, toes in stretching, or the chest in leaping.

Children may learn a great deal from observing one another's movements.

The Children Observing

We believe that children can learn a great deal from observing one another's movements. In gymnastics, peer observation is particularly effective because children are eager to show their work. While peer observation in gymnastics is very similar to that of dance and games, there are some differences largely due to the apparatus.

When children are observing their peers, tell them to:

1. Sit so they can see the "front" of the whole sequence.
2. Concentrate on one or two elements when observing. (These elements should directly result from the task; i.e., "Find three movements showing changes of direction." You should look specifically for changes of direction.)

When children are performing, tell them to:

1. Hold their beginning and ending shapes so that the start and finish are clearly defined when they are showing their work.
2. Take their time and avoid rushing through their sequence.

Evaluation

The methods used to evaluate gymnastics will likely be very similar to those used in dance and games. However, remember that the difference is that gymnastics focuses on how the body moves in relation to apparatus. How the apparatus is set up and used is important. Gymnastics also focuses on function and design of movement, as well as action, both alone and with others.

There are numerous tests designed to assess competitive gymnastic skills; for example, the Ellenbrand Gymnastics Skills Test, and the Harris Tumbling and Apparatus Proficiency Test. Because we are concerned with

Table 12.3

▼▼▼▼   ▼

Lesson grid

Lesson Experience	Concept(s)	Apparatus	Social	Link
1 Explore	Roll	None	Alone	New
2 Explore/create	Transfer of weight	None/small	Alone	Develop
3 Recall/create	Transfer of weight/ body parts	Small/large	Alone/pairs	Develop
4 Imitate	Body parts	Small	Alone/small groups	New
5 Refine	Body parts	Small	Alone/small groups	Develop
6 Create	Body parts/levels	Large	Pairs	Develop

Comments: Children worked well lesson 1; did not change tasks often enough lesson 2; large apparatus most challenging but recall needs work lesson 3; they copy well but head placement weak lesson 4; concentration poor (due to class party?) lesson 5; wonderful sequences in lesson 6!

▼▼▼▼   ▼

both process and product of skill acquisition, meaning the qualitative and quantitative aspects of movement, these tests are usually inappropriate. Our methods of evaluation should reflect what we deem important. We will be evaluating movement pattern and movement skill. Thus, formative rather than summative means should be used, with criterion references established.

Lessons

How much time was spent setting up apparatus? Was there sufficient apparatus for all the children? Should the introduction have been longer in the lesson? Were there too many basic tasks without enough extending and applying tasks?

These and other questions you have may be answered simply by examining your lesson plan. You may critique your lesson by listening to a tape recording or watching a videotape.

Evaluation after each lesson is wise so that you may effectively plan the subsequent lesson. You could assess such things as the appropriateness of progressions from floor work to apparatus, how readily the children grasped the movement concepts (and establish why it was so), variety in skills learned, or the progression from working alone to small groups. A grid may be helpful for you to determine some of the strengths and weaknesses of your lesson (see table 12.3).

Children's Skills

When we think of evaluation of children in gymnastics, we first think of evaluating their physical skill level. You will find that some children will quickly develop new skills. Other children may not be quite so talented, or, conversely, may be so skilled that they reach a plateau. You will need to decide what you believe is best to evaluate for formal reporting purposes: process, product, or a combination.

Table 12.4

▼▼▼▼   ▼

Sample checklist for skill development in gymnastics

Grade: _3_ Name: _Carl Hardy_   Date: _Feb. 3_

	Satisfactory	Unsatisfactory	Needs Work On
Running	X		
Jumping	X		
Leaping		X	
Rolling	X		
Balancing		X	
Taking weight on hands			X
Taking weight on other body parts			X
Body shapes	X		
Landing			X
Springing			X
Firm movement	X		
Sudden movement	X		
Sustained movement	X		

▼▼▼▼   ▼

Table 12.5

▼▼▼▼   ▼

Evaluation of the child

Date: _May 12_   Teacher: _J. Williams_   Student: _R. Hill_

As compared with peers:

	Stronger	Average	Weaker
Skill level	X		
Recollection, movement memory	X		
Creativity, innovation		X	
Continuity of movement	X		
Cooperation			X
Independence	X		
Conceptual understanding	X		

▼▼▼▼   ▼

To Do

Examine the graph in figure 12.4. On a scale of 1–10, what grade would you assign each child based on their December 20th performance?

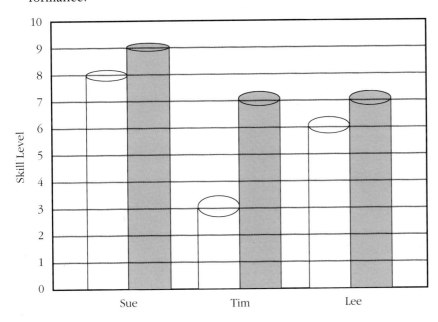

Skill Level

KEY:

☐ Sept. 20

▨ Dec. 20

Figure 12.4 What grade would you assign each child?

Since gymnastics is functional yet includes aesthetic elements it may be evaluated with respect to either pattern or skill. Was the cartwheel performed with a fully stretched body shape? Did the dive roll reveal a movement of flight? Were the arms neatly tucked into the body during the spin? These questions refer to the movement pattern. On the other hand, when equipment is used in gymnastics we may wish to evaluate how the body related to the equipment. How high was the box when the child traveled over it? How long did the child walk on the balance beam without looking down? Tables 12.4 and 12.5 will give you ideas of what to evaluate.

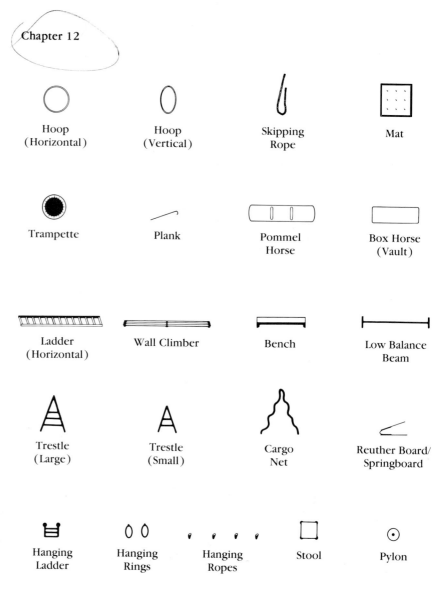

Figure 12.5 Gymnastic apparatus

Apparatus

Apparatus provides excitement and additional challenge in gymnastics. While small apparatus may be easily manipulated to meet the needs of differing skill levels, large apparatus provides the challenge of new heights. Here the child can swing, balance, hang, and grip. Figure 12.5 illustrates types of gymnastic apparatus.

Children may work with one piece, a combination of small pieces, or both small and large apparatus.

When each piece of small apparatus has been used in many different ways the children have built up a considerable movement vocabulary on each, the progression to work with two or three pieces of small apparatus arranged in a circuit will be simple (Mauldon and Layson 1965).

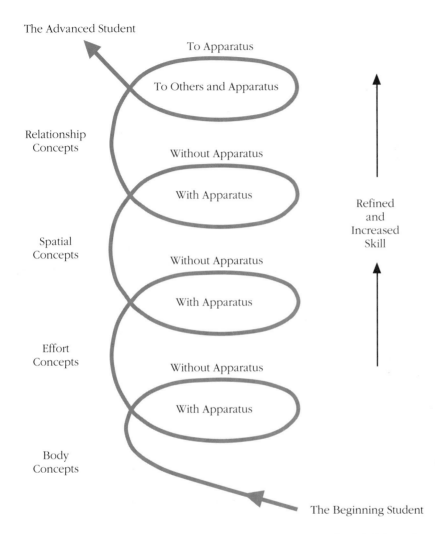

The Advanced Student

To Apparatus

To Others and Apparatus

Relationship
Concepts

Without Apparatus

With Apparatus

Refined
and
Increased
Skill

Spatial
Concepts

Without Apparatus

With Apparatus

Effort
Concepts

Without Apparatus

With Apparatus

Body
Concepts

The Beginning Student

Figure 12.6 When apparatus is initially introduced, there is a decrease in the quality of movement. After apparatus is used for a period of time, skill will surpass previous skill level

Progressive arrangements of apparatus are important so that children develop versatility and skill over a period of time (see figure 12.6). As the movement concepts presented progress from simple to complex, so too should the environment. This ensures not only a safe, challenging environment for the child, but also the necessary progression of apparatus arrangements required for effective skill development.

Skipping ropes, hoops, mats, and blocks are examples of small apparatus, which is easily portable and available in most schools. Small apparatus provides additional stimuli especially for young children who delight in traveling in relation to the apparatus as they jump, travel under and over, around, and through it. Older children may also enjoy using

Small Apparatus

it as it serves as a valuable intermediate step between working with large stationary apparatus. They will be challenged to discover the possibilities and limitations of each piece as you set challenging tasks.

Small apparatus provides a point of reference within the space and may help alleviate problems of line-ups and overcrowding. Children will work within their own space where the apparatus is situated. This will encourage spatial orientation, which is important to develop in the early years. Tasks such as "Jump across your mat," "Using hands and feet, travel around your hoop," and "Travel along the length of your skipping rope" will clarify the child's conception of space and how it may be filled.

Beanbags Beanbags may be used effectively in gymnastic lessons. They may be placed between the chin and chest so that children tuck in their heads as they roll forward or backward to maintain a curled shape. They may also be held in between the knees if legs tend to separate during rolling. Beanbags may facilitate a symmetrical jumping action by children placing them between their ankles.

Hoops Hoops may be used in various ways either as stationary or moving obstacles. Children love to roll hoops and run beside them, jump over them, or step through them as they roll. Hoops may be situated flat on the floor so children balance or transfer their weight over to the other side using various body parts. They may be walked around to reinforce a circular pathway or traveled along on feet or combinations of hands and feet. A hoop may be balanced vertically by placing a mat through it so that it stays upright. In this situation, children may freely travel over and through as they jump, crawl, and roll in various ways. With additional small apparatus such as small stools or blocks, hoops may be raised horizontally to allow traveling over, under, around, and through. Children may also balance inside them. Whichever way hoops are used, consider how much time children spend holding hoops for others.

Skipping Ropes Skipping ropes are available in most schools and they provide much challenge for movement. While skipping itself is a worthwhile activity, ropes may be used in ways similar to hoops: they may be placed on the floor in various shapes or attached to chairs or boxes to provide a "high jump" that may be traveled over or under in various ways.

Large Apparatus   Stools, ladders, benches, boxes, and horses are examples of large apparatus. Large apparatus is heavy and cumbersome. Apparatus, such as bars, springboards, trestles, ropes, and ladders is often taller, longer, or heavier than the children themselves, who will need to work together to lift, carry, and set it in place. Many schools have large climbing frames that attach to the wall. These "wall climbers," as they are called, usually require a few children working cooperatively to pull it away from the wall and secure it to the floor.

Large apparatus provides an additional challenge for children.

Although wall climbers and other large apparatus may seem very different from small apparatus, the same basic movements of locomotor and nonlocomotor activities are developed. The numerous small attachments (such as ladders and planks) are designed to add variety and challenge to large climbing frames and will reinforce and extend many of the skills previously acquired. However, large apparatus will provide the additional dimension of being able to support children's total weight at both low and high levels. Skills that were not possible on small apparatus may be performed on large apparatus. These include climbing, swinging, hanging, and rotating around an object at a medium or high level.

Suggestions for Apparatus Upkeep and Storage:

Mats, ropes, and hoops can be hung on a wall to be effectively stored.

Storage carts are useful for wheeling small apparatus onto the gymnasium floor.

A portable trolley (the size of your school's mats) allows for mats to be stacked and then rolled onto the gymnasium floor.

Mark one side of each mat to denote a "clean side." Clean sides should be stacked facing one another so that they stay clean.

Mats should be stacked carefully, not thrown on a pile.

Hanging ropes should **never** be knotted as they will fray from the friction and pressure of someone's weight.

Summary

The teacher's role is complex, as children should experience increased skill development and the enjoyment it will bring.

The methods a teacher must utilize to achieve this goal should promote continuous activity and encourage individual exploration and discovery that results in frequent success for the student (Canadian Gymnastics Federation 1977).

Review Questions

1. List five factors you will employ to ensure a safe gymnastic environment.
2. What are the advantages and disadvantages of children spotting one another?
3. What is the role of observation in the gymnastics program?
4. On what basis will you evaluate children in the gymnastics program?
5. How does the challenge of small apparatus differ from that of large apparatus?

References

Canadian Gymnastics Federation. 1977. *Coaching Certification Manual.* Ottawa: University of London Press.

Department of Education and Science. 1972. *Movement.* London: Her Majesty's Stationery Office.

Docherty, D. and A. R. Morton. 1982. *A Focus on Skill Development in Teaching Educational Gymnastics.* Canadian Association of Health, Physical Education and Recreation Journal. 48:6, 3–8.

Mauldon, E. and J. Layson. 1965. *Teaching Gymnastics.* London: Macdonald and Evans, Ltd.

Williams, J. 1974. *Themes for Educational Gymnastics.* London: Lepus Books.

CHAPTER

13

Learning Experiences in Gymnastics

While we do not wish to be dictated to by our lesson plan, an effective plan provides us with the initial source of guidance. Once with your class, you will be attending to various needs of the children and cannot expect to remember every task, activity, or arrangement of apparatus within the lesson. You will need time to interact with the children as the particular movement dictates. To be good teachers, we should not be preoccupied with what we'll say next to the whole class when one child requires our undivided attention. The plan should be used for quick reference during the lesson.

The age and previous experience of the children you teach will be the primary factors to consider when you design gymnastic lessons. The expectations you may realistically establish for their level of skill, the vocabulary you select for development, and the tasks that you spend the most time extending, applying, and refining are paramount.

If the children have had minimal exposure to gymnastics, you should first cover rolling, for safety reasons, whether they are in grade 1 or 6 (as outlined in Lesson Plan 1). However, the development of the tasks and the final stage of the lesson would differ because of the various needs, abilities, interests, and experiences of the children. Older children will progress more rapidly as their grasp of the concepts both cognitively and physically is more advanced. Thus, while each group may begin at relatively the same point on the gymnastic continuum, great divergence should occur over a period of several lessons.

Lesson Design

We must have a general idea of what we wish to cover before we plan a lesson. The general content should be based upon a selected movement concept, while also considering the needs of the children. While no movement concept can be developed in isolation, it will provide a basic framework within which the children will work. For example, if a class is asked to "Travel any way you like along the bench," locomotion is key, but direction, level, time, and relationships are also employed. The concept of locomotion here will provide the focus for movement development, and for this reason should be clearly presented to the children at the onset of each lesson.

When planning lessons, you will need to decide how much time the children will spend working on the floor, or small or large apparatus.

Whatever the length of lesson, the proportion of time allocated to floor and apparatus work has to be considered. When introducing a new idea the time spent working at floor level will be greater than that on apparatus but in consecutive lessons the working time will probably be equally divided. Once the particular theme has been fully explored at floor level the children will need a greater proportion of time to exploit the possibilities on apparatus (Mauldon and Layson 1965).

The movement concept should be clearly outlined and discussed with the children if a new concept is being presented. If it has been the focus of previous lessons then review is probably warranted even if it is a cursory look at the essentials. All tasks and resultant movement exploration and development should involve the application of the concept. True skill development will ensue, as the children's focus will be on solving specific movement problems. You should have a preconceived idea as to what types of responses will result, so that children may be appropriately guided.

Initial lessons should focus on relatively simple and familiar actions for the child. Movements should focus not only on the whole body as in running, jumping, and rolling, but also upon various body parts which require preparation for more stressful work. Stretching and curling as weight is transferred from one body part to another work the neck, trunk, and hip regions. Weight taken on the hands, shoulders, hips, and stomach tax the muscles of the upper body. Body parts may be stressed in locomotion with tasks such as "Travel with knees high," "Travel with springing actions and quiet feet," or "Lift your arms high to accentuate your leap."

If children are older or more advanced in their movement, the teacher may expect more complicated responses to more involved tasks. The additional elements of space and time may be added in initial lessons with tasks such as, "Travel backward with springing actions," and "Ensure that you use a sudden take-off as you leap and then balance."

Even when children have had a strong background in gymnastics, it is wise to begin with the more basic concepts of weightbearing and weight transference for review purposes. From there, you may then make decisions as to the movement concepts that will most effectively stimulate the children to increase their motor competency. For example, students may be adept at traveling and balancing on their hands in various ways. The introduction of apparatus such as benches, horses, and boxes for traveling on, along, or over, with weight on the hands, will further challenge the children.

In all likelihood, the children you teach will have had some gymnastic experience. They may have used the gymnastic apparatus within the school with little exposure to the movement concepts and vocabulary presented in this text. In this situation, children will require careful guidance during the lessons in order to fully appreciate the movement possibilities within each concept. If you use age-appropriate apparatus and social structures (working alone, with a partner, or small group), the children should find delight in your classes and their developing skill.

Movement Concepts

Apparatus

Apparatus is introduced to provide further stimulation within the theme. Young children usually require more time to discover the range of movements possible within a theme without apparatus, while older children may quickly indicate to the teacher their readiness for the additional challenge of obstacles.

You must carefully consider which pieces of apparatus will be most appropriate and conducive for the movement concept being developed. After children have explored the range and movement potential of the concept while working on the floor, an additional challenge of small or large apparatus provides further motivation and stimulus. It is extremely important that you select suitable apparatus for the children and that it promotes the range of movements that provide the focus of the lesson. For instance, if you select the theme of levels and tell the child to create a sequence of: travel at a high level, then at a low level, and balance at a medium level, the apparatus of a large box, a bench, and skipping rope will encourage appropriate responses. You should always ask yourself how you would respond to the task with the apparatus provided. If you would have difficulty with solving the movement problem with the apparatus suggested, then you can anticipate the children will as well. See table 11.5 for help with this.

Usually at the beginning of the lesson, little or no apparatus is used so that children will focus their attention completely upon the body. Some teachers allow students to take apparatus out and begin work before the class begins. Other teachers are adamantly against introducing apparatus until students are sufficiently limbered. As a teacher, you will find what works best for you and your class. Figure 13.1 outlines the progression we suggest for apparatus use.

Partner and Group Work

While young children may find success in working with another or others only after a good deal of time has been spent working on their own, older children may be physically and mentally prepared to collaborate with their peers in the earlier stages of skill development. This process of cooperation and collaboration may also be a valuable motivating tool for pre-adolescent children in the upper elementary grades. These children are sometimes self-conscious and find tremendous support and encouragement in working with others. The amount of time children may spend working with others, due to their own inclinations or the decision of the teacher, is shown in figure 13.2.

Creating Sequences

Children should be expected to create sequences that reflect the best movement they have performed that day. Sequences may involve the floor or a mat, apparatus, and/or other children. You will need to stress a clear beginning shape, good continuity of actions joined together, and the holding of a clear shape to conclude the sequence.

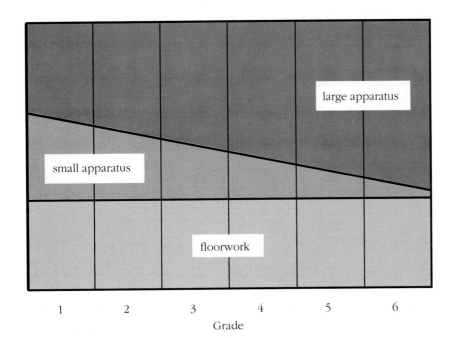

Figure 13.1 Progression in the use of apparatus

Children should be exposed gradually to working with others as they mature through the grades.

GRADE	1	2	3	4	5	6
Working Alone						
Working in Pairs						
Working in Small Groups						

KEY:

▨	Used Extensively
▨	Used Often
▨	Used Rarely

Figure 13.2 Progression in social structure

Sample Gymnastics Lesson Plan Formats

Format 1

Grade: _____

Movement Concept: _____

Gymnastic Actions: _____

Apparatus: _____

Introduction (3–5 minutes)

Movement Development (15–20 minutes)

1. Leg work

3. Whole body work

2. Arm work

4. Sequence work

Culmination (5–10 minutes)

(Note that apparatus may be used in any portion of the lesson. This format ensures that weight is taken on all body parts for a well-rounded movement experience.)

▼▼▼▼

Whatever the age and skill level of the class, the most difficult task for the teacher will probably be to find continuity of action within movement sequences. Children will tend to find a few movements that they enjoy and are successful with, but will probably have difficulty joining them together smoothly. Because gymnastics involves the sequencing of various types of locomotor and nonlocomotor movements, you will need to spend much time on ways in which isolated movements may be joined together.

Because children learn effectively from watching others and enjoy performing their work, you may wish to include a few minutes of observation. Some children may be eager to perform their sequences and will readily do so, while others may need your encouragement. "Let's watch all the children in this corner," or "This half of the class show us your sequences," may be all the incentive the children require. However, while you should provide as much encouragement as possible, children should not be forced to display their work, especially if they are not pleased with the result.

Lesson Plan Formats

As you progress as a teacher, you will find particular lesson plan formats more appropriate for your needs than others. Two examples are shown.

Format 2

Grade: _____

Movement Concept: _____

Gymnastic Actions: _____

Apparatus: _____

Introduction (3–5 minutes)

Movement Development (15–20 minutes)

1. Without apparatus

2. With apparatus

Culmination (5–10 minutes)

Sample Lesson Plans

The sample lesson plans that follow are arranged in order of difficulty from simple to complex. We begin with a basic lesson focusing on rolling and springing with small apparatus, and end with a lesson that is challenging in skill, apparatus, and social structure.

These lessons are not designed for a particular age group but are based upon an approximate social, cognitive, and skill level of a typical class of children. If you choose to follow these plans, keep in mind that adjustments (in vocabulary and sentence structure) will have to be made to the tasks so that they are appropriate for, and understandable to, your class.

Careful observation of the children as they respond to the tasks will be essential. At times children will generate new movement ideas that you may not have considered. Sometimes you may find your lesson digressing from its original intent into a new skill or concept. In order to capitalize upon the "teaching" movement, encourage this digression and work with the children—not against them. For example, you may follow Lesson Plan 1, but find the children become absorbed with twisting and rolling. Instead of saying "No, don't do that, do this!", it is wiser to capture their interest and promote further skill development by changing your springing tasks to "twisting" tasks.

Lesson Plan 1

Skill Focus: Jumping, rolling

Grade: Any gymnastically inexperienced group of elementary school children

Length: 20–30 minutes

Apparatus: One mat per child (if available) or grass

Objectives:

The children will be able to:

1. create stretched shapes in jumping
2. create round shapes that roll
3. absorb force by rolling after flight for safety reasons
4. sequence run, jump, land, roll, with continuity in movement

Movement Concept: Weight Transference

Tasks	Teaching Aids
Organizing	
Find a space all by yourself.	
Basic	
Run into empty spaces and jump whenever I clap.	Initially, clap with a predictable time span between claps. Later, claps may become unpredictable. Watch for jumps with good height. Encourage children to move continuously.
Refining	
Swing your arms up to gain height. Bend your knees to land quietly. Keep your head up; don't look at the floor when you jump.	Force should be absorbed by sudden curling of the trunk and knees after stretching in the air. You may want the class to watch someone who jumps with good form.
Push off the floor suddenly, stretching your body as much as possible when you are in the air. Remember to bend your knees when you land.	Watch children's use of feet and ankles to see if they really stretch in the air.

Fitness Fact

Running and jumping repeatedly will promote cardiovascular endurance and muscular endurance of the thighs.

▼▼▼▼   ▼

Extending

This time, on your own, run, jump, touch the floor with your fingertips, and repeat.	Encourage children to find rhythm in their movement. This will facilitate a smooth sequence of action.

Organizing

Get a mat for yourself and place it on the floor as far away from everyone else as possible.	Establish the most efficient way to get out the mats. Sometimes it is easier for two children to carry their mats together, rather than each child carrying one.

Basic

Find several curled shapes and see if you can rock back and forth on each one.	Stimulate children's ideas by suggesting various body parts to take their weight (e.g., stomach, back).

Refining

Make sure your shape is really curled. Tuck in knees, elbows, and head, and hold it tight.	Children may observe one another to check if shapes are curled. A beanbag may be placed between a child's chin and chest to ensure a tucked head if the body is curled toward the stomach.

Find a curled shape and rock
back and forth.

Extending

Begin with small rocking actions and increase their size to the point that it makes you roll over.	This may be easy for some children and more difficult for others. Assist those who need help.
Raise the level of one good curled shape so that you have a new base of support. Let gravity pull you down to roll. Make that shape again and repeat the action.	Weight may now be on knees or feet. Children will have to shift their center of gravity (hips) off balance so they roll.

Extending

This time make a stretched shape on one or two feet, then curl so that you roll.	Shapes may be stretched long or wide. Point out that elbows, knees, and toes should be really stretched.

Refining

Again stretch, then curl, but this time quickly bend your head, knees, and elbows before you land.	Stress the importance of not using hands to break the fall. Children should take weight on upper back, hips, and the side of arms and legs, not bony body parts.

Extending

Add a little jump before you roll so that you are really stretched, then really curled.	Give children a good deal of time to master this task before you go to the next. (It may take longer than you anticipated!)
Add a small run to your sequence so that you run-jump-land-roll.	Quick tucking of the body is necessary to safely roll. Curling of the knees and back are very important to absorb force.

Refining

Run very lightly, jump, land, and roll forward, backward, or sideways.	Remind children to continue their roll in the direction they were running (see figure 12.1).

Applying

Repeat your sequence over and over again, jumping then rolling into different spaces. Try to create a rhythm in your movement.	Watch children's use of space. Advanced children will roll quickly; slower children will roll with caution. Observation of others may help some children.

Because gymnastic apparatus provides a unique challenge in the elementary physical education program, you may wish to expose an inexperienced class to a variety of apparatus at this point. It is a good idea to allow them to freely explore the apparatus before you set specific tasks for them (see figure 13.3).

Tasks	**Teaching Aids**

Organizing

Please look at the diagram on the board. This is how we'll set up the apparatus today. Sandra's group, please leave your mats where they are, but put away everyone else's. John's group, please get two benches and two hoops and set them up. Terry's group, get the ropes out and set them up. Julie's group, please take out three trestles, two planks, and one box. Brenda's group, you'll need two trestles, a plank, two hoops, and a box.	Assist children in retrieving apparatus. Check to see if it's set up the way you asked.

Basic

Play on your apparatus as you like.	
Jump over, onto, or off of your apparatus. Remember to really stretch in the air and really curl when you land.	Help children find ways of using the apparatus. Encourage quality in jumping.

Organizing

Do the same thing on different apparatus.	
Now that you have used a variety of apparatus, find a piece that you like.	Ensure that all children are active and no one is waiting for a turn.

Applying

Create a sequence of jumping, landing, and rolling with your apparatus. Try to design your sequence so that you can do it twice without stopping.	Continuity of movement is important here. Help children design their sequences to ensure quality in jumping, landing, and rolling.

Observing

Let's watch this group perform their sequences. Watch carefully for good jumps and rolls.	Choose a group of children who are utilizing the apparatus in a variety of ways.

▼▼▼▼   ▼

Important Points

In Lesson Plan 1, children may have their first attempt in creating a gymnastic sequence. You should look for:

1. truly stretched shapes when they jump. Watch particularly for stretching in arms, thighs, knees, ankles, and toes.
2. truly curled shapes with heads especially tucked in (you may say to children "Look at your belly button as you roll" if they are curling forward).
3. absorption of force as children land through bent knees, ankles, and curled backs.
4. continuity of movement (smooth movement) in the sequence of run, jump, land, and roll.

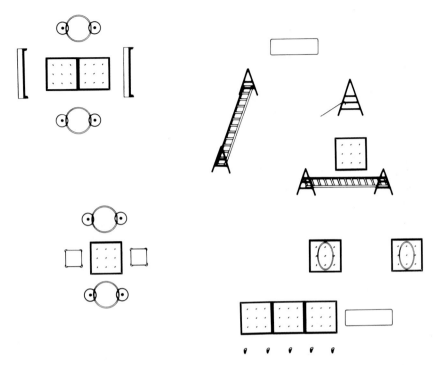

Figure 13.3 Apparatus arrangement for Lesson Plan 1

Note that every task within the lesson is naturally related to the previous task. The first task of run and jump requires vigorous activity and serves to warm up the children. Its purpose is also to encourage the kinesthetic experience of stretching and curling in order for weight transference to occur. The tasks then progress from simple rocking, to rolling, to rolling preceded by traveling on feet, with a moment of flight (in the jump).

Ways in which Lesson Plan 1 may be modified are presented in table 13.1.

The lesson as outlined should provide plenty of material for most classes. You may wish to vary the lesson with: **Possible Progressions**

1. Movement action such as:
   a. traveling in other ways than running (skip, hop, leap)
   b. turning in flight during the jump
   c. focus on pathway during the sequence
   d. focus on direction during the sequence (i.e., travel sideways, twist to roll forward or backward)
   e. focus on time-traveling quickly and rolling s-l-o-w-l-y

Table 13.1

▼▼▼▼   ▼

Modifications for Lesson Plan 1

Lesson Plan 1 Involved:

Running	Curling	Floorwork
Jumping	Rocking	A variety of small and large apparatus
Landing	Rolling	

Kindergarten–Grade 3

Lesson	Review material	New material	Apparatus
1	Running and stopping	Jumping Landing	Free play
2	Jumping Landing	Rocking Rolling	Exploring Jumping Landing Rolling
3	Rocking Rolling	Sequencing run-jump-land-roll	Small and large
		—or—	
1	Running and stopping	Rocking Rolling	Free play on large apparatus
2	Rocking Rolling	Running Jumping Landing	Over, off, and on large apparatus
3	Jumping Landing	Sequencing run-jump-land-roll	Small and large apparatus

Grades 4–6

Lesson	Review material	New material	Apparatus
1	Running and stopping	Jumping Landing	Over Off On
2	Running Jumping Landing	Rocking Rolling	Small apparatus with a partner
3	Rocking Rolling	Run-jump-land-roll	Large apparatus with a partner
		—or—	
1	Running Jumping Landing	Rocking Rolling	Free play
2	Sequencing run-jump-land-roll	Rocking Rolling	Small apparatus with a partner
3	Sequencing run-jump-land-roll		Large apparatus with a partner

▼▼▼▼   ▼

2. Partner work that includes:
   a. children performing their sequences at the same time, not matching;
   b. incorporating copying in matching, leading, and following, meeting and parting, or contrasting levels, directions, or timing of actions in any part of the lesson.
3. Children may be ready to explore the possibilities of incorporating apparatus not suggested in the lesson.
4. Lessons could involve both a partner and apparatus. However, the children should have previously been exposed to either a partner or apparatus so that they are not faced with two new stimuli at once.

Lesson Plan 2

This lesson focuses upon weight transference, where children perform stepping actions. To clarify this concept: steplike transference of weight can take place using a number of body parts; for example, in handstands and cartwheels, hands and feet alternately act as supports for the rest of the body (Mauldon and Layson 1965).

Skill Focus: Stepping with hands and feet

Grade: 3 or 4

Length: 20–30 minutes

Apparatus: Mats (one for each child if available)

        Option 1: Hoops

        Option 2: Large apparatus (see figure 13.4)

Objectives:

The children will be able to:

1. create narrow, wide, curled and twisted shapes
2. transfer weight onto various body parts
3. sequence three forms of weight transference showing different body shapes

Movement Concept: Weight transference

Tasks	Teaching Aids
Basic	
Travel any way you like on your feet. When I clap, stop, make a shape, and freeze. Hold it and travel again.	Stress good use of space and quick response to claps. Point out various shapes children have made and discuss whether they are primarily stretched, curled, or twisted.

Refining

As you are running think of what type of shape you'll make when you stop. If you make a stretched shape, stretch all your body parts. If you make a curled shape, really curl your body. If you twist, twist as much as you can.	You may demonstrate a weak shape and then have a child demonstrate a good shape. Point out the difference (e.g., placement of head, hands, feet). Also point out that a stretched shape may be wide or tall and thin (narrow).

Extending

Travel and freeze making shapes on your own. After you've made your shape, twist it so that you face a new place to travel.	Sequence work is beginning here. Continue to encourage clarity of shape. You may have to clarify twisting (feet fixed, body rotates) with the children.

Basic

Travel, using body parts other than your feet to take your weight.	Children may take weight on combinations of hands, head, knees, and back.

Extending

This time focus on the shape of your body as you travel. First, try making round or curled shapes, then try making wide shapes. Now have only your hands and feet take your weight. First, see what different ways you can find, then repeat the good ones, concentrating on the shape of your body.	Children may arch, spring from feet to hands to feet, roll, or cartwheel. Observe and help children clarify their body shapes.

Refining

Place your hands on the floor shoulder-width apart. Spread your fingers apart as far as possible.	Observe the hand positions of the children.

Fitness Facts

Weight on hands promotes muscular strength. If repeated long enough, this will promote muscular endurance in the arms and trunk.

▼▼▼▼   ▼

Option 1: Hoops

Tasks	Teaching Aids
Basic	
Transfer your weight from feet to hands to feet. Only your hands may go inside the hoop. What kind of shapes can you make when you do this?	Children should begin standing so that they create momentum for their hips to go up as their hands go down.
Refining	
Try really stretching your shape, as you take your weight on your hands and make your feet travel over the hoop.	You may tell children that stretched shapes are best when shoulders and hips are placed above the hands (in a line). Children should look at their hands.
Extending	
Place your hands in the hoop and make your feet go to the other side, but now sequence it: hand-hand-foot-foot.	Analogies such as "Stretch your toes to the ceiling," "Think of yourself as spokes of a wheel stretching out," and "Imagine you are a puppet with someone pulling the strings on your legs" may help the children achieve a true stretch.
You can also try placing both hands together on the floor, then landing both feet together.	Placing the hands far away from the feet may encourage a moment of flight before the hands touch the ground.
Experiment with placing your hands close to or far away from your feet.	Children may experiment with placing the hands in front of and behind their feet. This will encourage a front or a back walkover.

Place your hands in the hoop and make your feet go to the other side.

Basic

Find other ways of transferring your weight as you travel over or across the hoop. You may use feet only, or a combination of hands and head, knees and elbows, or any other combinations that work for you.

Having children observe each other may help them gain some new ideas. If quality movements are beginning to emerge, you may choose some for the class to observe.

Refining

Find some good ways of traveling over or across the hoop accentuating your body shape.

Stress smooth weight transference and clear body shape. Encourage twisted and wide shapes as well as more common stretched and curled shapes.

Applying

Create a sequence of three ways of transferring your weight over or across your hoop, showing at least two different body shapes.

Expect variety in skill level but quality in clarity of shape. Final observation will reinforce satisfaction of accomplishments.

Option 2: Large Apparatus

Tasks	Teaching Aids
Basic	
Explore getting onto or over your apparatus using stepping actions with feet and hands.	Check foot and hand pattern of the children.
Travel along or off your apparatus using a pattern of hands-feet-hands or feet-hands-feet.	
Extending	
Try to take a number of steps with your hands as you travel along or off your apparatus.	Some apparatus may not be conducive to this task. Children may take some or all of their weight on their hands (e.g., their feet may still be on the apparatus).
Now focus on curled body stepping actions as you travel on, along, over, or off your apparatus.	You may mention that when the body is curled, the center of gravity is lowered and balance is easier than when the body is stretched.
This time make stretched shapes using feet and hands to travel on, along, over, or off the apparatus.	Make sure that children really stretch their bodies.
Applying	
Create a sequence of stepping actions to get on, along, and off your apparatus. Show at least two different body shapes in your stepping action.	Watch for continuity of movement, and suggest ways to promote it through use of body shape and weight transference.

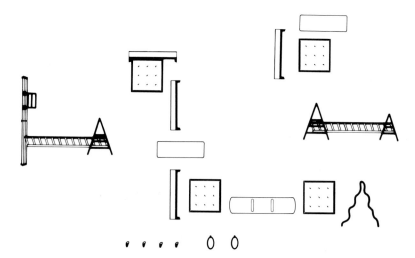

Figure 13.4 Possible
apparatus for Lesson Plan 2,
Option 2

Important Points

In Lesson Plan 2, children are exposed to weight transference with emphasis on stepping actions and body shape. The concept of body shape
should have been at least briefly introduced in dance, games, or gymnastics prior to this lesson. However, since weight transference may be
new to the children, Lesson Plan 2 will provide an introduction for further work in weight transference that is linked with other apparatus and
other movement concepts.

You will notice that in the first option (using hoops) the tasks are
more closed in that they lead to the specific movements of a handstand,
cartwheel, back walkover, front walkover, and round-off. These skills are
given less emphasis in option 2. If you desire to have greater emphasis
on these skills, the lesson may be modified through more closed teaching
methods. (One can achieve this through tasks such as "Take your weight
on hands only in a stretched shape.")

As you observe children working, take special notice of:

1. students who are especially weak or especially talented in their
   skill. They may need extra encouragement, alternative ideas, or
   time for refinement.
2. use of hands. When hands are placed on the floor to receive the
   body's weight, the whole palm and all fingers should contact
   the floor to create as large a surface area as possible. Hands
   should be placed shoulder-width apart for greatest stability.
3. children's shape. Clarity of shape is a major objective.

As in Lesson Plan 1 and, in fact, in all lessons you plan, tasks should
be arranged from general to specific and simple to more complex, always
reinforcing the movement concept of the lesson.

Ways in which Lesson Plan 2 may be modified are found in table 13.2.

Table 13.2

Modifications of Lesson Plan 2

Lesson Plan 2 Involved:

Traveling with different body shapes

Transferring weight onto hands and feet in curled and stretched shapes

Sequencing stepping actions with stretched and curled body shapes

Option 1: floorwork and hoops

Option 2: floorwork and large apparatus

The following progressions are modifications of Lesson Plan 2. If you are teaching kindergarten to grade 3, the children should spend most of their time working alone. In grades 4 through 6, partner and small group work will provide additional challenge.

Lesson	Review material	New material	Apparatus
1	Weight transference	Stretching Curling Twisting	Hoops
2	Stretching Curling	Stepping actions	Benches
3	Stepping actions	Twisting Curling Stretching	Large apparatus
		—or—	
1	Stretching Curling Twisting	Weight transference	None
2	Weight transference	Stepping actions	Hoops
3	Stepping actions	Stretching Curling Twisting	Large apparatus

Possible Progressions

It is suggested that you repeat this basic lesson with some changes so that the concept of weight transference may be fully appreciated. Remember that all concepts may be developed through partner or group work and/or variation of apparatus. The concept of body shape may be replaced by other movement concepts so that lessons could focus on weight transference of:

body parts

pathway

level

direction

time

The movement concept of body shape will also warrant further study. If you wish to explore and develop this concept in further lessons, then a natural progression will move into other areas such as body shape and:

    balance

    locomotion

    stressing body parts

    level

To gain further ideas for the development of the above concepts, refer to chapter 11.

Lesson Plan 3

    Skill Focus: Static balancing

    Grade: 4 (with previous experience with partner work)

    Length: 30–45 minutes

    Apparatus: One mat per child

    Objectives:

The children will be able to:

    1. balance with three different bases of support

    2. match a partner's balances

    3. create a movement sequence with a partner that matches and involves three balances

    Movement Concepts: Relationships, matching

Tasks	Teaching Aids
Organizing	
Find a space by yourself.	Make sure that the children are as far apart as possible.
Basic	
Travel and freeze as quickly as you can in your own time.	Every child should repeat this at least five times.
Refining	
Travel and freeze again, making sure you really concentrate on holding your freeze.	Ensure that children spread their arms, bend their knees, and place their feet shoulder-width apart to step quickly.

Fitness Fact

Traveling and stopping quickly to hold a shape promotes muscular strength, especially in the thighs, hips, back, and shoulders.

▼▼▼▼ ▼

Extending

Travel, jump, and land on only one foot and freeze. Try again, landing on your other foot.

You may have to discuss the necessity of a lowered center of gravity and absorption of force (bending of knees, arms wide) for children to be successful.

Organizing

Find a partner who is wearing the same color shirt as you are. Decide who will be *A* and who will be *B*.

Applying

B, match *A*'s running, jumping, landing, and freezing, and follow closely behind. This is cooperative, so *A* don't travel too fast and be careful when you travel backward. When I tell you, *B* will lead and *A* will follow.

You will have to tell children that the leader should never turn around to face the follower because the follower will have to turn his back on the leader. Children may tend to make this competitive rather than cooperative. Stress quality in pairs. Groups of three are acceptable if there is an odd number of children in the class.

Organizing

Group 1, please pull out the mats. The rest of you, line up behind Tim. Group 1, hand each person a mat. Place your mat as far away from anyone as possible.

Balance on your head with one or two other body parts.

Basic

Explore balancing on different body parts. You can try balancing on combinations of feet, knees, seat, stomach, shoulders, head, elbows, and hands.

Encourage children to try unusual combinations of body parts (i.e., head and knees or elbows and seat).

Extending

Continue balancing on different body parts, but increase the challenge by balancing on as few body parts as you can (i.e., one elbow and one knee, your head and one foot).

Concentrate now on balancing on combinations of hands and feet. You could try both hands and both feet, both hands and one foot, both feet and one hand, or one hand and one foot. Balance with your stomach facing the wall, floor, and ceiling.

Remind children that their base of support will need to be wide if they have two or three body parts on the ground. The lower the center of gravity, the more stable the body will be.

The children may benefit from observing one another or you may need to give them ideas by demonstrating yourself.

Applying

Find your best balance on hands
  and feet.

Balance on your head with one or   Watch carefully that children do
  two other body parts.   not injure their necks. There is
                                  diversity of opinion as to
                                  whether weight should be taken
                                  on the top of the head or near
                                  the hairline. However, children
                                  should never take their weight
                                  on their foreheads, as this is
                                  dangerous to their necks.

Extending

Balance on head and hands only.   Children's fingers should be
  Where should your hands be   spread apart with palms on the
  placed in relation to your head?   floor. The head and hands
  (See figure 13.5.)   should form a triangle.

Applying

Find your best balance on your   Encourage children to hold very
  head with one or two body   still.
  parts.

Create a movement sequence of   You may have to circulate
  three balances: your best   throughout the space and
  balance on (1) hands and feet,   provide public feedback to
  (2) head and other body parts,   children who are challenging
  and (3) any other balances. Put   themselves. Discourage
  them in any order you like.   simplistic balances on one or
                                  two feet. Encourage interesting
                                  shapes.

Refining

You'll need to figure how you can   Variety is desired here, with
  move from one balance to   purposeful movement in
  another. (This task could be the   between shapes. Children's
  basis of a lesson in itself.) Will   bodies should be "tight"
  you travel (e.g., roll) in between   throughout the sequence, rather
  balances or do all three   than "shape-relax-shape." Look
  balances on one spot?   for continuity of movement
                                  where the shape is held because
                                  of its aesthetic interest.

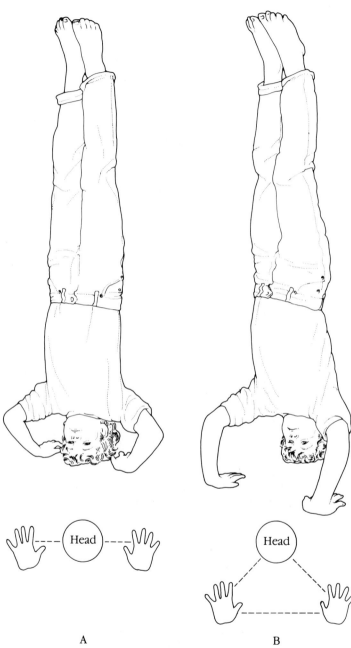

Head - - - Head

A   B

Figure 13.5 Which has better placement and provides better stability?

Organizing

Find a partner that you haven't worked with. We can have a group of three if there is an odd number. Show your sequence of three balances to your partner.	Pointing out that there could be a group of three eliminates the problem of one child feeling left out. Children should sit far enough (10 feet) away from their partner to clearly see the balances. Stress that those showing their work should take their time.

Applying

Create a matching sequence of three balances. One is your partner's favorite from your sequence, one is your favorite from your partner's sequence, and the third can be a new balance or one from either sequence.	You may need to present or review the concept of matching (see chapters 2 and 11). Ensure that the children understand the directions. You may want to use one pair as an example.

Refining

Ensure that you have a beginning shape and a way to get into your first, second, and third shape. Usually matching sequences are performed side by side. Decide if this is how you want to do it, or if you want to face each other, face different directions, etc. Practice your sequence over and over until it is "polished."	Students will need to be told to take their time and hold their shapes clearly. Observation of various spatial combinations will help children appreciate how movement looks differently with a variety of "fronts."

Option 1

The teaching method at this point could become quite closed. You may believe it is very important for children to develop some specific, "traditional" gymnastic skills. Thus, these tasks are presented with little choice for the student; however, they are still intended to accommodate a diversity of skill levels.

This sequence of tasks is designed so that the students will develop skill in both the headstand and the handstand.

The movement concepts are body parts (head and hands) and body shape in the action of (static) balancing.

Tasks	**Teaching Aids**
Basic	
Take your weight on your head and both hands, forming a triangle with these three body parts.	Make sure that the children's fingers are spread out and their palms are on the floor. Check students' head placement; their weight should be in between their foreheads and the tops of their heads.
Simplifying	
Keep your body curled as you take the weight onto your head and hands. You may want to try a frog stand, where your elbows rest on your knees.	Students will have greater success if they try this slowly. First one elbow goes on one knee, then the other. Reinforce the concept of "strong hands."
Extending	
You were working on a curled shape balancing on your hands and head. Now try slowly raising your toes to the ceiling so that you form a stretched shape as you balance.	Reinforce the stretching of the trunk and leg muscles to the ceiling. Tight muscles are extremely important.
(Children who can easily do a headstand may be challenged by creating twisted or wide shapes as they balance on their head and hands, or by moving into a headstand with straight legs.)	Can they perform the action with variation in time?
Basic	
Take your weight on your hands only. Remember hands should be shoulder-width apart.	Children should not lock their elbows, yet their arms must be strong.

You may want to try a "frog stand," where your elbows rest on your knees.

Extending

Is it easier to do a handstand starting with your weight on your hands and feet or just your feet? Try it both ways and see if you can figure out the answer and a reason for it.

You could put children in pairs to observe one another for hand placement.

Since our center of gravity is in our hip area, we want to use the momentum of our hands going down to get our hips to go up. Students should not begin with hands and feet on the floor; it requires more strength to get their feet up.

Children will also need to be told to place their hands near where their feet were so that the downward momentum is utilized. Otherwise the momentum is down and forward—a waste of energy.

Refining

Take your weight on your hands again, but imagine that someone is pulling your toes up to the ceiling, like a puppet. Really stretch! Make sure your stomach is tight; point your toes! (Children who have learned the handstand may work on creating various shapes as they balance: walking on their hands [dynamic balance], traveling sideways as in a cartwheel to "get into" the handstand, rolling backward into a handstand [back extension], or moving from a headstand into a handstand.)	You may wish to physically pull a student's ankles upward.

Option 2

Apparatus: One bench for 4–5 children

Task	**Teaching Aids**
Organizing	

Find a partner that you've never worked with. We may have a group of three.	Stating that you may have a group of three will alleviate the problem of someone feeling left out.
Join another pair so you have a group of four or five.	Ensure that children carry the benches properly. The groups should be well spread apart and the benches far away from the walls.
Two of you get a bench and bring it back to your space. The other two or three, place your mats on either side of the bench (see figure 13.6).	

Applying

By yourself and using the bench, try some of the balances you or your partner created.	Children may place some body parts on the bench and others on the floor (i.e., head on the floor, feet on bench) or all body parts on the bench (i.e., head and hands).

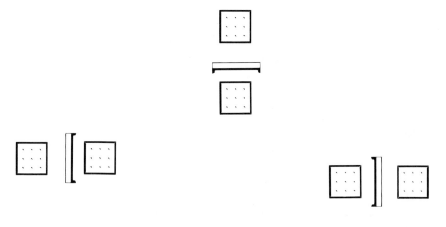

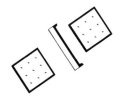

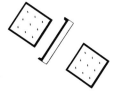

Figure 13.6 Benches and mats for balancing sequence

Extending

Working with your partner again, adapt the sequence you did on the floor, matching one another, so that you now use the bench. One balance must be totally on the bench, another off, and the third balance some weight should be on the bench and some on the floor.

You will have to observe, circulate, and provide guidance when children need help.

Refining

Work on matching your movements as closely as possible.

▼▼▼▼   ▼

Make a balance with the bench.

Important Points

In Lesson Plan 3, balancing is first explored alone, then with a partner, then applied through matching on the floor and finally on large apparatus. This lesson is not intended to serve as the initial experience in balance but rather to illustrate how balance, partner work, and apparatus may be interrelated.

Take notice of how the tasks are arranged. While each basic task offers new guidelines, the refining tasks involve a partner and extending tasks require matching movements. Thus, the first applying task is a basic review and requires synthesis of what has previously been accomplished. The final applying task again involves matching movements but with the additional challenge of apparatus.

Table 13.3

Modifications of Lesson Plan 3

Lesson Plan 3 Involved:

Floorwork
Partner work
Partner work on small apparatus

Kindergarten–Grade 3

Lesson	Modification
1	Floorwork → partner work
2	Floorwork → small apparatus
3	Floorwork → small apparatus → large apparatus
	—or—
1	Floorwork → small apparatus
2	Floorwork → large apparatus
3	Floorwork → partner work

Grades 4–6

Lesson	Modification
1	Floorwork → small apparatus → large apparatus
2	Floorwork → partner work → alone on small apparatus → partner work on small apparatus
3	Floorwork → partner work → alone on large apparatus → partner work on large apparatus

As you observe children within this lesson, take special notice if they are cooperating as they are matching. Matching may occur as children travel and balance beside or behind/in front of one another (traveling beside is the easiest). Timing is important when matching and may be very difficult in some actions.

Possible Progressions

Lesson Plan 3 could be utilized as it is written. However, it is very likely that there is too much material for one lesson. It could be modified for children in kindergarten through grade 3 by simply omitting the partner work. If you use this lesson with children in the upper elementary grades, you may conclude the lesson when children have created matching balances, and involve the benches in later lessons. You could develop many progressions, as outlined in table 13.3.

Lesson Plan 4

Skill Focus: Jumping, springing, swinging

Grade: 5 (experienced, relatively skilled children)

Length: 30–45 minutes

Apparatus: Large apparatus such as boxes, benches, horses, reuther boards/beatboards, trampettes, ropes

Objectives:

The children will be able to:

1. show flight with no apparatus
2. show flight with flight-assisting apparatus
3. show flight with flight-assisting apparatus adjacent to other small and large apparatus
4. sequence movements that involve flight
5. use good judgment in selecting movements to perform

Movement Concept: Flight

Tasks	Teaching Aids
Organizing	
Take a mat into your own space.	
Basic	
Travel around the room using flight to get over the mats as you come to them. Change your method of traveling when you like.	Stress good height, through use of arms and legs in take-off and landing. Encourage quality movement.
Refining	
Try to stay in flight as long as possible by keeping your head up when you are in the air and when you land.	Children tend to look at the floor when they jump.
Extending	
This time after you land with flight, roll. You should jump or hop before the mat so that you can roll on it.	Note children's use of space. They should use whatever mats are free.

Refining

Try to spring and land with light feet.	Stress good use of knees, ankles.

Basic

Travel across your mat by rolling forward, but precede the roll with a small jump before your hands contact the floor.	This is the basis of the dive roll. Stress good spring in knees and stretching of the body during flight.

Refining

Make sure your chin is tucked into your chest so that the back of your head touches the floor first. Aim for height, not distance.	Children may practice this by rolling over a crouched partner.

Extending

This time take a small run before you roll and finish your roll with a jump.	Stress quick curling and stretching, with lots of spring in knees and ankles.

Basic

Find a movement you can do well where you quickly transfer your weight from feet to hands to feet in some way.	Children may perform a headstand, handstand, cartwheel, or other movement.

Refining

Make the movement very quick so your hands are in contact with the floor for as short a time as possible.	Children will have to use their arms and shoulders effectively to produce spring.

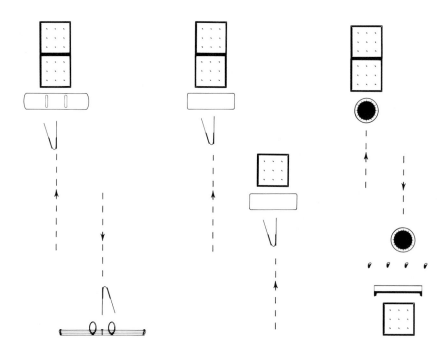

Figure 13.7 Possible apparatus arrangement for Lesson Plan 4

Extending

Take a short run before you perform your movement and delay putting your hands on the floor for as long as possible, so that you have flight. This may come before, during, or after the movement.

Stress quick stretching and curling and "tight" bodies. Children may require quite a long time to develop this skill. Observation of others may serve to illustrate important points.

Organizing

Get into your groups of five. When I hand you a card, please set up the apparatus (as shown in figure 13.7).

Check that apparatus is in good condition and that "runways" all going the same direction.

Basic (with flight-assisting apparatus only)

There are different types of flight-assisting apparatus: the reuther board, the springboard, the trampette, and ropes and bars. All of these will help you gain flight to different extents. Try the boards and trampette with two-foot take-offs, placing your feet in various points on the apparatus, and trying to gain height or distance (up or out).

Point out that force must be projected down so that the body will be sent up. Try to go to the shortest line up.

Refining

What things did you discover? (Allow time for discussion.) Go back to the apparatus, trying to incorporate what we've talked about.

Taking off with both feet is best because more force is projected down. The reuther board tends to project the body forward, the springboard up and forward, and the trampette, up.

Extending

At your station, use the apparatus. Use it to gain height and find a movement you can do after you land. Think about what you are going to do before you begin the movement.

Stress safe, thoughtful movement. Children's variation in skill level may be dramatically different. A crash mat may be used here if you think this will help the children progress.

Basic (with flight-assisting and other large apparatus)

Find a station that you'd like to work on. Work on ways of using the flight-assisting apparatus to get on or over the other apparatus.

Apparatus may be set up in a variety of ways. See figure 13.7.

Use your flight-assisting
apparatus to gain height.

Refining

Note which body parts you are
using. Keep hips and trunk
"tight" as you try to gain more
flight.

Give assistance to children,
providing ideas and guidance
for improved movement.

Extending

Find a good movement as you
travel onto or over the
apparatus. Add another
movement either before or after
you have gained flight.

Children with lower skill levels
will likely add movements
before their flight (i.e., they may
roll to the trampette). Children
with higher skill levels will
likely add movements after
flight (i.e., cartwheel after
vaulting a box).

Applying

Create a movement sequence where you use at least three pieces of apparatus and employ flight at least twice.	Stress continuity of movement and how children travel from one piece of apparatus to another. Observation may occur so that children may see each other's work.

▼▼▼▼   ▼

In Lesson Plan 4, children are exposed to the advanced concept of flight. **Important Points**
It cannot be stressed too heavily that this concept is appropriate only for
older students or students who have already acquired a good deal of
bodily control in gymnastic movement.

You will note that the lesson provides a gradual progression from flight
on the feet, to flight on various body parts (primarily hands and feet), to
flight assisted by apparatus, and finally, flight in relation to large apparatus. The important things for you to note as children progress in flight
are:

1. that children are constantly mindful of safety in all situations.
2. that children have "tight" bodies during flight.
3. that children are in fact, ready to progress to the next stage
   before you offer additional challenges.

As was the case in Lesson Plan 3, Lesson Plan 4 was written with a great **Possible Progressions**
deal of material, so that you may utilize the lesson in whole or in part.
The lesson could conclude before flight-assisting apparatus is introduced or before flight-assisting apparatus is used with other large apparatus.

Ways in which the lesson could progress from the applying task are:

flight in partner work/matching

leading and following

contrasting

meeting and parting

assisting flight

If you have reached this point with your children, they are well-skilled
and a class of whom you should be proud.

Summary

Finding the "right" progression of concepts for your class will require your sensitivity and good observational skills. At times you may find repetition of tasks and practice will most benefit the children; at others, the children will "feed you" what guidance they are ready for. Above all, share the success and pride in the work of the children!

Review Questions

1. Discuss the purpose of each of the three parts of the gymnastics lesson plan.
2. Write a progression of tasks for run, jump, land, roll.
3. Which will you teach first—weightbearing or weight transfer? Provide your rationale.
4. What types of gymnastic actions will increase arm strength?

References

Mauldon, E. and J. Layson. 1965. *Teaching Gymnastics.* London: Macdonald and Evans, Ltd.

Related Readings

Capel, S. 1986. Educational Gymnastics Meeting Physical Education Goals. *Journal of Physical Education, Recreation and Dance.* 57:2, 34–38.

Docherty, D. and A. Morton. 1982. Focus on Skill Development in Teaching Educational Gymnastics. *CAHPER Journal.* 48:6, 3–8.

Williams, J. 1974. *Themes for Educational Gymnastics.* London: Lepus Books.

CREDITS

Photographs

All photographs unless otherwise credited © Jennifer Wall and Nancy Murray. **Page 38:** By permission of The Laban Archives, University of Surrey, England; **page 151:** Royal Bank Junior Olympics; **page 159:** © Sherry Suris/Rapho/ Photo Researchers, Inc.; **page 271 left:** © James L. Shaffer; **page 358:** courtesy of Robert Watson, The Regina Leader Post.

Illustrator Credits

C. Clark Heugel: **pages 16, 17, 18; figures: 11.4, 13.5.** Precision Graphics: **Figures: page xii, 1.1, 1.2, 1.3a & b, 2.2, 2.3, 2.4, 2.5, 2.6, 2.7, page 91, 3.4, 3.5, 4.1, 4.2, page 132, 5.1, 5.2, 5.3, 5.4, 5.5, 6.7, 7.1, 7.2, 7.4, 7.5, 7.6, 7.9, 7.10, 8.1, 8.6, 9.1, 9.2, 9.3, 9.4, 10.2, 10.7, 10.8, 10.9, 10.11, 10.12, 11.1, 11.2, 11.3, 11.5, 11.6, 11.7, 12.1, 12.2, 12.3, 12.4, 12.5, 12.6, 13.1, 13.2, 13.3, 13.4, 13.6, 13.7.**

Line Art

Chapter 6:

Figure 6.2: Courtesy of Diane Fagan.

Chapter 9:

Figure 9.4: From D. Jones, "Teaching for Understanding in Tennis" *Bulletin of Physical Education* 18(1):29–31, 1982. Copyright © 1982 British Association of Advisers and Lecturers in Physical Education, London, England. **Figures 9.5** and **9.6:** From A. Gentile, "A Working Model of Skill Acquisition with Application to Teaching." *Quest* Monograph 17.3–23, *Learning Models and the Acquisition of Motor Skills.* Copyright © 1972 Human Kinetics Publishers, Champaign, IL. Reprinted by permission.

INDEX

68557